Community Journalism

THIRD EDITION

Community Journalism
Relentlessly Local

Jock Lauterer

The University of North Carolina Press
Chapel Hill

Designed by Heidi Perov
Set in Minion and MetaPlus types
by Keystone Typesetting, Inc.
Manufactured in the United States of America

This book was published with the assistance of the H. Eugene and Lillian Youngs
Lehman Fund of the University of North Carolina Press. A complete list of books
published in the Lehman Series appears at the end of the book.

Unless otherwise noted, all photographs are by the author.

Excerpt from "Cosmos and Kingdom," in Elizabeth Sewell, *Signs and Cities* (1968),
published by the University of North Carolina Press.

The paper in this book meets the guidelines for permanence and durability of the
Committee on Production Guidelines for Book Longevity of the Council on Library
Resources.

Library of Congress Cataloging-in-Publication Data
Lauterer, Jock.
Community journalism : relentlessly local / by Jock Lauterer. — 3rd ed.
p. cm. — (H. Eugene and Lillian Youngs Lehman series)
Includes bibliographical references and index.
ISBN 0-8078-5629-0 (pbk. : alk. paper)
1. Community newspapers. 2. Journalism. 3. Reporters and reporting.
I. Title. II. Series.
PN4784.C73L28   2006
070.1'72—dc22
2005020667

10 09 08 07 06   5 4 3 2 1

All across this land the lights are burning late at newspaper offices in towns with papers perhaps you've never heard of: the Bee *of DeQueen, Ark., the* Pilot *of Southern Pines, N.C., the* Independent *of Hillsdale, N.Y., and the* Herald *of Jasper, Ind. These are the so-called small newspapers of our country. But they are small in size only, as you will discover as you read on. This book is meant to honor those late-night candle burners, the men and women of* community *journalism. This third edition is dedicated to 92-year-old Virginia Rucker, who, as this book goes to press, is still writing for the Forest City (N.C.)* Daily Courier *and keeping me straight.*

Virginia Rucker of the Forest City (N.C.) *Daily Courier* and one of her lifelong pupils.

Contents

Foreword

Community newspapers are thriving. Of the 9,321 newspapers in the United States, about 97 percent are considered "small" or community papers. These include weeklies, dailies, ethnic newspapers, papers devoted to religion coverage, gay and lesbian papers, and papers targeted to parents, senior citizens, military personnel, and other special-interest groups.

Jock Lauterer is there to cheer all of them on. This book, now in its third edition, has been used nationwide by professors in their journalism classes and by journalists wanting to brush up on their Journalism 101 skills.

Lauterer, an award-winning former North Carolina community newspaper editor and publisher, teaches community journalism every semester at the University of North Carolina at Chapel Hill, where he also directs the Carolina Community Media Project.

His book includes insightful, down-to-earth tips on covering one's community inside and out. Lauterer doesn't just talk about community journalism. He gives real-life examples from his own and others' experiences in the nitty-gritty, day-to-day world of community journalists. Many of those experiences are described in his "From the Trenches" segments.

In "Your Town; Your Turn" at the end of various chapters, Lauterer lists ideas for further discussion. In the chapter on news (Chapter 7), he suggests the following: "Think about your paper, or a target paper. Find an example of how the community journalism response to a local news event was different from that of the nearby big-city daily and area TV." In the chapter on interviewing and writing (Chapter 10), he gives the following idea: "Pick a person at random right now. . . . Study her eyes, hands, mouth, hair, walk, clothes, how she 'looks out of her face.' Take notes and write about it."

Lauterer's writing style is personal, warm and humorous.

In his discussion about features (Chapter 8), for example, he writes, "[Features] are the garlic to the sauce, the flower on the table, clean sheets on the bed, an unexpected kiss, a phone call from a dear old friend. . . . We could probably get along without these things, but their surprising presence uplifts and enriches us."

Students like Lauterer's informal style of writing.

"Lauterer's book is easily the best textbook I've ever read. It was interesting, informative, and I actually looked forward to reading it," a student in my Community Media class at Kansas State University said.

"Lauterer's conversational writing style made it feel like you were listening to an old friend," said another.

Lauterer's passion for community newspapers is evident throughout his book, but he has no patience for those who are satisfied with the status quo. He looks to the future with up-to-date information on technological changes in the industry and helps newspapers come to grips with challenges such as how to cover and fairly reflect their increasingly diverse communities.

This edition of *Community Journalism* will help prepare journalism graduates for their journey beyond the classroom and will provide a refresher course for those who are veterans in the profession. This book should be included on the shelves of all of those who claim to be community journalists.

Gloria B. Freeland is director of the Huck Boyd National Center for Community Media and assistant professor in the A. Q. Miller School of Journalism and Mass Communications at Kansas State University in Manhattan, Kansas.

BY JERRY BROWN

Introduction
The Community Newspaper: An Essential Institution

I learned to appreciate the weekly newspaper in a south Alabama outhouse, where, when the Sears, Roebuck catalog was used up, the thoroughly read Clarke County *Democrat* served a dual purpose.

In its essential if earthy fate, the newspaper was doubly appreciated.

Of course, by the cool college years, most of us felt we'd outgrown our community papers, loaded as they were with wedding write-ups that might run to half a page, pictures of dead snakes, five-legged calves and grotesquely shaped or whopping vegetables and lots of ads for hernia trusses, earthworm farms and "lost or strayed" cattle.

One of my journalism professors disabused many of us of our condescending notions about those publications. In a course titled "Community Newspaper," which he developed and taught for about three decades, generations of students learned that most of these papers weren't the cornball rags sneered at by city dudes. They were thriving business enterprises—though nobody would have guessed it—and most of the editors were more skilled at their craft than we'd appreciated. Dealing fairly but frankly with neighbors and friends, we came to understand—first in the classroom and then through experience—can be tougher than reporting from the lofty perch of a metro newsroom. Such journalism requires the highest levels of courage, diplomacy and dedication.

Community paper editors always run the risk of making people mad and losing subscribers and advertisers, but the greatest threat to their livelihood would be to blink when the tough stories must be published. In the long run, people appreciate a real newspaper, with accurate, plain-style news stories, features that reveal new facts about supposedly familiar people and places and an editorial voice that speaks about critical issues while avoiding personality clashes. Among the booster sheets and the shoppers, such newspapers stand out as the best of their breed. Furthermore, these good papers have an opportunity to develop an individual identity, a distinct voice. I confess to a fondness for what we used to call "country correspondence," written, usually by ladies, who "motor" into town, who cover their communities like kudzu and who are blessed with editors who do not correct their idioms or tinker with their nonstandard grammar.

Those of us who've grown up and moved away may laugh all the way from the mailbox about who's canning what vegetable or which epistle the preacher took for his text Sunday or who's had visiting relatives or is down in their backs, but we can't resist that news. We also scan the obits and the wedding and anniversary stories, but I doubt if many of us realize we're encountering true grassroots journalism.

Big, bland dailies owned by dollar-driven corporations can continue to learn lessons from their small-town counterparts. To paraphrase Tip O'Neill, all news is local. Of late, for instance, the departure of National Guard units brings to our doorsteps a war that we hear national TV-studio pundits talking about. And national election coverage always involves issues close to home.

Of course, this tendency to localize national news can go too far. I heard one old newsman say that when a former U.S. president departed this life, his editor told him to localize it, so he submitted this lead: "Harry Truman, who once flew over our state in an airplane, died yesterday."

I don't want to Rockwellize the hometown press, because right many papers are truly awful, but you don't have to look far to see that this country is blessed with many great community journalists, who cover every aspect of their communities and are, in fact, leaders. They influence political agendas, serve as mirrors of their readers' lives and literally embody journalism. They're savvy, determined and resilient—and even your average, garden-variety local editor knows more about a county's communities than does any other single citizen.

Community journalism is, for better and for worse, personal; readers know the folks at the newspaper by name. They know to expect somebody from the paper—probably the editor, who may also be the publisher and the chief ad salesperson—to pop up with a pad and a camera whenever vehicles wreck, courts convene, school boards meet and politicians bloviate. (And dumb and probably defeated are those office seekers who blow off community papers as lacking an impact on elections.)

Moreover, readers look for the newspaper to provide public notice of land transactions, sheriff's bookings, tax dodgings, weddings and divorces and, most importantly, changes in fishing and hunting laws. Smart advertisers know that newspapers that attract readers also are critical to commerce—and thus the unique institution survives. The National Newspaper Association, which serves community papers, has about 2,500 members, proof that community journalism is thriving and providing a complement to regional and national dailies and to television and online news sources. Like night baseball and ice cream, the local weeklies or small dailies ain't going away; their reach exceeds most folks' grasp of their influence. If you are among those who believe I am overstating or sentimentalizing the impact of these community newspapers, just publish a controversial story, column or photo in one (or misspell a name in an obit) and see what reactions you get around town and on the country roads.

In the main, the role-model community newspapers I am describing have built their readership and sustained their influence by delivering news that is strengthened by institutional memory—in other words, a knowledge of local, state or regional history that determines and shapes the news content. Chain

Family matriarch Quintenna Boone Hampton breaks beans while a grandson shows off a pocket knife. "The character of place is defined by its newspaper," writes Jerry Brown.

ownership, with its inevitable turnovers and preoccupation with profits, often, though not always, erodes this foundation. However, that traditional groundsill of small papers is still appreciated, still needed, often missed and occasionally restored.

From my perspective as a former editor of weeklies, a community without a newspaper is like a church without a pulpit or an altar. Something is missing—a familiar voice, a sense of home, a continuity. The character of place is defined and confirmed by its newspaper, and these country cousins in the great family of the democratic press are just as essential to our way of life as their more citified—though, I concede, equally important—media relatives.

True enough, publications and plumbing have changed. We now have narcissistic blogs; e-mail in-boxes clogged with dumb, dirty and deceptive ads; hit-and-run happy-talk local TV news; and shouting, pontificating studio pundits. But we also have community journalism, as counterpoint and a truer grounding in journalistic values. Flashier media may be hogging the limelight, and outhouses may have disappeared, but there are still fish to wrap, puppies to train and birdcages to line. But, first, that community newspaper gets read.

Jerry Elijah Brown has been dean of the School of Journalism at the University of Montana since 1999. He edited a weekly in southwestern Virginia for three years before returning to Auburn University, where he taught for 20 years.

Preface
The Newspapers of the Blue Highways

The only newspaper in the world that gives a damn about Yerington.
—Motto of the *Mason Valley News*, a 3,700-circulation weekly of Yerington, Nev.

Since the publication of the first edition of *Community Journalism* in 1995 and the second edition in 2000, I have had the rare opportunity to see the country as few community newspaper editors or publishers get to do. The book has afforded me the opportunity to lead workshops at colleges, universities and press associations all over the nation. For a former co-founding editor-publisher who for 15 years rarely went beyond his coverage area, the last 10 years has been a real education for me. Though I shouldn't have been surprised, what I found delighted me. For in every state I encountered scores of excellent "small" newspapers run by enlightened community journalists whose passion for the work and whose splendid output will quickly disabuse you of the erroneous myth of small newspapers' inferiority.

This is extraordinary, given that too few institutions of higher learning offer classes titled "Community Journalism." Neither is there the equivalent of a seminal text, such as an AP *Style Book of Community Journalism*, nor is there a widely accepted gold standard of excellence for the field, such as the *New York Times* serves for the major metro dailies.

So, from whence cometh these enlightened community newspaper folk with their wonderful newspapers? I have long suspected that that like any grassroots phenomenon, great community journalism is organic. It just . . . *is*.

But that explanation, while poetic, fails to satisfy the student of community journalism or the professional who is ready to raise the bar. So this edition will attempt to get its arms around the factors of community journalism excellence by providing real-life examples. In a new best practices chapter (Chapter 20), I'm calling on some of my favorite community newspaper leaders to put it in their own words. In the end, I'm hoping that their wisdom will inspire you to do your best work starting right now, right where you are.

The beginner asks: Just what is community journalism anyway . . . ? Is it some newfangled gimmick . . . ? Is it "rural civic journalism?"

Community journalism, in form if not in name, has been around from the time of our founding fathers—and mothers! Though the practice is old, the term is relatively new. "Community journalism" got its name from long-time

Montana editor-publisher Ken Byerly during his tenure as a professor of journalism at the University of North Carolina at Chapel Hill from 1957 to 1971.

In a letter written a year before his death, at age 90 in 1998, Byerly pecked away on an honest-to-God typewriter to tell how the name emerged: "When I came to the J-School the title that I inherited for one of my courses was 'Country Weekly Newspaper Production,' or some such. I didn't like it as the course was more than that. Another name you would hear back then in the trade journals and at J-Schools was 'Hometown Newspaper.' I didn't like that either because the number of good weeklies in city suburbs was growing rapidly. The title just didn't fit suburban papers. And nationally and in J-Schools they were talking only about weeklies and semi-weeklies. This didn't fit either as good dailies in small cities with circulations up to 5,000 and even 10,000, and sometimes in suburbs, were successful because they stressed local and area news, editorials, pictures, features and such that their readers couldn't get from big city dailies.

"So I mulled over the idea of a better name, and finally came up with 'Community Journalism.' It seemed to fit these weeklies and small dailies. Anyway, the dean agreed with me and the name of that course was changed to Community Journalism. Shortly after that [in 1961] my book, *Community Journalism*, was published [by Chilton]. It sold well and the name caught on. It became the name for the small dailies as well as weeklies and semi-weeklies."

And Byerly, true to form, ends with a prickly admonition: "It troubles me though that some J-School profs now include larger dailies of 30,000 circulation or more under the name of 'community newspapers,' which they are not."

He's talking about me there, for I include dailies with circulations up to 50,000 among the ranks of community papers.

These are the newspapers of the Blue Highways, off the interstates perhaps, journalism as practiced by weeklies and small dailies with an intensely local focus. Fully 97 percent of U.S. newspapers fit this description. So if you're a student of journalism, it's very likely you will be working at a community newspaper.

And yet, most graduates emerge from university journalism schools and schools of mass media and communication largely untrained and totally unprepared for what they encounter at papers of that size and nature—all the while that they're awaiting that call from the *Washington Post* or the *National Geographic*. The common misconception is that the community paper is a small version of the big-city daily. Nothing could be further from the truth. Little wonder then that newcomers find the community newspaper to be a bewildering journalistic briar patch.

And it's important to remember, as John Neibergall said in the introduction to the first edition of this book, this is not journalism for everyone. So beware, because your author, a former community newspaper editor-publisher, thinks it's tougher, more demanding and, as some would say, far more rewarding.

But remember this also: We are not better; just different. The differences between

You know it's a community newspaper when you can't tell the editors and publishers from the production team. Unloading newsprint at *THIS WEEK* (Forest City, N.C.), the author (in overalls), then co-publisher and co-editor, is surrounded by the work crew that includes, clockwise, assistant pressman Jackie Arrowood (in Elton John T-shirt), co-editor and co-publisher Ron Paris, business manager and co-publisher Bill Blair, and pressman and business partner Don Lovelace. (Photo by Joy Franklin)

us and TV and big-city dailies are so profound, as one community newspaper editor says, "we might as well be a different species."

Try thinking about journalism in a fundamentally different way: throw out your preconceptions about TV journalism or big-city newspaper stakeouts for "sources." Get down. Get close to the earth. Get real.

Think about newspapers where reporters, editors and photographers are citizen-journalists, intimately involving themselves in the welfare of the place, in the civic life of their towns, participating as active members of the very community they're covering.

As a community journalist your approach is personal. Focus on one so-called real person reading your story. Picture his or her face as you tell him or her about the tax increase, the Little League game, the Girl Scout field day.

Then it's one person reading the story. Or looking at your picture. There's no "mass media." Only one person at a time reading the story, absorbing the photograph. Effective communication happens intimately, privately, quietly. 1:1. The personal approach.

I believe all small newspapers are community newspapers, even if they don't subscribe to the ideals presented in this book. In other words, these papers are sleepers that haven't yet awakened to what the late Nelson Poynter called their "sacred calling"—the responsibility, nobility and legacy of community journalism.

Throughout this book you will be meeting hundreds of real-life community newspaper men and women who care enough about their profession, our calling, to share their wisdom and experiences. You will also meet the staff of the *Bugle*, a mythical community paper that serves as a literary device, allowing me to put Community Journalism 101 lessons into parable form. The stories are absolutely true to the spirit of the scene and history. And in many cases, "Mark" or "Rachel" is your humble author, who, along the way, has made every mistake in the book, and then some.

While this book is intended to be used as a text and workbook for university students studying community journalism, it is the author's aim that it serve also as a survival manual/field guide/handbook—a support mechanism providing sustenance for those of you already out there in the trenches. I mean it to be an affirmation and a validation for all the long hours and crazy times, when you're feeling very alone, trying to stay sane and creative out in the boonies, or up against a thorny ethical dilemma when there seem to be no mentors, role models, allies or anyone else who's been through anything like this before. When it's late at night and it's just you and the problem, you and your fingers on the keyboard at deadline, you in bed in a cold sweat wondering if you did the right thing—take heart; we're all in this together. There are legions of enlightened, caring and dedicated professional community journalists who have gone before you and succeeded against great odds. And so can you.

Acknowledgments

This book itself is a community venture. It has reached publication only through the inspiration, support and encouragement of a community of friends. I can take credit only for having been in the right place at the right time. My most heartfelt thanks go to three models, mentors and friends whose personalities run through this book like a clear note: editors and professors Jim Shumaker and Ken Byerly, both now deceased; and the late Charles Kuralt, fellow Carolinian and special inspiration. To my former "partners in crime" at the Forest City paper, Ron Paris and Bill Blair—Long live the spirit of *THIS WEEK*!

Thanks to Virginia Wesleyan President Billy Greer for providing me a nurturing work space when the idea for the book took root at Brevard College (in Brevard, N.C.) in the late 1980s. Thanks also to former fellow workers who contributed good photos and wise guidance: Ron Paris, Joy Franklin, Pat Jobe and Maggie Lauterer.

I am indebted as well to Steve Bouser, Jeff Carney, Bill Collins, Rod Doss, Dewaine and Bobbie Gahan, Loren Ghiglioni, Linda Gilmore, Joe and Emmaline Henson, Kenny Irby, Jim Kevlin, Torsten Kjellstrand, Steven Knowlton, "Stretch" Ledford, Kelly Leiter, Dave Marcus, O. Louis Mazzatenta, John Winn Miller, Daniel Morris, Laurie Quade, Garrett Ray, Bill Reader, Gene Roberts, Jim Sachetti, William Shaw, Vicki Simons, Uzal Martz and Mark West; also to Woody Marshall and the gang at the Macon (Ga.) *Telegraph*, David Woronoff and the crew at the Southern Pines (N.C.) *Pilot*, the Allens of the Wake Forest (N.C.) *Wake Weekly*, Pam and Renee Fikes (formerly) of the Idalou (Texas) *Beacon*, Ed Harper and the staff of the *State Port Pilot* of Southport, N.C., and Jeff Byrd and his folks at the Tryon (N.C.) *Daily Bulletin*.

This third edition is enriched by insightful contributions by Joe and Dana Shaw of the Southampton (N.Y.) *Press*, Chris Frear and Sharyn Maust and the staff of the Bedford (Pa.) *Gazette*, Don Smith of the Monticello (Minn.) *Times*, Bob Buckel of the Azle (Texas) *News*, Andrea Hurley of the Marthasville (Mo.) *Record*, Grey Montgomery of the Junction City (Kan.) *Daily Union*, Patsy Speights of the Prentiss (Miss.) *Headlight*, Tim and Jeremy Waltner of the Freeman (S.D.) *Courier*, and Jeff Brady of the Skagway (Alaska) *News*. Additional thanks to Tom Mullen, Dwight Sparks, Tom Terry, Ben Carlson, Kerry Sipe, Robin Johnston, Bart and Hoover Adams, Frank Fee, Priscilla M. Brown, Phil

Meyer, Peirce Lewis, Kathy Gelman, Bill Horner, Michael Palmieri, David Fritz, Bill Rollins, Leonard Pitts Jr., Federico van Gelderen, Hal Tarlton, Michael Sellett, Bill Meyer, Ted Vaden, Rebel Good and Tommy Thomason.

And a special note of credit and appreciation for the many community journalism students over the years who "road tested" this text and who contributed to this edition with their own research. Whenever possible, I have attempted to name them in the text. Thanks also to Jerry Brown at the University of Montana for his colorful introduction and to Gloria Freeland for her enthusiastic foreword. A particular note of appreciation to the folks at Kansas State University for believing in the vitality and fundamental importance of community journalism from the get-go. It would be difficult to overstate the importance of the Huck Boyd National Center for Community Media at Kansas State, which has spearheaded the national renaissance of acceptance for the craft. Carol Oukrop and John Neibergall, bless you: You inspired me to create a center for community newspapers in my home state. And thanks also to the North Carolina Press Association and the 182 community newspapers of the Old North State for helping to make that dream come true.

I would be remiss if I didn't acknowledge the sustained support and encouragement received from colleagues at the School of Journalism and Mass Communication at the University of North Carolina at Chapel Hill—not just for this book, but also for the Carolina Community Media Project. Without Dean Richard Cole (who suggested back in the early '80s that I write this book!) none of this would have happened; Cole has been a champion of the Carolina Community Media Project from the very start.

And, lastly, a heartfelt thanks to my wife, Lynne Vernon, whose own love and enthusiasm for quality community journalism keeps me on my toes.

ONE

The State of Community Journalism

What Is Community Journalism?

Invariably, when people ask, "What is *community* journalism?" I always feel as if I should be able to respond quickly, "Community journalism is . . . A, B and C."

But, being "American by birth, and Southern by the Grace of God," I can best answer the question "What is community journalism?" with a story—for storytelling is one of the South's greatest legacies.

And the story itself, told in the first person, came from Governor Mike Easley himself, in his inaugural address to the North Carolina Press Association, the very month he took office, January 2001.

Shortly after Easley was elected governor, he needed some downtime to recover from the rigors of the successful campaign of 2000.

So he took the ferry boat from Southport in his native Brunswick County to his vacation spot at Bald Head Island.

On the way across the sound from Southport to Bald Head Island, Easley spotted the boat's captain sitting on a copy of the local community newspaper, the *State Port Pilot*, a prizewinning weekly out of Southport.

Repeat, a weekly—and, at this point, a three-day-old weekly.

But the news would be new to Easley; so the governor-elect asked the captain if he could borrow the paper to read during the boat trip—and the captain said, "Yes."

Easley read the paper, heartened by, as he put it, "seeing all those faces and names I knew . . ." So, by the time the boat had gotten to the dock, the governor-elect wasn't finished with the *State Port Pilot*.

Easley asked the captain, "Can I keep the paper?"—clearly expecting the old salt to defer . . .

But this is the response he got: "No," said the captain flatly, "I haven't finished with it yet."

Definition: Small Is Beautiful

A community newspaper is a publication with a circulation under 50,000, serving people who live together in a distinct geographical space with a clear local-first emphasis on news, features, sports, and advertising.

A more liberal definition of community journalism will include papers serving not just "communities of place" but also communities of ethnicity, faith, ideas or interests.

The use of a centralized printing operation, called "clustering," is one way that community papers contain costs. Here, at the Franklin (N.C.) *Press*, owned by Community Newspapers Inc. of Athens, Ga., multiple papers are printed each week. Staffs, seen here from several papers, also gather for occasional group workshops.

You know community journalism when you see it. The heartbeat of American journalism. Journalism in its natural state.

Here's the way one kid put it: After taking my community journalism class, George Butcher concluded, "If people are the most important thing on the planet, then community is what life is all about. Following that logic, community newspapers are among the most important publications on the planet."

Faces and Names; Names and Faces

Picking up two random copies of my old weekly, *THIS WEEK* (now a healthy 10,000-circulation daily in western North Carolina), I was greeted by a couple of stories on inside pages that say everything about what community journalism is . . .

The first story was about an annual spring academic awards banquet held at one
of three high schools in the paper's coverage area. After a synopsis of the principal's congratulatory speech, the writer listed the names of all 80 high school students—and their parents' names as well! The 33-inch story was accompanied by a large photograph of the group. Large enough—four columns wide—so you could clearly make out the face of each kid.

On another page I found a 30-inch news release from the local arts council detailing the opening of *Alice through the Looking Glass*, an original production involving 80 area kids. Again, every single character and every single young actor was listed—and yes, this story, too, was accompanied by a four-column-wide photo.

In the words of 1998 Pulitzer Prize–winning weekly newspaper editor and co-publisher Bernard L. Stein of the Riverdale *Press* of New York City, "Our job is to cover the everyday lives of ordinary people."

Relentlessly Local

Beyond the beltway—far from the stakeouts for the latest news celebrity, shouted interviews-by-ambush, "Gotcha quotes" and pack journalism—there exists another kind of newspaper journalism. Small-j journalism, some call it.

It's the kind of journalism practiced by newspapers where the readers can walk right into the newsroom and tell an editor what's on their minds. It's the kind of newspaper that covers the town council, prints the school lunch menus, leads the sports page with the high school football game, tells you who visited Aunt Susie last week and runs photos of proud gardeners holding oddly shaped vegetables.

The paper is loaded with weddings, anniversaries, engagements, police blotter reports, sports statistics, births and obituaries—all with one common denominator: The emphasis of the paper is local first, or what late CBS legend Charles Kuralt called "relentlessly local."

We call such papers "community newspapers."

Though the label may be new to some, the practice and form have been around since the first wooden hand presses cranked up over 200 years ago in this country. That rich tradition is strong in every state; I like the motto of the Quakertown (Pa.) *Free Press*: "100 percent local since 1881." In the words of editor Jim Sachetti of the Bloomsburg (Pa.) *Press-Enterprise*: "Local?—It's the only game in town."

Though such papers are small, their impact is large.

Daily Proof That Their Town Was Still There

When the great flood of April 1997 ravaged the town of Grand Forks, N.D., the Grand Forks *Herald* kept on publishing, in spite of the fact that the entire downtown was under water and the newspaper office was devastated. The 35,000-circulation Knight Ridder daily kept on keeping on. Publisher Mike Maidenberg recalls they decided, "We're going to publish something, no matter how primitive." For two months, a nearby elementary school on higher ground provided a computer lab with old Macs and "little chairs for our middle-aged butts," quips Maidenberg. The staff, many of whom had suffered the same fate as many of the readers, camped out in rented RVs by the school in order to put the paper out. Each day the paper was e-mailed to its sister paper, the St. Paul *Pioneer-Press*, where two editors put the *Herald* together. Once printed, the papers were flown 300 miles back to Grand Forks in time for 11 A.M. free distribution. "People couldn't believe it," Maidenberg says. "The city had burned, the town was flooded, the paper office destroyed, and yet—here was the newspaper!" Editor Mike Jacobs said afterward that the newspaper in a weird way became the virtual community, providing the daily proof that their town was still there. The *Herald* staff won a Pulitzer for public service in 1998 for their dedication to their craft and service to their community. Even after the recovery, Maidenberg says readers with complaints didn't forget. A typical barb might be softened like this: " 'I'm so mad at you about [you name it], *but*, I'll never forget what you did for us in the flood.' " And when longtime publisher Maidenberg retired, the mayor proclaimed Saturday, Dec. 13, 2003, "Mike Maidenberg Day."

You Are Here

Upon entering any shopping mall, the newcomer is sure to be greeted just inside the mall's entrance by a large map or schematic model showing the location of the various shops and food courts. Then the shopper orients him- or herself by finding the big red dot bearing the inscription "You Are Here."

It would strike me as being eminently worthwhile if we in community journalism could but pinpoint our location so precisely in the American journalistic landscape.

And I use the inclusive "we" here with good reason. For 15 years I was co-founding editor-publisher of a pair of community newspapers in North Carolina. Though I am a journalism teacher now, I like to think of myself as a Once and Future Publisher—for I intend to have a piece of another community paper before I'm through. So it is not with a detached, ivory tower point of view that I began asking: What is the state of community journalism? For I too am a stakeholder.

Two States of Community Journalism

The very topic itself, "The State of Community Journalism," could be taken semantically at least two ways. That title implies a question: What is the current situation regarding community journalism in the United States? As in the State of the Union address, or Ed Koch's famous line: "How'm I doin'?" We'll look at the big picture first, and then zoom in for the break-out numbers. Relax, you mathphobics, the arithmetic will be simple.

THE NATIONAL PICTURE: DAILY DILEMMAS, WEEKLY STRENGTH

> It was the best of times, it was the worst of times.
> —CHARLES DICKENS, *A Tale of Two Cities*

Dickens could have been writing about the newspaper industry during America's post-9/11 era, midway between the millennium and the 'teens, when big dailies see their readership continue to slide, small dailies struggle to find their identities, and weeklies quietly flourish.

Make no mistake about it: The people who are running the growing weeklies (any paper that comes out less than four times a week) are not smoking fat cigars, sitting back in their chairs with their feet on the desk. They are, as the expression goes, busting their humps.

That being said, the numbers are in: As this book goes to press, looking at figures from the mid-'90s till now, *there are more weeklies, reaching more people, with a higher average circulation*.

Who'd a-thunk it? Weeklies, long deemed the redheaded stepchild of the media industry, making a go of it, doing an end run on the stumbling big guys.

BY THE NUMBERS

Community newspapers (defined as weeklies and small dailies) dominate the U.S. newspaper landscape. There are 9,321 total newspapers, 9,104 of which are small newspapers. Here's the breakdown, according to the *2004 Editor & Publisher Year Book*:

Dailies. 85 percent (or 1,239 of the nation's 1,456 daily newspapers) have circulations of under 50,000 and are thus classified as "Small Newspapers" by the American Society of Newspaper Editors (ASNE). Because of their local news emphasis, I call them community newspapers too. These small dailies reach 44 percent of all daily readers.

Furthermore, of the 1,239 small dailies, 85 percent (1,047) have circulations of under 25,000. On the other hand, overall, only 15 percent (217 dailies) fall into the classification of "big" dailies, papers with circulations in excess of 50,000. Again, the "big/small" line in the sand comes from ASNE, not me.

Weeklies. In addition, there are 7,865 weeklies (including twice-weeklies and tri-weeklies, but excluding shoppers) with an average circulation of 7,467 readers, reaching 50.2 million readers, for a near all-time high in readership, according to the Newspaper Association of America figures.

Urban alternative weeklies such as the Portland (Ore.) *Mercury*, with its political/arts and entertainment niche marketing, have enjoyed strong growth recently. Notice the paper's spunky focus: "News · Culture · Trouble."

Now fold in other types of often-overlooked community newspapers, including (again, from the 2004 *E&P Year Book*) along with circulation numbers for the largest circulation categories:

- 112 alternative community papers, reaching 7.5 million readers
- 188 black community papers, reaching 5.4 million readers
- 135 ethnic community papers
- 39 gay and lesbian community papers
- 137 Hispanic community papers, reaching 6.2 million readers
- 103 Jewish community papers
- 116 military community papers
- 114 parenting community papers, reaching 5.2 million readers
- 125 religious community papers
- 92 senior community papers

Totals. Add it all up and you'll find that 97 percent of the nation's newspapers are "small" or community papers, while only 3 percent are "big."

The 9,104 "small" newspapers reach 108.9 million readers.

The 217 "big" major metro dailies reach 38.2 million readers.

Kind of makes you think differently about the word "small."

Now, most likely there is overlap in readership. (At our house we subscribe to three papers: one major metro, one large community daily and a weekly.) We are probably not alone; clearly more research is needed in dual readership statistics and patterns.

A SNAPSHOT OF ONE STATE

But the title "The State of Community Journalism" could also be interpreted as a declaration, as in: Wyoming, the State of Community Journalism! For friends, as Bob Dylan said, "you don't need a weather man to know which way the wind blows."

In the Tar Heel State where I teach, North Carolina's statistics on community journalism mirror the national figures: 182 out of the 189 newspapers, or 96 percent, are community newspapers by my definition.

The breakdown goes like this:

- 141 weeklies, semi- and tri-weeklies (75 percent of the state's papers are weeklies)
- 48 dailies, including:
  - 3 major metros with circulations of 100,000 or more
  - 5 big regional dailies, with circulations of 50,000–99,999, which still pay a considerable amount of attention to local news, even if "local" is 10 to 30 counties!
  - 40 community dailies, with circulations of under 50,000 (85 percent of the state's dailies are "small")

ONLINE STATS

Of the 189 newspapers in the state, 135 have Web sites, of which 127, or 94 percent, belong to "small" newspapers.

OWNERSHIP

Of the state's dailies, 88 percent are chain or group owned.

Of the state's 141 weeklies, 73 (52 percent) are still family or independently owned. That's a fairly remarkable figure these days: the majority of the state's weeklies are still in local hands.

GOT LOCAL?

According to a reader survey done by Belden Associates for the North Carolina Press Association, 81 percent of those polled said they read a newspaper in the last week. The 2000 N.C. Statewide Readership Study also underscores what other similar surveys have revealed:

- *People want local news.* 61 percent listed Local Community News as the "most important" part of the paper.
- *Local news is the most read part of the newspaper.* 62 percent said they look at the Local Community News "regularly"—more than any other section.
- *Readers trust their newspaper over other media.* 75 percent of adults said their newspaper has the most accurate information on community events, compared to TV, radio and the Internet.

Trends: The View from Here

What are the changes and trends in our business? Here are some, maybe not all, of the dominant themes that I keep bumping into:

- The survivability, growth and acceptance of community journalism in all its many forms
- The changing American demographic landscape
- The technological revolution
- The loss of independent voices in the publishing world, coupled with the corporatization of America
- The resurgence of community journalism in higher education

SURVIVABILITY, GROWTH AND ACCEPTANCE

"Nothing is more important to American journalism than the editor who sees the people he covers every day."

Those wise words come from Eugene Roberts, professor at the Phillip Merrill College of Journalism at the University of Maryland at College Park, who delivered a speech to the 2004 winter meeting of the North Carolina Press Association, asking, "What's Next for the American Press?"

Roberts, a UNC-CH grad, got his start at the Goldsboro *News-Argus* in Wayne County, eastern North Carolina, where he was the farm reporter, responsible for the well-read feature titled "Rambling in Rural Wayne." The column contained, Roberts recalls, "family reunions, recipes for sage sausage, sweet potatoes who looked like Gen. Charles de Gaulle . . ." So "the world could be exploding but the Rambling in Rural Wayne had to come out."

Prior to his teaching career, Roberts served as the legendary executive editor of the *Philadelphia Inquirer* for 18 years. On his watch, "the Inky" won 17 Pulitzers. Subsequently, he served as the managing editor of the *New York Times*. Though his fame was made at large papers, Roberts hasn't forgotten his roots, or how important community papers are.

"Community newspapers are extra important," he says. "They ought to thrive and flourish."

The Vanishing Newspaper is the attention-getting title of Professor Phil Meyer's new book. Speaking to a journalism workshop in 2004, Meyer was *upbeat about community papers*, saying, "Specialized media for specialized audiences are doing better, which is good news for small newspapers and not-so-good news for larger newspapers."

Meyer predicts that if major metro dailies don't right their ship, the last newspaper will hit the streets in April 2043. Give or take a month or two.

The "specialized media" about which Meyer speaks is a huge growth area of our times. As has been said, "We no longer ask, 'Is it newsworthy?' Instead we ask, 'To whom is it newsworthy?'"

Niche journalism and target marketing are in. At a national journalism educators' conference in 2004, the International Newspaper Marketing Association reported, "There is a profound shift in consumer and advertiser markets from mass to niche to one-to-one—meaning more targeted newspapers aimed at more targeted markets."

Community newspapers: in the right place at the right time with the right stuff.

Not surprisingly, then, there has been an explosive growth of the ethnic press. The fastest growing sector is most probably the Spanish-language press, according to the Freedom Forum *News* quoting Maritere Arce, assistant editor of *El Diario La Prensa*: "We've proved we have a winning formula that [mainstream newspapers] don't have and can't execute without us . . . We're in a strong position," she said. *El Diario*, a 54,000-circulation New York City daily dating back to 1913, is published right under the noses of the *New York Times* and the *Wall Street Journal*. Arce predicts the number of Hispanic newspapers will rise rapidly.

Kirk Whisler, founder and first president of the National Association of Hispanic Publications, agrees, noting that the number of Spanish-language weekly newspapers jumped from 74 in 1970 to about 250 by 1999.

"Explosive" circulation growth has followed. According to "The State of the News Media 2004: An Annual Report on American Journalism," published by the Project for Excellence in Journalism, "The circulation of Spanish-language dailies in the United States has more than tripled from 440,000 copies sold each day to 1.7 million."

In my home state of North Carolina, where AP estimates the Latino population grew to 350,000 from 1994 to 2004, there were at least five new Spanish-language newspapers start-ups in as many years. And that's being conservative. The true numbers of Latino newspapers are hard to track, in part because of the cultural distrust that many Latinos have for authority. So, many Latino papers exist out there under the radar of their traditional mainstream state press associations.

ACCEPTANCE

Across a broad spectrum, community papers and especially weeklies are gaining national legitimacy in ways never before imagined. At last, *Editor & Publisher* has begun producing a yearbook dedicated exclusively to weeklies. *E&P*'s better-late-than-never recognition of the value, power and contributions of weeklies is a welcome sign of a larger national groundswell. People are beginning to get it: community journalism is hot.

Yet, even now, the bias is so heavily prejudiced in favor of dailies that you can still look in the edition of the *E&P Year Book* devoted to dailies only and see state maps with little white triangles on various counties standing for: "County Seats Without a Newspaper." What they're really saying is, county seats with *just a weekly*. The "bigger is better" bias is still around. Many state press associations still refer to their weeklies as "Non-Dailies." To get the idea of how silly and insulting this is, imagine referring to the *New York Times* and *USA Today* as "Non-Weeklies."

"Far too many of us suffer from an inferiority complex," says Swansboro (N.C.) weekly *Tideland News* editor Jimmy Williams, "which keeps us from doing a better job and also keeps us from enjoying the time we spend doing it."

But don't think for a minute that Williams is suffering from feeling like a second-class newspaper citizen. In 2002, Williams' paper was named the "Nation's Best Small Community Newspaper" in the National Newspaper Association's Best Newspaper Contest.

CHANGING AMERICAN DEMOGRAPHICS

When politicians speak of the "two Americas," they could be talking about the new demographics of our land: some very rural small towns withering on the vine while other towns—whether they want to or not—are burgeoning into bedroom communities, "exurbs" just down the four-lane from new office parks around the urban beltways. (We'll take a closer look at this phenomenon in Chapter 6.)

Though the number of weekly newspapers serving these "two Americas" has declined over the last 30 years, there has been an increase in the last 10 years. Also, the number of newspaper copies read and the average circulation of weeklies have been climbing steadily. Thus, weeklies are now larger, smarter and better read.

This is not widely appreciated, for weekly people are so busy putting out the next paper that they don't have much time for public relations—nor do they need it. Growth in circulation numbers has been driven by healthy and growing communities. "In the '90s, two million more Americans moved from metro centers to rural areas than migrated the other way," according to a *Time* magazine issue headlined "Why More Americans Are Fleeing to Small Towns."

Americans are living in "the age of the great dispersal," writes David Brooks in his book *On Paradise Drive: How We Live Now (and Always Have) in the Future Tense*. Brooks notes that "the truly historic migration is from the inner suburbs to the outer suburbs, to the suburbs of suburbia." For instance, while the population of Atlanta grew by 22,000 during the '90s, Brooks points out that Atlanta's 'burbs exploded in the same time period by 2.1 million. And it's happening all over the country.

To take another example, not far from my writing retreat in the southern Appalachians, a new golfing community is going up, with approximately 2,000 new homes slated to be built. Who's going to live here? Certainly not the natives. No, it's Joe and Marge from Akron, who are retiring early and selling their home (and their snow-blower) for a small fortune, which in turn can buy twice as much of a house and lot in rural North Carolina. This new demographic is significant to my friend Jeff Byrd, the publisher of the nearby Tryon *Daily Bulletin*. For these potential new readers are not doddering old poops in wheelchairs; they are "young poops," in their mid- to late 50s and early 60s, still healthy and looking forward to the best years of their lives. Byrd's formidable challenge is to get these new folks to become stakeholders in their new hometowns, and thereby to read the *Bulletin*.

In many areas of the Midwest, where small rural farming towns are drying up, publishers face a different challenge. Bill Meyer, award-winning editor and publisher of three Kansas weeklies, says, "Small towns have lost their retail trade center identity. There are fewer local stores to advertise shoes, automobiles and such. What do we do about it? To survive we must shift gears and do something different. Newspapers that don't adjust to the times won't be around long. The answer doesn't lie in e-mail or on the Internet. It comes to those who provide interesting feature stories about local issues and people."

LOSS OF INDEPENDENT VOICES

> The challenge that faces us in the next few years is saving the news business from the news business.
> —PETER SUSSMAN, journalist, from the Freedom Forum Calendar

Gene Roberts, whom we heard from earlier in this chapter, says that chain ownership, practically unheard of in the '50s, is changing the landscape of American journalism for papers both large and small. Of the nation's 1,456 dailies, 80 percent are now chain owned, according to Roberts. He acknowledges that when the big shift began occurring in the '80s, quality did improve among some chain newspapers. But, he laments, "other chains began expecting greater profits."

Roberts thinks this corporatization of American journalism means that "the business side is in clear control of many phases, either by committee or corporate decree," as "profit pressures force top managers (to) get more distant" from individual papers and local editors and publishers are "forced to focus on corporate goals rather than journalistic excellence."

"Newspapers are destroying themselves in order to keep profits unnaturally high," he observes, citing "under-funded, under-financed newspapers" as being common nowadays. In recent years, he claims, "more corporations began practicing 'accordion journalism,'"—contracting news staffs and news holes to fit the demands of economics. "Newspapers are making such a mistake by cutting back on their newsrooms," Roberts charges.

This has resulted in, among other things, a "diminishment of governmental coverage and international news." Roberts wonders, "Consider the danger if the majority of the voting public becomes more isolated from international news," or if newspaper owners who have a monopoly decide that governmental news is boring?

"It is possible that newspapers will fail if they don't provide critical, necessary civic reporting," Roberts says. But he is high on community journalism and cautiously hopeful about the rest of the industry. "Our business is safe if we remember what our business really is—to collect news and information and present it intelligently." And reversing the trend, American newspapers must not neglect governmental reporting, where, Roberts says, the news doesn't break so much as it oozes.

Author Phil Meyer (*The Vanishing Newspaper*) says big dailies are in trouble because at many publicly owned chains the bottom line has become more important than the headline, and quarterly earnings mean more than news content. At the worst, these owners raise prices, reduce quality, and take the money and run—what Meyer calls "harvesting your market position."

Management, more often than not at chains, that cares mostly about the bottom line (I call them "bottom-feeders") has become skillful at producing cheaper newspapers.

Meyer's Newspaper from Hell Scenario goes like this: Management introduces a *smaller web size*, which reduces costs for newsprint but creates a *shrinking news hole*. Because news is devalued in this corporate culture, management then begins hiring *less-skilled journalists*, whom it can *pay less and train less*, which in turn leads to *greater staff turnover*, about which ownership doesn't care, but which the folks in the local newsroom trenches are left to deal with.

Meyer says he wants to help turn things around by looking for "new ways to measure profitability so long-term investors are more willing to take a long look instead of milking the paper dry each quarter."

"Newspaper companies have the resources to fight [this trend]." But Meyer wonders, "Do they have the will?—that's the question."

As more papers are purchased by "groups" and become chain owned, the trend is having what media observer and *New Yorker* magazine writer Ken Auletta calls a "profound impact" on community papers.

"When you look out of the window of a jet flying at 30,000 feet, people on the ground look like ants," Auletta told a community journalism conference held in 1998 at Oswego State University of New York.

It is this "people as ants" corporate perspective that bothers Auletta, and it bothers me, too. From 30,000 feet up (or 1,000 miles to the north, east, south or west), whole communities—and the individuals living in them—become objectified, their issues and dreams, their very identity, trivialized by distance and the almighty bottom line.

"You can't be at a distance and know the truth," says developmental psychologist Lynne Vernon-Feagans.

Here is the big challenge for many chain-owned community newspapers today. As more papers come under the corporate thumb of distant owners, how can the conscientious community paper maintain its primary covenant with its community—and still keep the corporate front office happy with ever more demanding profit margins?

Independent community newspaper publishers (33 percent of publishers in my home state) are watching. Says publisher David Woronoff of *The Pilot* of Southern Pines, N.C., "The perverted corporatization of community journalism in some ways is reaffirming of what we do."

The flip side of this is: Corporate has gotten the message that Local is Hot because it's market driven. "There's gold in them thar hills." Why else would so many chain-owned major metro papers be trying to gobble up the successful community weeklies ringing their cities?

THE TECHNOLOGICAL REVOLUTION, YAWN

Our choice of labels is revealing about how far we've come as a culture with regard to technology and media. In the '90s we called it "emerging technology" and "new media." How quaint. Now, it's just our *stuff*, the tools of newspaper storytelling.

At even the smallest of weeklies today you can find the technological marvels that not so long ago were beyond a community journalist's wildest dreams. Nowadays e-mail, cell phones, laptops, digital cameras, photos off the Web, "Googling" sources, pagination straight to plate and online sites are simply the way we do it now. The first wave of the digital revolution has passed, and we're still in the storytelling business.

ONLINE

According the latest figures from the Newspaper Association of American, nearly 1,500 North American daily papers have Web sites, which show great potential for attracting that elusive young reader. More than 55 percent of Internet users, ages 18 to 34, get their news online weekly, according to a UCLA study cited in *The State of the News Media 2004*.

Further, 83 percent of newspaper Web users said these online sources were their top Internet source for local news and information. Not surprisingly, NAA reported in 1999 that of the Web sites belonging to daily papers, 75 percent were operated by "small" dailies.

For a close-up look at one state, consider mine. Of the 189 newspapers in North Carolina, 135 have Web sites, of which 127, or 94 percent, belong to "small" newspapers—including many weeklies.

Though nobody seems to be making a killing at it, online journalism has begun to hold its own. According to *The State of the News Media 2004*, though many Web sites are "now at the point where they can claim profitability, it will still be years before the Internet becomes a major economic engine that is paying for the journalism it contains."

Online is here to stay, if for now as only an accessory, a sexy alternative to our ink-on-paper, hold-and-fold mainline product. While many community papers seem only to be staking out their cyber-turf with make-do, mediocre content, others have created visionary, excellent sites. Online's future seems assured if only for one reason: kids love the Web. Young readers, the very group that seems *not* to be reading traditional papers, *eat up* online papers. (See Chapter 15.)

Off the Back Burner: Community Journalism and Higher Education

When recently asked by a learned scientist what I studied, I responded, "Community journalism—you know, small newspapers."

To which the researcher replied in genuine surprise, "Oh?! Are there any of those left?"

"A few," I said, allowing myself a private smile.

That anecdote captures the sort of myopic vision of the American journalism landscape common to many college and university-level journalism programs. Particularly during the '80s, as college and university journalism programs vied with one another to place graduates at so-called prestigious big-name major market media outlets to enhance their ranking and appeal, many "J-schools" either abandoned or simply overlooked community journalism.

But in doing so, they threw out the baby with the bath water.

In a country where 97 percent of all newspapers are defined by the profession as being "small," it is a stunning paradox that community journalism classes are not offered at more colleges and universities as a vital part of a practical, comprehensive journalism curriculum.

Fortunately, the last 10 years have seen a virtual renaissance across the land in community journalism higher education. New programs, new classes, new endowed chairs, new publications, new initiatives—and just recently the formation of a first-ever national-level association of like-minded community journalism professors—have all combined to move the field of study off the back burner of academe and to the front of the stove where the topic is now hot stuff.

Meeting in Toronto, Canada, in August 2004, a group of 25 journalism educators launched the first-ever Community Journalism Interest Group dedicated to

- invigorating and inspiring educators in community journalism by forming a national cohort of like-minded scholars sharing their ideas, findings and work on an annual basis
- fostering, encouraging and rewarding superior academic work in community journalism through an annual competition that would identify and showcase the best research papers and creative teaching ideas
- moving the field forward by supporting and affirming excellent teaching, publications and research in the field

- stimulating new affiliations, research and publications by nurturing and mentoring young academics in the field

- making a positive difference in the profession of community journalism by forging new partnerships and building new bridges between the academy and the profession, and by producing significant and practical research immediately useful to the profession.

KANSAS STATE UNIVERSITY

In the last 10 years at least a dozen universities and colleges I know of personally have launched community journalism courses, classes and initiatives, while several others have created centers for the study and advancement of community journalism.

Kansas State University has proven to be a national leader in the area of community journalism. Since 1993, the Huck Boyd National Center for Community Media at Kansas State's A. Q. Miller School of Journalism and Mass Communications has run the premier national-level symposium titled "Newspapers and Community-Building," co-sponsored by the National Newspaper Association Foundation and held in conjunction with the annual NNA convention, where professors studying community journalism share their latest findings. The HBNC is led by director Gloria Freeland, and the journalism school is led by director Angela Powers. Former director Carol Oukrop, who, along with executive director John Neibergall, pioneered HBNC in the early '90s, still teaches there. Neibergall now works in development at Bethel University.

From 1993 to 2000 the Huck Boyd Center published the community newspaper *Showcase of Excellence*, a hefty 72-page compendium of the winners from each year's National Newspaper Association Better Newspaper Contest. Kansas State also pioneered free, on-site journalism workshops around the state and an innovative journalism SWAT team concept that brought community journalism students to aid small papers where editors or publishers needed time off. While all three programs have been discontinued due to resource issues, the Huck Boyd example impressed many of us. Indeed, that's where I got my inspiration.

SOUTH DAKOTA STATE UNIVERSITY

You can't write about community journalism higher education without paying tribute to South Dakota State University, home of one of the nation's premier pioneer programs.

Engraved on the front of the program's 1950-era building are the words, "Printing and Rural Journalism." Professor Richard W. Lee, retired head of the Department of Journalism and Mass Communications, says though the printing curriculum is gone, the old "Rural Journalism" is very much alive in the form of community journalism. South Dakota State doesn't have a formal community journalism class per se, but the principles of community journalism are mainstreamed through all classes in the four sequences of the Department of Journalism and Mass Communications, involving 250 students within the College of Arts and Sciences.

Professor of journalism Lyle Olson says, "We have what some have called a model to mid-sized journalism program (continuous accreditation since 1948). Our mission always has been to train journalists for smaller market newspapers."

In the last site visit for accreditation, former San Jose *Mercury News* executive editor Jerry Ceppos (whose own paper won a Pulitzer for public service), said, "If the Pulitzer were to given to educators instead of practitioners, South Dakota State University might win the Pulitzer [for public service] because of the number and scope of its activities within the state of South Dakota."

Because of the rural nature of the state, every paper in South Dakota is a community paper, Lee says (only 11 dailies but 131 weeklies). Even the state's largest paper, the Sioux Falls *Argus Leader*, has a circulation of right around 50,000, placing it still within the ranks of community papers.

Lee points to 1,600 SDSU journalism grads, almost half of whom (approximately 700) are working in community journalism in South Dakota. "They're under every rock," he says with a chuckle. "The great thing about this job is that you're really in constant touch with your graduates. And that's fun."

For a time SDSU also the headquartered the International Society of Weekly Newspaper Editors, producing a monthly newsletter for some 200 members, plus a quarterly newsletter, *Grassroots Editor*. The quarterly is now produced by Chad Stebbins at Missouri Southern State University in Joplin, Mo., where ISWNE is headquartered.

In 2000, SDSU took on a new goal, which, according to Lee, was to create "the strongest Native American journalism program in the nation." The "American Indians in Journalism" program features Native American faculty members, a Lakota/Dakota Conference Room that reflects the cultural traditions of the local Native Americans and a curriculum aimed at tapping into the traditional Native American gift for storytelling and applying that innate talent toward narrative journalism. The program's slogan is "The School for Native Americans to begin journalism careers."

THE CENTER FOR COMMUNITY JOURNALISM

In 1998, at Oswego State University (part of the State University of New York), a new Center for Community Journalism was launched under the direction of Mary Glick. After an ambitious debut that included statewide television video conferences, the center created a national listserv and began offering summer workshops in various aspects of community journalism, led by the CCJ's infectious workshop leader John Hatcher, in conjunction with the journalism programs at the Roy H. Park School of Communications at Ithaca College and the State University of New York at New Paltz. However, as this book goes to press, the CCJ has been forced to regroup. After launching CCJ, Glick left for a job at the American Press Institute; and when in 2003 funding dried up for the CCJ, Hatcher decided to pursue his doctorate. According to SUNY Oswego's Assistant Provost Michael Ameigh, the CCJ is in transition as it reassesses its role and capabilities. Writing on the CCJ listserv, Ameigh, who is also the assistant director of the CCJ, says, "Things may have slowed down a bit, but the enthusiasm for what we are all trying to do in this age of limited resources has not waned."

CCJ is currently headed by Carolyn Rush, deputy to the president of Oswego. Meanwhile, the journalism program that CCJ spawned continues to flourish at SUNY Oswego, where Linda Loomis is head of the journalism program and faculty liaison to the CCJ, writes that CCJ "continues as a lively advocate the grass-roots press. It provides working professionals with onsite educational programs, training staff members at community newspapers throughout New York State in the latest techniques in reporting, editing, and design. The CCJ also is the co-sponsor, with the New York Press Association, of an initiative for better newspapers that invites NYPA members to submit their publications to a multi-disciplinary team for written critiques. Oswego State students benefit from having the CCJ on campus, where they can have access to community newspapers from around the state, interact with professional journalists, and participate in internships offered through the New York Press Association and other newspapers that are connected to the CCJ."

OTHER INITIATIVES AND PROGRAMS

Here are some additional notable developments of the period 1999–2004:

- In a groundbreaking initiative, the Ayers family of the Anniston *Star* of Anniston, Ala., has donated the daily newspaper to the University of Alabama where College of Communication and Information Sciences Chairman Ed Mullins proposes to "change the landscape of journalism education and community journalism by establishing a 'teaching newspaper' as part of a new master's program in Anniston, Ala." Mullins says he thinks the partnership and the UA-Tuscaloosa master's degree in community journalism is a first of its kind in the nation.
- Professor Tommy Thomason at Texas Christian University has created an extremely successful community journalism training program in conjunction with the Texas Press Association in which hundreds of small daily and weekly journalists have benefited from lively workshops at TCU.
- As this book goes to press, the University of Kentucky has received funding for the creation of an Institute for Rural Journalism and Community Issues, with Al Cross serving as director. The UK School of Journalism and Telecommunications is led by director Beth Barnes who is very excited about this new community journalism initiative.
- The Poynter Institute for Media Studies in St. Petersburg, Fla., now offers seminars with such titles as "Reconnecting with your Community."

• The American Press Institute began offering seminars in 2004 geared toward community newspapers with titles such as "Managing the Weekly Newspaper," "Editing the Weekly and Community Newspaper" and "The Executive Development Program" (for community newspaper leaders).

A COMMUNITY COLLEGE GETS IN ON THE ACT

As this book goes to press, one new community journalism distance education initiative is being launched by a community college in North Carolina. Beginning in the fall of 2004, students were able to take individual online classes or earn an associate degree in community journalism from Central Carolina Community College in Sanford (<www.cccc.edu>).

The new initiative came after the urging of several community newspaper publishers and with the support of the state press association. The program's lead instructor, Mavis Carter, says she thinks the program will appeal to older, more local students who for various reasons might not be able to attend a major college or university but who want to go right to work at their hometown papers. Publishers say they hope such graduates-turned-reporters will be more apt to stay put at a hometown paper.

What does this signal to the leading J-schools at major universities? That we're not supplying a consistently reliable pool of new graduates excited about community journalism and willing to work in less than major metro venues? Stay tuned.

The classes offered include principles of community journalism, communications law and ethics, news gathering and reporting, writing for mass media, feature and editorial writing, basic photojournalism, news editing, and journalism theory and production.

Carter explains that cccc is growing the program as a work in progress, with the inaugural class of community journalism students taking the "principles" class first, then moving on each semester to one or two newly designed classes. The program culminates with an internship at a community paper.

CIVIC AND/OR PUBLIC JOURNALISM

Major metro dailies getting on the local bandwagon and giving it their own spin and name has brought the national spotlight on local coverage—and therefore community journalism. But big city daily newsrooms being told to care by fiat can only hope to duplicate the day-in, day-out "humanistic journalism" practiced by community newspapers.

Big papers (at the corporate level at least) have realized (if only privately) that they have much to learn from the burgeoning, successful, savvy community newspapers ringing them and city central.

Civic journalism guru Jay Rosen of New York University was on the Pennsylvania State University campus to give an address titled enticingly, "I Don't Know What

Civic Journalism Is, and Neither Do You." During the question-and-answer session after the excellent presentation, the subject of community journalism arose. And the NYU associate professor challenged the audience, "What IS community journalism?"

Mike Duffy, one of the associate editors from the student online community newspaper, took up the gauntlet. I held my breath, but I needn't have worried.

"Community journalism . . . ," Mike responded easily, "it makes the community and the newspaper more real to each other."

"More *real* to each other," Rosen repeated, and nodded thoughtfully. He was impressed. And so was I.

AND CLOSER TO HOME

And finally, your author has been blessed with meaningful work. In January 2001 I became the founding director of the Carolina Community Media Project at the School of Journalism and Mass Communication (with seed funding from the Carolina Center for Public Service) at the University of North Carolina at Chapel Hill. Through teaching, research and outreach, the project seeks to support, enhance and empower the state's 189 community newspapers and their online sites. The project is dedicated to the proposition that strong community media help strengthen communities, and that communities—rural and suburban—with a vital civic life and a sense of place are key to high livability in a free democratic society. (More on the project in Chapter 22.)

On the Importance of Being from Ernestville

On the first day of class, the college instructor can ask where students are from, and many will lie. Well, maybe "lie" is too strong a word—but many will not be entirely accurate—they will not tell you the name of their town if they think it is "small," but instead will default to the nearest large city.

Why is that? Maybe the answer lies with those students from small places who do proudly tell you exactly the names of their little towns, no matter the size. The answer has to do with civic pride, an old-fashioned notion perhaps, but a priceless commodity these days. To be proud of your place is to be a stakeholder, a steward, a trustee—warts and all. As the old saying goes, "It's a poor frog that won't praise his own pond."

For without civic pride there can be no positive civic identity, the myriad factors that lend each place that "sense of place"—why living in Portland, Ore., is so dramatically different from Portland, Maine. And it follows that without civic pride and identity, civic life itself is in peril. Ours is a participatory society whose maintenance is dependent on so-called ordinary people embracing their roles as citizen stakeholders. George Bernard Shaw captured the civic engagement imperative

Don't let anyone tell you small papers won't take on tough issues. In 1990, the Washington (N.C.) *Daily News*, a 9,562-circulation family-owned community daily, won a Pulitzer for investigative reporting. Publisher Ashley "Brownie" Futrell Jr. proudly displays a copy of the *Daily News* announcing the award. The paper was hailed for exposing the local governmental cover-up of cancer-causing pollutants in the town's water supply.

when he said, "I am of the opinion that my life belongs to the community, and as long as I live, it is my privilege to do for it whatever I can."

Community newspapers serve a vital role in this dynamic. Says New York weekly co-publisher Bernard Stein, "The most important job of community newspapers is to persuade people that their lives are important." Stein asserts that empowerment leads to civic engagement. "It's my conviction that what we do is crucial to the maintenance of a real democracy."

The way we make democracy work is through transparency, checks and balances, and by talking, talking, talking. Community newspapers should be all about "building a civic culture of conversation," says media ethicist Donald Shriver, president emeritus of Union Theological Seminary at Columbia University.

For without civic life, the very fabric of our democratic society is at risk of succumbing to apathy and alienation.

Charles Kuralt knew the importance of maintaining civic life. In a 1985 commencement address at the University of North Carolina at Chapel Hill, the legendary CBS newsman said, "It was on this campus, all those years ago, that I first became faintly aware that there is, in this state, and in this nation, and in this world, an association of men and women, who, while they may not even know one another, might still be called a conspiracy of good people."

I'd like to think that there is also such a thing as a "conspiracy of good papers," whose good works (again, using Kuralt's words) "in concentric circles, as if from a pebble tossed into a pool . . . spread outward to the farthest corners of our state, and far beyond its boundaries."

That's the real significance of the 9,104 small newspapers toiling away off the interstates—each one covering local government, the school board, the high school drama club production, the Rotary Club, the zoning debate, the sporting events, the births, the engagements, the weddings, the anniversaries and the deaths, the very life of each place between those pages.

This is what Walter Lippmann was referring to when he said, "A free press is not a privilege but an organic necessity in a great society."

A conspiracy of good papers.

And it's all local. Relentlessly local.

TWO

With Apologies to Nike, but Why Just Do It?

One Journalist's Love Affair with Small Newspapers

> There are no small parts. Only small actors.—MILAN KUNDERA

In community journalism, as in acting, there are no "small" roles. And there's no such thing as a "nondaily," or "just" a weekly, either. Especially if you're the editor of that paper, every issue is very real, and there are no conditionals. So, we say:

- There are 3,000-circulation weeklies.
- There are 10,000-circulation weeklies.
- There are 12,000-circulation twice-weeklies.
- There are 14,000-circulation tri-weeklies.
- There are 3,000-circulation dailies published Monday–Friday.
- There are 15,000-circulation dailies published every day.
- There are 40,000-circulation dailies with an extra-big Sunday edition.

And those are just some of the examples and configurations.

The bottom line is: They *are* community newspapers. From now on, when we talk about newspapers in this book, we'll be specific, defining the paper in terms of its publication frequency, circulation, and ownership, if it's pertinent, and perhaps the population of the area it serves.

So it's understood that if you see the word "small" in this book, it's in a positive context. Take for instance, the Jasper (Ind.) *Herald*, a terrific community paper with a circulation of 13,851 in a town of 10,000 people. In ads seeking a photo intern, the *Herald* describes itself as a "small and beautiful paper." With an attitude like that, no wonder the *Herald* is one of the top "small" newspapers in the country.

Though we call it community journalism now, it still requires that you test the outer limits of your underarm deodorant. From an eight-page weekly on up, the so-called small-town newspaper requires all your guts, sheer grit, creativity and energy.

Big-city newspeople who harbor pipe dreams of buying that little weekly in rural Pennsyltucky and settling down to the leisurely pace of Rotary Club editorship with banker's hours had better wake up—because that's what a pipe dream is: pure fantasy. My workday averaged about 14 hours a day during my 15 years as co-publisher and co-editor. And whole weekends off were rare. A newspaper is a living thing. Just ask any newspaper widow or widower.

In the words of award-winning Kansas editor-publisher Bill Meyer: "I've never seen a good editor who was also a good golfer."

AT HOME IN THE BACKSHOP

As I write this, I am leaning on the light table in the production room of the Whiteville *News Reporter*, a 10,213-circulation family-owned twice-weekly in "deep eastern North Carolina"—one of my many stops this summer on the Community Journalism Roadshow (see Chapter 22 for more on the Roadshow). The experience out of the classroom keeps me honest while it grounds me. As the paper is being prepared for press, all my senses come alive here: the sweet, acrid smell of the backshop, the whir of the negative-developing machine, the crank and clank of the copy camera easel, the whoosh of vacuum on the copy camera back, country music in the background, faces of the strippers and opaquers lighted by ghostly illumination from the light tables, the prolonged zzzzzaaaap of the plate burner and the clunkaclunka of the plate developer.

The backshop is my home. I was raised in this briar patch. When I was a kid hanging out in the backshop doing odd jobs, they called the likes of me a "printer's devil." The paper became my nursery room. As a burr-headed, whistling newsboy, I couldn't get enough of the dusty, fusty confines of the Chapel Hill *Weekly* with its friendly Dickensian counting house of a shop, all a-clank and a-clatter with the busyness of collecting, collating and printing the news.

The printer's devil liked the backshop so much he decided to own one, and so a college degree and a career as a community journalist ensued. In 1969, along with two partners, I started a weekly, *THIS WEEK* (Forest City), in rural western North Carolina. Within five years we had moved to larger offices, purchased a press and bought out the competition semiweekly. By 1978 we had grown into a 60-page weekly, and that fall we went daily, renaming the paper the *Daily Courier*. Yearning for another weekly, in 1980 I sold my interest to my partners and started a second paper with two young optimists in another community. We published this paper as a free broadsheet weekly until 1982, when we converted to paid and twice-weekly. But the major recession of that year crippled us. After selling in 1983, I found my way into university teaching. (See Chapter 23 for two case studies of community newspaper start-ups.)

Never far from the newsroom or the backshop, I continued to freelance columns, features and photographs to the local community paper. All the while I began paying particular attention to the state of community journalism as only someone who had sat in an editor's chair for 15 years could do.

I started noticing things.

First, that during the recession of the late '80s (when major dailies were hemorrhaging, laying off reporters and folding at an alarming rate), the community papers seemed to be surviving in far better shape. Fewer layoffs, fewer papers folding, less decline in ad revenues and circulation relative to the big boys. Plus,

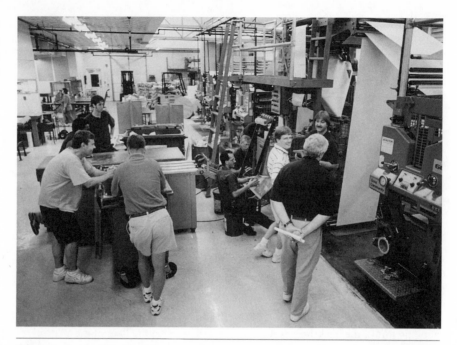

Working hard and playing hard: The crew at *The Pilot*, of Southern Pines, N.C., summer 1999, puts the paper "to bed" at about 11 P.M. Are we having fun yet? You can tell from that grin on the face of publisher David Woronoff (third from right).

community papers were hiring all through the recession. Perhaps not at the boom-town rate of the '60s to the '80s, but there weren't hiring freezes either.

The same pattern was repeated in the most recent recession. As veteran publisher Rebel Good of the 6,000-circulation tri-weekly Elkin-Jonesville (N.C.) *Tribune* said, "We didn't go boom in the '90s, but then we didn't go bust [in the recession that followed] either."

Secondly, community papers seemed better insulated not only from the vicissi-tudes of the economy but also from TV's insidious influence. In this online age of instant global communications, this satellite-enhanced Information Age in which it seems everybody has a Web site and we're all regularly "CNN-ated," how can a small-town newspaper survive? Haven't the Web and TV rung the death knell for commu-nity papers? Has the global village abrogated the need for the village news?

A flourishing community journalism industry says a resounding "no!" As it turns out, community newspapers have embraced online journalism. (See Chapter 15 for details of how farsighted community papers have capitalized on their online edi-tions). According to the Newspaper Association of America, fully 75 percent of the U.S. daily newspaper online sites belong to "small" or community dailies. Online editions are cranking out local news—our bread and butter.

Happily for us, people are hungry for and in need of information about their community, its concerns and their neighbors.

So until CNN can come up with a permanent uplink from Crooked Creek, Possum Trot and Gobbler's Knob, papers like the *Bugle*, the *Argus* and the *Tattler* will continue to prosper.

In the words of cowboy poet Baxter Black: "Small town papers often thrive because CNN or the *N.Y. Times* are not going to scoop them for coverage of the 'VFW Fish Fry,' 'Bridge Construction Delay,' or boys and girls playing baseball, receiving scholarships, graduating, getting married or going off to war. I think of local papers as the last refuge of unfiltered America. A running documentary of the warts and triumphs of real people unfettered by the spin, the bias and the opaque polish of today's homogenized journalism. It is the difference between homemade bread and Pop Tarts."

WE AIN'T AFRAID OF WORK

The plates for the Whiteville *News Reporter* are ready now and are being loaded onto the big light blue Goss Community press, the flagship of community papers everywhere. I can't help but think back to my favorite pressman, Babe Yount of the 13,326-circulation tri-weekly Waynesville (N.C.) *Enterprise Mountaineer*, whose Goss was emblazoned with two big signs on the press's folder: "U.S.S. YOUNT" and "We Ain't Afraid Of Work."

The press operator, who you'd better get along with because he or she can make you look like either a king or a goat, fires up the press, which takes off like a chained locomotive. To stand beside a running press is to be in the presence of the essence of our trade. After all, before it was "the Media," was it not "the Press?"

I still prefer the latter, for it evokes the power, energy and vitality of the printed word rifling through the giant machine . . . the oily pungent smell of printer's ink, washer and solvent . . . the dry tang of paper dust that tickles the inside of your nose . . . the concrete floor vibrating slightly as the press thrums a staccato chunkachunkachunka . . . the solid schuss of paper blurring through the units . . . the steady whining whir of metal rollers . . . and the sticky, tacky hiss of rubber rollers meeting, meshing and parting.

Standing at the end of the press, watching the stream of neatly stacked papers shooting off it, I can't help but be reminded again why I am, and always will be, a newspaperman. And, above all, a small-town newspaperman. A community journalist.

WE BLEED INK

When 77-year-old Bill Meyer, the editor and publisher of three Kansas weeklies, received the highest lifetime achievement award from the International Society of Weekly Newspaper Editors, he said, "If a doctor told me, 'You've got two weeks to live,' I'd answer with, 'That gives me time for two more issues.'"

What Is a Community Paper? One Editor's Perspective

Vicki Simons is the former director of the Center for Community Journalism at Oswego State University in New York. Before holding that post, she, along with her husband, Tony, owned the Hillsdale (N.Y.) Independent *and built it into a healthy 9,715-circulation 100-page twice-weekly. Simons is also a past president of the New York Press Association. The following comments are excerpted from her introductory remarks opening a teleconference on community journalism held at the* ccj *in Oswego. In her introduction Simons said that community papers could be described as weeklies and small-circulation dailies; then she went on to illustrate her point in detail.*

. . . But even without defining it or working in it, you *know* instinctively what community journalism is: It chronicles and comments on the every-day topics that shape peoples' lives in our neighborhoods and in our towns; it involves reporting on all manner of personal tragedies: fires, auto accidents, crimes, children fighting ghastly diseases.

But it is also chocked full of reports on the offsetting triumphs of life: There are profiles of courage, accomplishment or simple good-heartedness. Notice is taken of time volunteered, money donated, anniversaries attained, awards conferred—documentation of the events, activities, meals, meetings and gather-ings where the glue of the community gets applied.

Much of the mainstream or mass media turns its nose up at this kind of cov-erage. By their lights it's not important or significant enough to make the cut. But in terms of real effects on real peoples' lives, *this* is where the action is.

It's pretty obvious that this nose-close-to-the-ground reporting gives commu-nity journalists an up-close-and-personal view of their communities. That makes us more accurate, by and large, than the bigger media.

It's always a revelation to me when the bigger media come into our coverage area to report a story. It is rare we don't pick up a host of small mistakes, a name misspelled, a place misidentified, some other local sense misrepresented in some fashion.

Not that community journalists doesn't make mistakes too—of course we do. But when we do we have people at the deli counter, or the laundromat or the dining room table *telling* us we got it wrong.

At best, our thresholds for accuracy and responsible reporting are greater be-cause we are a part of the community we cover, not outside it.

But there is a danger here as well. Does this community connection make us too timid to do the difficult stories . . . ? Too familiar to recognize the emerg-ing trend?

This is the real front line of community journalism: sorting out the degree, for example, to which we function as community boosters, or community watchdogs.

Linda Gilmore is the former assistant director of the Huck Boyd National Center for Community Media at the A. Q. Miller School of Journalism and Mass Communications at Kansas State University. She is currently an assistant editor in the publications unit of Kansas State Research and Extension. In 1998 she wrote the following commentary in answer to a nagging question.

Recently I was challenged by the publisher of a large metro daily to explain how the Huck Boyd Center defined "community journalism." He believes that what they do at his large paper can be called community journalism. I didn't want to say otherwise, but I also didn't want to agree completely with him. I found myself fumbling around to describe what we really mean when we say community journalism. I even found myself getting defensive about it.

Because, when it comes right down to it, I really believe that community journalism is truly practiced in smaller newspapers—weeklies and small-market dailies. That's not to say that metropolitan newspapers don't serve their communities in different ways. But a "community" of half a million people just doesn't seem to quite fit the definition.

The term "community" implies that the people who live there have certain things in common: a common frame of reference, common knowledge about infrastructures and people and systems. It also implies a certain interactiveness, an accessibility to all.

James Carey talks about communication in terms of "sharing, participation, association, fellowship and the possession of a common faith." He goes on to say in the same article, "A ritual view of communication is not directed toward the extension of messages in space but the maintenance of society in time; not the act of imparting information but the representation of shared beliefs."

A person can only share and participate with so many people at a time. When a community becomes too large for most of the people to share those things, then perhaps it is not truly a community. Most large cities are actually made up of many smaller communities. In those settings, the people there share many things in common that others in the city as a whole don't share.

What all this has to do with community journalism is this: in the small towns and cities of America, the local newspaper is one of the links that connects people to each other. It is one of the ways that the community is maintained. It is part of the local discussion on issues that concern a community.

In a large city, the newspaper can only represent so many views at a time. Certain special projects, or a diverse letters to the editor section can bring more voices into a paper, but the audience is still measured in the hundreds of thousands.

There are other differences that I believe apply to the definition of community journalism. Often a community newspaper must rely on its own limited resources. The publisher who challenged me has the resources of a large newspaper chain behind him. If he faces unexpected disaster, those resources are at his disposal, at least to some extent. If some of his staff gets sick, there are people who can fill in. It may be hard, and require long hours, but the manpower is available.

At many community papers, if the editor gets sick, there's no one to fill his shoes. If the building burns down, he has to rely on the good graces of the local bankers and hope they will back him in rebuilding. If most of the staff eats tainted fruit and comes down with hepatitis A, there is no one to put out the paper. All these examples really happened at community weeklies I'm familiar with.

But somehow, in spite of these obstacles, the paper comes out every week, or every day, as the case may be.

In the small communities I know, the publisher and editor and reporters are recognized on the street and the members of the community can take them to task, or praise them, about something in the paper. The people at the newspaper belong to the same local organizations and churches as the rest of the community, their kids attend the community's schools and play softball in the community leagues. For the most part, the people at the newspaper fall into the same economic bracket as most of the community members. There is an accessibility and interactive quality that is lacking at most larger papers.

Looking at this year's Pulitzer Prize winners, I was pleased to see that community journalism is represented. The Grand Forks *Herald*, which won the public service award, is a community paper, though it has the resources of a huge corporation behind it. But it exemplified what community journalism is all about during last year's devastating flood. The staff of the paper were experiencing the same effects as the rest of the community and suffered just as much loss. They managed to put out the paper anyway.

The winner for editorial writing, Bernard Stein, is a community journalist in New York City. His paper, the Riverdale *Press*, serves a community within the larger city. It has long been an outstanding example of community journalism.

One of the finalists for editorial writing, George Pyle of the Salina (Kan.) *Journal*, is another fine editorialist. He is often at odds with the opinions in conservative Kansas, but he is a part of his community and holds to his mission of challenging people to really think about the issues.

A member of the Pulitzer Prize Board is also a representative of community journalism: Edward Seaton is publisher and editor-in-chief of the Manhattan (Kan.) *Mercury*. The *Mercury* serves a town of about 45,000. The Seaton family has owned the paper for a long time, but Seaton's ties to his community haven't prevented him from becoming involved in the Inter-American Press Association, an organization that works for press freedom in Latin America, or the American Society of Newspaper Editors (ASNE), of which he is president this year.

All this finally comes around to my final point about community journalism.

Providing the news and information that helps hold a community together doesn't preclude telling the hard stories or voicing unpopular opinions. Community journalism isn't synonymous with mediocrity. This year's edition of the *Showcase of Excellence* (an annual Huck Boyd Center publication of the year's finest community journalism from around the country) is proof of that, as are this year's Pulitzers. Community journalists are doing their jobs, with distinction, day in and day out, usually with little recognition. It's time that journalism educators and the newspaper industry recognized the significance of community journalism and encouraged continuing excellence.

In the future, when challenged to define community journalism, I plan to be ready with a definition and an explanation. I will leave defensiveness behind and will move ahead to promote a better understanding and greater respect for the journalists I serve.

Your Town; Your Turn

Whether you're a student of community journalism, or a reporter, editor or even owner, here's a little sensitizing exercise.

1. Go into your backshop. Close your eyes. Listen to the place. Catalog the sounds and smells. How does it make you feel? Write down the experience.
2. Go talk to the press operator. Find out about his (they used to be "pressmen") family, his history, how he got started, how long he's been with the paper, what he thinks of it. Ask him his opinion of how you could be doing a better job. But be forewarned; press operators are characteristically long on honesty and short on tact. It is one of their greatest occupational virtues; a press is a no-bullshit machine. Consequently press operators come equipped with what the late great Jim Shumaker was famous for calling "a 100 percent foolproof iron-clad bullshit detector."
3. Think back to how you got into this game. How has the business changed since then? How have your standards and your dreams changed? Where do you see yourself in five years? In 10 years?

THREE

What Am I Doing Here?

Speaking of Professional Identity Crises

When Bob showed up at the arts center on Main Street, he was already agitated. He had some other assignments to do—and this one, a seemingly insignificant check presentation, felt like a waste of time.

Four middle school students had won awards for their creative writing.

Big deal, Bob thought to himself. The paper's editor wanted a story and a photo, though Bob thought the whole thing was pretty lame.

He arrived at the arts center in a sour mood, spoke to no one, but watched as the parents, teachers and principals stood chatting in happy clusters around the main room of the arts center.

What losers. Privately Bob scoffed at the scene. He had bigger fish to fry. Didn't these little people realize how important he was?

The superintendent of the county schools spoke about the significance of good writing.

The director of the arts council spoke about the relevance of effective communication.

Each principal—all four of them—enumerated each school's efforts to promote excellence in the written word.

Bob was becoming increasingly agitated.

Then each student was called forward, handed a modest check and asked to say a "brief word."

As this ceremony dragged on and on, Bob began to fidget noticeably. He shifted his weight, sighed audibly, rolled his eyes and looked at his watch . . .

Finally, when he could stand it no longer, Bob was heard exclaiming to himself—loud enough for several people on either side to hear—"*What am I doing here?!*"

Be Here Now

Actually, that's a very good question.

What *was* Bob doing there—at that arts center check presentation in that small town served by that little newspaper . . . ?

The answer should have been this: blooming where he was planted; doing his job to the best of his ability *regardless* of the circumstances or setting.

Why is that? Because how you perform in challenging settings has everything to do with your future—because if you are under the impression that immediately after graduation (based solely on your family connections, good looks and charm) you are going directly to the *New York Times*, ESPN, *National Geographic*, *Sports Illustrated* or *Entertainment Tonight*, then hats off to you, bucko.

What *Do* We Do?

Comedian Howie Mandel likes to open his routine by asking audience members what they do.

"What do you *do*?" he demands simply.

Systems analysts, middle managers, and the like, have a hard time explaining exactly what it is they really *do*.

"Oh, so you analyze systems," says Howie in mock fascination.

"Well, not exactly," comes the embarrassed response.

"Well, then, what?" asks Howie with childlike innocence while his subject wriggles under the bright lights.

And the audience goes nuts as the poor soul stumbles all over himself trying to put into simple terms what he spends eight hours a day *doing*. He can't do it—because he's never thought about it before.

What do *we* do?

If we in community journalism can't say very quickly what it is we *do*, then it's a safe bet our work reflects that lack of identity, purpose and vitality. So right away, before we talk about the nuts and bolts of writing, editing and producing a community newspaper, let's figure out what it is we do *do*, so that if Howie Mandel were standing here today pointing his finger at us and saying, "Editors, publishers, reporters, photographers, advertising sales people of community newspapers . . . *what do you do*?" we would respond positively in a chorus of unity, in the words of the late Charles Kuralt of CBS fame, that it's our job *to be relentlessly local*.

A Dogfight on Main Street

According to the late Ken Byerly, author, professor and publisher, there's an old saying that captures the "local first" dictate of community journalism: "A dogfight on Main Street is more important than a revolution in Bulgaria."

"If we can't find a local angle, we will not touch the news—no matter how large it is," says Ed Harper, editor of the *State Port Pilot*, a 9,000-circulation family-owned weekly in Southport, N.C. Speaking with community journalism student Lauren Rippey, Harper said, "Our stories on 9/11 featured local people who had connections with someone who was killed or survived. And any stories on Iraq are of servicemen with Brunswick County roots."

The community daily has a special challenge. Many daily editors say they want their paper to be all-local, but that the news hole is too big, forcing them to use wire

The enlightened community newspaper is intimately involved with building its community through consistently positive coverage that also strives to be accurate, comprehensive, balanced and fair. No wonder community journalism is so challenging. The spirit of our work is embodied in this photo of a victorious Special Olympics athlete being held up by a real-life professional athlete while the happy boy's coaches respond with applause and support.

copy as filler. In their defense, many other community daily editors point out that readers expect a daily to carry nonlocal news—and that in some cases, the local community daily will be the reader's only source of printed news. So there is an obligation to print state, national and international news in the community daily.

However, the paper's local imperative should never be forgotten. Speaking with community journalism student Cullen Stafford, Kinston (N.C.) *Free Press* managing editor Lee Raynor put it this way: "Everybody wants to know what's happening in Afghanistan or Iraq, but what they really care about is whether or not their garbage will be picked up on time." The *Free Press* is a 13,000-circulation daily owned by Freedom.

The same week in 1999 when John F. Kennedy Jr.'s plane was lost in the Atlantic, the 5,050-circulation Tryon (N.C.) *Daily Bulletin* led with the death of an outstanding local college student, killed in a traffic accident. The lede read: "One of Polk County's leading young adults was killed in an automobile accident during the early hours on Tuesday morning in Spartanburg County." In his traditional front page column, *Bulletin* publisher Jeff Byrd noted, "The loss of Meredith McCallister this week for our community, like the loss of John Kennedy Jr. for the nation, leaves so much sadness, so much loss of potential. Our hearts like those of every person down every lane in Polk County and Landrum, go out to the McCallister family today . . ."

There is a vital, organic and synergistic interaction between various constituencies within the community, as well as between the community and the newspaper. In Danville, Pa., Geisinger Medical Center is the town's largest employer. Reflecting on the delicate relationship, former Danville *News* reporter Bill Reader put it like this: "When Geisinger sneezes, Danville catches a cold."

When Brevard, N.C., passed a liquor-by-the-drink law, it was the banner P-1 head in the twice-weekly *Transylvania Times*—and so it should have been. For the nearby big-city daily, the Asheville *Citizen*, which led with war in the Balkans, as it should have, the little Brevard story was on page 24 along with a smattering of other stories from the 17 other counties the *Citizen* tries to cover.

The *Citizen* may have scooped the Brevard community paper by two days or so, but to what end? The detailed story, in full length came out later, and it was the 30 inches the story deserved and the local readers wanted. In short, people in Brevard got their first news of the vote's outcome by word of mouth, by radio, by TV, and then maybe from the Asheville paper. But for the full story, Brevard readers waited until the Monday "*T-Times.*"

The Role of the Community Newspaper

Nobody should be covering Pottsville, Pa., better than the *Republican*; nobody should be covering Dixon, Ill., like the *Telegraph*; nobody knows Rutherford County, N.C., like the *Daily Courier*; nobody should get better coverage of the local Little League playoffs in McCook, Neb., than the *Daily Gazette*. Nobody.

At their best, community newspapers satisfy a basic human craving that most big dailies can't touch, no matter how large their budgets—and that is the affirmation of the sense of community, a positive and intimate reflection of the sense of place, a stroke for our us-ness, our extended family-ness and our profound and interlocking connectedness, what Stanford's Nadinne Cruz calls "the Big WE."

In these days especially, the role of the community newspaper and humanistic journalism is very much more subtle, important and far-reaching than one might suppose. The sheer accretion of relentlessly local coverage of the city council, the planning board, Boy Scout field days, church suppers and even Aunt Maude's 100th birthday all add up to a shouted YES for Our Town. An affirmation of the community's identity and its vision for itself, a way of saying over and over again in words and pictures a fundamental truth that keeps getting lost—that, yes, people are all that matter.

Community newspaper editors, publishers, ad reps, business people, reporters, photographers . . . students of community journalism: Put that on your wall. *People are what matter.* If you're not already doing so, live and work by that slogan—and watch your work and your product take off, your staff morale soar and your community relations improve.

Less Is More

In further trying to define ourselves we might start by saying what we don't do. For instance, a lot of us aren't daily. In fact, up until recently even we ourselves called ourselves "NON-dailies."

Too many of us tend to define ourselves by what we perceive as our limitations. As in: Philadelphia, Charlotte, Denver, LA are the Big Boys. And we, by extension— the Brevards, the Danvilles, the Tryons, towns perhaps you've never heard of—we're the Little Guys. As in: Little is Less.

Please, don't insult yourself. Such pigeonholing is demeaning and self-defeating. Let's come at it from a different tack. As in: Less is More and Small is Beautiful.

To the enlightened community newspaper, small is beautiful and less is more because it operates within "the human scale," a term that recognizes that people flourish when given one-on-one attention. But that 1-to-1 ratio is difficult to maintain in all transactions. However, the alternative is untenable.

The antithesis of the human scale is being caught on LA's Ventura Freeway in 10 lanes of mad commuters at rush hour, where human values deteriorate very quickly. Total strangers shooting at one another? Not my idea of community. By contrast, the small town has the human scale automatically working for it. You can make it work for you, too.

Here's how small is beautiful and less is more can be a boon for the enlightened community newspaper.

- A community newspaper can turn on a dime, make major decisions about coverage, editorial policy, news judgment, editing, cropping and advertising— without going through layers of needless bureaucracy and personnel.
- And because of the lack of layers, the access to the top is usually easier. Unless it's a poorly run, slack chain operation, the editor or publisher is Norm or Nancy in the next room, empowered to make decisions quickly.
- Because it is small, it doesn't cost a fortune to start and equip a community paper with the latest technology. (See Chapter 15.)
- Everybody does more. Generalists are needed. So it's a great place for (1) beginners who need to learn the holistic art of newspapers; (2) older folks who want variety because it's never boring at a community paper since you're always doing something different; and (3) people who care about the final product and want to maintain journalistic and artistic control over an entire project—all the way from conception to pressroom.

- Small is beautiful because you can limit your coverage area. Instead of spreading yourself too thin (as the big papers are trying to do with so-called local Neighbors editions—thinly disguised attempts to copy us!) we can spread ourselves THICK. In most cases the exclusively local weekly, twice- or tri-weekly is more valued by its readers and perceived by the community as being more caring and possessing more personality than the daily. That's why a great community newspaper can compete successfully against a large metropolitan daily. And that's why so many big-city dailies are scrambling to localize their coverage with zoned editions and Neighbors tabs. Doesn't that tell us something? One canny media observer even has a term for it: Professor Olin Briggs of Central Missouri State University calls it "the de-massification of the mass media."

Today the buzz is all about "niche communications." Your community is your niche. When Ron Dalby was general manager of the 6,500-circulation tri-weekly *Frontiersman* of Wasilla, Alaska, he said that pulling the plug on the wire service machine was "the best thing I ever did."

Conversely, when an all-local nondaily converts to daily and is forced by sheer need to add wire service to fill the voracious news hole, a strange thing can happen. Because national and international news tends to overshadow and dilute the local coverage, the reading public is liable to assume the editors no longer think that the local news is important. Community newspaper editors and publishers considering such a conversion should beware.

Why Size Matters

"Small is beautiful" is not just a smiley-face platitude. Research backs it up.

Psychologists have found that when, in any particular setting, there are *too many people* in a given geographical unit, and *not enough roles to fill*, some people feel worthless, nonessential to the setting, and at worst, alienated.

On the other hand, when in a setting there are *not enough people* to fill all the needed roles, many—if not most—people not only feel valued; they feel cherished.

This "human scale," in which everyone has a role, provides a valuable method for thinking about the dynamics of human aggregates. For our purposes that can mean the size of the town or the newspaper—or, for instance, the size of the school.

Think back to your own high school experience.

Psychologists have known for some time that high schools with student populations under 1,000 produce kids with a better sense of self-worth and well-being. It's because they get to do more.

In the wake of the 1999 Littleton, Colo., high school massacre, *Time* magazine asked, "Is Smaller Perhaps Better?" Kathleen Cotton, a researcher at the Northwest Regional Educational Laboratory in Portland, Ore., told *Time*: "It doesn't matter what category you measure, things are better in smaller environments. Shy kids, poor kids, the average athletes—they all are made to feel like they fit in."

Kids at smaller schools and in small towns are more likely to be high achievers than kids from huge schools and cities, according to behavioral psychologists Roger Barker and Herbert Wright of the University of Kansas in their landmark study of Oskaloosa, Kan., (current pop. 1,074) in the '40s and '50s. Barker and Wright call this positive scenario the "under-manned behavior setting," in which the yearbook editor might also be the head cheerleader; or in the small town, the school janitor might be the town mayor.

The opposite scenario, in which there are too many people and not enough valued roles to fill, is called the "over-manned behavior setting." People in this setting, who are not exceptionally talented in any area, may feel that they have no purpose, no calling, nothing that sets them apart. Only the exceptional athletes make the teams, only the smartest scholars make the Key Club, only the best actors get to star in the senior play.

It is not difficult to grasp why average students in huge high schools and some people in large cities can become invisible, and fall through the cracks of society, until they become all too visible tragically when they lash out in frustration against a society that they perceive doesn't care about them.

You can see how this applies to our line of work. Imagine yourself a new reporter in a newsroom of 400, a not uncommon number for a major metro newsroom. How are you going to know everybody? You aren't.

You may remain a "stranger in a strange land." Veteran reporter-photographers *who have never met before*, but who have worked for years in the same building, are often teamed up for story assignments. If you want to work in that setting, you need to know this dynamic.

If, on the other hand, you want to know all the folks with whom you work, then community journalism is the setting for you. If you want to know and be known to the community you cover, then community journalism is for you. And if you want to feel vital, needed and valued at a newspaper—right out of J-school—then community journalism is for you.

By the way, you might want to start where Baker and Wright did—in Oskaloosa, Kan. The community paper there is the Oskaloosa *Independent*, a 2,125-circulation weekly, which is one of only three papers in the state that dates back to territorial times before statehood in 1861. Publisher Clarke Davis, who also owns the weekly in Valley Falls, says, "There's a strength in weeklies because of the emphasis on local coverage."

Community in the News

"Community" is a hot topic because American culture has taken a philosophical swing toward all things more personal. America's yearning for inclusiveness is reflected in the public demand for products that make the consumer feel recog-nized, affirmed and a part of something intimate and worthwhile. The examples abound: user-friendly personal computers, "human scale" architecture such as Camden Yards or the neotraditional neighborhood, the two-seater roadster and microbreweries.

One theory has it that the growth of this "communitarian" spirit is due in part to a backlash to the "me-first '80s." Nowadays, people crave inclusiveness, to be a part of a real community, a town with a strong sense of civic identity, a sense of place.

As individuals we want and need to be recognized, valued and heard in the context of our towns. However, a city has a hard time being a community. While a city can offer many products and amenities, it must work harder than a smaller place to make its inhabitants feel accepted, nurtured and cherished. (For more on community, see Chapter 6.)

Danielle Withrow, town planner of Forest City, N.C., says that people crave acceptance, inclusiveness, being part of a real community, a place with a strong civic identity. We want to be recognized, valued, heard and affirmed in the context of our Home Towns. American citizens have come to insist that home must be more than Exit Ramp 45.

Thus, it is not surprising to find that within any major metropolitan city, various "communities" can and do flourish by nurturing and articulating their core values to their members. Affinity groups can range from the philosophical-intellectual (Portland, Oregon's community of poets), ethnic neighborhoods (Charlotte's Greek Orthodox community), to ethnic-sexual orientation groups (the Irish-American Gay, Lesbian and Bisexual Group of Boston). Each has its own identity, and each has very often a niche "community" newspaper to package news of specific interest to that constituency, while articulating and reinforcing the community's core values in an intimate, inclusive way that larger media can only mime at best. This would account for the success of the many different kinds of niche newspapers serving specific communities within larger population areas.

THE *NEW PITTSBURGH COURIER*

African-American newspapers are a perfect example of papers that, while they may serve a community of place, more importantly serve a community of another kind—in this case, a community of ethnicity.

Some 3,500 black newspapers have been published since the first American black newspaper, the *Freedom's Journal*, rolled off the presses in New York City in 1827, according to Roland Wolseley in *The Black Press, U.S.A. Editor & Publisher* lists 188 black newspapers in its 2004 *Year Book*.

Historically, these papers have been pivotal to the national black community in several ways. Going back a century or more, not only did they affirm the race by publishing positive stories about African-Americans (or stories that the main-stream press ignored), but they also were pioneers in the civil rights movement

Serving a community of ethnicity as well as a community of place: editor-publisher Rod Doss of the *New Pittsburgh Courier* says, "The other media tend to talk *about* our community . . . we talk *to* our community."

before the term "civil rights" existed, according to a 1992 article in the *Washington Journalism Review*.

Now largely in decline, compared to the huge circulations of the '40s and '50s, the leading black newspapers have repositioned themselves by producing relentlessly local coverage.

The *New Pittsburgh Courier*, founded in 1910 and published twice weekly since 1988, may not be the national powerhouse of its heyday in the late '40s. After succumbing to economic pressures in 1966, the paper was acquired by the owners of the Chicago *Defender* and reborn as the *New Pittsburgh Courier*.

Listening to Editor-Publisher Rod Doss, you get the feeling this is a paper coming to terms with a new mission and a new identity. Its community, once national, is now intensely local. Its audience consists of upward to 30,000 readers in the greater Pittsburgh area—a far cry from the 400,000 high-water mark of 50 years ago. Nonetheless, the *Courier* is a paper with a purpose.

Doss, a dapper, middle-aged man with the voice of a crooner, says, "This newspaper is very important to this community." One of the paper's primary functions is "to be a voice and to allow voices within the community to be heard." Ultimately, the paper wants to portray the "Black community" accurately, as Doss sees it, with a capital "B," "to dignify a race of people"—the way many African-Americans are not

portrayed in the mainstream white press, he says.

So how does the *Courier* compete with the great Pittsburgh *Post-Gazette* with its circulation of 248,000? Strategic news judgment, explains Doss. The big papers have to present a scattered sort of "shotgun approach" to what news they deliver, "but here at the *Courier*, we rifle in," Doss says. "And of course our readers know what they're getting.

"The other media tend to talk *about* our community . . . we talk *to* our community . . . we say 'we,' and we say 'us' in our stories, and the reader knows who we mean.

"We carry a certain sense of dignity about our community. We do take a positive outlook. There are so many people who are committed to their community, to their churches, to their families, and regrettably they're never portrayed as such in many of the media. This is a story that needs to be told."

As if to illustrate that point, Doss opens the *Courier* to a Lifestyle page that contains a 24-inch story about an annual community achievement awards banquet. It is illustrated with 10 two-column photos (containing 10 people) and a larger four-column horizontal photo in which at least 40 members of the Rodman Street Missionary Baptist Church are out in force to support Rev. Delano R. Paige, who was named minister of the year at the banquet.

For 28 years a nonprofit agency named Hand in Hand has been promoting black community achievement in Pittsburgh. How much coverage did this story get in the Pittsburgh *Post-Gazette*? Doss responds, "None that I'm aware of."

Of this kind of coverage in the *Courier*, Doss vows, "It's what it's all about. . . . We cover the interests and pursuits of our community that never see the light of day in the other media. . . . We make the community come alive. . . . It's a positive reflection on them and their community that they would never otherwise see."

Saturday's edition is keyed on the Democratic primary election of the spring, and there are two full edit pages, including an editorial endorsement of candidates, accompanied by a large listing for clear and easy reading of the editor's choices. There are many black candidates, and they receive support from the *Courier*. This is not taken lightly by candidates or readers. (Many white politicians advertise in the *Courier*.)

But most notably, Doss is aware of the *Courier*'s responsibility and of the paper's political clout: "It's an important role [endorsing candidates]. I think the community looks forward to it. I've known people to carry our list of endorsements into the voting booth and vote just as we recommend.

"But that comes after time . . . of being responsive . . . it's that believability . . . they [the readers] *trust* what we have to say."

And what of the future of the *New Pittsburgh Courier*, in the shadow of the mighty *Post-Gazette* and the upstart *Tribune-Review*? The Pittsburgh newspaper wars are legendary.

Doss is philosophical. "There's a niche market here. We just have to hone in on it." His readers live in scattered pockets all over the four-county region, in diverse neighborhoods, which makes it all the more challenging to cover those "communities within communities."

Doss is upbeat about the future. "We do have a plan for the future, both locally and nationally," he says. As with so many other things in community journalism, time will tell. But one thing's for sure, if you want to know what's going on in the black community in and around Pittsburgh, you've got to read the *Courier*. Rod Doss is banking on that formula. (For more on ethnic community newspapers, see Chapter 19.)

The Community Journalism Perspective

Regardless of differences in subject, specialization, setting or circulation, all community publications share a common denominator. Their perspective, focus, balance and news judgment are driven by local interests first. The Nigerians even have an expression for the concept, according to Associate Professor Anthony Olorunnisola of Penn State. The Yoruba proverb, "T'iwa ni t'iwa; t'emi ni t'emi" (Ours is ours, [but] mine is mine), when applied to community journalism, could be extended like this: "The national news is OK, but how does this story apply to me?" Americans have an expression for it too. "All politics is local," said Tip O'Neill, the late congressman from Massachusetts.

If there's such a thing as a universal community journalism formula, that's it. Whether the reader is in Lagos, Nigeria, or Lost Creek, Mass., he or she needs to know how the international, national or state story is going to affect his or her life directly. In practically every big story, there's a local angle to be found. As we will see in Chapter 7, 9/11 proved that.

Who's Who in the Zoo: Types of Newspapers

Broadly speaking, there are two types of traditional weekly and daily community papers: the independently owned community paper and the chain-owned paper.

The weeklies are usually exclusively all local; while the dailies are often a mix of state, national and international news, with local predominating. Students often wonder why dailies carry nonlocal coverage. The answer is twofold. First, many readers historically expect state, national and international news in their daily paper (and many editors think that it's the daily's duty to deliver it). Second, it's all but impossible to generate enough local copy every day to fill up a full-sized daily newspaper.

- *The independent or family-owned weekly, twice-weekly, tri-weekly.* The owner has an investment in the community as well as the newspaper. The level of involvement between ownership, staff and community is profound. For the beginner, this is the best place to find a job. You'll learn more, and they'll treat you like family. But fewer and fewer of these papers exist now, as the chains pressure them into selling. Some of the remaining independent family-owned papers are legendary in their areas, and their owners are fiercely resolved to hold off the chains. But the pressure of big bucks is too much for many owners.

- *The chain-owned weekly, twice-weekly, tri-weekly.* In this instance the publisher is not the owner. Although chain-owned papers can be a good place for a young journalist to get a start, at their worst they can be plagued by uninvolved management, low-grade talent, a bottom-line focus, and draconian edicts handed down by a distant, remote owner who cares about little except the P&L (profit and loss) statements. There are many exceptions to this; in the best cases, the chain has allowed the former owner-family to stay in place as editors and managers.

- *The urban alternative weekly—'zines.* This is the newest type of community paper to emerge recently, mainly centered in urban areas, catering to a tight target market of young Generation X intellectual arts people. The focus can include causes, lifestyles, the environment, guerrilla local politics, leisure, music, poetry, and so on. The "look" is often edgy, employing "garbage fonts" and Seattle-inspired "grunge graphics" that aim at projecting a hip and with-it image. The ownership is usually independent and not overly concerned with profit and loss. The attitude is usually unapologetically to the left. Example: the *Mercury* of Portland, Ore., with this motto under the flag: "News. Culture. Trouble."

- *The "We Yam What We Yam" Community Dailies* (circulations of under 20,000). With apologies to Popeye ("I Yam What I Yam"). These dailies are the true community newspapers of the daily world. Many of them still run all-local fronts. In the United States, there are more of these dailies than of any other category. It's useful to also think of these newspapers as teenagers, with all the glories and foibles of that age.

- *The Last of the Mohicans* (20,000–34,999). In honor of James Fenimore Cooper's classic tale. These are the dailies still small enough to maintain their essential personal nature but starting to get the feel of the larger daily. They're mixing in national and international news with what's local. So front pages might have abutting stories on the city council arguing over dogs running loose beside reports of car bombings in Iraq. If their community and their circulation grow without direction, their days are numbered.

- *Little Big Papers* (35,000–49,999). These papers get their name from the classic movie in which Dustin Hoffman plays a heroic yet diminutive character who is abducted and then adopted by Native Americans; his tribe honors him for his courage by dubbing him "Little Big Man." In our world, these are growing community newspapers, still classified by the American Society of Newspaper Editors as "small newspapers" but feeling their muscles. Like Hoffman in the movie, these papers are caught between two cultures, that of the community paper and that of the larger regional daily. Newspapers this size may often begin to lose sight of their original reason for being—of what made them great in the first place. If they start setting their sights on other goals instead—usually the constantly increasing profit margin—they risk losing their connection with their community or constituent communities.

- *Regional Big Dailies: The Damned-If-You-Do and Damned-If-You-Don'ts* (50,000–99,999 circulation). Papers this size try to give everybody a little coverage, but are spread too thin over too large an area, so they can never make everybody happy all of the time. It's a catch-22. Are they community newspapers? Some would say not. It depends on the individual paper's orientation. So papers in this category are like Jekyll and Hyde; in any given encounter, the public doesn't know if it's dealing with a community paper or a big-city paper (because the paper itself isn't sure of its identity).
- *The Major Metros.* Big-city papers with circulations over 100,000.

What the Community Newspaper Is

You're no doubt familiar with the paradigm of the Cup Half Empty versus the Cup Half Full. How you fare in life is generally a function of your perspective and attitude. It's all in how you look at things. Whether you're working at the paper or studying it, think about the community newspaper along those lines. First, make a list of what the paper is. Remember, keep it positive. As award-winning photographer Emmet Gowin says, "Pessimism has no muscle."

For example, our hypothetical weekly community newspaper—for fun we'll call it the *Boogersburg Bugle*—is relentlessly local, small, a second read, accessible, leading and online.

Relentlessly Local. For the readers of the *Bugle*, the paper is their primary source for in-depth local coverage. They get the details of everything from Little League games to school bus routes to city council coverage to Girl Scout cookie sales winners exclusively in the *Bugle*.

Small. As in Small is Beautiful. It keeps it manageable, humane, personal and personally satisfying. Reporters can drive around their primary coverage area by car easily in one day. The paper isn't so bulky that it breaks the bank to mail.

Second Read. It therefore follows that, most likely, the *Bugle* is the second newspaper in the house if the reader wants complete state, national and international news. That's not our job. And it's not our problem.

Accessible. Most community papers don't employ armed guards with video monitors at a security desk out front. Any reader or advertiser can walk in the front door of almost any community paper in the land and immediately find the editor, the publisher, a reporter, a photographer or an ad salesperson. This accessibility is one of our greatest strengths. It reinforces the human scale, serves as a reality check for personal values, as well as responsible and fair news judgment, while encouraging professional accountability. (See Chapter 5.)

Leading. Whether or not its editor or publisher realizes or acknowledges it, a community newspaper is involved intensely with its community, always leading, teaching, reflecting and telling the community about itself. The words of esteemed Brevard College mathematics professor Rachel Daniels fit this model; she says, "You're never not teaching." The same is true for the community paper. We're never not leading. Whether the paper's cumulative impact is for good or not is a function of the editor/publisher's vision of the paper and the community. It's a lot like being a parent. Once you have a child, it's not a matter of choice. You are a mommy or a daddy, and that kid isn't going away. How you choose to parent makes all the difference—in your child's life and in yours as well. Like a great mother or father, the enlightened community paper relishes its unique role in helping its community grow in healthy and appropriate directions.

Weekly, Twice- or Tri-Weekly. The publishing schedule is your friend. More often than not, you have more time to spend on any given assignment than your counterparts at the daily. You have more time to do the interview, more time to write the story, more time to craft the package. And the less the frequency of your publication, the longer the shelf life of your paper. A weekly is liable to sit around on the coffee table for a week, whereas with a daily, it's very likely to be daily-in, daily-out.

Online. Just because your paper isn't a daily doesn't mean it can't have a great Web site. Many weeklies have cool online editions. Check out <stateportpilot.com>. (More on this in Chapter 15.)

What the Community Newspaper Isn't

First Read. The community paper doesn't provide the first news coverage of breaking news from the state, national and international beats. Nor should it! Isn't that nice? The *Bugle* doesn't need to support a foreign correspondent in Bangkok. (However, if a local kid becomes an exchange student in Bangkok, that's another matter.)

Big. The larger the paper, the more it costs to support, produce, print, deliver and mail. We are also not the nearby big-city daily, so quit trying to be like it. Ever see an older woman desperately trying to look like a teenager? Bleached hair, fake bake, tight pants, too much makeup. It's obvious to everyone that she's straining to be something she's not. How sad that she doesn't embrace the appropriate beauty of her age with grace and dignity.

TV. We are not TV. Go ahead and let the big-city dailies try to copy TV; it isn't working. The community newspaper has something that both TV and the big-city dailies don't and can't have: true personal community authenticity in your town. This is your turf. Exploit that strength.

What the Community Newspaper Should Be

Bill Fuller, former community journalism editor and now a Tallahassee-based newspaper consultant, likes to say that community newspapers have to be vital. Vital to their community and vital to their advertisers (see Chapter 17), while striving to be better still. We should be taking advantage of our medium's innate, traditional strengths of in-depth storytelling in both words and pictures. Be true to your school; do your best at what you're best at, namely, thoroughly local coverage. And finally, we should be watching the technological curve and staying educated for the future.

The Downside of Community Journalism

Just as big-city dailies have distinct disadvantages, there can be a real downside to our profession. Community newspapers can represent the worst of our business. We are smaller, and undeniably we have fewer resources—fewer reporters per newsroom, fewer computers, fewer photographers, fewer state-of-the-art cameras—along with less financial support, both for the papers' production and for salaries. Relative to big-city daily folk, beginning reporters, photographers and ad salespeople make less until they rise to editorial, advertising and publishing positions with managerial responsibilities. For a beginner with big dreams, this can be discouraging.

Furthermore, many small-town papers seem to attract and harbor the washed-up derelicts of our business; community papers at their worst become sort of a stale backwater for the flotsam and jetsam of journalism. This results in poor management, terrible writing and uninspired photography: a community paper that resembles the journalistic version of a zombie. It just keeps coming at you, dead or not.

On the Chain Gang

The proliferation of chain ownership, particularly in the nation's community dailies, has spawned a farm system not unlike minor league ball clubs. If managed well, this can be a good thing. But horror stories abound.

The most egregious practice common among many chain operations is that of not replacing a newsroom staffer when that person moves on for whatever reason.

It's an insidious way of disguising what amounts to a layoff while sucking the remaining newsroom staff dry, keeping them hanging on, working them beyond their capacity, all the while tempting them with false promises of a rehire when management actually has no intention of filling that vacant seat. Predictably, such overstretched newsrooms have low morale and high turnover.

Consequently, young journalists in training miss the entire point of community journalism. They never get involved with the community. Often, they privately assume a condescending attitude toward the community, a superior attitude toward the readers. They're at the paper only long enough to get some experience under their belts; then it's on to the next rung on the corporate ladder.

This sad system can be exacerbated by lazy editors who have bought into the fallacy that their publication is "just a little paper," and therefore less of everything is not just OK, it's the norm. Quality, precision, professionalism, the pursuit of excellence—all suffer because sloppy editors have sold out.

This situation is often compounded by a publisher who is a "bottom-feeder" of community journalism, caring nothing about professionalism or the community but only the all-sacred bottom line. Little wonder that community journalism doesn't get the respect it deserves. When a recent outstanding graduate of a major journalism school announced her intention of joining the staff of a fine weekly paper, one of her former professors reacted with, "Surely you don't intend to stay in community journalism . . . ?"

Pressing for Decent Pay: You Get What You Pay For

How can publishers expect quality college grads (with car payments and school loans) to come to work at a community paper for $8.50 an hour and stay long enough to mature into editorial leadership roles? Do the math; that's below what some consider the poverty line. So it's no wonder that enthusiastic young people try community journalism, go hard for a couple of years and then burn out. A former reporter from the local 25,000-circulation chain-owned daily who waited on the author at a local restaurant said candidly, "I can make more [money] waiting tables than working 65 hours a week at the paper." When publishers grouse about high newsroom turnover, they need think about that.

For the quality-conscious young professional working at an uninspired community newspaper, the going may be tough. If you're not getting creatively nurtured, constructively edited or professionally encouraged, remember this: you are paying your dues, and your experience will serve you well. When you do choose to move on, wherever you go, what you've gone through will help. Many a big-city daily managing editor will tell you that there's no better beginning than to work on a community newspaper. (For further advice on how to stay sane and creative in a nonsupportive community newspaper environment, see Chapter 24.)

*Before Steven R. Knowlton became an author and an associate professor of jour-
nalism at Hofstra University's School of Communication in Hempstead, N.Y., he
received one of his lasting life lessons while serving as editor and part-owner of
a Maine weekly newspaper. He calls this parable: "A Romance of the Columnist,
the Police Chief and the Diner: How a Hotshot Young Cityside Reporter Got His
Comeuppance."*

Reporters on metropolitan daily newspapers often harbor a fantasy—most pro-
saically, it is to go to law school, more fancifully, it is to write a great novel, or,
most wonderfully of all, it is to own their own paper. The notion of someday
eking out a noble living with a shirttail full of type, a mouthful of irreverent wisdom and a heart full of deep compassion has sustained many a journalist for periods unfathomable to anyone who has never made or missed deadline,
successfully interviewed a grieving parent or gotten a handwritten thank-you
from a third-grade kid you've made a front-page hero.

Someday, the reporters say to each other and to the back-bar mirror after
work, someday I'll chuck the daily madness and Own My Own Paper, routing
the rascals, comforting the afflicted, keeping a watchful eye on a grateful world.
Dreaming gets no grander. Sometimes, people actually try for it, usually in their
middle years or later, winding up their careers where journalism began and
where in many ways it is still its purest and its best, in smallish towns and communities, publishing newspapers with circulations of a few thousand.

So I was unusual in that before I was 30, I was living the dream on the rocky
coast of Maine—with a few bucks and a bit of credit, I bought half of a struggling weekly and with it the gloriously long hours, the romantic poverty, the
pride to bursting-point of press day, when the best of me that I could commit to
type came roaring off the press 20 or 24 pages at a time. At the time I bought my
paper, I was a journeyman reporter, self-confident to the point of arrogance and
altogether dead certain that my 10 years at big dailies and the wires would inevitably translate into more and better readers, nobler American journalism and
greater glory for all.

Before I was 32, I was dead broke, out of business and deeply humbled by a
small town in rural Maine, home to lobstermen and clam diggers, shopkeepers
and shoemakers, cops and schoolteachers and civil servants—a tough, resilient
people, impenetrable as a lead-gray winter sky, folks with deep roots and long
memories.

There's a joke in Maine that a friend told me once over coffee in a well-
meaning effort to keep me from tripping on my own big-city shoes. In it, a New
Yorker who had moved to Maine decades before asks his Maine-native friend
what it takes to be considered "from Maine." The native gently tells the ex–New
Yorker that his 20 years in Maine don't qualify. "But how about my children?"

asks the "newcomer." "They were all born here. They're Maine natives, aren't they?" The New Englander answers, "If your cat had her kittens in the oven, would you call them biscuits?"

I laughed at the dry, rustic humor, finished my coffee and went back upstairs to the four-room store clerk's apartment that we had converted into the newspaper office. We had jammed three typewriters and old wooden desks to hold them into the larger of the apartment's two bedrooms, and had put the leased typesetting equipment into the smaller one. We had made a darkroom out of the kitchen, sealing it off with towels and duct tape to keep the dark from getting out. And in the large front parlor, we had put the makeup tables, waxer and everything else it took to turn notes and quotes and too-few ads into a quarter's worth of weekly wisdom about Downeast Maine, the coastal strip from Machias on the Canadian border down past Mount Desert Isle and Bucksport to Belfast and on to the summer playground of Camden.

We had a full-time staff of four, including the ad salesman, but not counting the high school typing-class whiz who set most of the paper's type on Mondays and Tuesdays after school. Plus, like most weeklies, we had a dozen or so local correspondents, nonstaff writers who were paid embarrassingly few dollars to produce a few hundred words a week on the comings and goings of their communities—who was in the hospital, whose offspring had enlisted in the service, who had houseguests from out of town, and so on. They were almost always dreadfully but colorfully written, frequently in longhand, and, in my case at least, generated great ambivalence as to whether they should appear in the paper at all. The columns took up valuable space, and both the authors and their copy were a nuisance to work with. On the other hand, the columns contained dozens of names, which translated into dozens of badly needed newsstand sales, and were a convenient place to fob off hundredth birthdays and baby christenings I had neither staff nor stomach to give the full coverage the relatives wanted.

Most such columns were written by gossipy old ladies, but I took it as a matter of big-city sophisticated pride that if I had to be burdened by such, we could at least have a little variety. An English teacher in a local community college provided 500 words of plausible erudition, an expatriate from Washington wrote about national politics with remarkable insight, and a fellow named Ty Cooper, who ran a bait shop, wrote pieces of wildly uneven quality about the changing life of the Downeast fishing and lobstering families. It was one of Cooper's columns that taught me volumes about newspapering in a small town.

Late one summer, as the tourist season was winding down and folks were starting to hunker down for the long hard winter of much snow and little income, Cooper's weekly column was about an offshore squabble in which one lobsterman's boat was shot full of holes and sunk by another lobsterman in a quarrel over the number and location of the two men's lobster traps. Nobody was named in the piece, which pleased me well enough, since while I found Cooper's wry account screamingly funny, I had been Downeast long enough to know that lobstering was serious business and that lobster pots represented far more than the source of a fine dinner on the one hand or the base for an L. L. Bean–kitsch coffee table on the other.

I called Cooper at the bait shop and questioned him closely about the incident and his sources, but he swore as to its absolute veracity and even explained why there was no police record of the aquatic showdown, since lobstermen rarely saw fit to avail themselves of the urban lawmakers' sense of justice. In truth, I had a residual nagging doubt, but figured what the hell, it was Tuesday, crunch day for us, the column was already in type, and the boats weren't even very well described—one red stripe above the waterline on the one, two narrow green ones on the other, barely enough to tell them apart in Cooper's tale of High Noon on the High Seas. We ran it.

The next afternoon, after another late night of getting the paper out, then sleeping until noon in celebration of another issue on the streets, I strolled up to the police station to see what malefactors had been apprehended since last we checked, and to chat with the chief. He was an amiable ex–state trooper with a raconteur's gift for timing and the telling detail. It had become a high point in the rhythmic cycle of weekly newspapering to sit for an hour or so with him in his small, dark-paneled office, listening to tales of the lighter, as well as more chilling, moments of a Downeast cop's 30 years on the road. So I breezed into his office and plopped down in my accustomed spot, a black leather armchair with a small tear in the seat cushion and brass-headed upholstery tacks worn shiny and smooth. "What's up, chief?" I said by way of greeting. "Have you got the bad guys all rounded up?"

Now, during much of life, three or four seconds isn't a long time, and the chief's silence probably didn't last much more than that, but the dead quiet of the room seemed to take an eternity to break. Then the chief looked up from the latest issue of my pride and joy, opened to Cooper's copy, and froze me with a glare that I'd never seen but that other cops had told me was legendary. "You . . . stupid . . . bastard," he said finally, and I was amazed how clear his diction was since I could barely see his lips moving. "I ought to shut your goddamn paper down."

"Excuse me, chief, but what did I do?" was the best I could muster, hoping it didn't sound sarcastic, because I didn't mean to be flippant, but was way too spooked to try the line out in my head first, and way too rattled to trust my own conversational skills.

"You . . . got . . . the . . . wrong . . . damn . . . boat."

The "wrong damn boat" of course, involved Cooper's story of the lobstermen's quarrel. After a few minutes of the most blistering verbal hiding I'd ever received, the chief explained, as one might explain to a naughty but slow-witted child, that Cooper's story was all backwards, that one of Cooper's friends was one of the figures in the story, and that the chief's own brother was the other.

The men had quarreled for years, their respective families for generations. The
chief had hoped it was finally over. Now, thanks to my ignorance, Cooper had
let the evil genie of generational hate out of the bottle again.

I hazarded an interruption. "Maybe you already know the story, chief, or
think you do, but nobody's named in that story. There's nothing to identify anybody. If Cooper screwed up, I apologize, but there can't be any real harm done."

"How many lobster boats around here have a red stripe just above the waterline?" the chief asked me, no longer livid because a decent man can stay angry
with a fool only so long. He stuck his right forefinger—his trigger finger, I
noted—into the air and counted. "One, my grandfather's."

I slunk out of his office and back down the hill toward the sanctuary of my office, stopping in the diner for a midday coffee and muffin that was the usual
breakfast after the weekly exhaustion of giving newspaper birth the night before.

"Hi, Linda. Coffee and blueberry," I said with none too much cheer to the
diner's waitress and half-owner, a pleasant woman in her early 30s who was also
my newspaper's landlord.

She didn't glare as the chief had. She didn't look at me at all, in fact, so I didn't
see how red her eyes were until much later. She just turned on her heel and went
off to scrub down the other end of the counter, which had apparently suddenly
become very, very dirty.

Her husband, Dennis, moved over opposite my place at the counter. "Don't
talk to Linda," he said evenly but with obvious checked anger. "She's been crying
all morning. Because of what you wrote about her brother-in-law."

In half-hearted self-defense, I asked, "What brother-in-law? I don't know
Linda's brother-in-law. I didn't know she had a brother-in-law. What did he do?
Get arrested or something? Dennis, you know I can't keep people's names out of
the paper if they get busted." I rattled off several more sentences, which clattered
to the Formica countertop and lay there like so many pickup sticks.

"Ty's story about the boat-sinking," Dennis said. "She's terribly embarrassed,
and mad, too, that you said her sister's brother sank that other guy's boat. You
got it all wrong."

I could muster nothing more eloquent or profound than "Oh, Jesus" and
swept a hand through my hair so I could stare harder at the countertop. I had
known that Linda's family, and Dennis's too, for that matter, had been in Downeast Maine for generations. I didn't know about the sister's husband, but it was
no surprise that she had one or that he was a lobsterman.

What else I didn't know, of course, was that the brother-in-law had two Kelly
green stripes painted on his boat, just above the waterline. To these and a fistful
of other details, I told Dennis weakly, "I didn't know."

"You are probably the only one around here who didn't," he said. "You'd better leave now. Get your coffee down the street."

The paper didn't fold that week, though it could have, and the earth didn't crack open and swallow me up, though for a day I wished it would. I was glum enough for a day—self-pitying would be a fair enough way to describe it—then I righted myself and yelled at Cooper for screwing up his boat story. He stuck to his guns, joined the chorus in calling me a fool, and said he'd just as soon quit writing the column anyway unless I wanted to start paying him cash for it.

I was flummoxed again because I figured we'd been paying him ten bucks or twenty bucks or whatever for his column. Not so, Cooper said, adopting the increasingly familiar tone of the wise man trying with waning patience to explain the obvious to the town dunce. It turns out the guy who sold me half the paper had worked an off-the-books trade with Cooper—the column, plus half a cord of firewood now and then, in exchange for a $50 display ad for the bait shop.

I'd love to say this story was an epiphany, that the scales fell from my eyes and I suddenly agreed wholeheartedly with Rousseau and his conviction of the wisdom of the common folk. But that wouldn't be true, either. After a few weeks, we resumed getting decent cooperation from the cops, and after a few more weeks I returned to getting my coffee at Dennis and Linda's diner.

We limped along another year before the paper finally folded with a thud almost nobody else heard but which still hurts with a pain usually associated with the death of a pretty good friend or fairly close relative. But I still hadn't lost all my arrogance, so I blamed everybody but myself for the failure. The economy, the chief, Cooper, of course, Gerald Ford, who was president at the time, Richard Nixon, who wasn't but whom I still blamed for almost everything. Epiphany is too strong, too sudden a term for the learning that the sunken boat story provided.

In the 20 years since then, I've been beaten up a lot, both at other small papers and at some bigger ones, and greatly humbled in realizing how arrogant and brash are the young, even when they are, as I was, bright and clever and "fast copy"—perhaps the most highly regarded of all big-city reporters' virtues. And I don't know about Rousseau, but I do know that there's a great deal of difference between small-town papers and metro dailies in the way they fit into their communities. And while I love, truly love, the *New York Times* and the *Washington Post* and what they stand for in American journalism and American democracy, there's an intangible something, almost familial, about community journalism.

I think I am almost old enough to own my own paper again, a small weekly, perhaps somewhere on the New England coast.

Your Town; Your Turn

1. If Howie Mandel were to ask you, "What do you do?" what would you say?
2. If you're a professional, examine your paper. What kind of community paper

is it? Does it have a vision? Of itself? Of the community? Can you put it into words? If you're a student, analyze your hometown paper.

3. If you're working at a community paper, ask yourself this: Why are you in this business? How'd you get started? What do you like and dislike about the community newspaper business so far? If you're a student, why are you taking this course? What attracts you to community journalism?

FOUR

Whose Paper Is It Anyway?

Having a Paper Must Be Like Owning a Cow

The old farmer, stopping by the newspaper office to renew his subscription, noted that the young editor seemed to be there working at all hours. "Son," he observed with characteristic folk wisdom, "having a newspaper must be like having a cow." And seeing the editor's puzzlement, he explained, "Well, y' gotta milk 'er twice a day, and you can't go off."

Nowhere is the difference between the community paper and the big daily more apparent than in the area of ownership. We're not talking about corporate ownership here, but the community's emotional and philosophical ownership.

Up until now we've been talking about how you and your paper relate to the community; now we're turning the mirror on ourselves. How does the community look at us? How do our readers regard the paper?

First, and most importantly, it's not the paper. It's their paper. Everything about community journalism is personal, even the way the readers regard their paper.

Repeat. It's *their* paper. Or more personally, you're likely to hear "*My* paper." Even if *you're* the owner, it's *their* paper. Lose sight of that fact and fail; recognize and capitalize on that attitude and soar.

Possession Is Three-fifths of the Way There

Your readers are possessive about their paper because that's the nature of small-town people. They're also possessive about their high school football team, the school marching band, Little League, the way the church is run, what happens in the county courthouse, borough council, planning board and town hall. It's their town; it's their paper.

Miss a delivery, do something they don't like in the paper, or change something that's been long-standing—and you'll hear from the readers.

"Where's *my* paper?"

"What have you gone and done to *my* paper?"

"If you don't believe a community newspaper plays a vital role in peoples' lives," says production manager Daniel V. Morris of the Waynesboro (Pa.) Green County *Messenger*, "talk to our secretary at the front desk . . . ask her what would have happened if Mabel on First Avenue didn't get her paper on time!"

By now, some of you are shaking your heads. But big-city daily papers and TV

stations hire ad agencies and PR firms to try and figure out how to get their readers
and viewers so committed, involved, possessive and even jealous. That's not a
problem for us in community journalism. Half the time the readers act like we work
for them.

A constructive way of looking at that makes the publisher more of a public
servant than an entrepreneur out for a fast buck. Nothing wrong with a buck.
Nothing wrong at all. Fact is, the more you recognize, accept and buy into your
paper's unique relationship with the community, the more bucks you'll have.

And the rest of you—editors, reporters, photographers, ad people—listen up.
While your highest calling may be to the principles of journalism or the bottom
line, you too work for the reader.

Back in the '80s when his men's running teams stayed busy winning national
junior college cross-country championships, Brevard College coach Dave Rinker
often addressed the sports information director as "Boss." And when asked why,
Rinker, now the track and cross-country coach at James Madison University, replied with a grin, "Because I work for everybody." As it turns out, that's not true at
all, but it is the generous, non-ego attitude of a proven winner.

A Newspaper's Greatest Resource

A community newspaper's greatest resource is not its printing press or its fine
facility. Neither is it the deep pockets of some owner, be that local or chain. A
newspaper's greatest resource is the reader, pure and simple.

Hoover Adams is one successful newspaperman who knows what his readers
want and has been giving it to them for years. Adams' formula of relentlessly local
coverage has paid off for his five-days-a-week afternoon Dunn (N.C.) *Daily Record*.

It's not often that a community newspaper gets glowing spread in a national
paper like the *Wall Street Journal*. But in August 2001 that's exactly what happened
to the *Daily Record* when the *WSJ* featured the family owned, 9,832-circulation daily
for its record 112 percent market penetration in its primary market—the highest
penetration marks for any U.S. daily newspaper audited by the Audit Bureau of
Circulations.

The headlines in the *WSJ* crowed, "Practically Everybody In Dunn, N.C., Reads
the Daily Newspaper—In an Electronic Age, It Wins with Blanket Coverage of
Hometown Goings-On."

Reporter Patricia Callahan's in-depth story lauded the *Daily Record*'s founder,
then 81-year-old Hoover Adams, for his newspaper's successful formula of faces and
names—or to put it another way, names and faces.

The following week editor-publisher Bart Adams, in his column headlined "Will
Journal Article Give Us the Big Head," responded in part: "Some of our readers may
fear . . . that all this attention will give us . . . a serious case of the big head. . . . But in

At the community newspaper, you are accessible to your readers in a most open-door sort of way. If someone wants to send you fresh roadkill in floral greenery, they can and will. The author ponders how to run this "'possum to the editor." (We didn't; it was unsigned.) (Photo by Ron Paris)

the community newspaper business, with limited staff and little time to do any one thing, there is always some typo or awkwardly worded sentence to bring us down to size pretty fast. Besides, the attention does not tempt us to rest on any laurels; it makes us want to work harder to earn your trust. It makes us more committed to covering local news as thoroughly and accurately as we can."

Adams wrote that he wanted his staff to think of themselves as citizen-journalists, involved in the welfare and civic life of the same community they were covering: "Because the owners of this newspaper all live and work right here, this has always been our philosophy. Still, our circulation success is only possible because the Dunn-Erwin area is such a great community. That sounds like pandering, but this community really is unique. So many smaller towns have turned into bedroom communities for larger cities. And when this happens, there is less interest in local happenings and institutions.

"While Dunn and Erwin do have more people who commute to [nearby cities] than we used to, we still have a strong sense of community. And we all want to do our part to keep it. We buy barbecue-plate tickets and let teenagers wash our cars in church parking lots. We're here for the long haul and we don't want to see our children move away for a decent job. In short, we are in this thing together. And it is the job of *The Daily Record*, among other things, to help us remember that.

"... My father's take ... is to print lots of names. In a memo to the newsroom around 1980 he wrote: 'If I heard this morning that President Carter is coming to Angier, the first thing I'd want to know is the names of the people in Angier responsible for him coming, who's making the arrangements, the names of everybody in Angier involved in the preparations. I couldn't care less about his speech—only how his visit affected Angier and Harnett County.'

"He, of course, is exactly right. What counts is people. As to our circulation success, and the subsequent national attention it has brought to this community and this newspaper, there are many people to thank: there is my father who continues to be the soul of this paper. There are all *The Daily Record* staff members who work so hard each day under tight deadline pressure. There are the scores of carriers who make it possible for our work to be seen. And there are the businesses and individuals who choose to reach their best customers and prospects by advertising in this newspaper.

"But the people who deserve the most thanks are our readers. You make it all possible. And if you ever think we get a case of the big head, give me a call and straighten us out."

Personalities and Community Newspapers

Newspapers are individuals, too, with distinct personalities. The longer you're at a paper, the more you'll recognize the paper's true nature. A paper's personality is usually the function of two factors: ownership and the community itself. We're going to look at communities in more detail in Chapter 6, but here's the *Cliff Notes* version to get you thinking.

Just as surely as people have vastly different personalities, towns also possess varied personalities. Cosmopolitan, cultured, open minded, forward thinking—or ingrown and root bound, suspicious of new things, outsiders and change. Financially busting at the seams, holding its own, or in decline. Is the town friendly and optimistic or grumpy and grim? Some communities welcome strangers and newcomers with genuine charm and early acts of friendship. Others take pride in studiously ignoring newcomers. Some communities make you prove yourself before they'll take you in—then once accepted, you're blood kin. Others will never accept you no matter how long you live and work there.

Where does a community get its collective personality? Study the area's ethnic, cultural, religious, commercial/financial and historical background, and the answers will reveal themselves to you.

A played-out Pennsylvania coal town dominated by a central and eastern European culture is going to have a very different personality than a culturally thriving, tourist-oriented vacation community in the Smokies of western North Carolina with a Scots-Irish population base.

Community/Paper: Yin/Yang

It stands to reason that newspapers reflect the personalities of their communities. Grumpy town, grumpy paper. And conversely, a thriving town with high livability is likely to have an enlightened, creative, involved and high-quality paper.

This is important to know if you are soon to be a college graduate and are considering a first job in community journalism, or if you are already at a community paper and seeking a change, or if you are a community journalism vet ready to move on and perhaps buy (or start) "your" own paper.

Mark these words: Save yourself a lot of time, bucks and stomach lining by researching the target community before you commit to a move. Because if you don't find out these personality factors first, you'll surely find them out later, when it will be too late to avert a bad move.

Where do the people come from? Are newcomers and change welcomed or shunned? What is the attitude of the residents toward themselves? Do they like their town or look down on themselves? There's nothing worse than a place filled with self-hate and loathing. Do they all shop 30 miles away in the big city? If they do, you probably don't have an ad base.

What do they think of their government, their schools, their hospital, their social services? What's the local governmental picture like? Who's who in the zoo? Is there a political machine that runs the town? If there is, you better know about this up front.

Is there a college in town or nearby? What's the state of the arts in this town? What kind of social-action programs exist? What is the dominant ethnic background? What churches predominate and how does that affect behavior and attitude? Where do people work? Is the town and area's population growing or shrinking?

The Paper's Ownership

In addition to being a reflection of the community, a newspaper tends to be a mirror image of its ownership and the publisher's attitude. As we heard from media scholars Gene Roberts and Phil Meyer, while there are several forward-thinking, community-involved chains across America, there are many others that take as much out of the community as possible, putting back as little as possible. These are the bottom-feeders of community journalism. They're not fooling their community; readers usually openly dislike these papers. No wonder folks who work at one of these paper remind you of Eeyore. You remember, the sad donkey from *Winnie the Pooh* who moped about expecting (and getting) the worst. There's one such sad newsroom I know of that publisher David Woronoff describes as "58 Eeyores." (Woronoff, on the other hand, runs a happy shop, as we will see in Chapters 12 and 20.)

Before you take a job at a paper, do some research on the ownership. If it's a

family-owned paper, what is the family like? What do people in town think of the
paper and the owners? Do reporters like working there? What's the turnover like?
What are the newsroom dynamics like? Does it seem like a happy shop? The same
goes for a chain paper, but you also need to determine the chain's reputation and
direction. Compared to management at other papers, how do they pay and treat
their people?

You will have an uphill struggle imposing your personality on the town's personality, or on the personality of the existing paper. The wiser route is to find a
community and a paper that already matches your personality. You'll live longer,
and your stomach lining—not to mention your loved ones—will thank you.

Community Newspaper Personalities and Aging

Like people, newspapers have life spans. They age. A bumptious new community
weekly run by a bunch of enthusiastic whippersnappers may evolve into a larger
weekly, then be forced to go twice-weekly or tri-weekly, or even afternoons five days
a week; "semi-daily" some call this.

Why do newspapers change?

Change can come from within or without.

Sometimes owners, publishers and editors see opportunity for growth in changing the format and printing schedules. More often, it's because the paper has grown
along with the community's commercial areas, and must respond or lose out to
competition. A newspaper that doesn't keep pace with the needs of its advertising
community is no longer growing. And if it isn't growing, then it's in decline, and
may be even dying a slow death.

When a community newspaper dies, or folds, it's usually the result of the economic decline of the community and the inability of its ad base to support the
media outlet (especially in a competitive market). But sometimes internal mis-
management plays a part. If a chain closes a community paper, there can be a
variety of reasons at work, but typically it has to do with declining revenues and
lackluster projections for any future growth.

It's important for the professional to determine the age of the target paper. Is it a
dowdy old gray mare out to pasture? A frolicking teenager afraid of nothing? A
settled and conservative middle-aged business-as-usual type? Or a wise old owl
getting better with age?

When a Paper Changes Hands

Like a divorce ripping apart a family, the most traumatic thing that can happen to
a paper, short of folding, is a change in ownership. Especially if the change is

from family-owned indy to chain. Then everyone in the newsroom is thinking more about their own jobs than quality journalism, and the paper goes into what developmental psychologists call "arrested development." No growth will occur until the new ownership shows its true style and things settle down—which can take years.

So ask yourself, is your target paper on the brink of a personality identity crisis? Is it about to change publication schedule or ownership? Identifying all these character traits of the paper will save you needless grief, and it will enhance your working there and empower you with your relationships.

Other Voices; Other Newsrooms

William E. Shaw, fifth-generation publisher of the Dixon (Ill.) Telegraph, says it took him years to realize who really owned the paper. The following is excerpted from his presentation to a symposium titled "Community Newspapers and Community-Building," co-sponsored by Kansas State University's Huck Boyd National Center for Community Media, held in conjunction with the 1994 National Newspaper Association Convention in Orlando, Fla.

"There Goes Our Republican!"

Each morning I re-assume my role as publisher of *The Telegraph*, Dixon, Illinois' daily newspaper. It is a job and a title that has been held in my family for many years. My father and his father before him were newspaper publishers their whole lives. This unbroken string goes back 143 years to my great-great-grandfather who joined the Dixon *Telegraph* in its first year of publication.

Folks in town know the Shaw family well. Our name is synonymous with this newspaper. My original newspaper ancestor greeted Abraham Lincoln as he passed through town on his way to debate Douglas. Not only greeted him, but helped Lincoln plan his debate strategy. My grandfather gave Ronald Reagan his first job, as carrier boy for his hometown newspaper.

Through the years we have continuously published *The Telegraph*, never missing an issue or episode. The chain of events that has shaped our community has been faithfully chronicled in our pages over our five generations of family stewardship. *The Telegraph* embodies the past history of Dixon as well as channels the energies that will lead the community ahead toward an uncertain future.

Each day brings with it new stories and headlines for *The Telegraph*. When we come to work in the morning, we have no inkling about what news will be bannered across our front page. However, when the day is done, the spontaneous events of the day will be permanently recorded in our official record.

In this era of newspaper chains and publicly-held newspapers, the ownership of most newspapers has become far-removed from their constituency. Most people no longer know who owns the local newspaper published in their community. Some newspaper owners do not even know anything about the communities served by their newspapers.

But even in our case, where our family has operated this newspaper in this town for so many years, I wonder about the essence of ownership. An incident happened about seven years ago that challenged my notions regarding a newspaper's investor's role respective to newspaper ownership.

In an effort to expand our family business, to keep pace with an expanding family, we have purchased several newspapers in communities of Illinois, Iowa and Wisconsin. One such newspaper, the Bureau County *Republican*, is located in the town of Princeton, Illinois, scarcely 30 miles south of Dixon. I held the position of publisher of that newspaper for five years, immediately preceding my return to Dixon in 1986.

A few months after I left Princeton a fire broke out in the same block as our newspaper plant. The gas explosion quickly consumed the building next to ours and flames leapt onto our roof.

Afterwards, our publisher, Bob Sorensen, who succeeded me in Princeton, reported the disaster in which our newspaper almost changed from a news object to a news subject.

Bob rushed to the scene in the early evening and began removing computers and valuables from our building. When the fire began threatening our plant, he could do nothing but watch the firemen conduct the valiant fight. While watching in terror, Bob heard a lady shriek in a loud voice:

"There goes our *Republican!*"

It's funny how, in a moment of panic, a thought can crystallize in one's mind. When Bob shared that comment with me, we both realized that the lady sincerely believed that her newspaper was about to burn down. In fact, the whole community probably felt that way. The Bureau County *Republican* belonged to the people of the community. We merely owned the rights to manage the company that published it.

For four years that comment haunted me. Even back in Dixon, where our family had been plying its trade for nearly a century and a half, did we really own the newspaper? Of course we did. Our newspaper holds the record for continuous family ownership in Illinois. We have toiled, sacrificed, saved and invested our blood, sweat and tears for all that time.

But in a larger sense, the newspaper has always belonged to the people of the greater Dixon community. If we are to be a healthy newspaper, we must hope our local citizens perceive that they own *The Telegraph*. It is *their* newspaper.

Fortunately, the firefighters put out the blaze on the roof before *The Republican* was destroyed. But the distraught woman's cry—"there goes our *Republican!*"— burned in Shaw's mind, all the same. In 1993 the lesson of the trial by fire inspired publisher Shaw to put together an "Owner's Manual" for *The Telegraph*, which is distributed to new and old subscribers as well as advertisers. In the intro, Shaw opens with these words: "In the larger sense, you readers own this newspaper. By subscribing to *The Telegraph* you have hired us to produce a newspaper that lives up to your standards. We have prepared this Owner's Manual for you to better utilize 'your' newspaper. . . . We are also eager to hear from you about how we can improve 'your' Telegraph. Feel free to give me a call or write me a note with your ideas."

From the Trenches: Another Lesson by Fire

It was a typical Friday morning at the Greene County *Messenger* in downtown Waynesburg, Pa. Daniel V. Morris, production manager at his father's 6,000-circulation weekly, was busy working toward a Monday deadline when the fire alarm went off and the scanner squawked, "Company 61 report to your station, a structure fire at the Blair Hotel."

Morris recalls: "The secretary and I did a double-take, as we realized the fire was in our building. . . . We went outside and looked up at a third-floor window which was billowing smoke. The landlord said it was probably a grease fire. After flames shot out of the window, we knew it was time . . ."

They unplugged all the machines, phones and computers. "Like a madman I plucked every wire form every socket, stacked hard drives on top of scanners, disk boxes on top of disk boxes . . . ," Morris says.

Then a wonderful thing happened.

Morris tells the story:

As I turned back toward the door with an armload of equipment, I was stunned to see dozens of people lined up to carry the stuff to Lord knew where.

A young man said, "We're taking your things across the street to Waynesburg Floral. Rusty Rice has everything prepared to house them for the moment."

The young man took the equipment from my hands, as did the others. They didn't know they were carrying thousands of dollars' worth of delicate equipment in each armload. Although I knew they were unaware they were carrying every essential newspaper equipment, I somehow trusted these people. Bankers, lawyers, store owners, kids and employees from the competing daily newspaper carried the equipment across the street. Then we shifted our attention to the main office. . . . The group of community "ants" assembled behind the secretary and myself as we handed them every loose item. People carried out mammoth filing cabinets and other furniture with ease. Smoke began filling the office as we got the last items we needed . . .

Pittsburgh television stations shot video and interviewed our staff. They reported our fortunate escape, but couldn't convey the sense of community we felt. The community just saved "their paper" and we all knew it.

A local businessman, Shirl Headlee, came by to console my father and the editor. Shirl reminded us of the kindness the paper had shown when his building supply business burned three years earlier. Shirl handed us a key to an empty store in the strip mall he and his family owned and said, "Make yourself at home."

Several people who had pickup trucks observed what had just taken place. They began to load our equipment into the trucks and like some crazy parade, we were off to Central Plaza. After a few hours unloading and moving equipment, we were exhausted . . . just then, Shirl strolled in with cheeseburgers and fries for everyone. He told my father not to worry about the rent; they'd work something out. "Right now," Shirl said, "you've got more important things to think about."

By that evening, we were a functional newspaper once again. The Monday deadline seemed impossible, but we made it.

The fire story dominated the cover and was accompanied by a full page that let people know where their paper had moved. An editorial page was transformed into a thank-you to all who helped during the crisis. The experience should show anyone how much a community newspaper means to its community.

On one day in July, people who are generally taken for granted were transformed into a team that was determined to help. On one day in July, we learned, once again, what the word community is all about.

It's been 10 years since the fire, and the Greene County *Messenger* continues to flourish, having found a second home in Shirl Headlee's donated building. Daniel Morris' dad subsequently sold the paper to Calkins Media, but Morris remains at the helm of the paper as general manager.

A Newsroom Accessibility Study: Less Is More

> Only the mediocrities of life hide behind the alibi "in conference." The great of this earth are not only simple but accessible.
> —ISAAC FREDERICK MARCOSSON, 19th-century American journalist

It's difficult to find a weekly, semi- or tri-weekly anywhere in this land with a newsroom that is not at least relatively open to the public; most, in fact, are what can be called "wide open."

So why is it that when daily newspapers reach a certain circulation size they begin shutting down the newsroom to the public, citing concerns about "safety" and "theft" as the justifications? Don't smaller newspapers with their open newsrooms face the same issues?

Yes, so get over it, says Pulitzer Prize–winning Bronx, N.Y., co-publisher Bernard Stein of the weekly Riverdale *Press*. He vows, "You have to be *open*—and be *known* to be open."

According to community journalism student Christina Rexrode, the easy access to the newsroom of the Asheboro (N.C.) *Courier-Tribune* was a conscious decision. Says Asheboro *Courier-Tribune* columnist and former editor Bob Williams: "You can't live in some ivory tower and then claim that you're writing what the public is thinking. How are you going to know what they're thinking if you're not talking to them?"

Williams, a lifelong resident who has worked at the paper since 1969, writes a slice-of-life column that runs on the front page four days a week. Where do many of his ideas come from? Right through the front door of the 16,300-circulation Stephens Media Group–owned daily.

Also, it is reasonable to suggest that there is a critical link between newsroom accessibility and journalistic community accountability. When asked to define a "community newspaper," I propose we distill it to one factor: newsroom accessibility during regular office hours.

That is to say, can the public walk right in and talk to editors, reporters and photographers? Or must they be screened, vetted, given a badge, let through a security system—or are they denied access completely?

Why does this matter? Because there is reason to suspect that big-city papers, by invoking the mantra of community, are really wrapping themselves in the flag of authentic community newspapers in hopes that some of the neighborliness-by-fiat will staunch the circulation hemorrhaging.

As has been said, true community journalism has been defined as the style of intensely local-first coverage provided by papers with circulations of not over 50,000. But circulation numbers are only a start; there must be another factor of community-ness that can be measured. That factor is accessibility. Accessibility is one of the most critical defining factors in determining a newspaper's "community quotient."

That is, how physically accessible is the newsroom to its readers during regular office hours? Is there a security system in place to bar the very public the newspaper purports to cover? Are reporters and others on the staff protected and therefore detached from and out of touch with the readers? How easy/difficult is it for the public to get in touch with editors, reporters and photographers by phone? Do telephone callers get sent to "Telephone Hell"—a computerized and depersonalized answering system? Are newsrooms ivory towers? Or are newsrooms open and folks can walk right in?

THE PENNSYLVANIA ACCESS SURVEY

Let's take the newspapers of one state as a case study. A survey conducted by your author when he was at Penn State reveals that the smaller the newspaper (by circulation size), the more access readers are likely to have to newsrooms.

The Penn State study was conducted over a six-month period in 1999. One hundred percent of Pennsylvania's 80 dailies and 80 percent of the state's 184 weeklies were surveyed (monthlies, shoppers and newspapers without newsrooms were excluded from the study). In all, results were tabulated from 86 percent of the state's newspapers.

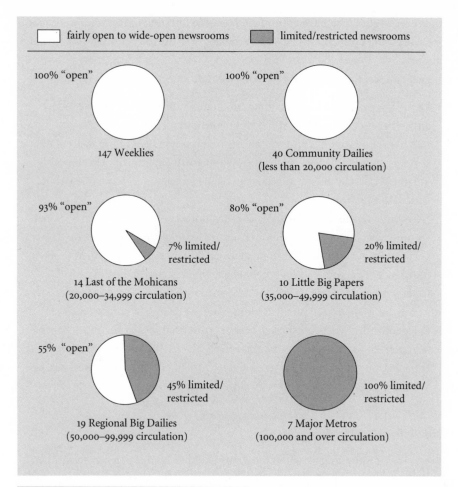

The author's survey of the public's access to 147 weeklies and 80 dailies in Pennsylvania, conducted in 1999. When newspapers are smaller—and call themselves community papers—readers are more likely to gain entry to newsrooms and interact with staffers.

Editors, publishers, reporters and photographers classified their newsroom accessibility according to one of three degrees of access/inaccessibility: "wide open," "fairly open" or "restricted/limited." All questions pertained to regular office hours only.

"Wide open" means that readers can walk right in to the newsroom and see whomever they want without being stopped.

"Fairly open" means that readers check with a receptionist first, but don't encounter locks on the newsroom, with access to the newsroom still easy.

"Restricted/limited" means that the newsroom is locked or has some form of security system, electronic or human. These newsrooms, which may be on a separate floor, are off limits to readers, unless they receive official clearance, sign in, get a visitor's badge or have an appointment. Newsrooms in this category may also use the receptionist to screen the visiting readers by detaining the reader and calling up to the newsroom where the editor or reporter in question has the option of "coming down," or of remaining inaccessible by saying to the receptionist, "Tell them I'm not here" or "I'm too busy."

Respondents were also asked questions about:

- Phone Usage: Only a tiny fraction of the state's papers used computerized answering systems, and paper size didn't seem to matter.)
- Neighborhood Safety: Editors at only two newspapers out of the entire state said they thought they were in somewhat unsafe locations. Conclusion: This judgment call may be too subjective to be of any relevance; more research is needed in this area.
- Newspaper Ownership: The three classifications of ownership were: National Chain Ownership, a large group with out-of-state offices; Small Group Ownership, out-of-town but in-state ownership of 20 or fewer papers; and Independently/Locally or Family-Owned. Of the state's dailies, out of all 80 papers, 37 papers, or 46 percent, were owned by national chains; 19 papers, or 24 percent, were owned by small groups; and 24 dailies, or 30 percent, were independently owned. Of the 147 weeklies contacted for the survey, 16 papers, or 11 percent, were owned by national chains; by far the largest group was the 81 papers, or 55 percent, that were owned by small groups; and 50 weeklies, or 34 percent, were independently, locally or family-owned.

THE RESULTS: THE WEEKLIES

Every single responding weekly in the state was either "wide open" or "fairly open"—with the exception of one paper, which had its press shoehorned into its tiny building in such a way that visitors had to walk right by the press to get to the newsroom!

The breakdown was almost a dead heat between "wide open" and "fairly open" in the weeklies. Seventy-five weeklies, or 51 percent, were "fairly open," while 72 weeklies, or 49 percent, were "wide open."

So the weeklies were "open"; that will come as no surprise to any student of community journalism.

But the issue was more complex with the dailies.

THE RESULTS: THE DAILIES

Eighty-one percent, or 65 of the dailies, were "wide open" or "fairly open." Of the 19 percent, or 15 of the dailies, that were "restricted/limited," where was the battle line between access and inaccessibility?

It appears to be in the mid-50,000 circulation area.

To make it easier to grasp, the state's daily newspapers have been divided into categories according to circulation. The numerical divisions are according to the Pennsylvania Newspaper Association's Keystone Press Awards, and circulation figures were computed according to the PNA formula, but the names are the author's. (The PNA formula is weekday daily circulation plus 10 percent of either the Saturday or the Sunday edition, whichever is largest.)

MULTUM IN PARVO (MUCH IN LITTLE)

Now, here is what I found out about accessibility at these papers: The larger the paper, the less the access. The smaller the newspaper, the more the access. Again, less is more.

- The Major Metros (with circulations over 100,000). All seven of the big-city newspapers in Pennsylvania had "restricted/limited" type newsrooms. (Interestingly enough, four out of the seven were chain-owned; the others were independently owned.) So there didn't seem to be a link between ownership and access in this area; they were *all* off limits.
- The Regional Big Dailies: The Damned-If-You-Do and Damned-If-You-Don't's (50,000–99,000). Fifty-five percent, five out of the state's nine DIYD/DIYD regional big dailies, were "restricted." Three were "fairly open," and one was "wide open." So, viewing the cup half full, we could say these types of papers in Pennsylvania were 45 percent fairly open. (Ironically, the four "open" papers were owned by national chains; and the five "restricted" newspapers were a mix of one national chain ownership, one small group owned and three indies. Go figure.) Nevertheless, it is clear from the 55/45 split that *this category of newspaper is the real battle zone for access.*
- Little Big Papers (35,000–49,000). Of the ten Little Big Papers in the state, two were "restricted," five were "fairly open" and three were "wide open." Predictably, the ones in this category, still faithful to their roots as community papers, were 80 percent "fairly open" or "wide open." And of the two "restricted" papers, the editor of one said it's been like that since the '70s and no one can remember why . . . while at the second "restricted" paper, that publication took on a corrupt city hall, and according to the editor, "There was a real Wild West atmosphere here in the '70s." This group included four national chain-owned papers, three papers owned by small groups and three indies.
- The Last of the Mohicans (20,000–34,999). Only one of the state's 14 papers in this category had a "restricted" newsroom, and that is in part because of building configuration. So, 93 percent of this category had "fairly open" to "wide open" newsrooms. Relative to ownership, this group was made up of seven national chain papers, three small group-owned papers and four indies.
- The "We Yam What We Yam" Community Dailies (under 20,000). The true community dailies were 100 percent "fairly open" or "wide open." Of the 40 papers in the state in this category, 22, or 55 percent, were "fairly open," while 18, or 45 percent, were "wide open." The breakdown on ownership: 17 were national chain-owned, 12 were small group-owned, and 11 were indies.

Now, listen to the words of Pennsylvania newspaper folk when asked about newsroom accessibility. First the weeklies:

"We *have* to be open . . . we're a *community* newspaper"
—Kim Capitano, managing editor, the Pittston *Sunday Dispatch*.

"Nothing should come between us and the readers."
—Wade Fowler, publisher, the Perry County *News*

"There's no door on my office—that's how open *we* are."
—Vickie Peters, editor, the Albion *News*

"Access is the whole crux of what this paper is all about. There's absolutely hands-on immediacy. . . ." At the larger dailies, "there's a grim sense of taking themselves too seriously . . . when the product becomes more important than people. Though we're very proud of our product, we never lose sight of our priorities; people come first."
—Bobbie Kopicki, managing editor, the Honesdale *Weekly Almanac*

On getting criticism from readers who come into the newsroom to give him grief: "You hate to hear it . . . but it's good. It keeps you on your toes. How else are you going to keep in touch with the community and the community with you?"
—Jim Webb, publisher, the Boyertown *Area Times*

"You walk right into our palatial offices which consists of three rooms . . . baseboard heat. If there is a fire in that front room, we are cooked, as there is no other way out!"
—Carole Boynton, editor, the Conshohocken *Recorder*

"Our office is located in a two-story frame home on Main Street, and more resembles a home than an office. That makes the visitors and three-member staff feel quite comfortable."
—Douglas Teagarden, publisher, the Claysville *Weekly Recorder*

"Our office is *open*. Even the squirrels walk in—human and otherwise."
—Gwen Stockwell-Rushton, editor, the Doylestown *Patriot*

"Our office is so accessible you don't even have to be a human being to get in—the wind blows the front door open."
—Andrea Hurley, former news editor, the Mercersburg *Journal*

Elizabethtown *Chronicle* publisher Wanda Reid felt it was important for her reporters "to live in the town where they report because they are more accessible . . . because—*excuse me*—they *are* serving a public need."

Edith Hughes, publisher of Gateway Press, Inc., agreed. Her 15 weeklies in the Pittsburgh area were either "wide open" or "fairly open." She said, "American newspapers are becoming too corporate when they build newspaper offices lately."

She regretted the passing of the gonzo, Frisbee-throwing "You'll-never-believe-what-I-just-got!" kind of newsroom energy that said in effect, "We're all in this together."

IN THEIR OWN WORDS; THE DAILIES

"A lot of daily papers are having an identity crisis," said a former Pennsylvania daily newspaper woman who asked not to be identified: "The mid-size dailies are trying to be metros and the metros are trying to be communities!"

But many small or "community dailies" were as equally dedicated to open accessibility as the weeklies:

"We make a point of being open. Community journalism is what we're all about," said Marty Wilder, managing editor of the 12,800-circulation Bradford *Era*. But she noted that other larger dailies were not so open: "I see that at other newspapers, even me, a newspaper person, I see their inaccessibility and I don't like that. And I think that's why newspapers aren't being read as much . . . there's an alienation there."

"Wide open and proud of it," is how co-owner Ed Christine of the 3,900-circulation Danville *News* described their situation. "We shouldn't put locks on [newsroom] doors."

Indeed, the folks at the 10,000-circulation Huntingdon *Daily News* reported that "the locals come right in the back door."

Building configuration affected access in some places. The smallest daily in the state with a restricted/limited access newsroom was the 28,200-circulation Sunbury *Daily Item*, which had a second-floor newsroom. Readers had to get cleared by a receptionist before they could go upstairs.

But building configuration didn't always stand in the way. At the 12,100-circulation Shamokin *News-Item*, which also had its newsroom on the second floor, managing editor Jake Betz reported folks "come on up anyway."

Another form of exclusion occurs when newspapers relocate their offices out of downtown. "If you're located out of town, across from the mall, you're not exactly accessible—even if your newsroom *is* open," said Pottstown *Mercury* editor Nancy March, whose 30,000-circulation paper was "fairly open." She said she thought newspapers in remote locations have distanced themselves from the heart of the community, greatly reducing walk-in traffic from the public. "Very often the people who need to talk to you in person the most can't."

The 29,000-circulation *Centre Daily Times* of State College was one such "fairly open" paper located out of downtown and across from the mall, requiring that the public drive out there to hand deliver items. Assistant city editor Kakie Urch recalled a visit from a reader in tears dropping off an obituary of a friend. "How do you say 'no'?" Urch said. "It's like having a customer in your living room."

The 50,400-circulation Johnstown *Tribune-Democrat* was sure of its stance on accessibility: "We consider it a special responsibility," said editor David Levine.

"We've got a special mission in the community," and he added that access is central to the concept of involved community journalism.

No one screened the calls of editor David Troisi at the 35,900-circulation Williamsport *Sun-Gazette*. And his "wide-open" newsroom "makes us totally accountable," he said, acknowledging, "It's a pain sometimes, but it means we're a part of the public. Even if they disagree with you, you learn something."

Publisher and editor Dennis Hetzel's "fairly open" 50,400-circulation York *Daily Record* had a street-front newsroom in a new building in downtown York. According to Hetzel, this was no accident. When they moved into a new building, they could have chosen the third floor with a great view. "But we picked the first floor. I don't want people to have to take an elevator. Access is too important a factor. Being at street level is important." On the balance between access and security concerns, he said, "We figured, it's not broken, so we're not trying to fix it."

RESTRICTED/LIMITED ACCESS: A BUNKER MENTALITY

At many major metros, an adversarial "us vs. them" attitude could be detected, along with a certain paranoia. An editor at a major metro large daily with an off-limits newsroom explained, "It would be great if we could be 'wide open,' but we're in the business of making people angry . . . all it takes is one person . . ."

During one conversation with another editor from a major metro daily, he referred to readers as "civilians."

Going restrictive to the max: at least two papers were requiring passes for employees to go from one part of the building to another.

"I hate it," confided one editor.

CONCLUSION

We newspaper people go into our readers' living rooms, but some of us recoil at the thought of their coming into our newsrooms. How dare we expect access into their lives when we deny them entry into our world? Is it any wonder larger papers are experiencing a disconnect? At community papers we see that open access is an important part of the corporate culture. An equation might go like this:

- Major Metros: Access Denied = Alienation/Disconnect
- Community Papers: Access Permitted = Inclusion/Connection.

The accessibility factor is a strong indicator of the newspaper's "community-ness."

For large, big-city papers claiming to be community newspapers, the study suggests why disconnects exist.

Mid-sized papers contemplating a switch-over to restrictive security systems should think twice.

And for smaller community papers with open access to newsrooms and personnel, the access study findings should be an affirmation; they are doing the right thing.

True community journalism, both in its pages *and* in its newsroom, is *inclusive*.

15 Things Every Person Working at a Small Newspaper Should Know

- Whether you know it or like it or not, you're doing community journalism.
- A community newspaper is not just a smaller version of a big-city paper.
- Jayson Blair and Jack Kelley wouldn't have lasted a week at a decent community newspaper.
- Your mantra is "Local, local, local," followed by, "All stories are local."
- The purpose of your paper is to serve your community—pure and simple.
- Regardless of who you've been told owns your newspaper, your paper's true owner is the community.
- Your job title is only a beginning.
- You don't have to wait until you get to the *Washington Post* or *Sports Illustrated* or *National Geographic* to do your best work; you can do it now.
- Small is beautiful. Believe it; don't wish it away.
- You may not get rich, but your psychic pay will be enormous.
- Everybody has/is a story.
- The "middle of nowhere" is the center of someone else's universe.
- When journalists say, "There's nothing going on here," they are telling you about the space between their ears.
- Every story will lead to another story. It's all connected. Just pay attention and trust.
- The doors of your newsroom should be just as open as the doors of the homes, offices and meeting rooms of the people you expect to cover.

Your Town; Your Turn

1. Define in as many ways as you can the factors that contribute to the personality of your community. Then, in a 30-word lede, define your community: "Boogersburg is . . ."
2. Do the same thing with your newspaper. What kind of a paper is it? Does it have a happy shop? What's the attitude of the owner-publishers toward the community?
3. Where is your newspaper in its life span? Is it on the verge of a midlife crisis?

FIVE

About That Little Old Lady from Dubuque

The New Yorker We Ain't

When the svelte and urbane *New Yorker* started up in 1925, its editor, Harold Ross, wrote grandly in his opening essay, "*The New Yorker . . .* will not be edited for the old lady from Dubuque."

Well, friends, in case you haven't figured it out, we *are* writing for the little old lady from Dubuque, Iowa; Dixon, Ill.; or Dunn, N.C.—in a manner of speaking. You can do sophisticated and cosmopolitan work now where you are, but never forget that little old lady; she's your reader too.

Reality Check Aboard Flight 1041

High over the eastern seaboard, the Washington to Miami USAirways flight 1041 cruised at 37,000 feet, the passengers enjoying their drinks, taking in the views, dozing or reading newspapers. Even the flight attendants had time on their hands.

"Excuse me, sir," said a young flight attendant to a businessman, who had put his large Northeastern metro daily down and was gazing out the window. "Is that your paper?" she asked politely.

"Yes," he replied.

"Can I read it?" she asked.

"Well, I need it back," he noted.

"That's OK," she replied brightly, "I just want *Dilbert* and the front page."

And she said it in exactly that order. As in, entertainment first, a little news second.

The young flight attendant was as good as her word, returning the *News* in under five minutes, having summarily dispensed with a weighty 68-page broadsheet newspaper with a 68-page tab weekend insert!

Sometimes your reader might not be just the little old lady from Dubuque; she might be a young flight attendant.

Canary in the Coal Mine

Deep within that same edition of the *News*, a letter to the editor noted that 30 years ago 60 percent of the people between ages 18 and 29 read newspapers every day. Today the figure is less than 30 percent and falling. The letter writer then presented reasons she thought many readers have stopped turning to newspapers:

It is not the readers who have changed but the newspapers.

Twenty-five years ago, you could read in most papers how to bake a cake and fix

a car, as well as news of your community. Youngsters would eagerly scan the paper looking for their names and photos.

Today, newspapers everywhere blame TV and our education system for eroding readership. Some sponsor newspaper-in-the-classroom projects in a bid for younger readers, while others opt for mindless contests to increase circulation. Glitzy and expensive graphics and color are also employed to heighten reader interest. Meanwhile when average readers send heartfelt but amateurish letters to the editor, the letters are trashed. When a school teacher asks if someone from the newspaper can cover a Columbus Day play, she gets the brush-off. Church news is relegated to the religion page. Press releases must arrive three or four weeks in advance (absolutely no phone calls), and there is no guarantee of publication.

Today's editors and reporters are more sophisticated and better educated than those of yesteryear. They rarely grow up in the cities and towns they cover, and they keep their bags packed as they hop from paper to paper in their quest for a career on a large daily. They do not share the values, lifestyles or history of their average readers.

If newspapers are serious about recapturing readership, then they should become reacquainted with their readers. While TV, time-starved lifestyles and lower SAT scores do play a role in declining readership, the elitist approach taken by more and more newspapers is what's really turning people off.

Boom. There you have it. The canary in the coal mine has dropped dead. What more of a warning do we need? That concise critical analysis of what's wrong with newspapers today came not from a media specialist, not from a professor of journalism and mass communications, but—you guessed it—from the little old lady from Dubuque!

Read and Weep

In an era when some doctors are prescribing something called "*news fasting*" (no TV, newspapers, online news outlets, magazines or radio for two weeks), those who care about serious journalism have just cause for alarm.

Community newspapers are a part of that monster term, *the media*. People tend to lump us together with all the other weird dysfunctional family members—Jerry Springer et al. Do we deserve the blanket condemnations? Maybe, maybe not. But we'd better know what people are thinking and saying out there. Here are the points most often heard from people—*readers*—complaining about the media:

• The media are not involved with the community. They project a holier-than-thou attitude. As the letter writer noted, reporters are like free agents: keeping their bags packed, selfishly advancing their own careers, always looking for that

Who's your audience? Somebody's mama, in hairnet and apron, has walked down the gravel driveway with her cane to get the mail and her newspaper. She'll carry the paper back to the house and read it on the front porch. Keep her in mind when you write.

big move to the next big market. They have no roots, no links to the community, and no intention of making any. It's called "parachute journalism."

- The media's collective attitude toward the smaller and disenfranchised or minority communities is detached and condescending. Small towns are all too often described in stereotypical terms such as "sleepy" and "nestling." The major media companies cover small towns only when there's a disaster or bad news.
- The major media are sensation-driven. TV news especially is "angst-pandering," as singer-songwriter Bill Byers puts it. The adage is still the rule: "If it bleeds, it leads." TV example from 8 P.M. teaser: "Boy struck by javelin at track meet. Details and film at 11." We have to wait till 11 to find out if the kid lived? Who is the kid? Is that sort of coverage serving the public's right and need to know? No, it's prurient, ghoulish titillation and the worst kind of infotainment. It is not news. Paul Duke, former *Washington Week in Review* host, addressing the National Press Club, lamented the current state of the media, noting the "tabloidization trend," "giving vent to rumors" and resulting in "an orgy of speculation," as well as the "endless hype and puffery of TV."
- The media are arrogant and self-righteous, overlaying events with opinion when

given the slightest chance. Paul Duke cited a poll that showed that 70 percent of respondents felt the press "got in the way of solving problems."

- The media sometimes act as if they care about people and the community, but really they don't. "Neighbors" editions are disingenuous attempts by major metros to win over outlying market areas surrounding the center city, thinly disguised maneuvers designed mainly to sell ads, expand circulation and insinuate major metros into someone else's territory, or to prevent competition from entering what they see as their turf. Neighbors editions have proved to be a good way to head off or at least compete with shoppers. That's $hoppers with a dollar sign. That's their real reason for existence; the community news value is of little concern to the paper.

- The media are impersonal, inaccessible, unaccountable and uncaring. Not surprisingly many people think daily newspapers are not to be trusted. According to the Pew Research Center for the People and the Press, the percentage of people who believe what they read in their daily newspaper has declined from 80 percent in 1985 to 59 percent in 2003, according to figures cited in *The State of the News Media 2004* by the Project for Excellence in Journalism.

How much regard do media show for the people they cover? A "USA Snapshot" from *USA Today* depicted the decline. In 1985, 35 percent of respondents said the media do care about the people the report on. That dropped to 21 percent in 1999. And, in 1999, 67 percent said they thought the media *don't care about the people they report on*—up 19 percent from 48 percent in 1985.

On Being Neighborly

Arrogance and elitism don't cut it in community journalism. Consider the story of the former big-city newspaperman, an experienced veteran from a major Northeastern daily, who bought a small coastal Southern weekly. Within six months of coming to town, Mr. Big Britches had alienated most all of his readers and every single one of his advertisers. He was brusque, perceived as unfriendly, business-first, openly arrogant, inaccessible and condescending to the natives. He may have had peerless credentials and stunning clips from New York or Washington, but along the way he had failed to develop that fine talent they don't teach in big newsrooms or J-schools—how to be neighborly. As every experienced community journalist knows, in a small town there are only so many people to alienate until you've pretty much touched every household. So it didn't take long for word to get around town; the new man was a self-inflated stuffed shirt who looked down on the locals as mere groundlings, hardly worth his eminent editorial brainpower. How different it might have turned out for the new editor-publisher had he treated everyone as if they mattered—whether they were bankers or bagboys, cooks or county commissioners. They were all readers and advertisers or potential advertisers and readers—in other words, his customers.

CARE

For a community newspaper to work at its optimum pitch, there must be an active reciprocal relationship between the town and press. That is, a good faith sense of give and take.

When phoning, e-mailing or walking in unannounced, community members should never feel belittled, marginalized or treated as a nuisance, but rather they should feel welcomed and valued.

In turn, the paper and its people must be genuine, active stakeholders in the well-being of the community. Staffers must authentically care about the place in which they work. That cannot occur by fiat, or by a directive from management.

The sign in front of Carl Stoltzfus' plumbing company in rural Pennsylvania carried this motto: WE'RE LOCAL AND WE CARE.

With that attitude, combined with quality workmanship, it's little wonder that Carl had all the business he could handle.

Carl's credo gets right to the core difference between community papers and other larger metro media outlets. Take that word "care" and break it down.

The acronym CARE serves as a simple but useful formula for understanding the covenant that should exist between the paper and its community.

C stands for Community, as in Community First.
A stands for Accessibility and Accountability.
R stands for Responsibility.
E stands for Even-handedness, Equanimity, Egalitarianism and Elitist-NOT.

- *Community.* As community journalists, we are first and foremost community minded and community oriented. Our coverage is our community first. Call it the community imperative, an intense curiosity about all things close to home, a dedication to finding the relevant local angle, why this matters to us, and how to craft our work so as to contribute to a stronger, healthier community.
- *Accessible and Accountable.* As community journalists, we are accessible and open to our readers, as they are to us; there should be very few barriers, physical or otherwise, between main street and the newsroom. In community journalism it's useful to think like this: *A stranger is just one of your readers you haven't met yet.* Further, as community journalists, we are pledged to be accountable to our sources, to the community at large and to ourselves for what goes in the paper with our name on it.
- *Responsible.* As community journalists we are responsible to to our readers (our community) to bring them the complete, accurate, fair and balanced story to

the extent we can make it so. We do not shout interviews, commit guerrilla driveway journalism or engage in paparazzi photojournalism. We do not "shoot and scoot," "run and gun," which feels more like *hit and run*, thus re-victimizing the victims. We *do* conduct humane and civil interviews; we *do* treat people (aka: sources) as the human beings they are, and *not* as expendables.

- *Even-handed.* As community journalists, we try to do things with Equanimity, with a spirit of Egalitarianism. Our stories cumulatively reflect the realization that positive growth occurs when our news judgment springs from a perspective that could be boiled down to "We are all in this together," as opposed to "Us vs. Them." This final part of our mission statement negates any possibility of media elitism.

What Readers Want

At a journalism conference in a session titled "What Do Readers Want?" University of Tennessee–Knoxville College of Communications dean emeritus Kelly Leiter cut right through the fat and the small talk with this oration delivered at a machine-gun pace:

"What do readers want? They want local news! They want to know who got married and who got born; they want to know who bought the old Leiter place out on Route 4 and are they really going to put a Motel 6 out there? Is the planning board going to approve that chemical plant? They want to know what the school board is doing with all that money raised by the new sales tax; who's going to play quarterback this week in the high school football game and why that stupid coach put him in in the first place; what streets are going to be torn up next week; they want health stories but only as it applies to them—like how to find a good rest/retirement home. They want local news and they want lots of it!"

Leiter finished his preachment by saying with a grin, "If I could, I'd tell every managing editor to get your newsroom together at the end of the day and have them start chanting the mantra: 'Local . . . local . . . local . . . ommmmmmmm.'"

Leiter also told of his interview with a 75-year-old grandmother: "When I asked what her favorite part of the paper was, she surprised me when she said, '*Sports*—I got two grandsons who play high school football, and by God I wanna see their names in the paper!'"

The Readership Study

Predictably, when readers are asked what they want from their newspaper, the response invariably is "more local news." But it's more complex than that.

After researchers at the Readership Institute at Northwestern University asked 37,000 readers in 2001 what they wanted from their newspaper, the institute produced an impact study that outlined definitive methods newspapers could use to attract and hold on to readers.

"Content emphasis, service excellence and brand relevance have great potential, separately, to build readership. Together, as part of a newspaper's readership strategy they have tremendous potential," says the institute's director, John Lavine, as quoted in the ASNE Small Newspaper Committee 2004 booklet "*Implementing the Impact Study: What Small Newspapers Are Doing.*"

According to the booklet, the Readership Institute also conducted research at 100 dailies of all sizes to determine how successful dailies are "combating the problems of declining circulation and readership." (Note: the Readership Institute impact study research did not include any of the nation's 7,865 weeklies, twice- and tri-weeklies, perhaps because they are doing so well with their readership.)

The institute's "How-to-do-it" guidelines, veritable reader-based criteria for excellence, provide an extremely useful road map for evaluating your newspaper and determining what changes might be appropriate.

CONTENT MIX: INTENSELY LOCAL

- The newspaper has a good strong blend of news topics: *intensely local*, government and politics, lifestyle, education, religion, etc.
- Consider how well marquee pages, such as the front page, convey this variety.
- Enterprise, or news the newspaper discovers (i.e., not event based), is a significant part of the mix.

IN-PAPER CONTENT PROMOTION

- The newspaper points readers to content inside the newspaper that day (includes rails, strips, boxes, refers).
- The newspaper points readers to content in upcoming days.
- The promos are attention-getting and effective sell-pieces.

VARIETY OF WRITING STYLES

- The newspaper uses forms in addition to the inverted pyramid to tell stories and convey information—e.g., feature-style approach; Q&A; breakout boxes; graphics; lists.

CLARITY

- Stories have a point, get to it quickly and are clearly written.

- Where to, how to, how much, whom to call, directions, locator maps, where to go for more information on a subject (e.g., Web sites, books, TV programs, etc.).
- Listings, briefs, etc., are organized and presented for reader utility, i.e., in ways that respond to interests of readers and how they use information.

LOOKS OUT FOR READERS' INTERESTS

- Reporting institutional stories in ways that are relevant to consumers/citizens.
- Less of what the town council decided and more of how it affects people, what it means to them.
- At a basic level, gives readers things to do, and is helpful.
- At a higher level, is a watchdog.

SOMETHING TO TALK ABOUT

- Content that would make readers want to share it with a friend or colleague: "Hey Martha" stories, things you can imagine the local talk radio show picking up, water-cooler fodder.

PEOPLE LIKE ME

- The newspaper is for and about average people in this community.
- Stories about ordinary people.
- Photos and content that reflect the life of the community.

CONTENT THAT WOULD INTEREST YOUNGER ADULTS (18–24)

- Events that would appeal to them.
- Issues that concern them.
- Stories and photos featuring them.
- Issues of general interest that include their perspective.

THE NEWSPAPER EXHIBITS PERSONALITY

- It stands for something.
- It gives people something to talk about.
- It is more than just a chronicler of news and information.
- The newspaper conveys that it cares about the community and readers (evidence could include an editor's column addressing reader concerns; stories focusing on the future well-being of the community; ample letters to the editor).

- Headlines are strong, crisp, inviting.
- The newspaper approaches routine stories with enthusiasm and creativity.

Roping In Those Elusive Young Readers

Give kids what they want: coverage of them and the stuff they care about. (And make sure it's online, as well.)

Twenty-something Ann Malik of Barrington, R.I., was spotted with a week-old copy of her hometown weekly, the Barrington *Times*, which she had packed and brought with her 600 miles to the family beach house in North Carolina. When asked why she thought the 5,000-circulation *Times* was such a good community paper, she exclaimed, "Everybody reads it! If you don't, you feel out of the loop."

Words to warm the cockles of an editor-publisher's heart.

An extremely successful and popular feature of the semiweekly Franklin (N.C.) *Press* that gets young readers into the paper as writers, story subjects and readers: a weekly rotating column and mugshot from a different high school journalism student reporting the high school news or reflecting on some aspect of high school life. The column is coordinated by the high school journalism teacher, and the writing is an important part of the class curriculum. It costs the paper nothing but commitment. Editor Barbara McRae and Franklin High School journalism teacher Lee Berger say it's a win-win situation for everybody.

Looking in the Newspaper Mirror, Uncomfortably

Ted Vaden is editor-publisher of the 22,000-circulation twice-weekly Chapel Hill News, *a McClatchy-owned community paper in the North Carolina college town. After a thought-provoking workshop on newspaper fairness, Ted wrote the following in his weekly commentary, "Editor's Desk."*

You probably didn't notice it, but there were a lot of journalists in town last week.

More than 600, to be exact, attending the annual Winter Institute of the North Carolina Press Association. That giant *fshhhht* sound you heard from Franklin Street Thursday night was that of beers being opened for reporters and editors after celebrating the prizes they'd won at the newspapers' annual awards ceremony. The local economy—at least that of our bars and restaurants—was much healthier thanks to last week's inundation of newsies.

Journalists are famous carousers, but there was more than partying going on in the proceedings at the Friday Center. In fact, much of what we heard was pretty sobering. Journalists are worrying a lot about credibility these days, in the wake of the infamous Jayson Blair episode at the *New York Times*, when a cub reporter was caught making up stories about the Washington sniper shootings and other national news. Some of you probably also saw the excellent movie, "Shattered Glass," about a reporter for *The New Republic* who similarly published fictionalized reportage. Our industry is not held in the highest regard.

All this was brought home to us at last week's conference by Bob Haiman, former executive editor of the St. Petersburg *Times*, who has led a project on newspaper fairness for the Freedom Foundation, a newspaper industry think tank. In focus groups around the country, readers told Haiman they find newspapers unfair for these reasons:

- Factual errors and inaccuracies. "The public says it sees scores of mistakes in our papers every day," he said. "If you want to be perceived as fair, then start by getting the facts right."
- Unwillingness to admit errors and correct errors fully. It's hard for readers to make a complaint, and we're chary of apologizing. "If you make a mistake, you don't just correct it, you apologize," Haiman said.
- Reporter ignorance or incompetence. In an increasingly techno-world, "some reporters just don't have the expertise to do the job. Reporters don't know enough."
- Cultural bias and insensitivity. Our staffs don't reflect the diversity of the community; not just racial or ethnic identity, but also political, ideological and even religious. "The average news staff has lots of people who call themselves liberal or moderate and far fewer who identify as Republicans," Haiman said. "Lots of people [in newsrooms] are only casually churched, but far fewer are Christians or orthodox Jews."
- Inadequate time and space devoted to "good news." "We want to know what's going wrong, but we also want to know when something's going right and what's working well," Haiman paraphrased readers. "If you don't tell us about both, you're only giving us half of what's going on in the community."
- Preying on the weak and the defenseless. This is the thrusting-a-microphone-in-the-face-of-a-car-wreck-victim syndrome.
- Use of unidentified sources in news stories. "They don't like allegations or attacks that are not accompanied by a name," Haiman said. "The promiscuous use of sources was at the heart of the Jayson Blair affair."
- Unwillingness to admit that sometimes there's no big story here. Once we invest reporting effort in a tip, we feel obliged to write a story, even if there is no substance to report.

To most of the above, the Chapel Hill *News* pleads: guilty as charged. We do let a maddening number of errors get into the paper, and we have too high a tolerance level for mistakes. Our reporters are generalists—by necessity, I submit—not educated in the intricacies of the beats they cover. We do not adequately reflect the increasingly diverse culture of this community. We're more liberal than conservative, certainly (but so is Chapel Hill/Carrboro).

We do make an unceasing effort, day in and day out, to scrub out the errors, guard against biases, double-check and second-guess our reporting and develop as professionals. We subject every story to two readings—a luxury for a small paper. We try to hire the best—two former *Daily Tar Heel* editors, currently— and give them training. And we check in with you, our readers, by holding regular reader forums, although we could do that more frequently.

But we're never good enough. Our ultimate safeguard against unfairness ultimately is you, the reader, and we hope you'll feel free to let us know how we're doing. Our reporters' phone numbers and e-mail addresses are listed at the end of stories, and we regularly publish a box showing how to reach editors and reporters. If you have a problem, you can start with me, by e-mailing <editor-@nando.com> or calling 932-2030.

And thanks for reading us, despite the flaws. We do care.

Other Voices; Other Newsrooms

RPS IN TEXAS

Media folks living Inside the Beltway have a term for the rest of us, Out Here. "RPS . . ." It stands for Real People . . . Ordinary folks, Joe Public, Suzy Citizen, the Little old Lady from Dubuque.

Then, there's Duke Ellington's perspective. He said, "The people are *my* people." I'll go with the Duke, because I hope, deep down, we're all RPS . . .

I was reminded of this yet again during a gig with the Texas Press Association. A workshop for community newspaper journalists, the small-town newspaper boys from the capstone canyon country, the community newspaper women of the desert prairie.

Newspapers with such colorful and descriptive names as the Earth *Weekly News*, the Hart *Beat* and the Jasper *NewsBoy*.

Where newspaper offices may be located in a converted bank (where the vault is used for storage) or a in a part-time florist shop where they keep the flowers fresh in the broken commode in the back . . . or where the bullet holes in the front office plate glass window serve as a graphic reminder of a long-ago reader's dissatisfaction with an editorial political endorsement.

It's a part of the country where plain speech is appreciated. At one weekly on production day, co-publisher and editor Debra Wells of the 1,241-circulation weekly Fritch *Eagle Press* places a sign on her door:

"If this is Wednesday, I ain't talkin' to nobody about nothin'!"

These are the folks that face the tough decisions of everyday small-j journalism in an in-your-face, situational ethics kind of way. Everywhere there were lessons.

Photographer Richard Porter of the 7,800-circulation Plainview *Daily Herald* arrived at a fire the same time as the first firefighter, who unrolled the hose and

RPS in Texas: In 1955 Margaret and Bill Wilkerson started the Idalou *Beacon* in their garage. Curiously, they named the paper after a lighthouse, though Idalou, population 2,074, is located in the flat, dusty panhandle of Texas, a thousand miles from the nearest ocean. Regardless, pictures of lighthouses adorn the walls and the paper's business cards. Go figure. The 681-circulation weekly *Beacon*, later bought by Renee Fikes, shared a former bank building with the local Chamber of Commerce and a tanning parlor. And talk about public access: This is the typical weekly situation. Walk in the front door and you're in the "newsroom." Keep going another couple of steps and you're in the "backshop." Additionally, the old bank's former night safety deposit box serves as the *Beacon*'s after-hours drop box. Update: As this book goes to press, the town has grown to 2,500 and the *Beacon*'s circulation has climbed to an even 1,000, says Jona Janet who bought the *Beacon* in February 2003. How many people does she have on staff? "Uno. Just me. I *is* the staff," replies the irrepressible Janet, who comes from a Texas community newspaper family and had a career selling printing equipment but always dreamed about having her own paper. "I love it, man," she vows. "It's a wonderful lifestyle." Why is the *Beacon* such a success these days? "I'm highly visible," Janet declares. "I go to everything—meetings, ball games, cheerleading camps, school events. I'm there!" (Photo by Princess Butler, courtesy of the Idalou *Beacon*)

shouted at the reporter: "Hook me up!" Porter, used to being a member of his community as well as a journalist, didn't think twice. He hooked him up.

Melinda W. Bigelow of the 3,800-circulation daily Kilgore *News Herald* told about going to a rest home to take a "routine" picture and then on her way out seeing in front of the rest home an old man in a wheelchair raking leaves. Aha! Now there's a photo. She took the picture. It won an award. "But that's not what made me feel good," she said, "—not nearly as much as the look on that man's face when I went back to the rest home with ten copies of the paper . . . that's why we do what we do."

But imagine working in the same town you grew up in. Reporter Burlon Parsons of the 4,679-circulation daily Wharton *Journal-Spectator* said, "I work in the town where my first-, second- and third-grade teachers still live . . . and when I make a goof, they'll see me and say, 'Now Buuuur-lon, that's not the way we taught you to do . . . ' "

Community journalists shouldn't need focus groups to reconnect with their readers. Award-winning publisher and editorial writer Bob Buckel of the 4,880-circulation weekly Azle (Texas) *News* wrote a gun control editorial (in *Texas!*) and was greeted on the church steps the following Sunday by a reader who buttonholed him: "I know I can't change your mind," the man said, "but I'm sure gonna' try." Bob says he just smiled and replied, "I understand how you feel . . ."

And when we were all talking being raised in the backshop and how the newspaper had been our second home, Charles "Mac" McClure, editor of the twice-weekly *Wimberley View*, outdid us all with "I was spanked with a pica pole!"

There is nothing in my business that can beat rubbing shoulders with the Real People of community journalism. I return to the classroom renewed by their dedication to the craft, refreshed by their sense of humor and inspired by their grace under fire.

Your Town; Your Turn

1. Talk to the reporters in your newsroom. What is their attitude toward the paper? Do they see it as just a rung on their professional ladder? A place to learn and grow? Their dream job?
2. How are the staff members of your newspaper involved with the community beyond their professional contacts? How many of them consider the community their hometown?
3. Find an example of angst-pandering news presentation. Is it coming from your newspaper or some other media source?

SIX

About the Community in Community Journalism

As we seek the self-unraveling clue—
A sense of place is but the beginning.
—ELIZABETH SEWELL

Newspapers don't publish in vacuums; they exist in places. And places can be just as individual as people. The student of journalism would be well advised to assess the "sense of place" about a prospective job destination, and along the way learn something about "placeness."

"All communities, like people, have an . . . attitude!—the psychological character of a community—and you can spot it a mile away," says Danielle Withrow, town planner for Forest City, N.C., and advisory board member of the Carolina Community Media Project. The individual community's self-image will be revealed, she asserts, when you listen to people talk about their towns—whether it's the old money, the culturally elitist county seat or the hard-working, blue collar mill town with an inferiority complex.

Definitions

What exactly is a city, a town, a village, a community? After all, aren't these words ones we think we already understand? Interestingly enough, it turns out their definitions are vague and subjective. From Susan Mayhew's *Dictionary of Geography*, we learn that a city is a "large urban center functioning as a central place which can provide very specialized goods and services. There is no worldwide agreement over limiting figures of population size or areal extent for a city."

The same goes for a town, which Mayhew describes as "a relatively small urban place. No limiting figures of population or areal extent are agreed upon." It's equally vague for "village," defined thusly: "Just as there are no definitions for the population size which delimits a 'town' or a 'city,' so there is no limiting size for a village."

And the definition of community is even more challenging. Some wag once said, "There are 99 definitions of community, and they're all good."

Maybe "community" is so nebulous and complex (or simple and intuitive) that getting at its meaning is like when someone once asked Louie Armstrong to define jazz. The great Satchmo just shook his head and is reputed to have replied more or less in this way: "*Jazz?* Man, if you have to ask, I can't help you."

Wrestling with this definition for years, I can only conclude that "community" is a contested notion, and that there are degrees of authentic community-ness, ranging from intense to pretty shallow.

But thanks to town planner Withrow, we can break community down into three distinct types:

- Communities of place
- Communities of ideas
- Communities of ethnicity

COMMUNITIES OF PLACE

We all live in geographically bounded communities of place. The traditional terri-torial definition of a community fits here. From Meyer and Brightbill's text *Commu-nity Recreation*: ". . . a group of people living in the same area under the same local government and laws . . . bound together by a common environment and held together by psychological as well as economic, social, and cultural bonds. Because of their common interests, needs and concerns, they create for their own use, institu-tions of governmental, educational, economic, recreational and religious nature."

Zen potter Kenneth Beittel writes that a community can be defined as usually a smaller contiguous population center where individuals feel cherished for their selfness, share core values and social mores and possess a highly defined sense of place and a strong civic identity.

Social psychologist Amitai Etzioni writes that communities are essentially "webs of social relations that encompass shared meanings and above all shared values."

Dr. Martin Luther King Jr. put it most eloquently when he said, "We are caught in an inescapable network of mutuality, tied in a single garment of destiny."

Or in the words of the old proverb from Cameroon, "Rain does not fall on one roof alone."

That statement of community takes on added weight, coming from an African country containing 200 ethnic groups speaking 80 languages, according to the *National Geographic Atlas of the World*.

COMMUNITIES OF IDEAS AND ETHNICITY

Then we're familiar with communities of ideas, faith, and interest because we hear the lingo all the time: the intelligence community, the university community and the farming community. Though they cross spatial boundaries, these affinity groups have unity because of shared values. The term is usually used in an ideal context. Thus, one rarely if ever hears of the "prison community," the "drug abuse community" or the "pornography community."

Communities of ethnicity are aggregates that are bonded by blood and common history, though they too may be geographically scattered. We hear of the Hmong community, the Latino community or the Greek community, and so forth.

But it is reasonable to suggest that there are also *faux communities*: Here of late
the word "community" has been abused, cheapened and diluted by the inappropriate use, as in the Internet or "virtual community," the gated community, and
references to major metropolitan cities as communities.

And Satchmo himself might agree here: communities are essentially small—and by small we mean a human aggregate that is humane, one that pays attention to the selfness of its numbers, one in which citizens feel cherished and realize their worthwhile-ness. As research has shown, small nurtures; large alienates.

This "human scale" is naturally preserved in towns, the author suspects, until the population range exceeds about 50,000. After that, the small town, with its sense of place and civic identity, becomes a city. And a city is a different animal.

Often you will hear "community" used as a mantra, as a blessing, and often as an appeal—sometimes a blatant public relations ploy to invoke unity when perhaps there is none—as when the mayor of Detroit (pop. 4.5 million) says on TV and radio that he hopes "the community of Detroit" will come together to stop the ritualized arson of "devil's night."

Detroit is a community? No, Detroit is a city. But "city" doesn't have the inclusive, sacred warm appeal of "community." To belong to a community is to belong to a congregation—what Stanford's Nadinne Cruz calls the "Big We."

You can have that Big We feeling in a city, but it's in diverse and individual neighborhoods. Etzioni calls such a city a "community of communities."

But can community be said to exist when people, its so-called members, can fake their identifications, spew hate, cause harm to others, and then disappear without consequence—as in the Internet "community"? Doesn't being a member of a true community require accountability?

Next, can community be said to exist when that place is restricted to all but an ex-clusive clientele—as in a gated "community"? These places didn't grow organi-cally, as did most traditional authentic communities—around a railroad, a river or the intersection of trading paths. They are manufactured to make the developers money.

While gated communities may indeed provide some of the benefits of the tradi-tional community, they are a marketing device. They're *developments*, pure and simple, given fuzzy-wuzzy handles to entice buyers.

How Places Grow

Thankfully, "place" has been defined more concretely. Mayhew describes a place as an "identifiable location . . . on the earth's surface . . . endowed with meaning by human beings."

Most American places—towns and cities—owe their existence to very humble beginnings, according to Peirce Lewis, Penn State professor emeritus of geography, the most common being primitive access, whether it be a navigable river or the intersection of Native American trading paths. Settlers, following the line of least resistance, turned those trading paths into post roads. As the town flourished into a city, trolley and rail lines extended outward, allowing folks to live beyond the old nuclear city center (example: the Main Line out from Philadelphia).

The access to public transportation spawned the "first wave" of suburbanization, which flowered in the 1950s, according to Joseph Wood, professor of geography at George Washington University, He speaks of "the Ozzie and Harriet kind of suburb—with the station wagon invented for just this sort of lifestyle."

Wood's "second wave" occurred when retail followed the housing patterns outward, developing along old streetcar lines, creating linear patterns. This led to the formation of the shopping plaza of the '50s, the first shopping centers in which each store had its own entrance, and parking was all out front—the precursor of today's covered malls—which pulled customers away from the old downtown department stores and ultimately led to their demise. (Wood notes that the department stores tried to carry a little bit of everything to serve people who still lived downtown.)

The first bypasses were also built in this era, designed to help ease traffic flow away from congested downtowns. But according to Lewis, these ring roads had an unintended consequence. These new bypasses, intended to preserve and enhance the old nuclear downtown, instead attracted new residential and then retail development outward from the town center—hence the suburbs—forever altering and diminishing the appeal and the influence of the traditional American downtown.

Wood's "third wave" has office centers following the retail and residential to places of high accessibility—in other words, office parks out along the beltway, corporate "back offices" (not the head offices) out here near the new 'burbs instead of downtown. Woods notes that as more women have joined the work force, proximity has made the jobs they take more attractive because it cuts down the commute time and the drive time to school, ball field, grocery store, and so on. Is it any surprise out here along the beltways of our cities that the gigantic covered malls sprawl? If you live in one of the 'burbs, work nearby at the office park, shop right there at the Sprawl Mall, why bother to go downtown? Thus, individual 'burbs or exurbs become their own cookie-cutter homogenous "bedroom communities" without much of a sense of place, much less of "community."

Furthermore, when the new Sprawl Mall painstakingly re-creates with ersatz charm a so-called small town, you know something bizarre is happening in America's collective sense of place.

The New Urbanism

If there is a "fourth wave," Wood thinks it's the "new urbanism" defined as the so-called planned neo-traditional communities like Reston, Va., or Seaside, Fla., in which developers design in "compact, walkable, mixed-use cities and towns," where everyone lives, shops and works right there, but no one is actually from "there." Not surprisingly, the new urbanism has its critics. However, a proponent like Timothy S. Mescon, writing in the August 2002 issue of *Arrivals* in-flight magazine, will say, "New Urbanists support regional planning for open space, appropriate architecture and planning, and the balanced development of jobs and housing. They believe these strategies are the best way to reduce how long people spend in traffic, to increase the supply of affordable housing and rein in urban sprawl."

Well, that sounds great, but we all can't live in such places.

If the author might be so bold as to suggest a "fifth wave," it is that of "exurbia," the new autocentric sprawl nation of ours in which exurban nomads living in "gated communities" think nothing of living one hour or more from where they work (or maybe it should be: working one hour or more from where they live—because it seems working is more important than living). I call such folk 'exurban nomads' because they belong to a car culture, which in itself is a culture of alienation. How much affinity for their "community" do these road warriors have? As it turns out, not much.

The New Exurban Nomadic Culture

Clemmons, N.C., is typical of the emergent exurbia. Burgeoning from 7,500 to 16,000 residents in the last 10 years, the pleasant town serves as a bedroom community for the nearby city of Winston-Salem. But publishing a community paper in a community without a sense of community is a tall order. So the Clemmons *Courier*, a 2,400-circulation weekly owned by the Evening Post Publishing Co. of Charleston, S.C., is chock full of local news and pictures that readers would never see in the nearby major metro daily.

But while the town owes its rapid growth to its proximity to the big city, that very location dynamic has filled the town with people who don't care about local events, public affairs or civic life. They are not stakeholders; they are campers.

Publisher-editor Dwight Sparks told community journalism student Vicky Bouloubasis, "We're certainly in the heavy shadow of Winston-Salem. People here still associate with Winston-Salem, and we suffer because of that."

The exurban nomadic culture troubles Sparks, who observes, "When I first came here, I was amazed at the way people moved in and out. Moving vans were on the road all the time. We would sell a subscription, and people would move the next month. It's still a community that doesn't have deep roots. This is not a permanent home . . . they're on their way to somewhere else."

This peripatetic nature, call it "America the Transient," concerns urban geographers like Stephen Byers, a former editor and now associate lecturer in the Urban Studies Program at the University of Wisconsin–Milwaukee, who notes that the average American moves every 4.3 years.

Where Community Newspapers Fit In

Penn State geography professor emeritus Peirce Lewis says that all places, all communities, regardless of their character, face "the challenge of change" and usually this means "the challenge of growth." This is where community newspapers come in. Lewis believes that the involvement of and leadership from the local newspaper is critical if the community is to successfully take on growth and development issues before they get out of hand.

For Lewis fears that without proactive regional planning and zoning, the natural course will be unfettered urban sprawl, with its housing, traffic and societal headaches. He warns that if left unchecked, such "growth" will result in what he calls the "galactic city" (Los Angeles or the D.C. to Boston "megalopolis" comes to mind). Picture a city with ring roads after inner and outer loops circling ever outward connected by radial arms and where office centers, corporate "back offices," suburbs and retail service areas have followed roads willy-nilly without a whole lot of thought.

Can a Newspaper Create Community?

Media observers note another dominant growth area, that of the suburban community paper right in the backyard of the large metro daily. Such a paper faces a formidable challenge in establishing a sense of place when a suburb is little more than a highly transient bedroom community for the nearby city. Publishers can't just draw a circle around a bunch of neighborhoods on a map and proclaim that area a community, Associate Professor Gene Burd of the University of Texas–Austin told a seminar on community newspapers and community-building, sponsored by Kansas State University and the National Newspaper Association.

A publisher attending that seminar lamented his position. Like the folks at the Clemmons *Courier*, he publishes a paper in an area—in his case, just outside St. Louis—where "people just don't seem to care about our community. They move in, buy a house, work in the city and only sleep in the house. They couldn't care less about our town."

If people living side by side have no sense of community—that is, a separate and distinct identity—a newspaper has a long, uphill struggle in trying to inculcate those values. It will take time, risk and financial commitment, along with consistent, solid local coverage. The publisher has to bank on the formula that the accretion of many good works over a period of time will pay off in the end.

But for a paper in this dilemma it's not enough to just put out the news week-in and week-out. The paper will have to be proactive in nonconventional ways of promoting itself and the community. It must find new and nontraditional ways of selling itself, of selling the community to the community and of educating the newcomers about the social context in which they've chosen to live. (See Chapter 20 on the subject of best practices.)

Happily for community newspaper publishers, there is such a thirst for local news that it makes competition viable. There are plenty of success stories out there.

When asked, "How do you compete with the Philadelphia *Inquirer*?" the late editor Marshall Rothman almost laughed. "What's the *Inquirer*? We've got absolutely nothing in common," he said in 1999. "You've got two different species." Rothman's Philadelphia *Leader*, a 30,000-circulation free weekly publishing in the shadow of "the Inky" for 40 years, serving the neighborhoods of Mt. Airy, West Oak Lane and Lower Cheltenham, is now edited by Doug Wallen.

Other Voices; Other Newsrooms

When William J. "Jeff" Brady, founding editor-publisher of the Skagway, Alaska, *News*, graduated from the University of North Carolina at Chapel Hill in 1978, he was not only young but also brash and full of spit and vinegar.

In his own words: "I was just out of college, and I was going to change the world—or at least southern Alaska."

He was also adventurous enough to leave his native South for a start-up thousands of miles away. Taking the small nest egg his mother gave him, Brady put his dog and everything he owned into a van and struck out across the country, purchasing used typesetting equipment in the Seattle area, before pushing on north for Skagway.

Brady had discovered Skagway, an 1890s gold rush town, during a college spring break in 1974, and decided he wanted a paper there.

But when the mayor of Skagway heard that the young man just out of college was going to establish a newspaper in his town, he advised Brady, "If you're gonna start a paper here, you'll need a set of brass knuckles and a body guard."

But Brady is made of stern stuff. His paper just celebrated its 25th anniversary.

Just getting the paper out is a wilderness adventure; the twice-monthly *News*, an 8–16-page, 800-circulation tabloid, is printed 100 miles away in Whitehorse, Yukon Territory.

Journalism student Christina Rexrode quotes Brady as saying, "I like to tell everybody that I have the best commute in the world." He explains that his trip to the printer takes him through 30 potential avalanche slide areas and crests at a 3,300-foot mountain pass.

His circulation of 800 doubles in the tourist season, when Skagway becomes the 16th-largest cruise port in the world. His annual visitor's guide, styled like a paper from the gold rush era of 1898, is very profitable, Brady says, providing two-thirds of his annual revenue.

His pages are peppered with stories that reflect the wild nature of his state. As an example, Brady shows his interviewer a front page of the *News*. The lead story is about a glacier outside of town making an unexpected move, which caused local flooding.

Explaining the paper's role in the community, he says, "You have to be part cheerleader. But you have to be the first draft of history too."

Rexrode also notes that the Skagway *News* is a one-man show. Brady comments, "There are three computers: one for me, one for business and one for a reporter—when I have one."

And he says he likes to have college interns for the summer, if they don't mind sleeping on the newsroom couch.

Your Town; Your Turn

1. How would you define your hometown? Choose three words to describe its character.
2. Take a walk in your town. Go somewhere you've never been before. Take notes. Take photos. What's new?
3. How many communities are you a part of? List them.

SEVEN

News
9/11 Was Local News Everywhere

Nothing Ever Happens Here?

No matter where you go in the country, ask to see a community newspaper's edition from 9/11, and you're likely to find at least one local angle story of the faraway tragedy: most obviously and painfully, if a local family lost a loved one when hijackers crashed jetliners into the World Trade Center Twin Towers, the Pentagon and a remote field in rural southwestern Pennsylvania.

But the effects of 9/11 were experienced first hand by thousands of other so-called ordinary people in many ways too: local residents who knew people or who had family members who worked in New York City, D.C. or Pennsylvania and talked about how they survived and of their reactions to the day's events; local civic, church or school groups visiting or touring in those cities at the time; and local people who actually witnessed and photographed the tragedies and e-mailed photos and stories back to their hometown newspapers.

Many of these stories and tips came into community newspapers unsolicited, from local readers compelled to tell their stories and share their experiences. And because of most community papers' characteristic accessibility (via the front door, real humans answering the phones and a lower volume of e-mail), contributing readers were able to tell their stories immediately to receptive newsroom staffers.

As farfetched as it sounds, 9/11 seems to have touched every community in the land. That realization came slowly to most places far removed physically from New York City, D.C., and Pennsylvania—especially with 9/11 falling on a busy deadline Tuesday for most weekly newspapers.

"When it first happened, it [the news] was . . . *out there*," says Mary Hart O. Blackburn, co-publisher of the semiweekly Wallace (N.C.) *Enterprise*, waving her right hand toward the distant North. "But within two hours we realized this is . . . *at home*."

Bill Rollins, associate editor of the nearby weekly Warsaw-Faison *News*, chimes in, "Then it was *our* story; it was *our* town."

Close to Home

The first-time visitor to the Bedford *Gazette* has to look hard to find the 10,000-circulation small-group daily in the historic little town in southwestern Pennsylvania: Right at the art deco Gulf station, right at the big tree,

Sharyn Maust of the Bedford (Pa.) *Gazette* remembers 9/11 as "the day all hell broke loose." Flight 93 crashed less than half a minute by air time from the community paper's office in rural Pennsylvania.

right again at the small sign, and you approach the *Gazette* building from the rear so that the long, low steel-sided building is liable to be mistaken for an automotive body shop. But regardless of how humble or remote the *Gazette* may seem, it and several other Pennsylvania community newspapers were in the eye of the storm on 9/11 when hijacked Flight 93 came down almost literally in their backyards.

Flight 93 crashed an estimated 26 seconds of air time west of Bedford.

"The day all hell broke loose" is how *Gazette* associate editor Sharyn Maust describes Sept. 11, 2001—a day that started like many others, with a front page carrying headlines about a local fire, the death of two teens in a car accident and concerns about West Nile virus.

Maust, a 31-year veteran at the *Gazette*, had worked late as usual the night before and was awoken Tuesday morning before 10 A.M. by a phone call from a friend telling her to "get up and turn on your TV." Maust says she watched the smoking Twin Towers in shock, with the growing feeling that "they're not going to stand, I just had this feeling, they're not going to stand up to that fire." She shakes her head, "And then the Pentagon! . . . And when they said Pennsylvania, it's like: uh-oh, where the hell is it? And then when TV said Shanksville . . . it's almost like an electric jolt. It's where?! Crap! Like every other reporter, you think, 'Oooh, oooh, let's go do

something.'" Although the crash site was 25 miles away and across the county line,
Maust realized, "It's so close, you gotta go."

Local witnesses, including "somebody's mom on the other side of the building" had seen the hijacked Boeing 757 flying low and erratically over Bedford. Just after 10 A.M. the jetliner had crashed into a grassy field 10 miles east of Somerset at an estimated speed of 500 miles per hour, killing all 33 passengers, seven crew members and four hijackers.

After checking in with executive editor Chris Frear, Maust and reporter Paul Rowan headed west across the mountain on Route 30. "Of course, we didn't know where the hell it was," she says, though "the guys at the Bedford airport said it couldn't be too far because they heard it [the explosion]," and "people all the way down the mountain said they heard it."

Rowan and Maust decided to split up and, in Maust's words, went "blundering about the countryside," until they got close to the Flight 93 crash site. However, law enforcement officials had already shut down the site.

"More and more reporters were showing up," Maust says. "We were up to the wazoo in reporters." In order to deal with the crush of media, Maust says authorities bussed the press to a hill several hundred yards away overlooking the crash site.

From there, Maust and Rowan saw that the jetliner had slammed into the edge of a large meadow and "had splattered into the nearby woods, setting them on fire. But there was nothing . . . to see," Maust recalls, as if reporters expected to see bodies being removed and parts of the airplane's fuselage littered about.

"It was pretty much like a burning dump site," Maust explains, "a black heap at the end of a huge V-shaped hole in the ground." Using a very long lens, Rowan got a color photo of the crash site, which would be prominently displayed on the next day's front page.

The two *Gazette* staffers returned to Bedford midafternoon to help put the paper together. And Rowan, who was not shooting digital yet, had to rush his crash site film to the local drugstore for one-hour processing.

The next day's *Gazette* carried a banner headline: TERROR HITS HOME, with two large AP photos of the Twin Towers and a wire story. Then below the fold came Rowan's photo of the Flight 93 crash site and the local story written by *Gazette* staffers, along with AP reports, in which they quoted Mark Stahl of nearby Somerset, one of the first people arriving at the scene: "There's a crater gouged in the earth, the plane is pretty much disintegrated. There's nothing left but scorched trees."

The inside pages of the 9/12 edition of the *Gazette* were filled with stories about the local reaction, heightened local security, how the local hospital and emergency personnel were prepared to care for the survivors had there been any, how local businesses gave their employees time off to watch the TV coverage and deal with the shock (so many locals had actually heard the explosion). Plus there was a story about a former *Gazette* intern who worked at the Pentagon but had been away from the building that fateful day.

Ironically, other local news—mundane by comparison—had to be covered that day too: a local murder trial, a new cookbook being released, schools opening again, the local civic club's meeting, and "of course the world of sports goes on," Maust says.

While Maust and Rowan had been out in Somerset County covering the crash the morning of 9/11, feature editor Vicki Henry stayed behind at the *Gazette* office because she "had to handle the normalcy. Somebody had to answer the phones. It was very panicky there for a while."

As the week wore on, Maust says, "we had to figure out how to cover the story." There were only so many times they could go back out to the crash site, and there wasn't much new to learn there, so the story turned into one about the spontaneous memorial for the victims and the candlelight vigils and memorial services being held.

"The people are the story," Maust says, "if not the victims, then the families. As always, [people] is what it's all about."

Then as weeks passed, the story got old, Maust says. "After a while the story became the story, with reporters interviewing reporters." She didn't return to the crash site for a full year. And later, when it came time to enter clips for the annual state press association contest, Frear declined to submit any of the *Gazette*'s copious coverage of Flight 93—perhaps in deference to the Somerset *American* of Somerset, Pa., the community paper closest to the crash site.

Don't Ever Say: Nothing Ever Happens Here

Chris Frear, the editor of the New Jersey Herald, *a 19,600-circulation daily in Newton, N.J., was the executive editor of the Bedford* Gazette *on 9/11. Here are his reflections on that day.*

The nation's most important news can happen in your backyard. No matter where you work in journalism, your newspaper either has been or will be the newspaper of record for a major national event. Just ask around.

We learned that again at the Bedford *Gazette* on Sept. 11.

At the time, we didn't know that it was the final flight or the story of the passengers' heroics. But we knew it was now a local story. The kind of moment that gives a reporter or editor both a pit in the stomach—can we do it again?—and an adrenaline rush—time to chase the story.

The first report of the morning came from inside the newsroom; a plane had crashed into one of the Trade Towers. My instinct was that a small plane had gone off course, either a mistake or a misguided individual. So, get CNN on the tube and check it out. Run through the usual checklist: Find out if there are any local connections to the pilot, the flight, the standard rundown.

I watched for a few minutes and, seeing and hearing nothing to indicate it was

something more serious or sinister, went back to work. There are always plenty
of eager eyes to watch breaking news; they'd keep me updated.

Then came the gasps, cries, cursing. The second jet, a second tower.

Something serious, something sinister was in progress. But what?

It was full-time in front of the television, consulting with other editors and directing reporters to start making contacts. What are our story angles? Who from the area was working or visiting in New York? What contacts could we make?

The Pentagon hit came a half hour later. A full-scale attack was under way. Where else would it strike and how many times? Everyone available was working on a story or making contacts for coverage. Routine pages were stripped and redesignated; a decision on how many pages to add to the paper would come later.

From covering bank robberies I learned that two elements are vital: get on the scene as fast as possible to start reporting and be patient. Take the time to get it right and to give the story time to develop.

Then came the phone call. So many tips and alerts at a small newspaper come from readers, salespeople, friends and family. Over the phone, on the street. "Did you hear . . . ?" As with any small newsroom, phone calls from the community are part of the news chain. People feel connected to the newspaper, so they call with tips and information. True at any newspaper but intimately true—and important—at a community newspaper.

This one told us that a plane had crashed near Somerset, 45 minutes to our west by the Pennsylvania Turnpike.

By this point we weren't ruling out anything, but this one didn't fit immediately. A crash near Somerset was nothing obviously strategic. Was it a random small plane crash? Or were planes dropping from the skies?

In any case what was a story of monumental national importance had now become a story for on-the-ground reporting.

As we redirected reporters, called by cell phone to reposition them, the calls from off-duty reporters and editors followed. Two key editors—Sharyn Maust and Paul Rowan—had worked late the night before and had probably slept just a few hours. They both called to ask what I needed and let me know they were coming in. Those are the calls of the professionals that reminded me what a compelling profession journalism is, and what a great group of people I worked with.

One of the duties of an editor, though, is directing rather than doing. Frustrating at times, because any journalist is drawn to the business for the allure of the action, being at the scene. But it was more important for me in such a dynamic situation—who could tell what more was going to hit and when and where—to act as the hub for the newsroom.

The different part about a newspaper business is that not only are you responding to the event, you're also responding to competition. You have a story to tell, and you have to tell it better than the others. So even in a disaster, when the common response is to join together to solve the crisis, you're competing.

There's camaraderie in the field, of course, but there's nonetheless the element of competition.

You can prepare for these moments. Most small newspapers don't train for them, or for power outages and the like. But you can be prepared. Paul and Sharyn and others on the staff were prepared.

Elizabeth Coyle, whose compassion and sense of justice marks all her work, was already in the field, talking with people, drawing out stories and reaction.

Sharyn, a keenly intelligent observer of people and events, was already a veteran of covering murders, fatal accidents, Ku Klux Klan rallies and corrupt officials and ready to cover whatever the events threw at us.

Paul, a copy editor but the best photographer on staff, pulled off the photo of the day for us. One of the still-smoldering crash site. Most of his photography skills are self-taught, a result of hard work and experimentation, just more evidence of the desire that Paul brings to the job every day. It took a long lens—that he had bought and learned how to use on his own—and some reportorial gumption to get to the scene, but he got the shot.

As the hours passed without further attacks and the shape of the events became clearer, we narrowed our focus to what is now known as the Shanksville site, Flight 93's impact, and the results of that.

Nothing ever happens here? Don't buy it. Sure, in rural America you cover events with cows and meetings about sewerage systems. The *Gazette* does. And well. But if Flight 93 had flown a minute more, it would have landed in Bedford County.

We now live in an era when events on the scale of Sept. 11 seem more likely to happen than not. When your turn comes, make sure you're prepared. Treat every assignment—obituary, news brief or dairy cattle show—like the world's going to be reading your copy. Because one day they will be.

9/11 Anniversary

How do enlightened community papers handle news differently from many major metro media outlets?

The best answer comes from Joe and Dana Shaw of the Long Island, N.Y., Southampton *Press* where Joe is editor and Dana is the photographer. For the first anniversary of 9/11, they featured a local woman, Kathy Gelman, whose brother, Tom, a New York City firefighter, had died in the collapse of the Twin Towers. Kathy had graciously agreed to an interview and photo session.

Dana recalls the photo session as follows:

With any assignment like this, I was, of course, nervous. This is a person who lost a family member, and because we are doing a story about it, they are forced to relive it, publicly. I told her how sorry I was.

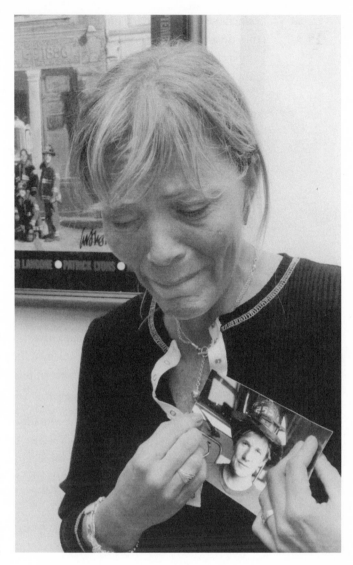

To print or not to print? The enlightened community newspaper handles a sensitive photo like this in a special way. Wanting to run the image and yet concerned about its impact on the person shown in emotional distress, Dana and Joe Shaw of the Southampton (N.Y.) *Press* tossed and turned most of the night until the newspaper couple came up with a solution acceptable to everybody. (Photo by Dana Shaw, courtesy of the Southampton *Press*)

I noticed that she has a painted print of a photograph of her brother with his fellow firefighters in front of the Brooklyn firehouse where he was stationed. I asked her if she had a photograph of her brother, and she did. She brought it out—it was a photo of her brother in his fire helmet. She looked at the photo, spoke about her brother a bit, and I started shooting.

Then she broke down.

I continued to take photos; I felt that it was important to show how the pain of losing a loved one, especially in a horrible situation like Sept. 11, would never go away. That one year later, and for the rest of her life, the pain of losing her brother will never leave her. I thought that needed to be seen.

Still, I apologized to Kathy for putting her through that. I knew that nothing I said would make anything better. I felt bad that I had taken her photo at a very vulnerable time, but in my mind people would see Sept. 11, 2001, as a human tragedy, a terrible waste of life, not just a terrorist attack, not just an event that would change the way that we live in this country; but it would emotionally alter people involved forever.

I went back to the paper and told my editor, Joe Shaw, who also happens to be my husband, that I had taken a very emotional photo. I showed it to him and asked if he thought it was too invasive.

We discussed it. The last thing we wanted to do was have something that seemed exploitive. That was not what I was going for, and that was not what the story was about.

Joe and I talked about it in bed for a long time, and we both lay awake for a good part of the night. Whenever an ethical journalism dilemma comes up, we will discuss it at home in private time. You never stop being a journalist even after you go home for the day. You want to do the right thing and do right by your readers. It's the most important thing. Losing sleep is just part of the job.

Joe suggested that we call Kathy and tell her about it and see if she was comfortable with us running the photograph. That is highly unusual. We don't usually do that, but under the circumstances we thought it was the right thing to do.

Joe called and spoke with Kathy, explained the photograph and the story, and made it clear what we were hoping to accomplish with both. She agreed and the photo ran.

How the Shaws handled this sensitive situation speaks volumes about how the enlightened community newspaper approaches the subject of news. Your author calls it "benevolent objectivity"—that complex mix of accuracy, access, compassion, responsibility and accountability that makes community journalism so important to the American media landscape.

Think Globally; Report Locally

If you need a visual model for community news judgment, try this:

News is like a hurricane: the closer it gets, the more important it becomes to you.

Every late summer and early fall, hurricanes rake the U.S. East Coast: Hazel in '54, Andrew in '92, Fran in '96, Floyd in '99, Isabel in '03, Ivan in '04. One of the largest was Hugo in '89.

When in early September 1989 a low-level tropical disturbance deep in the Caribbean first made the national weather news, editor-publisher Bill Collins of the 9,000-circulation weekly Summerville, S.C., *Journal-Scene* took little notice. But within 10 days, the storm assumed a force unparalleled in recent history. From the satellite photos Hugo looked like a giant's fist poised to deliver a roundhouse right to the Southeastern coast.

Summerville, just outside Charleston, was directly in harm's way.

In the next 48 hours, Collins would live through an unforgettable nightmare of

monsoonal rains and high winds that all but destroyed his community. That little
blip on the weather map had turned into the biggest headlines of the century, and many papers would be hard-pressed just to get to print at all that week.

Collins, who camped out at the *Journal-Scene*, says he vividly remembers roofs blowing off all around town within sight of the newspaper office, how his own roof rattled and groaned, how his building shook as if with fright. And how they managed somehow to put out the *Journal-Scene* that week in spite of trees down all over town. "Summerville looked like a bombed-out war zone," Collins recalls. "But thank the Lord no one in our town was killed."

Repeat: Our town.

For community newspapers, that's the nature of news. News is like that hurricane; the closer it gets, the more important it becomes to you, your town, your newspaper.

Enter the Hugonauts

In the aftermath of Hugo, national news organizations from the big TV networks to the major dailies sent teams into the Carolinas, and specifically into the Charleston area. Along with the influx of others taking commercial advantage of the area's plight, the media earned the local moniker of *Hugonauts*. And when they had "covered" the story, and national interest seemed to grow weary of angry lowland residents standing forlornly outside destroyed houses, the media went back home to the big cities.

Bill Collins stayed. He lives there. He cares. Summerville is his town.

That's the major difference between community journalism and the major media. They usually show up in your town only for a disaster; then when it's over, they go home. But for the area's community newspapers, the Summerville *Journal-Scene*, the Goose Creek *Gazette*, the *Coastal Times*, the Myrtle Beach *Sun-News*, the story continued. And it continued for years after the national media spotlight turned elsewhere. Here's the nut graf:

Because they're the home team, community newspapers collect, report, handle, write and package the news in a fundamentally different way from any other news medium.

Remember Bill Collins, holding on that dark night in the *Journal-Scene* office, praying for "his town."

Think about the folks at the flooded-out and burned-out Grand Forks, N.D., *Herald*, putting out the paper even though many of the staff had lost their homes to the great Red River flood of spring 1997.

For us, news is not some detached, impersonal set of occurrences happening to nameless, faceless news sources. What a terrible word: source. Join the human race, folks—we're talking about people here.

At a community paper, news is not events happening to inanimate objects. News is people, your people, and how the changing world affects their everyday lives.

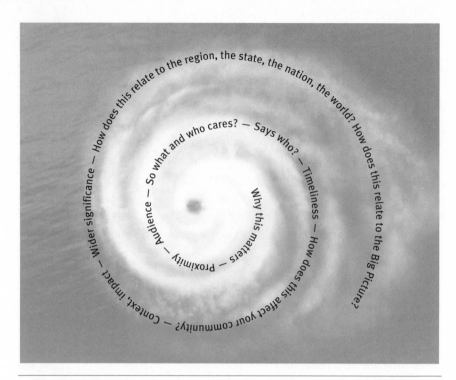

Local news is like a hurricane; the closer it gets, the more important it becomes to you and your community. You and your newsroom are in the eye. Shown are the factors that community journalism must weigh in tackling a story of consequence. What stands immediately before us can extend outward to ever-greater significance, making the local a part of what is global.

News is your people being caught up in events. Our job is to record that changing human condition in such a way that we provide not only an accurate and fair representation of what happened, but also understanding, compassion, context and, one hopes, growth.

In addition, great community news coverage (take the Hurricane Hugo or Red River flood example again) provides a place for community sharing, healing and growth. Both the Summerville *Journal-Scene* and the Grand Forks *Herald* became platforms for a communal rite of passage, a dependable scrapbook that said to its community: Look, you stayed here and took it and you survived. We (including the paper) may be small, but we're still standing. Once a community and its paper bond through such an experience, you have the makings of true and lasting communication.

The Community Journalism Spin

The closer to home, the more important. In community journalism, we don't talk about our "market" or our "primary coverage area." We talk about and to Our Town. We live in Our Town, and we report the news, and we *still* live here.

To put it succinctly, community journalists belong to the AAA Club: We strive to 101 be *Accurate*, and because we are *Accessible*, we are more *Accountable*.

That's quite a difference from the "shoot and scoot" style typified by much of the big-city media. If you're a victim or a source, sometimes that can feel more like "hit and run."

Dave Marcus, editor of the 38,000-circulation Salem (Mass.) *Evening News*, says that doing news at a community paper is tougher because of the Accuracy/Accessibility/Accountability dynamic. "The notion of precision is just as important —in fact—maybe even *more* important in a community newspaper, because if you have the wrong location of the park, then a lot of people know right away," he says, imagining the disgusted reader finding the error. "Who are those idiots? They don't even know where Bordenstein Park is!"

"Precision," maintains Marcus, "is very important. So you have to have big-city standards, but also the need for small-town connections with the readers."

The dynamic can be visualized as a spinning or swirling pattern, which may remind you of a a hurricane. You're in the eye, and you ask yourself key questions as the factors of news judgment swirl in and out from you and your location. Maybe such a model will help you grasp the concept of community newspaper news judgment.

Spinning Out; Spinning In

You and your community are the "eye of the hurricane." As you think of the outward spiral model of local news judgment, also be aware that the "spin" can come *at* you. Sometimes national and international news swirls in and touches your community. If you're lucky (and your readers like and trust you and the paper), you will discover a great local angle on the "big story" of the day.

As the old saying goes: Bring the story home for your reader.

In the wake of the 1999 Littleton, Colo., high school massacre, local folks in the small town of Avon in central New York noticed that one of the grieving Littleton teenagers on the cover of *People* magazine was a former resident who had recently moved to the West with her family. A tip to veteran sports editor Jack Haley at the Livingston County *News* in Geneseo, N.Y., started the story rolling for the 5,878-circulation weekly. The paper was able to secure permission from AP and *People* magazine to reprint the cover to accompany their own story about the young woman's ordeal.

Now *that's* bringing a national story home. Ben Carlson, who wrote the story for the *News*, recalls with considerable satisfaction scooping the nearby major metro, a Gannett daily in Rochester, caught flatfooted by the enterprising little *News* staff. (Carlson is now managing editor of the Brunswick *Beacon*, a thriving 17,000-circulation weekly in the beach community of Shallotte, N.C.)

What Is News Anyway?

The best community newspapers are unapologetically and enthusiastically local. Here's a way to visualize the concept:

If a newspaper's news perspective could be called "community framing," it would be like a photograph taken from a geosynchronous satellite high over the United States, zooming in from space to really close to Your Town—and everything that happens within that picture frame—that is

different,
interesting,
honorable,
odd,
fascinating,
significant,
infuriating,
controversial,
confusing,
curious,
laughable,
fun,
odd,
noble . . .
   is . . .
      NEWS.

News can also be broadly defined as an event that has one or all of the characteristics given below. The following time-honored list has been called the *factors of news judgment,* and you can use this to help you assess the newsworthiness of a story or story idea.

Timeliness
Audience
Impact and Proximity
Significance/Importance
Magnitude
Prominence
Disaster/Tragedy
The Odd or Unusual
Conflict and Controversy
Human Interest
Humor

From the CBS Evening News to the Summerville *Journal-Scene*—we all use this list, albeit intuitively at times, to determine:

What is the lede?
What is this story really about?
Who cares?
What is the most important thing?
What is the head?
How do we play or place this story?

Remember, the community journalism response to news is profoundly different from that of the big-city daily. Again, not necessarily better, just different, and therefore more effective for our context. Here's how the above list takes on a community journalism spin:

NEWS AND THE COMMUNITY JOURNALISM PERSPECTIVE

Timeliness: It's been said the media are in the new/s business, not the olds business. News—as in new information. CNN is the apotheosis of this credo, in which the "data stream" of the 24-hour news cycle is constant and unrelenting.

In community journalism, form follows function. If your paper is weekly, then it's one thing. If it's twice- or tri-weekly, then it's something else again. If your paper is daily, then it can carry breaking news. The less frequent the publication, the more explanatory and in-depth it should be. The longer we have between the news event and the time we hit the streets, the more we should be putting things in local context and providing background for our audience.

That's how we compete with the big daily and TV. The nearby TV station might give the story in your town 30 seconds; the big daily four inches. You can devote 20 to 40 inches—the whole front page if you're the editor and want to.

Audience: When you buy a house, according to the old saying, you look for three things: location, location and location. It's the same in community journalism. Your location is your audience, and your audience is in your face. It's very specific. It starts here, from your desk in the newsroom, and ripples out to the edge of your coverage area. Perhaps that's the county line.

If it happens to anyone within the county, then it's news. And, similarly, anyone in the county can become news and generate a news story (or a feature, or a sports story, or a sports feature, or an editorial or an editorial column or a . . . you get the picture).

Our audiences are what geologists call "site specific." Writing for the Lowcountry community of Summerville with its Gullah influences requires a different understanding of the local people, language and dialect, culture and historical background than writing for a newspaper in rural central Pennsylvania, where the influences are predominately Germanic with virtually no African-American influences at all.

Impact and Proximity: During the summer of 2004 news broke of the government's proposal to redeploy 70,000 U.S. troops stationed overseas. Although it was a national story, it may not have caused much of a stir in areas without stateside military bases. But you can bet it was big news in Summerville, where much of the local economy is based on spillover and from folks working at the Charleston Naval Base and Supply Depot. If the United States brings thousands of troops home, where are they going to be stationed? You got it: local news peg—local story.

It's a given truth in our business that anything that impacts your community is going to impact your paper too. If the Charleston Naval Base has a huge increase in population, it will impact all of Summerville, including the *Journal-Scene*, which will likely gain circulation and advertising. Talk about the trickle-down effect: if you're a cub reporter at the paper, this could mean you get that raise.

Bottom line: The community paper possesses an inherent intensity of community involvement that simply can't be matched by any outside big-city daily or area TV, no matter how neighborly they try to be or how chummy they may appear on camera. Their survival is not inextricably woven into the fabric of your community; yours is. Professional intensity is a function of caring. Caring comes from an honest sense of our connectedness. Small communities are profoundly connected.

Magnitude: The larger the crowd at the Christmas parade, the more people at the conference football playoffs, the bigger the voter turnout, the more money raised for United Way, the faster the car was speeding down Main Street—the community journalism response to this factor of news judgment is similar to that of the other media, except that we try to place it in a local context.

Prominence: Important people always are news. But in the community journalism world, important means Big Frog/Little Pond. So it's all relative. If the chairman of the county commissioners is pulled for suspected DUI, that's extra big news in your town. How your paper handles that story will have repercussions beyond just that edition. For instance, if you whitewash it or don't print it, you risk a complete loss of public credibility because everybody will have heard about it already by word of mouth. Consider the old saying: I already know the news; I just wanted to see if the paper had the nerve to print it. On the other hand, if you do print the DUI story and sensationalize and overblow it, you may have to live with the consequences.

Disaster and Tragedy: Just as the rest of the media, the community paper must report on disasters and tragedies—crimes, wrecks, fires and so-called acts of God. But here again, the community journalism response to human suffering is notably different. For us, it's a matter of balance. How much gore to describe or show in pictures? Do we publish the name of the rape victim, of the accused? Do we publish pictures of dead bodies? People grieving over burned homes? For the big-city papers and TV, this is standard fare. Why should we be any different? The answer is: the personal approach. Before you run any such story or photo that you think might contain content that would hurt people, use this rule of thumb: What if this were a member of my family? What if this were my daughter lying dead on the pavement? My grandmother's name in the paper as the rape victim, my father depicted crying hysterically in front of his burned-out home? Think twice. This is

Driver survives

Carl Vernon Gourtney, of Austell, Ga., was seriously injured Monday when the White Tractor he was driving lost its brakes on Coxes Creek, according to Trooper T.I. Adams, of the N.C. Highway Patrol. Gourtney went into surgery Monday afternoon upon his admission to Memorial Mission Hospital in Asheville. Adams said the tractor/trailer, which is owned by Camelot Distributing of Atlanta, was a total loss which Adams estimated at $60,000. Adams also estimated heavy damage to the load which was canned goods and other grocery products. Adams said the truck slid about 200 feet after overturning in the same curve where three motorists were killed last fall. One trucker on the scene was overheard to say, "It's enough to make you want to quit." [Photo by Pat Jobe]

A tasteful handling of a wreck scene: The photographer, McDowell County (N.C.) *Express* news editor Pat Jobe, puts the emphasis on the rescue workers, many of whom are local volunteers. At least eight rescue workers can be seen aiding the truck driver trapped in the wreckage. The driver is alive at this moment. But what if the driver had died after the photo had been taken? Would you have printed the photo then? Luckily, Jobe didn't have to wrestle with that issue, because the driver survived.

your town. And these are your people. What ends are served by publishing sensationalistic photos of human suffering or using lurid descriptions in hard-news stories? Think how Dana and Joe Shaw handled that photo of Kathy Gelman weeping.

These are basic news judgment questions every community newspaper must grapple with and define, ahead of time if possible. The best of papers have policies on such subjects, and young reporters and photographers learn these matters of philosophical style in due course. For instance, no, the *Express* doesn't run photos of dead bodies. That means if you go to a wreck where there's been a fatality, you take the shot from a discreet angle. Yes, we name the accused in a rape trial but not the victim. When it comes to grieving victims at tragedies or people hurt in auto accidents, allow them their dignity as best you can. At a disaster site, don't ask victims, "So, how does it feel to have lost your son [your home, your wife, etc.]?" We see enough of that reprehensible reporting on what late cartoonist Jeff MacNelly called TV's "Nitwitness News."

When taking photos, try to get permission either before or after shooting; or when your intrusion would be in poor taste, take such photos from a distance with a telephoto lens—and then huddle with your editor before the photo is run. At the shoot, it's better to concentrate instead on the rescue efforts by firefighters, police and emergency personnel. We're not in this to sell papers by using prurient stories and gory photos.

Where do you draw the line? The line is always shifting. It's a judgment call. It's a gray area. And it requires a constant sense of balance. There are no right or wrong answers. On good taste and news judgment, the old "breakfast table rule" is still a good yardstick: If your reader can't read your paper and get through eggs over easy without losing it, then you've got a problem with good taste.

The public's right to know is not served by a bloody photo of someone's dead mama all over P-1. If you run such a photo, you have every right to expect "the solid waste matter to hit the climate control device." And remember, because it's a community paper, the kinfolk can walk right in the newsroom and knock you into next week. You probably deserved it. (More about controversial photos in Chapters 14 and 16.)

ON MINIMIZING THE REVICTIMIZATION OF VICTIMS

The following is excerpted from a report by Glenn Scott, Park Doctoral Fellow, the School of Journalism and Mass Communication at the University of North Carolina at Chapel Hill; it was published in the spring 2002 edition of Grassroots Editor.

South Dakota weekly newspaper publisher Tim Waltner thinks collegiate journalism student should experience life's public dramas as directly and vividly as he and his contemporaries do while running small-town weeklies. Waltner, publisher of the Freeman (S.D.) *Courier* and past president of the International Society of Weekly Newspaper Editors, predicts that many students would be impressed by the value that readers place on conscientious and compassionate reporting in communities that larger and less-committed papers and broadcasters overlook.

Waltner tells about the painful but necessary conversation he had with parents of a boy named Paul who accidentally shot and killed his good friend, Woody, on the day of a Super Bowl party. The boys had gone to pick up a pizza and came upon a gun that had been inside a portable cooler. Waltner says he didn't know the facts behind the tragic incident, only that it was an accident. But Waltner says he did know he had to handle the story somehow. Waltner knew the families. In fact, his daughter had been near the scene of the accident. It was a tragic story among friends, one that affected many people in a rural town. And though Waltner knew that his readers would accept a straightforward story, he worried about how the big TV stations and regional dailies might exploit the event. "Two hours before press time," he says, "I got this awful knot in my stomach." Waltner phoned Paul's parents and explained that he was going to print

Paul's name in the *Courier*. It was the kind of consideration that goes with the job at smaller papers. The publisher braced himself for a difficult moment, but the boy's father didn't blame the paper.

"Your responsibility is to print the truth," the publisher remembers the father saying. "And the truth is that Paul shot Woody."

As it turned out, Waltner's fears were unfounded; the larger media virtually ignored the story because by the time Waltner's weekly came out, the story was "old news" to the larger media outlets.

Paul was not charged in the accident, and since that time, the youth has rebounded so successfully, according to Waltner, that he helped design the *Courier*'s Web site.

—the stuff of an honest ending.

FURTHER FACTORS OF NEW JUDGMENT

Conflict and Controversy: Because your backyard is so small, the community newspaper reporter, editor and even the publisher often finds himself/herself between a rock and a hard place. Sorry kids, it goes with the territory. Local politics, public governmental affairs, law enforcement and the public schools all involve public tax funds and therefore need to be watched closely. The rule of thumb is to attempt to cover all as objectively and fairly as possible. When covering a controversial subject, make sure you get as many sides as possible represented in the story and that your report doesn't seem weighted one way or the other. This is especially important in community journalism, because the townspeople will make it their business to know as much about your private life as possible. Any possible perceived biases (whether or not they're true) or conflicts of interest will perjure your story's credibility. If you do have an ax to grind, admit it and bail out of the story quickly. If you're a young reporter and are working on a sensitive story, make sure your editor is closely involved in crafting the final product. If you're the editor and you're thinking about writing a scathing editorial, remember: don't write mad, and pick your fights with care. Are your arguments balanced and rational? Or shrill and strident? (More on this in Chapter 9.)

Unusual Occurrences and Odd Things: On a coffee shop dare, one of the local characters decides to take a head-first dive into the fountain on the town square . . . an old woman has had a pet groundhog named Roscoe living in her spare washing machine for 16 years . . . the community college president must kiss a pig in public because he promised he would if the soccer team went undefeated . . . a truck overturns and spills its load of chocolate syrup across Main Street . . . a woman fakes a heart attack to scare off a burglar . . . five convicts dig their way out of the county jail using nothing but a pair of nail clippers—these and thousands of other little stories fall under the news heading of unusual or odd occurrences. People have an insatiable appetite for variety, things that are different and perhaps odd. We as a species seek relief from the boring humdrum of daily existence. Some papers, during especially slow news times, are famous for running photos of farmers with potatoes that look like dogs, tomatoes that look like they have faces. Is there anything wrong with this? Not really, unless that's all you're running.

Human Interest: Broadly interpreted, this term has come to encompass stories or photos that tug on the heartstrings a little. A mentally challenged boy was lost for a day and then found lodged in a drainpipe. He was found by local rescue crews because, though he couldn't speak, he wore a silver bell around his neck, and they heard him ringing the bell. When the rescue was successful, it made a good news story, with an added dash of human interest. When one newspaper editor heard about the impending retirement of the local high school janitor, it didn't sound like much of a story until the principal told him that the old man loved to sit in the boiler room playing his banjo while tending the furnace. Ah, now we've got a human interest story, and a picture, too.

Humor: Some maintain the media's job is to inform and entertain. Humor is the finest form of entertainment, but it's not so easy to come by. It takes a reporter, photographer and editor with a sense of humor, too. One of the real hallmarks of smaller towns is their innate sense of humor. A good community newspaper can reflect that sense of fun. The rule of thumb: Don't produce humor at the expense of somebody's feelings. Making fun of people is not good form. There's a fine difference between laughing at someone and laughing with them. In news and feature stories, avoid sarcasm, satire and parody until you've got some experience under your belt and your community knows you. Satire inevitably will be read straight by someone who will not be amused. Reserve this form of humor for the editorial page, personal columns and commentary that is clearly marked as such. Examples? The eccentric old man who has stipulated in his will that he must be buried with his beloved '57 Cadillac Eldorado. The farmer who, when baling hay, playfully sticks a pair of boots in the center of the roll of hay, and then watches for passing motorists' reactions.

The Big Three: News, Features, Commentary

Everything written in your paper that is not advertising is one of three kinds of stories: news, features or commentary. How can you tell them apart? What are their distinct differences? Joy Franklin, editorial page editor of the regional big daily Asheville (N.C.) *Citizen-Times*, uses the following model to help young reporters and students get a grip on the forms and their characteristics.

NEWS

Lede: Lede is usually a summary lede (several of the 5W's and H).
Style: Story style is usually an inverted pyramid.
Timeliness: The story is almost always timely.

Purpose: It is written to inform.

Perspective: The reporter remains objective.

Location: It is found on P-1 mostly, but elsewhere as well.

FEATURES

Lede: Variety of ledes can be used.

Style: Narrative, often anecdotal, and other styles.

Timeliness: May or may not be timely. News peg not necessary.

Purpose: Written to entertain and inform.

Perspective: Can be either objective or subjective.

Location: Usually section fronts, occasionally as a "bright" on P-1.

COMMENTARY

Lede: Variety of ledes can be used.

Style: Variety of forms and structure used.

Timeliness: May or may not have a time factor.

Purpose: Written to inform perhaps, but mostly to persuade.

Perspective: Opinion of editorial writer, or editorial board.

Location: Editorial page and, in the case of personal commentary, in set
locations in special sections: op-ed, lifestyle, sports.

All Politics Is Local; All Politics Is Stories

If news is like a hurricane, then local governmental affairs reporting could be called a veritable tempest. But it is not a tempest in a teapot. It is the very stuff of our calling as newspeople. Who else is going to provide in-depth, consistent and comprehensive coverage of city hall activities and meetings held by the town council, school board, planning council, borough council, zoning board and county commissioners?

Few beats covered by the community paper are more important.

The newspaper is there in proxy for the citizen who won't or can't attend the meeting. Such "public watchdog" coverage is one of a community newspaper's main functions. Stories generated by action by such boards directly impact our readers.

If the county commissioners are considering raising the county tax rate, just look at how the factors of news judgment kick in. The story hits our audience right in the wallet; they need to know all about it right now; why has the rate been upped? What's going to be done with the funds? Joe Six-Pack (who may never have read a county commissioners story in his life) wants to know, "How much am I going to have to pay?" There's going to be a howl of disapproval, perhaps at a public hearing.

"When is that meeting going to be held again? Where's that *Bugle*? I know I saw it here somewhere."

Local government stories are stories that matter to your readers. They may not know it right away, and they may not all know it at once, but it's vital that we be there at those meetings, providing coverage that goes beyond the mechanical reportage of agenda items one through five.

Avoid the 30-inch city council snoozer. Larry Atkinson, editor-publisher of the award-winning 2,848-circulation weekly Mobridge, S.D., *Tribune*, says his reporters used to "dump their notebooks" into the computer, making for deadly reading. Now the *Tribune* features multiple stories and sidebars to break up council stories, and Atkinson says readers seem to like that approach much better. For example, the *Trib* would do a separate story on how that proposed ordinance would affect Joe and Suzy Citizen.

f/8 and Be There

At one town council meeting that no newspaper deemed worthy of coverage, the board adopted a strict and sweeping sign ordinance. It wasn't until enforcement started kicking in that town businesspeople began reacting angrily. "How come we didn't know about this?" they lamented.

If the area community newspapers aren't providing vital watchdog services, it's very likely no one will. Historically, American newspapers in general and community newspapers specifically have been that public watchdog. Some consider our surveillance role to be almost a sacred calling. It is certainly not to be taken lightly, even though humorous, downright funny or odd things happen in council meetings—and they do.

In one town, the voters were preparing to vote on an ABC referendum, to decide whether beer or wine could be sold within the city limits. The town council, all elderly conservative white males, held a public hearing. One noted liberal citizen stood up, called the council members all a bunch of puppets, maintaining that the council was completely controlled by the conservative church down on Main Street. And to dramatize that connection, he tied a piece of string from a large ball to the table leg used by the council, and marched out of the room, unrolling the string as he went.

Where was he going, trailing that string behind him? There was only one community newspaper reporter in the room, and he and several curious onlookers followed as the man stalked out of the county courthouse, down Main Street to the church in question. There he tied the other end of the string to the front door. "That's the connection," he said emphatically. "This church jerks the string and the council jumps. And you can quote me on that."

You're darn right we can. Great stuff. One can only hope our reporter had a

camera with him. Hence the old journalism battle cry: "f/8 and Be There!" In other
words, the goal of the journalist is to witness the news in person—with a camera.
And how you set the camera (f/8 is an aperture setting) doesn't matter compared to
just Being There.

Your reporting model for this area of the news might well be the late Tip O'Neill's
famous motto, "All politics is local." When it comes to our business, we should add:
And all politics is local stories. State and national political stories impact our
readers as well. When the federal government mandated No Child Left Behind, it
impacted every school in the land. It's our job in community journalism to interpret these state and national stories by showing how such decisions directly affect
our communities.

Meeting Coverage: It Ain't Sexy, but It's Gotta Get Done

Many young reporters at small newspapers find themselves covering their first town
council/school board/planning board/county commissioners meeting with little
or no training.

With apologies to the popular "Dummies" guidebook series, here's what we'll call
"Public Affairs Reporting for Dummies." Credit University of Richmond journalism instructor Tom Mullen for cutting through the clutter with his handy-dandy
beginner's list—though Tom is quick to say "his" list is gleaned from a lifetime of
learning from other folks too. Even so, since we heard from Tom during a terrific
guest lecture, we'll call it:

TOM'S TERRIFIC TIPS FOR COVERING MEETINGS

- *Find out where you're supposed to go.* As silly as that sounds, it's critical. What
  building is the meeting in? What room? Where's the parking? How long will it
  take to get there?
- *Get there early.* It's a sign of respect for the gravity of the proceedings. And then,
  it's a very practical matter, too: Pick a seat where the sight lines are good and you
  can hear everybody at the table. Nothing looks worse than a rookie banging into
  the council chambers after the meeting is already well under way. If it's a small
  meeting, and you're one of the few observers, or the only reporter—that
  dynamic only magnifies your tardiness. On the other hand, if the attendance is
  high and you're late, you risk getting pinned down in the back of the room
  where you can't hear/see the action. Remember: No Access; No Story.
- *Dress appropriately.* Another no-brainer. But it's amazing how many media folk
  show up at relatively formal public affairs events dressed as if they're coming
  from a backyard cookout. Remember, you want to be invisible. Dress to blend.
  Guys: carry a tie in your briefcase. Some day it will save you. On the other hand,

if the entire council wears slacks and golf shirts, then you're safe to dress down, too. Just keep your eyes open and use common sense.

- *Do the research.* Get an agenda in advance. Go through it line by line. Don't go into the meeting clueless.
- *Make calls.* Especially if you're new in town. Call the people you're going to be covering. Introduce yourself with something like this: "I'm a writer for the *Bugle*, and I noticed this agenda item. Can you help me understand it so I can make better sense of it for my readers . . . ?" Don't be afraid to use your ignorance to help open doors.
- *What's the story?* Figure out what you want to write about before the meeting (but don't discount the possibility for novelty).
- *Remember, you are on display.* You're more than just you; you represent your newspaper. Be on your best behavior, and for heaven's sake, stay awake!
- *Bring extra pens.* The "Duh Rule," but often forgotten. Nothing makes a writer look dumber than having nothing to write with.
- *Number your notes.* "Org" (organize) as you go. Highlighters can help too.
- *Listen for great quotes.* Not just "killer quotes," but any lively direct quotes. They humanize and bring an otherwise sleepy meeting story to life.
- *Write for* RPS. That's "Real People," Also, PYR. That stands for "Picture Your Reader." If it helps you, visualize your Aunt Sadie reading your story and trying to make sense of it. Ask yourself, "Who cares?" "Who needs to know what I'm writing about?" and "Why do they need to know it?"
- *Eliminate jargon.* When council talks about "backflow effluent regulators," you need to say they're talking about sludge control. Speak English.
- *Laptops?* If you're using one at the meeting, start writing the story at the meeting—especially ledes.

Now you're ready to write the story. I call these:

MULLEN'S MULLINGS ON WRITING THE MEETING STORY

- *Avoid the agency lede:* Don't say, "City Council voted to raise taxes . . ." Do the math for the reader. Give the reader something right away, such as, "The average homeowner's taxes will go up $2,000 this year . . ."
- *Use the impact test:* How much does what's happening matter to my reader? Remember Aunt Sadie.
- *Use the "Would you read it?" test:* If you weren't the writer, would you read this story?
- *Use the "Put up or shut up" test:* If something's not clear to you at the meeting, it won't be clear in your story. It's your job to make things clear. After the meeting, don't be afraid to ask a council member, "What did you mean when you said . . . ?" It will make you appear dedicated to accuracy and precision, which of course you are.

It's a mortal fact lost on many young reporters: The older people become, the more they pay attention to obituaries. And the enduring irony is that many young reporters are required to write "obits."

Many an editor's reasoning goes something like this: Let the kid do it; we'll see if she or he can handle something so menial and plodding as writing clearly and accurately about a dead person.

But it's also a test—of accuracy, humility, enterprise and journalistic craft. Sad to say, but still many obituaries are boring, stereotyped or formulaic.

But obits don't have to be, well, dead.

Here, I've written my own obituary. Read and see if you don't get a feel for "the deceased."

LAUTERER OBIT

Jock Lauterer, a veteran photographer and teacher at the University who loved his work so much he was known for joking about wanting to die in the darkroom, got his wish Saturday.

Steadfastly refusing to retire, Lauterer, 89, was found early Saturday morning collapsed in the photo lab in his home at 122 Araya Lane, Chapel Hill. The coroner ruled heart failure as the cause of death.

Lauterer, a native of Chapel Hill, was the founding director of the Carolina Community Media Project and a longtime lecturer at the School of Journalism and Mass Communication at the University of North Carolina at Chapel Hill.

An author of 10 books, he worked for 15 years as editor-publisher of two newspapers he co-founded in western North Carolina. Lauterer also taught photojournalism at Penn State for 10 years.

"When he connected with teaching college," said his widow, Lynne Vernon-Feagans, "it was as if he was born again." Lauterer is also survived by a daughter, Selena, Portland, Ore.; and a son, Jon, Wilmington, N.C.

Services will be held at 2 P.M. Sunday, March 21, in the Community Church, 105 Purefoy Rd., the Rev. Charlie Kast officiating.

In lieu of flowers, the family asks that donations be sent to the Lauterer Scholarship Fund in care of the School of Journalism and Mass Communication at the University of North Carolina at Chapel Hill.

—30—

Typically, the obituary writer should include the following elements in the story.

• Name, age, address and occupation.
• Time, place, cause of death (if available, and if it's the paper's policy).
• Birthdate and birthplace.
• Accomplishments and honors.

- Education and memberships.
- Military service.
- Anecdotes, recollections of friends and relatives.
- Survivors (immediate family plus the number of grandchildren).
- Funeral or memorial service information and burial arrangements
- Flowers, special funds or donations in honor of deceased.

The obituary writer gets his or her material from at least one if not more of the following sources:

- Mortuary, funeral home
- Relatives and friends
- Newspaper clippings
- References (*Who's Who*)
- Police, coroner
- Hospital
- Attending physician

BRINGING THE OBITUARY BACK TO LIFE

"Appallingly short-sighted." That's what retired Colorado State journalism professor Garrett W. Ray calls sloppy and boring obituary writing. He and many canny newspaper editors know that the obituary page is one of the first and most well-read parts of the entire paper.

"Local newspapers are seeking ways to be useful and interesting to readers, to build community ties, and to gain market share in an increasingly competitive media mix. Strong local obituaries can help achieve these objectives; yet they are often among the newspaper's most neglected tools," Ray told one of the symposiums on "Newspapers and Community-Building" sponsored annually by Kansas State University in conjunction with the National Newspaper Association convention.

Ray thinks editors should remember that "we're in the business of touching ordinary lives in exceptional ways." On the topic of "Bringing the Obituary Back to Life," Ray advises community newspaper editors to write the obituary as if it were "a profile, a personality portrait of a living person." In his view, here are fresh ways to look at obituary writing:

- Think of obits as profiles that could be run as feature stories.
- Raise the status; give it to a good writer.
- Give special treatment to at least one good obit per issue.
- Give special attention to "ordinary people."
- Do your homework (seek out clippings, friends, etc.).
- Talk to more sources; ask better questions; listen for great revealing quotes, examples of character.

- Seek out the "marker events" of the life. The decisive moments. What did they care about, give their time to? What were they proud of, and what gave them pleasure?
- Listen for the "little stories," the revealing vignette. Never forget we're in the business of storytelling.
- Write feature ledes.
- Above all, be accurate.
- Finish with a tagline that includes the paper's name and date. This is crucial for the family, which will clip the obit for safekeeping.

"Routine obituaries can't convey how special a person was," Ray says. The Joliet, Ill., *Herald-News* realizes this, and so treats one obit each issue as a feature in a running story titled "Everyday People"—a regular feature about "people who might not have been famous but whose lives showed that there is no such thing as a common man or woman."

BUFFALO BILL WOULD BE PROUD

Here are some gems from the Cody (Wyo.) *Enterprise*, a twice-weekly 6,000-circulation community newspaper (founded over a hundred years ago by Buffalo Bill!) with the common touch when it comes to wonderfully written obituaries. To make it more personal, obituary writer Laurie Quade uses first names after full names at first reference.

"After graduating from Cody High School, Bob joined the Navy and served six years. He returned to Cody and married Jerry Read, the love of his life for 53 years.

"Bob had a love for the outdoors and fishing, which he loved to do with his buddies. He will be fondly remembered for the hours spent entertaining his family and the residents of the Long Term Care Center with his singing. Bob's life was shared by many who loved him."

"Ruth will be greatly missed. She leaves behind many great friends in the Big Horn Basin and Saratoga and those special friends she and Doyle shared during their winter retirement years in St. George, Utah."

Of a farm construction worker, the *Enterprise* obituary writer wrote, "He was a master mechanic, highly valued for his mechanical ability on any kind of equipment, his reliability and honesty."

"His second love was amateur radio. He was involved in the Cedar Mountain Radio Club and spent many fun hours talking to people around the world.

"He also loved hunting, which is what he was doing with his son on the day of his passing."

The Cody *Enterprise*'s society editor, Quade also handles the police and hospital news, takes photographs, writes a column and does the birth announcements, as well as the obituaries. "So I go from birth to death," she quips.

Quade has a definite philosophy on obituary writing. "It's a tribute to the one who passed away," she says. "It's their last hurrah, the last time they'll be in the paper, and I think their lives are worth more than just three grafs of 'She was born, she lived and she died.' It just pains me when I see that . . . because you know that an 89-year-old woman has lived more than three grafs."

She says she got her inspiration from obituaries from the turn-of-the-century community papers in Nebraska, when in her grandmother's time obituaries were "wonderful pieces of creative writing."

Quade's obituaries are "written mostly for the family and the friends left behind. I think it's sad when we relegate obituaries to the back pages, eliminate any adjectives and make people pay for them . . . I think it's very important, especially at community newspapers."

From the Trenches

I awoke in the middle of the night, a strange smell in my nostrils. Smoke. Where could it be coming from? And what was that reddish glow outside my window? Suddenly awake, I could see from my second-story apartment over main street— Franklin Street, Chapel Hill—that something large was on fire in the middle of the block.

A cub reporter-photographer for Jim Shumaker's Chapel Hill (N.C.) *Weekly*, I scrambled into my clothes, grabbed my camera, and hurtled downstairs and up the street. It was the Varsity Theatre. If it went, half of main street could go with it. The firefighters let me pass, and I shot some pictures of the firefighting efforts. But it was all smoke and darkness, and the actual fire was on the top and back of the roof. No way to get much of a decent shot, I realized with frustration.

Then as I was standing out on the sidewalk in front of the theater, I saw its manager emerging from the structure. The look on his face was what held my attention. Without even focusing or thinking, I popped off a direct-flash grab shot, catching the soaked manager and his glazed look of shock. I shot it from about 20 feet out. One shot. One single flash. I didn't want to bug the owner. He already looked upset enough as it was. I was lucky. The shot turned out.

Shumaker grunted his approval when he saw the photo and ran it front and center P-1. He liked it because the photograph depicted not so much the extent of the physical damage as much as it showed the human reaction to a news event. The look on the manager's face was more telling than a shot of the burned-out building. That was an important learning experience for the young reporter-photographer.

The pictures of the Varsity Theatre on fire were lackluster. But the shot of the soaked and shocked owner emerging from the ruined movie house told it all.

Your Town; Your Turn

1. Think about your paper, or a target paper. Find an example of how the community journalism response to a local news event was different from that of the nearby big-city daily and area TV.
2. Find an example in your paper of how the publication schedule affected how the paper treated a major news story.
3. What is your newspaper's audience? Be as specific as possible.

4. How does your paper treat hard news? Human suffering and grief? The depiction of death and dying? Does your paper have a set of standards for good taste and a stylebook for handling hard news? If so, what are those guidelines? Do they seem to differ from the big-city daily and TV? If the paper doesn't have one, why not? And what are some of the implied standards it uses?

5. Just for fun, see what you can do with a made-up death notice from a fictitious funeral home, given below. What's so special about Clyde? Turns out, plenty.

Fudnucker Funeral Home
"Rest Assured with Fudnucker"

NAME OF DECEASED: Clyde Cato Wiezcinski
ADDRESS: 14 Amber Alley, Chapel Hill, N.C. 27514
AGE: 88
CAUSE OF DEATH: Liver failure (old age)
PLACE OF DEATH: Home
TIME OF DEATH: 8 A.M. Wednesday, March 17
OCCUPATION: Janitor, Rathskeller.
SURVIVORS: Lily Beatrice Wiezcinski, of the home; two sons, Tom T. and Robert W., both of Graham; and four grandchildren.
FUNERAL ARRANGEMENTS: University Presbyterian Church. Rev. Robert Dunham officiating. Sunday, March 21, 2 P.M.; interment to follow.
ANECDOTES/NOTES: Liked to play his banjo after hours in the boiler room of "the Rat." Took in stray cats. Known as "the Cat Man of Amber Alley." Interviewed by the Chapel Hill *News* (Jan. 2001) when he was supporting 31 cats on his janitor's salary.
PERSONAL INTERESTS: Deceased was a long-time member of member of SPPBPA, the Society for the Preservation and Promotion of Banjo-Picking in America.
MILITARY SERVICE: The deceased was a veteran of WWII. Served in the U.S. Army and took part in the Normandy Invasion. Decorated for valor.
FLOWERS, MEMORIALS: In lieu of flowers, the family asks that donations be sent to the Orange County Animal Shelter in the name of the deceased.

EIGHT

Features
Pay Attention to the Signs

One That Didn't Get Away

The young feature writer stood puzzled at the open front door. An old man was supposed to meet him here for a feature about cider making. But Hoyle Greene wasn't in sight. Disappointed, the reporter turned to leave. But wait a minute—what's that sign by the mailbox? A jumbled bunch of nonsense. It said:

LOOK.ROWN
THE.HOUSE.
I.WILLB.W
ORKN.—>

Staring at the sign intently, the reporter began to understand. The old man couldn't spell very well and thought periods at the end of each word added weight. The message was starting to get through, as Hoyle Greene, all a-grin and eyes dancing, appeared from around the house where he had been working.

"Lahk ma sahn, young feller?" he inquired.

The reporter "lahked" it so much he took a picture of it. The old man who couldn't spell proceeded to teach the young man a world about apples, cider and making do with what you had.

Over the years, Hoyle Greene would become a vast sourcebook for the writer, and would eventually provide him the photograph that would become the jacket illustration for a book about the old people and the culture of the Southern Appalachians.

And to think the young reporter almost walked away from that sign.

The Community Journalist As Creative Writer

There's a memorable photograph from Edward Steichen's landmark photography exhibit and book, *The Family of Man*, depicting a clutch of small African children sitting by firelight listening in rapt attention to a village elder telling a scary story. Both of the old man's hands are raised to mimic open claws, his eyes are wide with excitement and his mouth is forming a toothy snarl. The children stare back open mouthed, hanging on every word of the story.

The art of storytelling, as old as our species, provides the basis for all newspapers. In the most fundamental sense, it is our reason for being and survival. (Even advertising, if you think about it, is about storytelling.) It's easy to lose sight of this fact in our age of online glut, TV gloss, hyper-grunge graphics and garbage

An open front door will allow readers to come see you—which they will, with all manner of "news." Hoyle Greene thought his big "Georgy red sweet 'tater" deserved a picture.

fonts in the magazines, and in glitz over substance in many newspapers that emulate TV.

Eugene L. Roberts Jr. (whom we will meet again as the Gene Roberts of "Wandering in Rural Wayne" fame) created a prize at his alma mater, the University of North Carolina at Chapel Hill, to reward annually the student journalist who is also a good storyteller. You can hear Roberts' words sing in the following challenge, engraved on the plaque:

> The Eugene L. Roberts Prize is meant to encourage and is dedicated to the story of the untold event that oozes instead of breaks, to the story that reveals, not repeats, to the reporter who zigs instead of zags, to the truth, as opposed to the facts, to the forest, not just the trees, to the story they'll be talking about in the coffee shop on main street, to the story that answers not just who, what, where, when and why but also, "So what?"; to efforts at portraying real life itself; to journalism that "wakes me up, and makes me see"; to the revival of the disappearing storyteller.

Tell the Story, Kid, Tell the Story . . .

You bring your story to life by using anecdotes, writing in the narrative style, delivering vivid direct quotes and hooking the reader with imagery.

If you're doing a story about poverty in Appalachia, don't cite statistics. That will make for a MEGO (My Eyes Glaze Over) story. Instead, find someone from the

Here's the sign our reporter-photographer found beside Hoyle's mailbox. It might take awhile to figure out the message.

region who is poor. Tell his or her story. Put a face on a problem, a name to a statistic. Through that one life story, you will say much more about poverty in Appalachia than all the stats in the world.

Pulitzer Prize–winning journalist Leonard Pitts Jr. says, "It's a way of humanizing issues by shooting it through the prism of one life."

Remember: Put a face on it.

Then you'll really be Showing, not Telling.

The late journalism professor emeritus Phillips Russell of UNC–Chapel Hill used to tell his writing classes, "If you're going to write about a bear—bring on the bear!"

Community Journalism and Features

Community journalism provides a unique platform for creative and engaging story-telling, especially for the enlightened community journalist. And because of the intrinsic characteristics of our papers, we have certain advantages over our big cousins from the major metropolitan areas.

First of all, the people we're writing about are more likely to already know us, or about us, so there's a ready familiarity working for us right away. We've got that all-important access. We're likely to have more time to devote to the interview and to the writing of the story. (See Chapter 10.)

In writing the story, we can be more personal. Many community papers encourage feature writers to refer to the source by his or her first name, instead of the impersonal-sounding AP Style "last name only" rule.

We're more likely to get to do the interview one on one, take our own photographs as well, and therefore have a better creative grasp on the story and package as a holistic entity. If we're lucky, we'll get to do the headlines and layout as well. Talk about total artistic control. Big-city feature writers would kill to get into the backshop to toy with the layout. Ever walked into a union backshop of a big-city paper and had the whole shop freeze in their tracks and just glare at you, daring you to touch anything?

And finally, we'll probably have the luxury of more space in which to run the story and/or photos. At the community newspaper level, feature writing is likely to be more personal, less harried, more holistically creative and far more enjoyable.

So, as the late great sportscaster Red Barber used to say, "We're in the catbird seat."

What Is a Feature?

Fluff? Puff? Filler? Fuzzy-wuzzy journalism? Some editors and reporters dedicated to only hard news would have you believe the feature is only "soft" news and a second-class story. Some people on the business side will be openly disdainful of features and maintain they're just taking up space better served with ads. In short, a waste of space.

But if that's so, how come *People* magazine is such a runaway success? What fills the pages of other successful magazines such as *Rolling Stone*, *Cosmopolitan*, *Ebony*, *Esquire*, and the *New Yorker*? Indeed, canny large newspapers and magazines are realizing that the increased use of features is one way to combat loss of readership to TV.

We may never be able to beat TV to the street with the printed news. But we can sure feature the competition to death. A well-written feature story may not be the lead story in the paper, but if you've done your job well, you can bet more people will read your feature than what's under the banner head. That's because people can't help but read a story with human interest, a feature with human appeal. If you're a reporter-photographer who is a "people person," features may be your strong suit.

The Form

As you recall, features can use a variety of ledes, can be written in anecdotal and narrative style, may or may not be timely, are written to entertain as well as to inform, may be either objective or subjective and are found all over the newspaper.

What usually separates news from features is that a feature contains information that is not vital to your need to know, as they say in the spy novel business. You can

probably live just fine without the information that Chubettes, the third fattest cat
in the United States, lives right down the road from you, and is on a diet. However, knowing about this fat feline makes life just a little more goofy and zany, and therefore bearable. It's been said that the highest form of bliss is living with a certain sense of the craziness of it all. Features may entertain, enhance our sense of livability, inspire us, underscore a sense of place and time and touch us deeply with the human condition.

Another factor of features: time. Many if not most features are what we call "evergreen." That is, the vital leaves of information won't fall off with time; they'll keep—depending on the story—indefinitely. There are usually limitations, but they are more forgiving than the time-demands on a news story, in which the facts turn brown and worthless with age almost immediately. For instance, the feature on Hoyle Greene's cider making is a good example of a relatively evergreen piece; it could be run any time all the way through the late summer apple-harvesting season.

Enterprise? Isn't That a Federation Starship?

Even old Captain Kirk and Jean-Luc Picard would tell you, the name Enterprise has its roots in self-reliance, pluck and what they used to call in football "broken-field running," or "razzle-dazzle." In other words, thinking quickly on your feet and employing all your senses and body parts to overcome adversity and to win.

Beginning reporters all too often expect the editor to provide all the answers, all the ideas, and all the guidance, plus loads of editing. However, at many community papers that is not the case. For a variety of reasons, you may be very much on your own—especially in the area of generating story ideas.

At many community newspapers you will be expected to conceive, background and write the feature. That means, find the story from scratch, figure out how to do your own research beforehand, set up and conduct a successful interview, possibly even take the photograph, organize and write the feature (and even critique your own work because maybe no one else will).

Enterprise—that skill or talent or learned ability for sniffing out features—will play a large part in your success as a journalist, be it at a community paper or a large paper.

"But there's nothing going on," whines the young reporter.

Imagine a pianist sitting down at the piano and saying, "There's nothing to play. It's just the same old 88 keys."

Or a guitar player looking at his guitar and saying: "It's just the same old six strings . . . and, anyway, I've played everything there is to play."

See? A community is just like a keyboard or a fretboard. Same number of notes, same number of keys, same number of strings—same number of people, the same faces, same ball games, same events, year after year. But that's where the sameness ends.

It's what you bring to the keyboard or the fretboard—the vision, perspective and attitude—that makes a difference.

As Bonnie Raitt or Emanuel Ax can tell you, six measly strings or the same 88 keys can keep you busy for a lifetime. The possibilities for novelty, complexity, rhythm, cadence and dynamics are limited only by the musician's inner vision. There is an infinite possibility for new-ness in the seeming sameness of just a few notes.

Everybody Has a Story

Charles Kuralt knew this fundamental journalistic truth even as a 20-something young reporter at the Charlotte *News* back in the '50s. (To CBS' credit, they've resurrected Kuralt's legacy in Steve Hartman's series "Everybody Has a Story.") And you can take advantage of the concept too. Frank Robertson, photo instructor at South Dakota State University, puts it like this: "It's the 'little people' who have the big stories. Famous people are boring. It's your neighbor across the street who has had the interesting life."

Consider, then, the infinite number of sheer story possibilities that must exist, statistically, in a community of say, oh, 6,000 people. Six thousand notes, if you will.

So get out there and show some enterprise, and don't let your editor ever hear you saying: "It's only a little town," or "It's only a weekly . . ." and "There's nothing going on."

Because when young reporters tell me, "There's nothing going on," I infer they're talking about *the space between their ears*.

Take for your inspiration veteran sports editor Ron Bracken of the State College (Pa.) *Centre Daily Times* who says no two games are ever alike. Even though the final score might be 4–2, and he's covered literally thousands of 4–2 ball games, Bracken says it's his challenge to find out what is *different* about this particular ball game he's covering today—"because there are thousands of different ways a ball game can turn out 4–2, and there's always something special about every one. You just have to find it," he says.

Where Do Features Come From?

If you're lucky, your editor will give you suggestions. But don't rely on that. In fact, it's really not mentally healthy to expect to be spoon-fed story ideas; it deadens your curiosity. As journalists, we find curiosity to be our main strength. And you have to know where to look.

"I can always find a story at a laundromat bulletin board," says photographer Suzanne Carr of the *Free Lance–Star*, a 44,000-circulation daily serving Fredericksburg, Va.

When Pamela Fikes was a reporter for the weekly *Beacon* in Idalou, Texas, she says she found a great story on "a flier on the window of the Dixie Dog, the only good place to eat in town . . ."

Here's a classified ad in the back of the paper that just begs for a feature story:

For sale: Wedding dress w/ many pearls & long train—never worn, $300, cost $600; bride & groom cake topper free to whoever buys the dress; also, girl's bridal attendant dress, sz. 8, white w/ pearls, never worn, $75, cost $150. Call . . .

NEWS EVENTS

Read the paper, yours and others. Find a news peg. What's going on and how does it affect people in your community. How does it affect one specific person? Put a face on the news. What's it like to raise a kid with Down syndrome in your town? Find a family and a kid willing to talk and be photographed. Look for the positive. What social services does your county offer the mentally challenged? Who are the people involved? Who pays for it? How has this family coped with the challenges? Features can and should provide inspiration when it's appropriate to reality. Charles Kuralt has said that a tidal wave of constructive, creative, social change can start from the ripples of one small pebble thrown into the edge of the ocean. Your features can be a real agent for positive growth in your community. Don't discount them. The accretion of many good works will make a difference. Don't you want to make a difference?

PEOPLE IN THE NEWS

Important people in your community are almost always generating news and features. A personality profile, an "inner-view" on almost anyone in a position of prominence is a worthwhile piece. How can anyone claim there's nothing to write about? You are surrounded by potential material.

Some community newspaper editors without higher professional inspiration tend to get dulled. That is, they fail to see the new things happening around them. If you're a new reporter, take advantage of your fresh perspective. Suggest personality profiles on leaders and outstanding citizens who perhaps have been featured already, but maybe it was years ago. Just because they've had one story done on them doesn't mean they're dead. What's new in their lives? If they're truly community leaders, they've probably grown and changed with the times, even if your editor hasn't.

NEWSROOM SUGGESTIONS

Once you get a reputation around the paper for being a good feature writer, you'll find that your colleagues will start coming to you with story ideas. The ultimate compliment is when someone from the backshop, the pressroom, circulation, or mailing comes forward with a comment and an idea. The wise reporter learns not to scoff too quickly at these folk. Their comments will be like a vision through a glass-bottomed boat, affording you a view of how the community may be looking at you, the paper and your work. Listen to their ideas with respect and respond graciously. If one of their ideas is good, it's liable to mean there are lots more where that came from.

READERS

A good feature writer at a community paper will develop a following. Don't get the big head. We're not talking about thousands of screaming fans, but a loyal core of folk who like your work and look forward to it. This can be a tremendous asset to you, especially when they begin to contact you with story ideas. You may receive notes in the mail or tips via e-mail or a phone call, but more than likely they will come when you're the least prepared. You may get hints at the grocery store, or while getting gas. And remember, you're never not a writer. Or, to put it more bluntly, you're always on duty. Got your pen with you right now? A writer is always at work. So be polite; readers are more likely to feed you story ideas once they like your work and find you approachable, receptive and respectful. And you don't have to use every single idea. Just thank them for the tip, and go on. But remember: What seems like a lame story idea at the time may eventually lead you somewhere worthwhile.

YOURSELF

Of course, it finally comes down to you. If you're new to this game, it may take awhile to learn how to sniff out feature story ideas, because many features don't leap out at you (remember, they may not be timely, new or vital). So they're not as obvious as news stories. Still, old-timers in our business seem to have no trouble finding feature story ideas everywhere they turn. What do they know that you don't? Not to worry; it's an acquired skill. And you have to want to do it. Carry a pen and notepad everywhere you go. Keep your eyes peeled. Suzanne Carr is right: Read those community bulletin boards—at the laundromat while doing your clothes, at the grocery store while shopping—and at church notice the church bulletin. Around town, listen to people talking. Call it creative eavesdropping. They may be talking about a story you can use. In other words, get your radar out and always be looking and listening. Develop a features ideas list with contact names and phone numbers and rank them according to priority of time and need to do. And be aware: In a small community one feature story often leads to another.

Dr. Jocko's Helpful Hints

- Before the interview, you should do as much background as possible on your source—on the person you're featuring, or on the subject you're writing about. Find out why this person is important to your community.

- Find out when the story is due. This isn't as dumb as it sounds. Because many features are timeless, maybe the editor is thinking about using it next week instead of this week. This will help you in your time management.

- Find out approximately how long it needs to be so you can craft the story toward a skillful ending. Features aren't like inverted pyramid news stories, which can have their bottoms snipped; news stories just stop. Features end. That makes a big difference to a writer.

- Find out where it's going to run. A front-page feature will have a different impact from something planned for an inside slot, or from a feature to anchor a section front. If it's to hold down an entire page, then you've got your work cut out for you.

- Find out if photos are to be included, and who is expected to take them. With photos, your story has an added dimension, and the added dynamics on the job. (You can't exactly take notes if you're making a photograph, right?) Without photos, you must use more descriptive imagery.

- Give yourself more time than you think you need to do the interview—and to write the story. Here's a basic truth of feature writing: Because there is no formula for writing feature stories (such as the inverted pyramid for news), both the interview and the writing will take—and deserve—more time.

BEFORE YOU START WRITING, ASK YOURSELF:

- Who is my audience? A sports feature will attract a different set of readers than a personality portrait on a classical pianist or a story about an old mountain man who lives in the woods alone except for Clyde and Lulabelle, his two bears. Also, ask yourself, who is my audience in the larger sense?

- Why am I writing this? Because it was assigned to me? If that's your only reason, no muse will get near you with a 10-foot pica pole. Your answer should be: Because I care. I'm curious, and this somehow affects my community or is a reflection of the community, and because people need to hear this story. It will help them, entertain them, make them laugh, or help them cope. You may want to write it because it will strengthen your clip file or add to your portfolio. That's not the best reason, but it may honestly be one of your motivations.

- What is the purpose of this piece? After our own agenda, the story itself may have a life of its own. One community newspaper writer did a story on a couple who were planning a home birth. The reasons were myriad: The reporter believed in home birthing; she knew the story and photos would be dramatic and unusual; and she realized how rare it was to have found a couple who gladly consented to the story and photo proposal. It was probably a once-in-a-lifetime opportunity for a writer. She was right. The baby turned out fine; the public's reaction to the piece was overwhelmingly positive; and the story won first place in the state press competition that year.

- What can I safely assume the readers already know? This is a tough one for community feature writers. You must know your audience pretty well. How well you know your audience will show up here. In doing the piece on the retired classical pianist, can I safely assume all my readers will understand all the classical musical terms my person is using? Maybe I better ask some follow-up questions and gently provide background information. How do you define Baroque music? The same goes for an old-time fiddler. Many of your readers don't know the difference between old-time string band music and bluegrass. Yet the differences are vital to understanding a fiddler's story. In both cases, let the source, the subject of the story, do the explaining. And, please, spare us the clunky amateur construction: "When asked to define Baroque music, Mr. Boznowski said . . ."

- How can I get the reader to stay with me to the end? Yes, it is hard for a beginner to realize yet again that his or her words aren't Holy Writ and that the reader isn't necessarily going to stay glued faithfully to every word all the way to the end. Remember, the comics page is calling. The crossword puzzle too. Worse yet, the reader might put down the *Bugle* and turn on the tube. You've lost your reader, and she has bolted. So before that happens, ask yourself how am I going to make the reader stay with me all the way? You have to seduce the reader word by word, line by line, until, voilà! it is *fini*. The story she is all done.

- And, finally, how do I want the reader to feel when he has gotten to the end? This question needs to be asked before you even put fingers to keyboard. It means, where am I going with this piece? Do I want my reader to feel sad, empathetic and filled with a sense of the difficulty of this person's situation? Or poignant, bittersweet, nostalgic? Maybe mad, outraged and indignant. Perhaps inspired, uplifted, empowered and filled with a sense of well-being. Words can do all those things. Isn't that the magic of writing?

THE IMPORTANCE OF IMAGERY

If you want your writing to improve dramatically, write from the senses: sight, sound, smell, taste, feel, intuition and common sense. Write sense-ually. It's called imagery, and when your writing emerges from your sensory impressions, you're Showing, not Telling.

People get hooked right away on writing that contains imagery because they can't help but relate when you start writing about this big golden South Carolina peach you've just bitten into—that's so bursting with juice you had to go stand over the kitchen sink to eat it. The peach is as fuzzy as your old teddy bear, and the juice runs down your chin and you have to laugh at the mess you're making. But you don't care because the peach tastes like summer . . .

People relate to sensual writing because they've got senses.

Stop reading. Look around. What are you seeing? Swing your eyes around the room, the deck, the woody clearing, the classroom, the canyon. Whatever. Look hard. How does what you see make you feel? Sheetrock smooth and uniform, log cabin rough and rustic, small windowless office sterile and trapped, a forest glade free and calm.

Now, what sounds do you hear? Close your eyes if you have to. Isolate the sounds of the radio playing light classical in the next room, the hum of an overhead fan, a bird song trilling outside.

The cup beside you; take a swig. Is the coffee dank and lukewarm or hot and sweet?

How does the old pottery mug you've had since 1988 feel in your hands? Smooth with age and chipped around the edges from years of rough wear and road trips. Best mug you ever had. Fits the palm of your hand like a custom-made tool.

If you're inside, get up and walk into the next room, close your eyes and smell. Of the Vidalias you fried for supper last night, of last winter's cold wood ashes in the stove, of the cat box that needs changing. If you're outside, what is that sweet, musky fragrance coming up from the woods? Old-timers call it sweetbush.

Those are the five senses. There are two more: the sixth sense, or intuition. After you've polled your five senses for their specific reaction, what's it all add up to? The total is indeed larger than the sum of the parts. As a writer, that's where your sixth sense kicks in. What do you intuit about where you are right now? Is it "good space"? Is there creative energy where you are? What is the light doing? Has any consideration been given to human scale and needs for peace and harmony? Or are you sitting in a classroom built in the '20s, no air conditioning, with walls painted institutional green? Or are you crammed in a tiny newsroom with depressing fluorescent and little window light? What sort of a Borg designed this place anyway? Pretty hard to be creative in such a space, isn't it?

The seventh sense is common sense. You'll need a lot of it in this business.

WHAT COMMUNITY JOURNALISM FEATURES ARE REALLY SAYING

Features are a whole lot more than just fluff, according to Bill Meyer, award-winning editor and publisher of three Kansas weeklies. Meyer, who has been honored with the International Society of Weekly Newspaper Editors' highest award, explains, "Small towns have lost their retail trade center identity. There are fewer local stores to advertise shoes, automobiles and such. What do we do about it? To survive we must shift gears and do something different. Newspapers that don't adjust to the times won't be around long. The answer doesn't lie in e-mail or on the Internet. It comes to those who provide *interesting feature stories about local issues and people.*"

Great feature writing can make the difference between an average and an outstanding community newspaper. The news, some maintain, is all pretty much the same. But features never need be repetitive. They are the garlic to the sauce, the flower on the table, clean sheets on the bed, an unexpected kiss, a phone call from a dear old friend . . . We could probably get along without these things, but their surprising presence uplifts and enriches us.

Features are a mirror held up to the community saying, "We're OK," encouraging people through examples of folks who have toughed it out. If our stories don't add up to doing good, and helping, then what good are we? In celebrating the ordinary, we lift up "the heroism of everyday life," says writer David Lamb in his book *A Sense of Place*.

Types of Features

THE BRIGHT

This is usually a short piece, 2–3 inches, with a cute twist and a punch line, seen mostly in larger papers and used as fill matter to enliven the front page. The appeal of this type of feature usually lies in the story's oddity. If done poorly, a bright strains at humor and can be vapid or cutesy. At community papers, many topics used for brights could be better used as longer features.

Example: A woman fakes a heart attack to scare off a burglar.

PERSONALITY PROFILE

Remember, what we're working toward is getting the Inner View of someone in your community, be he or she a mover and a shaker, a local artist, an outstanding teacher, or a town personality. If there's a news peg, then the personality profile puts a face on the news, a real person behind the events. Even in the small town, it's enlightening to gain insight on personalities behind the headlines. This story can be written in anecdotal form with a narrative style. Depending on your subject, you may find a single source sufficient, or you may want to involve as many people as you can. In either case, research and background your person. Beginner's Alert: Rule no. 1 is to stay out of the way of your subject. Don't upstage him. The story is about your person, not you.

Example: A local elementary school principal retires after 30 years. He's famous for handing out quarters to kids who bring him papers with A's.

NEWS FEATURE

At the community paper, the news feature is similar to the same style of story seen at larger papers except that, for us, this story can be written more informally and have a more personal feel to it. Unlike the evergreen features, the news feature usually has news peg that is timely. The story may have to be written under the same time constraints as a breaking news story it accompanies. Other news features have a harder edge to them. Again, it allows you to put a face on the news. After the tornado ripped through part of town, you might tell one family's ordeal of survival. Narrative anecdotal style works great here. Such personalized news features serve to reinforce your readers' commonality and sense of community-ness. In one small town where a long-awaited bypass project was lagging, two editors decided to inspect the 10-mile stretch on a bicycle built for two. The innovative approach yielded not only a hands-on story on the road's condition, but several humorous editorial columns as well. In addition, readers were impressed that the editors would undertake such a zany feat.

Example: When your town's veteran mayor decides not to run for office again, people want to know why. It turns out she prefers to spend more time with her husband, who for years has been an ungrudging "mayor's widower."

SPEECHES

Many inexperienced reporters tend to see speech stories as news stories only, but in fact visiting speakers can generate entertaining features. The trick is to find the local angle, that local "peg." When a local author who had made it big came to town to talk to the library club, one enterprising reporter found out who the author's third grade teacher was, and asked her what the author was like as an 8-year-old. The old woman shook her head in wonder and said, "Where did he learn to write like that? In my class it was all chicken-scratch." Again, in community journalism, the key is to find the local difference and ride it for all its worth. Yes, it takes more work. But anybody can sit in an auditorium with a tape recorder and go back to the office and pound out a passable story. It's infinitely more fun and worthwhile to find the local undiscovered nugget that lifts a speech feature out of the ordinary.

Say retired U.S. women's soccer star Mia Hamm comes to your town's middle ... give a speech. When she walks out on stage, the kids leap to their feet in a ... vation, and one girl thrusts a soccer ball toward her, which Hamm ... utographs: "Keep on Kickin'—Mia." Don't you think you've got a local ... human interest twist? Who was that kid and why does she idolize Mia ... e a soccer player? Did she watch the Olympics? As to Mia Hamm, what ... on? Buttonhole her after the speech and see if it made an impact. Does ... l the time? The kid might be the lede, and that could provide you with ... l angle but the vehicle as well.

Jane Jones, 12, had always wanted to meet U.S. women's soccer team star Mia Hamm. Friday she got her chance.

Speaking to East Rutherford Junior High School students yesterday, Hamm was greeted by a wild standing ovation—and Jane Jones with a soccer ball, which Hamm quickly autographed and handed back to the seventh grader. "It was a dream come true," Jones said with a shy blush afterward. "I love soccer and especially Mia Hamm. I guess you could say she's my idol."

Hamm, on a speaking tour across the country, said following the speech she was moved by the response. "Believe it or not, it doesn't happen that often," she said backstage. "I was genuinely touched."

Rules of thumb for speech stories: Always go in armed with as much background information on the speaker as possible. Get a program; it's loaded with info. Try to talk with the speaker after the speech for another local peg. Who invited the speaker? Get his or her reaction. And especially, watch the audience for reactions. Who's there and what do they think of the speech? Consider spin-off stories: The above piece might lead you into a story with local coaches, soccer moms and social psychologists. What's their opinion of how the success of U.S. women's soccer has affected young girls.

ARTS

This may sound like heresy, but arts coverage on the community level is every bit as important as—gasp!—sports. And look at how much space most papers, regardless of size, devote to that.

There is a real possibility for synergy on the community level between an enlightened newspaper and the area's arts community. Theatergoers, concert listeners and xhibit lookers are great readers. Support them, and they will support you.

In addition, if a community newspaper provides space and encouragement for a growing arts council or arts agency, the relationship can only be mutually beneficial. It's a proven fact: There's a connection between a great town, a great newspaper and a thriving arts community. It's all about livability.

On the community level, most performing and visual artists are not professionals. They belong to the local Little Theater, the Photography Club, the Community College Singers or the Arts Council Players. They're not in it for the money. They're in it for their own personal joy of self-expression and to enhance the cultural life of the community. That's why most community newspapers don't and shouldn't attempt to write critical reviews of community arts. It's pointless. Better to be positive and provide coverage, publicity and support for the people and groups giving of their time and effort.

The paper should engage in coverage before and after each event. Features prior to the event should include the 5W's, with heavy emphasis on the who, plus a synopsis. The easiest and most effective way to provide coverage after a production is with photos from the performance (or dress rehearsal or photo-call).

Story topics can include personality profiles of the lead in the play, the painter, and the dancer, usually before the production or exhibit. The intent should be to give the reader, the viewer and the theatergoer an inner-view behind the scenes. This insight before the performance, exhibit or concert enriches the audience members' total experience, as well as providing information that will help readers decide if they want to attend.

An arts feature requires that the writer know a great deal about the piece and the artist before starting the story. Read the book, see the exhibit, attend a concert, listen to earlier tapes, study rehearsals before the initial interview with the primary source. With regard to the arts especially, avoid the cold interview. You should have

A flourishing community arts program can be a good sign of active community growth and health. Enlightened community newspaper editor-publishers know these barometers are important. Editorial support for facets of community life can only help your paper grow as well. A broad cross-section of community people came together for this production of *Oklahoma!* The photo is what the late Ken Byerly called "a tree full of owls." For every one of these cast members, there are at least four family members who want copies of that edition of the paper. (Photo by Gerald Gerlach; courtesy of the Rutherford County [N.C.] Arts Council © 1972)

to turn in your press credentials if you find yourself asking, "So, what's the name of the play you're going to do?" The informed lead-in question should be more like "I understand *Cabaret* is set in Berlin just prior to World War II . . ."

The paper can also provide a platform for community arts by running an arts calendar and a regular arts page covering the activities of local artists and arts groups. The community newspaper also has a special role in encouraging emerging local artists by spotlighting unknowns as their talent and craft are developing. Also, some papers publish poems and or short essays suitable for the format.

Smaller community newspapers, notably weeklies, need not shy away from arts coverage because they fear they need to add an arts editor. You don't have to hire another staffer to effectively cover arts in your town. It should simply be included in someone's beat. Also, the real key is to get the various arts groups, the county arts agency or the municipal arts council involved in generating their own copy and photos.

The local community college, private college or university in your area is probably already doing that. One idea might be to have the director of the local college news bureau lead a workshop (co-sponsored by your paper) for the publicity people of the various arts groups and agencies on how to write and shoot for the paper. That's a win-win scenario. It's good PR for the college; it helps the arts folks, and it makes your paper look good while improving your coverage.

EDUCATION

The late editor-publisher and former community journalism professor Ken Byerly was so right when years ago he said: "Few things unite or tear a community apart as much as schools. The community revolves around its school. It is so vital that in many a small town, if the school closes, the town dies."

News of school closings, openings, hirings, firings, changes in curriculum, busing, lunchroom policies, new programs, choice of textbooks, expenditures, improvements, cutbacks—all provide grist for the mill. In addition to your regular news coverage of school board activities, the local educational scene provides an endless array of feature possibilities vital to your readers.

As in the case of the arts, the community newspaper has a unique role and responsibility with its education coverage. In short, nobody should be doing so much in-depth work as the *Bugle*. Your level of involvement should be intense. Ideally, as with arts coverage, education should be a beat. That way the community journalist gets a sure grip on the turf, knows the players and can see how everything connected to the schools relates.

Because education is such a hot topic nowadays it deserves more attention and space in our papers. The American primary education system is undergoing dramatic changes; community newspapers should be on the front lines. Story ideas abound:

- Which are most important to the development of our children: major league baseball players or teachers? So how come we aren't paying our teachers more? Great teachers don't do it for the money. So they need to be supported, encouraged and recognized. Features on master teachers, their philosophies of teaching and what works in the classroom can make a difference in how the teachers feel about the community. Each school's nominee for teacher of the year is a good place to start.
- At the urging of the veteran faculty adviser, the local high school newspaper began paginating its award-winning paper years ahead of the curve. (Do a personality profile as well?)
- Feature photos and thumbnail personality sketches of the new teachers joining the local high schools each August. Your readers are curious about these folks— and with good reason. Teachers are in the business of life changing.
- In the spring, profile retiring teachers who have taught long and well. If they're to be honored at dinners and parties, tie in your coverage with those events.
- Trends in education. Is public service being required for college graduation elsewhere? Is any school of higher education in your area already doing this? What is the nature of the requirement and how do the kids feel about it?

Features on school news can have great variety as well as community-building impact. When a local school sent a team of students to rural Mexico to teach English and help build a school, this is one of the pictures they brought back for the local paper. It's a storyteller.

- Amazing students. Develop a personality profile and "a day in the life of" photo coverage of the most profoundly disabled student who is excelling against all odds.
- Innovative programs that work. Say the local private college has instituted a two-week program for county eighth graders at risk of not finishing high school. Talk to the college administrator who dreamed up this notion. Why do it? Who's paying for it? Attend the camp, take photos, interview the kids, counselors, teachers, parents. Do follow-up. To what extent has the camp succeeded? How has it changed the lives of those involved?
- International students. Exchange students either in high school or college make for good features because they reflect so candidly in ways we can't see on the nature of American life. What do they like the most? The least? What do they miss? What's the funniest thing that's happened to them here? How has coming to America changed them? What will they take back with them?
- Class reunions in the summer. Talk with old-timers about how things have changed, and elicit from them their fondest memories, most memorable pranks, favorite teachers, and what they got from their experience at the high school or college. The best stories come out of attending a 50th anniversary dinner, taking notes as people are telling those stories and then buttonholing the folks afterward for permission.

One innovative newspaper provides coverage of the three area high schools by offering a page a month to each school's journalism class. The kids write the stories; a staff photographer comes out and takes the pictures the school editors have lined up. The entire highly successful program is coordinated by the community paper's editor and the respective high school teachers. The result is also posted on the paper's online edition with links to the high school sites. Little wonder that the newspaper wins educational coverage awards every year. But the best reward of all is the positive response from the community. Plus, you know you're doing something that TV and the big dailies can't or won't do.

COPING, HOW-TO AND NEWS YOU CAN USE

If there's a trend in print journalism, this is certainly it. Newspapers are picking up the magazine trick of niche marketing, being user-friendly to the reader, of giving the reader something he or she needs to know. Women's magazines particularly have been doing this for years; if the headline's a grabber, you've got to read it. How to Renovate Your Man, Nine New Great Ways to Make Love, Dating: What's Safe Anymore?, How to Turn On Your Creative Juices, How to Survive Your First Job When It's Not the One You Really Wanted, How to Enjoy the Beach if You're Fair-Skinned.

On the community level, the trick is to get a good topic, and then plug in all your local sources for authenticity and balance. For instance, say you decide to use the beach survival story idea suggested above. You could talk to a local dermatologist and other doctors about the danger of too much sun and the incidence of skin cancer, to a high school science teacher about the ozone hole, to local people who are sun worshipers and local people who are not—get their various perspectives on why they sunbathe or don't—and talk to a sociologist at the local community college about America's changing beauty standards. If "pale" is coming back in, why?

With "coping features" or advice and how-to stories, be sure to stay in the background as the writer. Let the source or the authority do the leading. No one likes to be given advice in a condescending way; and whatever you do, don't preach. Rather, you must be like a master puppeteer, always unseen, but in control of the flow.

Other related feature topics that adapt well to local-angle community newspaper treatment include the environment, health, science and the sexes. Such coping stories provide grist for the community paper's "Lifestyle" section. (See Chapter 11.)

From the Trenches

How do you get a story on someone who doesn't want to be interviewed—and how do you get a photo of someone who doesn't want to be photographed? Sometimes

the answer lies in saying just the right thing. And with different people, that right
something may be different.

Everybody in the county knew Aunt Kate Burnette as the grand old woman of Mackie's Creek. The 88-year-old matriarch prided herself on cutting all her cookstove firewood by herself with a trusty red bow saw.

I had to have the story and picture.

She didn't have a phone, so the only way to reach her was to drive out to her little house in the shadow of Mackie Mountain. There, I found her at her sawhorse, working outside the woodshed.

STAY OUT OR ELSE THIS MEANS YOU a front-yard sign warned.

I parked the car on the shoulder of the road, and got out. Before I got to her yard, Aunt Kate hollered, "I see you, you old bald-headed thing. You can just get right back in your car."

I was not to be so easily put off. "Aunt Kate," I shouted as politely as possible. "I'd like to talk to you for the paper."

"I get your ol' paper," she hollered. And then with a little grin, she added, "Use it to start fires with every morning! Now go on back to town."

I almost left, but then decided, having nothing to lose, I'd try appealing to her vanity. "Aunt Kate, I'm doing a book." I yelled, and let that sink in. "I'd like to put you in my book!"

You could see the old woman thinking, and then, almost shyly, she shouted back, not quite so loud, "Well, where do you want me to sit . . . ?"

I was in.

Don't Underestimate Your Impact

Any veteran reporter/photographer will confirm this: The first thing fire victims rescue from their burning homes—after the kids and the pets—is their photo albums.

Let the TV, the sound system and the computer burn—but grab the pictures.

These so-called common snapshots catalog the daily miracles of our lives: 4-year-old Jon hoisting his first big fish, 6-year-old Selena washing her bike on the day she learned to ride. Such seemingly trivial pictures provide the context of a personal and family visual history, and therefore are precious beyond reckoning.

Sometimes we journalists need to be reminded of that fact—that, and of the impact we have on the lives of the people we blitz in and out of.

Here it is: a black and white I shot back in 1982 on a visit to Christmas tree grower Joe Henson of Avery County, N.C.

Joe, a bearlike 60-year-old wearing a plaid shirt and a "wild bullrider" billed cap, is lifting a cherubic infant girl in his arms for the camera to admire. He holds the confident granddaughter with great tenderness, in contrast to his paw-like, work-rough hands.

Christmas tree grower Joe Henson and his granddaughter Sarah Elizabeth Hicks of Crossnore, N.C. in 1982.

If eyes can be said to sparkle, then Joe Henson's do burn, as if with an inner light of their own. A smile wreathes his handsome face, and he appears to be in the midst of another Joe-ism—perhaps telling me how when he started out growing trees his land was "so poor a rabbit had to pack a bag lunch to get across."

I was there in Crossnore doing a story on Joe and his Christmas tree farming back in '82 when Joe was a robust 60 and I a hairy 37.

Initially the story was to be sort of a business piece about how Christmas tree growing is so important to the local economy. But the story turned into a personal thing.

In a newspaper career spent interviewing the people of the Southern Appalachians, seldom have I latched on to a individual quite like Joe. Subsequently his story and pictures found their way into one of my books.

But time, events and sloth conspired to keep me away for many years. It wasn't until last holiday season, when a traditional Christmas Eve caroling event ended at Joe and Emmaline's, that we reconnected.

I found Joe, 75 now and fighting leukemia, stout and unbeatable as ever. He greeted me at the front door with a blinding smile and a bone-crushing hug.

My book, the one with Joe's story, occupied the place of honor on the coffee table. Its brown cover faded to beige by years of sunlight. And on the wall, a posed snapshot of Joe and Sarah, the cherubic infant (now a lovely teen), echoed my portrait.

Flabbergasted, I found I had a presence in this home.

Leukemia had lessened but not conquered Joe. "Too ornery to kill," Joe confided happily. Then: "You oughta come up and visit me this summer; I'll show you some trees!"

And I must have said I would, for Joe didn't forget.

And although I didn't make that visit last summer, I did remember Emmaline's

Don't underestimate the impact of your work. On Christmas Eve of 1997, Sarah Elizabeth Hicks and Joe Henson pose with the photograph taken of them by the author 15 years earlier.

mentioning how much Joe would value a print of my photograph of him and that grandbaby girl Sarah.

The assignment motivated me to find those negatives and make those prints.

On Christmas Eve, I had the profound satisfaction of surprising Joe and Emmaline with an envelope full of photographs: Joe and the child, Joe trimming his trees—framed against a clear sky with distant Grandfather Mountain off in the distance . . . "Paw Paw" Joe with his arm around 4-year-old grandson Jeremy, the latter wearing a bath towel as a Superman cape.

Emmaline told me, "We almost lost him this year." It was the leukemia. But Joe, who can't just sit in the house, still works the Christmas tree farm and cuts firewood for the family wood cook stove.

Back in May he had taken a turn for the worse and was rushed to the hospital in distant Asheville where he received a blood transfusion and was put on oxygen.

Joe, now telling me about it, fixed me with his burning eyes. "I had a visit from an angel," he declared with complete conviction.

From the next room my fellow carolers harmonized, "Hark! The Herald Angels Sing."

Joe again: "Something just come over me. I heard a voice saying, 'It's not your time yet,' and I've been getting better ever since."

Cookies and hot chocolate, a rousing version of "The 12 Days of Christmas" punctuated by more photograph making, and it was time to go. Again I promise to make that summertime visit to the old Christmas tree farmer.

"Why, you're the biggest liar in the world," Joe scolds me affectionately. "You *better* come on back!"

And I *had* better.

Do it, Lauterer. Flowers for the living.

In the words of Susan Smith of the South Dakota Press Association, "Being a success as a journalist doesn't necessarily mean earning big money at a large daily paper. It can be far more satisfying to tell a good story about someone about whom the community will enjoy reading (and that the subject will appreciate and cherish)."

Your Town; Your Turn

1. Find a dry statistical news story in your paper that could have been enhanced and made stronger if the writer had "put a face on it."
2. Analyze your paper. Clip all the features and rank them according to timeliness and their "evergreen" quality.
3. Make a list of your last five features. Remember where the story ideas came from. Is there a pattern? Where do you get your best ideas from? When does it happen? On the golf course? In the shower? Just before you go to sleep? Better keep a pad and pen handy.
4. Take a walk around outside the building you are in. Go empty handed but open sensed. Come back to your desk and write down as many of your sensory impressions as you can of what you saw, heard, smelled, tasted and felt.
5. Take your least favorite feature story and rewrite it with a new anecdotal lede.
6. Go buy a copy of *Cosmopolitan*. How many stories can you adapt and find local angles for at your community newspaper?

NINE

Editorials
The Rapier, Not the Sledgehammer

The Heat in the Kitchen

The brassy, outspoken high school biology teacher confronted the young editor as she was coming out of the local post office. Repeatedly thrusting one pointed finger at her, the teacher spoke as if to an errant first-year student who clearly needed to hear her superior wisdom: "About your editorial this week . . . why don't you just stick to what you're good at—which is writing features."

So . . . they didn't tell you it would be like this in J-school?

Welcome to the wonderful world of community newspaper editorial writing, where all your readers think they have the right to take a pot shot at you for anything you say; and indeed they do. And they will.

Editorial writing on the community level is an entirely different ball game from the insulated, isolated, anonymous editorial boardrooms of the big-city papers. There, editorial boards craft editorial policy, and editorial writers are likely to be nameless and faceless to their readers.

Not so with us. We get ambushed over the broccoli at Piggly-Wiggly. People know us, and they know where to find us, and they know they can get to us. If you say something that rubs folks wrong, you're going to hear about it quickly—and face to face.

The singularly peculiar nature of our business affords us the ability to reach the entire community with a single keystroke or the push of a shutter release button. Such power is not without its price: *The price of public access is public opinion.*

This doesn't mean you should shrink away from bold editorial stands. It does mean, as with everything else about community journalism, that you are professionally accountable and personally accessible.

Be bold when the issue calls for boldness, but choose your battles wisely. A community is a glass house. A loose cannon breaks many windows.

Why Editorial Pages Are Vital

Nowhere else is the difference more apparent between great, mediocre and just plain lousy community newspapers than on their editorial pages. A great community newspaper edit page is local, lively, timely and involved, but not strident, shrill or vindictive. The content is balanced—balanced between political viewpoints, personal perspectives, editorials, commentaries, cartoons and letters to the editor.

Sometimes images provide stronger editorial comment than words. The county's deplorable dumpster situation was best addressed with photographs—run on the editorial page.

Above all, the edit page does not shy away from discussion of important community issues—for debate is critical in our free society.

Jim Sachetti, editor of the Bloomsburg (Pa.) *Press-Enterprise*, a 22,000-circulation independent daily, says the editorial page is "the soul of the newspaper. It tells you if the paper gives a damn or is out just to print ads and make money."

Sachetti asks rhetorically, what is the importance of his daily editorials? "In the grand scheme of things, what does it matter? After all, we're just a small paper in a little town in central Pennsylvania." And answering himself, he says, "This whole country—the best place on earth to live—would not be what it is if it were not for a million small arguments such as this going on."

The editorial pages of thousands of community newspapers are what Sachetti calls "a 230-year-old bluebook." And he emphasizes, "You need to realize how important this is, however small your paper is."

It's what Walter Lippmann meant when he said, "A free press is not a privilege but an organic necessity in a great society."

Sachetti again: "Editorial writing must provoke people to share in some form of forum. This public dialogue is the vital goal of a good editorial page." Sachetti believes "opinion writing is critical to the history as well as to the future of this country."

On Writing the Controversial Editorial

Editor-publisher Jean Murph of the *Citizens Advocate*, a 5,000-circulation weekly in Coppell, Texas, says she lost no sleep at all writing an anti-Iraqi war editorial *before* the March 2003 invasion. "I had to write it," she explains, "—just as I have every week for the last 20 years." Murph reports that she had five readers in her largely con-

FORUM

EDITORIAL
Credit to the kids

It could be heard in Amanda Bohlen's voice — as emotions took over and her words fell off, replaced by tears.

It could be seen in Tara Pfeiffer's mannerisms — as she stood and spoke her mind unabashedly, pointing and gesturing towards teachers, parents and other students.

And it could be felt through the simple presence of nearly 30 other students on hand at last week's Freeman School Board meeting.

If ever there was testament to the magnitude of the financial problem at Freeman Public and the concern among its patrons, the impressive representation of students last week was it.

And those students deserve credit for their awareness, their courage and their presence of mind to know that what is happening at their school cannot go without comment.

Seated together at tables similar to ones they sit at every day at school during lunch, they listened closely to the board's approach to finding $125,000 to operate their school next year. They listened to parents and teachers plead with the board to opt out of the tax freeze and save several positions on the chopping block.

And they spoke; Not all of them, but enough to make their collective presence felt.

They made it clear they were concerned about the future of their school, even though a good number on hand were seniors and wouldn't directly feel any changes that may be coming.

They made it clear that they were concerned about what would happen to the quality of education at Freeman Public should positions be eliminated and class sizes increase.

They made it clear that a good number of their fellow students wish the board would opt out of the tax freeze. At least that would give the people a voice, they said.

Mostly, though, they made it clear that they have been paying attention.

Too often the young generation is wrongly accused of being apathetic and uninterested in the bigger picture, unwilling to take a stand, unwilling to be a voice, unwilling to show support for what they believe in.

All of those pretenses were thrown out the window last week, as the delegation of students made their presence known loud and clear, even if many of them just sat and listened.

A lot has been said in the 11 months since the board began discussing ways out of the financial crisis in Freeman Public's general fund. And some steps have been taken to alleviate the problem, even if it's in the short-term.

But until last week, the heart and soul of Freeman Public — the students who appear to have more pride in their school than many give them credit for — have sat silent.

Apparently, many felt it was time to break that silence last week.

FHS senior Matt Andersen may have said it best. A senior, he will not be around next year to feel the effects of whatever decisions the board makes.

"We want the younger kids to have the same type of education we had," he told the board.

That speaks volumes.

Not only does it say that the quality of education at Freeman Public is high, but also that it's appreciated by the ones directly benefiting from it.

And the fact that Andersen and the other students on hand last week would take the time and the energy to stand before their board, their peers and their teachers to express themselves says more than anything we've heard thus far.

It says the students are aware and, more importantly, concerned about what is happening at their school.

The ones who have, perhaps, been most forgotten about made it clear last week that they're listening.

The dialogue between the kids and adults must continue. That will lead to compromise, common ground and understanding as Freeman Public continues to try and find its way out of this financial mess.

We hope students will continue to exercise their powerful voice.

And we hope the tears of Amanda Bohlen, the testimony of Tara Pfeiffer and the presence of nearly 30 other students attending last week's meeting tell the board that the kids are paying attention.

They'd be wise to listen.

We all would.

J. Waltner

An emotional Amanda Bohlen, a senior at FHS, reacts to part of last week's discussion on proposed staff cuts at Freeman Public. Looking on is sophomore Brooke Hermsen.

Why not use photos to illustrate editorials—especially when they serve to strengthen the message—as in the case of this photo/editorial combination by Jeremy Waltner of the Freeman (S.D.) *Courier*.

servative community cancel their subscriptions, but she suspects those five disgruntled folks either are buying the *Citizens Advocate* in the racks or will be back soon.

The Cop-Out: The Canned Editorial Page

Because they're timid, burned out, lazy or simply don't care, some editors and publishers use nothing but canned stuff on their editorial pages. It's the editorial equivalent of the military field rations, MRE (Meals Ready to Eat)—barely digestible fill fodder. Clipped "guest" editorials from distant cities, etc. No local copy. Not one jot. There aren't any letters to the editor, either, because there's no reason for local folks to read the edit page.

Award-winning Kansas weekly editor-publisher Bill Meyer decries community newspaper editors who "never take a stand. They run clipped editorials, if any editorials at all. Or they buy marshmallow-impact columns from Goody Two Shoes that have the zest of tapioca pudding."

These zombie editorial pages are more widespread than community journalism leaders would like to admit. And the really bad thing about a canned edit page is that it sends to the community the worst possible message:

- This paper really doesn't think you're worth the trouble it takes to create a lively, local editorial page.
- We're lazy, and proud of it.
- And what's more, we don't care.

Lazarus! Rise Up and Walk

If you want to make your editorial zombie page rise up and walk like the biblical dead man Lazarus, it's going to take a holistic approach from the editor and the newsroom.

The editor has to commit to writing live edits on a regular basis.

Solicit guest editorials on relevant subjects from community leaders, similar to a "my turn" series pioneered by *Newsweek*. Accompany this with a headshot.

Get local writers on board as columnists. If they must be paid, give them a small honorarium or a free subscription. But in many instances community-minded writers will do this for the creative rush and the opportunity to get published as well as the possibility of doing something good for the town.

Assign weekly columns to each of your staffers in the newsroom, even your photographers. You'll be pleasantly surprised by what this can turn into. Accompany the columns with good headshots.

Encourage letters to the editor.

The only thing that can safely be canned is the editorial cartoon. If, however, you can find and develop a good local political cartoonist, all the better. But this is a rarity. So, if you run nationally syndicated cartoonists, be prepared for much of your reading public to assume that you and your paper endorse the political stance of the cartoonist on any given issue.

When Is an Editorial an Editorial?

Nothing in the newspaper makes people madder than something on the editorial page with which they disagree. However, shouting at the newspaper over the break-fast table is a grand old American tradition. Look at the history of American journalism; our early papers were all political and editorial opinion. Even so-called straight stories were larded with unashamed editorial opinion until well past the turn of the eighteenth century.

It wasn't until early in the twentieth century that newspapers began embracing the concept of objectivity and then separating opinion from straight factual reporting.

Nowadays we revere this concept as if it came down with the tablets from Mount Sinai. In current usage editorials have clear parameters.

To quickly review Editorial Writing 101:

- Ledes: A variety can be used.
- Form: A variety of forms and structures can be used.
- Timeliness: May or may not be timely.
- Purpose: Written to persuade as well as inform.
- Voice: Subjective, opinionated.
- Location: Editorial page in most cases.

Editorial Writing and the Community Journalism Spin

While some editorials are written to inform, explain, educate—and even at times to entertain—most are written to persuade. This subjective writing with a clear point of view is what separates editorial matter from newswriting.

Not so many years ago, newspapers were known as "the poor man's college." Newspaper editorials were supposed to be "molders of public opinion." That all sounds rather quaint now in the face of MTV video-editorials that reach a young, hip audience that doesn't read newspapers but gets off on rock. Add into the mix the glut of Internet voices, all with a point of view. Clearly, most big-city daily editorial pages have lost the exclusive, pervasive clout they once had.

But on the community journalism level, there will always be work to be done. Indeed, communities need strong opinions on local issues (which TV typically doesn't have time or stomach to address), unafraid champions of small, lost and worthy causes, and informed reflection on matters local and beyond.

Why are we writing editorials? What is our agenda? It should be that of the *Transylvania Times* of Brevard, N.C. On their masthead it says, "If it's good for Transylvania County, the *Times* will fight for it." Similarly, it is implied, if it's not good for the county, the *Times* will say so.

A good community newspaper editorial writer knows that there are five levels to editorial writing and reaction. From the outset, you ought to be shooting for level five.

1. Attention: The reader is "grabbed" and reads the edit. Maybe it's the headline; maybe it's your writing; most likely it's because the subject matter is something this person already cares about.

2. Comprehension: The edit is read in its entirety and stored in memory.

3. Synthesis: The reader then reflects on, or "processes," the information and data along with the opinion and argument.

4. Action: On that rare occasion, the reader realizes that the edit creates a desire to do something concrete about the situation. An edit on homelessness in your community prompts the reader to join a Habitat for Humanity work crew.

5. Reciprocity: We've already talked about the negative; let's look on the bright side. This is the most wonderful of complete cycles—when you the editorial writer are told by the reader that your editorial made him get out of his chair and pick up his hammer. Give yourself an "atta-boy." They can keep their Pulitzers; you've done a day's work. Because of the relative size of the goldfish bowl, the community newspaper editorial writer is more likely than his city counterparts to hear such positive feedback.

The KISS (Keep It Simple, Stupid) Rule

Editorials are usually confined to the editorial page, and to a "standing" or preset and predictable position, most commonly, top left. Editorial pages are also consistently positioned in the paper. People like predictability. If you start peppering your paper with edits all over the place, you risk alienating readers. Many media experts even frown on the so-called "front-page editorial," which is often used by editors when they want to trumpet an opinion. It's simply too confusing and risky to mix opinion with a page that purports to be objective.

There are other reasons to keep edits off P-1: It smacks of sensationalism, and it says, in effect, that you don't have much confidence in your edit page to get and keep the readers' attention.

Who writes editorials? That depends on the size of the paper. From medium-sized dailies on up, an editorial board formulates what the paper's opinion is on a given issue. The publisher, editor and editorial page editor usually make up this editorial board. However, it's a sore spot if half the newsroom disagrees with the editorial. And furthermore, some media critics claim readers don't understand the distinction between a newspaper's opinion (i.e., the editorial board's opinion) and that of a single writer.

On many smaller dailies and weeklies, editorials are written by a single editor. An editorial board is a luxury few small papers can afford. In much of community journalism, the editorial is simply the opinion of the editor, and that's it, pure and simple. It's not the opinion of "the paper." Newspapers can't have opinions; people have opinions.

So, if a small paper has several people writing editorials containing diverse views, they meet this challenge by having the editorial writers sign their edits. The simplest way is an initial tag line at the end of the edit. This way, an editorial page can comfortably reflect and accommodate diverse editorial viewpoints. It not only lets the reader know specifically who wrote the edit, but it also underscores the bedrock community journalism precept of individual editorial accountability. In this context, a newspaper won't have an editorial policy per se.

"Editorial policy" is much like legal precedent, and it can be defined as the body of opinions written over a period of time by a paper's editorial writers. Sometimes, an editorial stance is agreed on by the editorial board before anything is written on the subject. Whether it's the result of an editorial board, or a single writer, people in town generally are aware of the paper's position on a given issue. For instance, readers know the *Bugle* is pro-environment yet pro–balanced growth because the *Bugle*'s editorials consistently reflect that stance.

Uncle Walt's Advice

For over four decades, beloved veteran journalism professor Walter Spearman, of the University of North Carolina at Chapel Hill, gave legions of future newspaper editors the benefit of his benevolent spirit and generous vision. In his much-sought-after editorial writing class, the late "Uncle Walt" had this advice, which is especially pertinent for community newspaper editorial writers:

- *The rapier, not the sledgehammer.* When making a point, be precise, subtle and clever. Don't bludgeon the subject. It makes you look like a Robo-editor. Impress them not with your firepower but with the deftness of your argument.
- *Issues, not personalities.* Always concentrate on the issues of the question you're dealing with. Never go after personalities. If you've got a county commissioner accused of embezzling, the issue is misfeasance of office, the betrayal of public trust—not what a jerk you think the commissioner is.
- *Don't write mad.* Most beginners find it easier to write editorials (as well as songs and poetry) when they're upset, hurt or angry. If you're so bent out of shape you can't see straight, go ahead and write it, but throw it away. Then sit down, maybe later, and do it over again, this time without the shrillness. Remember John Belushi's classic "editorials" sketch on the old *Saturday Night Live* Weekend Update where he'd start out calmly and then get so worked up he'd go ballistic and have a heart attack. Looked pretty stupid, didn't he?
- *Avoid sarcasm.* Sarcasm depends on vocal delivery for its effectiveness. In other words, it's a sound gag. Because readers can't hear your tone of voice, somebody will read it straight and completely misunderstand your intent. Of all the literary tones than can be used, sarcasm is the most prone to be misread by some humorless clunk. Better to ditch the snide comments, parody and overly dry wit, and write it straight. Especially if you're a beginner.

Veteran editor-publisher Ken Ripley of the Spring Hope (N.C.) *Enterprise* is a perfect example of how one voice can make a big difference. His 8–12–page, 2,500-circulation paper is pretty much a one-man operation, yet Ripley has a wall full of awards honoring the editor-publisher for editorial excellence. A man not afraid of a good fight, Ripley says while "the news is the heart of the paper, the editorial page is its soul. And the paper is the spinal column of the community."

Not surprisingly, the *Enterprise* has a lot of spirit. Ripley bangs out a fresh editorial every week—no matter how late it is or how tired he is. It's just that important to him. Ripley, who describes himself as a "flaming moderate," says, "You've got to have a spine. We take pride in exercising leadership, stating our opinions, telling why this is important or why it is not important. The editorial page is a forum for the community to talk to itself. I'm trying to make people think. My role is to shape opinions—to shape attitudes that shape behavior—to take a stand."

Ripley's first law of editorial writing: "I operate under one dictum: the doctor's law (the Hippocratic Oath) of " 'First, do no harm.' " Another precept guides him as well: "The point of an editorial is to effect positive change."

The issues about which he editorializes aren't always as simple as stark black and white. In fact, they seldom are, he says, noting, "The older I get, the more grays I see."

Ripley editorials might be used to explain an issue, to offer guidance relative to an issue, to interpret a certain governmental body's actions to the reader, to give a pat on the back to the living or a tribute to a community member who has died.

Ripley calls his most effective type of opinion piece "the guided missile editorial"—limited, deliberately targeted "smart bombs" focused on maybe just one issue or more likely on one person—say, a specific city council member.

And finally, when he's exasperated, Ripley will roll out an "atom bomb editorial"—the most fun, he concedes, but to be used only when he's given up on a politician or a situation.

Ripley, who is described as a powerful figure in little Spring Hope (pop. 1,200), says, "I have the power to persuade. That the only power I have.

"When I die, I'm going to have the biggest funeral in town," Ripley grins. "Half the town will be there to mourn me; the other half to make sure I'm dead."

On the Power of the Press

Terry Calhoun, news editor of the Southport, N.C., weekly *State Port Pilot*, told community journalism student Lauren Rippey: "I was astonished after I wrote one of my first editorials, which criticized the performance of a city planner, when that planner immediately resigned. My previous [newspaper] experience was with a medium-sized daily, and most our sources wouldn't even acknowledge reading the editorial page. I keep a list in my car of the top 10 things that I believe I have contributed to the community in the way of change. I know, for example, that this county now has a nonprofit council on aging, and I know governmental giving has been de-politicized because of my work, not only in criticizing faults, but in offering positive solutions. One of my predecessors, when asked why he didn't run for public office, answered, 'I couldn't stand the loss of influence and power.'"

The Ultimate Show and Tell: Columns and Commentary

Having a regular column is not like looking in on the neighbor's cat for a week. It's there, waiting for you, week in and week out. Either you're thinking about it, or it's thinking about you. You're either thinking what will I write about next week or pondering whether the last one was worth about as much as a bucket of warm spit.

It's been said that having a column is like undressing in public. At first, it's downright embarrassing. But eventually you get used to the scrutiny. After several awkward disrobings, you learn to do it with style, one button at a time. Reveal yourself with restraint. Make it last. To be good at it, you need to have a little bit of an exhibitionist in you, with a smattering of stagecraft thrown in.

No part of community journalism baffles and eludes the beginner so regularly and thoroughly as column writing. Few young writers are naturally good at commentary, especially humor. Indeed, it is an almost impossible skill to teach. That's because it's a matter of accretion. Unless they have a singular gift or vision, young writers simply haven't lived enough to have worthwhile, meaningful stories or the vision to tell them—or they don't have the maturity to synthesize their life lessons and be able to write about them with clarity, humor, pathos and wisdom.

In spite of all this, at the best community newspapers, everybody in the newsroom is required to write a weekly column, regardless of training or background. In spite of the C+ quality of many of these columns, it's still the right thing to do. Here's why:

At big-city papers, they have great columnists who do nothing else. Their columns are fantastic. At community newspapers, if you're going to have a live edit page, everybody in the newsroom may have to pitch in. There's a real value-added bonus to this. At the community papers, columns need not be about knock-'em-dead writing. Because of their first-person voice and standing headshot, columns can, in the most personal way, give the newspaper a human face, a fallible real personality behind the P-1 bylines. This is the true subtext and value of columns in a community newspaper.

On the community journalism level, columns say: We are community. With every live editorial page, your paper will carry that reassuring message.

Below the flag of the 13,000-circulation daily McComb (Miss.) *Enterprise-Journal*, it reads, "The one newspaper in the world most interested in this community."

It doesn't matter if you're the hottest reporter on the paper; if you've got a column, you can't ignore the fact that you just did the laundry that included your kid's bright magenta crayon. You phoned Crayola, and they told you the way to get the stain out was by using WD-40 on the splotches.

Columns say: We're All in This Together and You Are Not Alone. Columns say that we're all pretty much alike; that there's someone else out there who thinks like you; that small things matter; that a single voice counts; that we don't take ourselves too seriously and that life is good—"in this time and this place," to borrow a favorite expression of State College (Pa.) *Centre Daily Times* past publisher Lou Heldman.

Columns say: Just because I'm a reporter or the editor doesn't mean I think I'm any better than you. I've just come back from vacation and the plants I left for the neighbor to water seem to have multiplied. The apartment looks like the set for the *Discovery Channel*. What's this? A note from the neighbor pinned to a six-foot-tall cactus reads, "We've moved to Arizona, and they won't let any plants into the state. I hope you can adopt or find good homes for these little buddies. Good luck!—the neighbors."

Former publisher Bob Allen of the *Wake Weekly* of Wake Forest, N.C., left his column out of the paper during a particularly busy week. Several days later, he was called out of the backshop to face an irate woman at the front desk, "Uh oh," Bob recalls, "I saw her face and I thought I was in for it . . ."

But here's what the reader said, wagging her finger in Bob's face: "Young man, if you don't put your column in the paper this week, don't even bother sending me the paper!"

Columns give your paper the human touch. By the way, what other kind is there? If the touch isn't personal, then it's impersonal.

The congregation may be seated.

Letters to the Editor

Major metro dailies such as the big 297,000-circulation Orlando (Fla.) *Sentinel* receive an average of 400 letters to the editor each day; it has room to publish about four to six. The other 394 don't get run, nor do the writers receive a response. How do you think that makes all those folks feel?

The *Bugle* will receive about four to six letters a week and run each and every one. How do think that makes those writers feel?

The human scale is again at work in favor of community newspapers. At our level there is a satisfying cause and effect at work in the dynamics of production. People are acknowledged as people, not units. The editor's rule of thumb should be: Run every letter when possible, and respond to every letter that you can't use. If the *Bugle* receives a letter that is inappropriate, the editor usually has time to phone the writer and talk about it.

This ideal breaks down once a newspaper or its audience gets beyond a certain size. There are simply too many letters for the space allotted and not enough editors to respond to all of them.

Once this one-on-one reciprocity breaks down, the human scale is swept aside, and even though the paper may now be daily and carry flashy full same-day color, the paper has lost something precious.

A responsive community newspaper with a lively editorial page can provide a platform for vital dialogue. During a snowstorm when the town lost electricity, the daily Hendersonville (N.C.) *Times-News*, with its own back-up generator, provided the only constant stream of local information and inspiration, as well as news and weather coverage to a community without power (no TV) for a week. The editorial page was chock-a-block full of letters. Says former editor Joy Franklin, "We are the voice through which the community talks to itself." Franklin is now editorial page editor of the Asheville *Citizen-Times*.

How a newspaper handles its letters to the editor can be viewed as a barometer of its community health. If you're not getting any letters, then either your edit page is a zombie, or readers have never been given a chance to write, or simply don't know how to go about it. A user-friendly explanatory box run regularly on the edit page should fix this.

Most problems with readers' opinions come from unsigned pieces, vicious personal attacks and libelous submissions. Since the newspaper is responsible for anything libelous on its pages, including even letters written by someone not on staff, the editor must be careful about potentially libelous content. Most papers won't run letters containing personal defamation or letters that aren't signed.

Unsigned letters, or anonymous call-in columns, are booby traps waiting to explode. If the writer or caller isn't courageous enough to sign his name, why should he be afforded the luxury of hiding behind the paper? When the solid waste matter hits the climate control device, guess who it's going to coat first.

So do you throw out all unsigned letters? Not necessarily. If you receive a letter on a compelling subject from a writer who did sign her name but requested anonymity, follow it up with a phone call, and if it warrants, arrange for a news feature or investigative piece to be done on the subject of the letter.

Letters to the Editor Policy

Does your paper have a reader-friendly, succinct letters to the editor policy? Here's a great one by Bill Reader when he was the editorial page editor of the Centre Daily Times, *a 29,400-circulation Knight Ridder community daily in State College, Pa., known locally as simply the* CDT. *Reader is now an assistant professor of journalism at Ohio University.*

The *Centre Daily Times* accepts letters to the editor about issues of local interest that are original to the *CDT*. Preference is given to letters regarding local issues and that do not focus on age-old debates. We encourage writers to follow these guidelines.

- Keep it short: Letters should not exceed 500 words. Longer letters are subject to editing, rejection or may be returned for editing. Longer letters may be excerpted in the newspaper but published in full on the *CDT*'s Web site: <www.centredaily.com>.
- Don't overuse the forum: A letter writer is limited to one letter every 30 days, so the *CDT* can accommodate as many different people as possible.
- Sign your letter: The *CDT* letters forum is only for signed commentary. Anonymous letters go in the trash. Letters that do not include a full name, address and telephone number also get tossed. Only your name and the borough or township in which you live will be published.
- Don't get personal: Getting mad at an opinion is fine, but don't take it out on the writer. The letters forum is for the exchange of opinions and ideas, not for making personal attacks. If your first draft contains anything along the lines of "He's the kind of person who . . ." or "The problem with people like that is . . ."? Go back and cross out the attacks.
- We reserve the right to reject: The *CDT* retains the right to not publish letters. As a rule, we reject letters only when they are deemed libelous, contain vulgar words, are illegibly written or make unverifiable claims of fact. We do not reject letters that disagree with the *CDT*'s editorials—in fact, we encourage people to disagree with us, and we publish such letters all the time.
- Please proofread: Letters containing a large number of spelling or typographical errors may not be published quickly, if at all. Please, proofread your letter before sending it.
- Original letters only: As a rule, we reject letters that are sent to multiple newspapers or are simply copies of letters sent to other people or agencies.
- No poetry please: The *CDT* rarely publishes poetry, not because we don't like it, but because the letters forum is intended for debate, not for artistic expression, and we simply do not have the room for poems.
- "Thank You" letters are welcome: The *CDT* is happy to publish letters thanking community groups and individuals for good deeds and services. The Letters of Special Thanks columns is published every Tuesday in "On Centre."
- Please be patient: When possible, the *CDT* publishes letters in the order in which they are received, verified and processed. Due to the volume of letters we receive, and our commitment to publish as many letters as possible, it could take as long as two weeks for a letter to be published. Shorter letters or letters on current topics are more likely to be published quickly. The *CDT* does not guarantee a particular turnaround time for letters to be published because of several variables, including: the number of letters on hand (usually about 20 to 30 are on deck); special projects that require grouping of certain letters (such as election letters or multiple letters on a common topic);

the time it takes to reach writers for verification and clarification; and last-minute news changes.

153
Editorials

But on the Other Hand . . .

Unsigned letters that are phoned in to the paper? Blasphemy! Or maybe not . . .
Bill Reader reflects on one of community journalism's ethical hot potatoes.

Just to raise a few journalistic hackles, here's a defense for anonymity. In particular, here's a defense of the practice of publishing anonymous public comments on opinion pages in newspapers.

A few newspapers across the country have anonymous call-in features, kind of like print versions of feisty talk radio. The forums are often called "Say So," "Your Turn," "30 Seconds." Readers call an automated voice mail system, vent their steam, and hang up. The newspaper prints the comment. It's all quite simple.

And problematic, apparently. At least for some.

The hounds of journalistic ethics are baying—or is it whimpering?—as these anonymous call-in forums creep onto the pages of newspapers throughout the United States. We are dropping jaws at the sight of these low-brow forums and railing against the fall of public discourse, the cheapening of free speech, the temptation of libel-suit seekers and the tainting of journalism's increasingly soiled existence.

All of which are legitimate concerns, at least from a knee-jerk perspective. But if you'll allow this hypocrite to offer some explanations, you may just see how anonymity is an important journalistic tradition.

I am a hypocrite because I often run with the pack on this issue. I'm an editorial page editor who rejects unsigned letters and discounts anonymous telephone calls, and in a previous job as a beat reporter I was the most vocal opponent to my former newspaper's inauguration of its own "hate forum." In my present job, I have no desire to initiate such a project.

But as a media scholar with an interest in public discourse, I am personally drawn to these features just as strongly as I am professionally repulsed. Because in those little snippets that make mean attacks on public officials, public policies, and public opinions, I almost always see the First Amendment in its purest, most basic form.

Though open to all, anonymous opinion forums cater mostly to the oppressed. It's a free country, sure, but not everybody feels perfectly comfortable speaking their mind and blowing whistles. In Washington, reporters recognize this and willingly offer influential people chances to speak their minds "on condition of anonymity."

The average person in Podunk enjoys no such luxury. And because it's hard to hide in Podunk, the powerless also tend to be voiceless.

Consider: In study after study trying to determine who writes letters to the editor, researchers have come up with the same answer: white, middle-aged, conservative, wealthy males. In essence, it's the same demographic that has been calling the shots since day one, a group that has never really been afraid to speak its mind and sign its name.

This is the same demographic, incidentally, that has run the newspaper business for some time, too. Birds of a feather and all that. Which over the years has built a very real wall between newspapers and the people they purport to serve.

That wall has locked out the old seamstress afraid to denounce the owners of the sweatshop where she works, the elderly couple fearful of reporting on the bully policeman who lords it over their neighborhood, the pregnant teenager who wants to tell the public that her schoolteachers harass her. That wall has allowed us to ignore the voices of a lot of people who have some very sobering things to say.

But in breaking down that wall, anonymous call-in forums also let in the riff-raff of public discourse, the cowards, the manipulators, the bitter and the mean. But then, a simple look at the history of signed letters to the editor reveal a similar pattern—anonymous or not, letters have always been predominantly negative and often venomous.

A common argument against anonymous opinion forums is the fear of libel. Those fears are unfounded. There is no connection between anonymity and libel—even signed letters can be libelous. Then there's the U.S. Supreme Court, which has upheld the First Amendment protections for anonymous commentary, most notably in the 1960 case *Talley v. California*, in which Justice Hugo L. Black wrote: "Anonymity has sometimes been assumed for the most constructive purposes. Identification and fear of reprisal might deter perfectly peaceful discussions of public matters of importance."

As for the history of that First Amendment, editors who reject the value of unsigned commentary might do well to read Cato's letters, the essays of Silence Dogood or the "Letter[s] from a Farmer in Pennsylvania." We know now who wrote these important and enlightening documents championing free speech, but it was their observations and opinions—not their names—that championed freedom in that revolutionary era.

Even less significant unsigned letters have been published through history. Grab a few rolls of old microfilm and spin through the days gone by of letters to the editor, and you'll find an awful lot of letters signed "a Soldier," "a Citizen," "a Local Woman" or "a Taxpayer."

Basically, the allowance of anonymity on editorial pages is a time-honored practice that has lost out to a modern conceit. Legal concerns are unfounded, and the moral certainty that anonymity is somehow damaging to society doesn't stand up very well against historical examples and modern reporting tactics.

If managed carefully and edited appropriately, anonymous comments—

whether submitted via telephone, mail, fax or e-mail—could add more than a little spice to a newspaper's opinion pages. Unsigned opinions could certainly enhance the public forum, which should be open to everybody who has something to say and not just to those who can afford to sign their names.

The Last Word

If you receive a stinging letter attacking you or the paper's performance or editorial position, take great caution before you allow yourself to respond in print. In some rare cases it may be appropriate to write a small "editor's note" beneath a misleading or vicious letter. But use this practice sparingly. It can make you appear mean spirited, as if you must have the last word. Use restraint. Otherwise you'll probably invite a letter-writing slugfest.

Here's a real-life editor's brain teaser (though the names have been changed): Imagine you are the editor of the *Bugle*. You have a city editor named Ralph who writes a regular weekly column. This week Ralph's column contains the following graf:

> I've been working at this newspaper for a year now and I can't believe the stupid calls I get from some dumbass readers. They complain about everything—from the 'Grip 'n' Grins' we don't run, if their paper is late, to simple misspellings. I'd like to see these whiners to come try to put out the *Bugle* by themselves just once—then they'd see how hard it is to put out a newspaper. To the readers who just don't get it: Screw you!

Scenario one: Ralph's column is printed in the paper before you have a chance to see it. Ouch.

Scenario two: Ralph's column lands on your desk before you've gone to press and you have time to do something about it.

What do you do? To the column? To the graf? To Ralph?

From the Trenches

From whence cometh the editorial "we"?

I don't know, but I suspect it originated from some editorial writer who either represented his newspaper's opinion or thought "I" didn't have enough clout.

For a small-town editor, "we" sounds pompous. My reality check came from one of my co-editors years back who heard me use that second-person possessive pronoun.

"We?!" Pat Jobe said with a derisive laugh. "Whaddaya mean *we*? You gotta rat in your pocket?"

PULITZERS IN SMALL PLACES

"Winning a Pulitzer Prize is like winning the Olympics or an Oscar. It's the best," wrote Rutland (Vt.) *Herald* publisher R. John Mitchell when the 22,000-circulation community paper's editorial page editor, David Moats, won the 2001 Pulitzer for editorial writing.

"It's even better for a small community newspaper to be among the finalists like the *New York Times* and the *Arizona Republic*," Mitchell wrote in his "From the Publisher" column on April 17, 2001. "It brings on tears, goose bumps and incredible emotions."

But win the little paper did—taking a risky stand by endorsing civil unions in a culturally conservative state. And Moats, a 20-year veteran at the *Herald*, told *Editor & Publisher* he saw it coming. "I thought, if there ever was a time I'd have a chance, this would be it," he said.

The gay marriage issue divided the state, the community of Rutland and the employees at the *Herald*, the publisher noted. But as the civil union law worked its way through the legislature, Moats "responded to the sometimes vicious rhetoric that deeply divided our state," Mitchell wrote.

"He was not shrill, mindful of how deeply Vermonters felt. He was forceful, however. The *Herald* (and its sister paper the *Times Argus*), through his editorials, were able to provide Vermonters with a clear view of the issue, which I hope furthered the debate. It is the kind of leadership a small newspaper should provide its community at such a volatile point in its history."

WHEN THE KKK COMES TO TOWN

As journalists we strive to remain objective, right? But there are instances when the typical objective newspaper coverage alone would do a disservice to the best interests of the community. Editor Jim Kevlin and the 36,000-circulation daily Pottsville (Pa.) Republican & Evening Herald *grappled with just such an ethical dilemma, as described in the following commentary by the editor. In 1996 the* Republican *purchased the Shenandoah* Evening Herald *of northern Schuylkill County. According to researcher Doug Eroh, in the heyday of the anthracite coal boom, Shenandoah was known as "the toughest town in the East." Says editor Kevlin, "Being an editor in hard coal country, you've got to be tough." Kevlin is now executive editor of the Norwich (Conn.)* Bulletin *and president of the Associated Press Managing Editors of Connecticut.*

When the American Knights of the Ku Klux Klan scheduled a rally on the courthouse steps in Pottsville, Pa., on Sept. 26, 1998, the first reaction in the Pottsville *Republican & Evening Herald*'s newsroom was a sense of helplessness in the face of this effort to mobilize the unseen hatred that exists in any community.

Then, the editors asked themselves: What would we do if Adolf Hitler came to town? Coverage decisions flowed from that question.

The traditional journalistic approach—interview the racist, then balance the comments with those of, say, a local minister—seemed inadequate, irrelevant, even repellent. Instead, we turned to state Human Relations Commission guidelines prepared to help communities counteract hate groups and used them to guide our coverage decisions.

The resulting editorials, articles and New Media adjuncts—audiotext and Web—provided our readers with the encouragement and means to resist the Klan's message if they chose to do so, including:

- A strong first-day editorial statement decrying the Klan, urging it to stay away—as recommended in the state guidelines—and giving readers a vehicle— an audiotext call-in line—to express similar sentiments if they wished. Further editorials encouraged people to participate in alternate events and to shun the rally.
- When a Unity Day Committee formed to plan the alternative events, a coverage plan was developed to fully publicize those efforts. This included a 5-by-full front-page "user's guide" to resisting the Klan. It included a "unity pledge" in coupon form for people to sign and mail in, a full-page, full-color "Support Unity Day" poster, and a purple-ribbon cut-out for people to clip and wear. (The committee urged people to wear purple, a symbol of compassion.)
- A Unity Day home page that included a story archive and links to anti-hate sites, an easy-to-return e-mail version of the "unity pledge," and pro–Unity Day images for children to print out and color.
- Daily news articles leading up to the rally that explored the Klan's goals and methods, profiled the lost souls that are attracted by the Klan's message, highlighted the county's ethnic diversity, and reported prominently on the developing counter-activities.
- A 5-by-full front-page package the day of the rally headlined "E Pluribus Unum," featuring the stories of people from varied races and ethnic backgrounds who had found a home and prospered in Schuylkill County.

On the day of the rally, a prayer vigil, a concert by a nationally known anti-hate musician, and numerous other counter-events were staged. The Pottsville-Berwick football game was rescheduled to coincide with and draw people away from the Klan rally.

Inevitably, perhaps, 500 people were drawn to the Klan event, but to heckle and challenge, not to encourage the 25 hooded figures who drove into town through a gauntlet of homes and businesses bedecked with purple ribbons. Above the rally site was a huge banner across the third floor of the courthouse: "Support Unity Day"; big purple bows decorated offices across the way.

When 90 minutes of police protection—as contained in the Klan's permit to gather—expired, the Klan members hurried to their cars and sped out of the county, their plans to organize a local chapter foiled.

An event that started as a threat to community life turned out to be an opportunity. The positive outcomes were many and, it can be hoped, lasting. The Unity Day Committee is evolving into a permanent countywide Unity Coalition. The next year, a full week of activities was planned to promote cross-ethnic understanding and amity. And the General Assembly created a new state day of observance, proclaiming the fourth Saturday in September "Unity Day in Pennsylvania."

The state Human Relations Commission said what happened in Schuylkill County—the immediate challenge, the alternate events, the formation of a permanent Unity Coalition—is a model for other communities to follow, and believes the steps taken here have discouraged future Klan activity. By contrast, a community in a neighboring county chose to ignore a similar rally and the Klan came back weekly. Once established, hate activity is difficult to uproot.

At one of the Unity Day Committee meetings, a local merchant recounted how he had visited Dachau during a trip to Europe: "Where were the German people?" a tour guide was asked during a walk through the gas chambers. "When they could do something, they didn't; when they would do something, they couldn't," was the reply.

If the question is ever asked in Pottsville, the *Republican & Evening Herald* can answer, when we could, we did.

Your Town; Your Turn

1. Remember the young editor zapped by the outspoken high school biology teacher? ("Stick to features.") What would be your response to such a comment?
2. Determine your or your hometown newspaper's editorial policy on some given local issue. How was it crafted? By a group or an individual?
3. Think back to the events of this week in your life. Write a personal column of not more than three double-spaced pages. If you've never written a column before, share it with a friend and ask for his or her honest reaction.

TEN

Interviewing and Writing

Tuttlemaus' Terrible Techniques

A local pianist who just returned from her Carnegie Hall debut stops by the *Bugle* to renew her subscription, and is spotted by her old friend the editor. They begin talking about the performance, and the editor suggests a follow-up story. "Actually," he says, thinking out loud, "it's a slow news day . . . could you give us an interview now?" The musician, a little surprised but mindful of the need for publicity, consents. The editor assigns an available writer from the small newsroom, Bob Tuttlemaus, a new reporter fresh out of J-school.

Tuttlemaus shakes hands with the pianist and explains he'd rather do the interview in the newspaper's conference room, but since that room is locked, he settles for the empty office of the vacationing circulation manager. Tuttlemaus seats himself behind the big desk and motions for the musician to take the chair facing him across the table. She hands the reporter a Carnegie Hall program (containing musical and biographical notes). He glances at the cover and doesn't look inside; he's too busy fumbling with the tape recorder and flipping his legal pad open to a fresh page.

The musician, sensing the beginner's nervousness, opens the small talk, asking Tuttlemaus how he came to the *Bugle*. Glad to talk about himself, Tuttlemaus explains that for his first job out of college he had to "settle" for a small paper, but that he doesn't see much difference between working at a community paper and a big-city daily, where he clearly thought he deserved to be. He regards the town as "kinda' hick" and with a desultory shrug adds that the *Bugle* "is an OK place to start." Then he proclaims, "Besides, the way I figure it, a crime story is a crime story is a crime story, and a fire story is a fire story is a fire story." He tells the pianist he won't be staying at the *Bugle* very long; he has bigger fish to fry.

Tuttlemaus turns on the tape recorder, picks up his pen and asks his first question. "So, where were you born?"

Ninety minutes later, the interview (laced with questions such as, "So, what kind of music do you play anyway?") is over, and the musician is leaving.

"Hey, Bob, wait," says an older reporter. "Did you get her picture?"

"Oh, yeah," Tuttlemaus stops the departing musician. "Gotta' take your picture." Grabbing a camera, he di-

Establishing rapport early in the interview is critical to the success of the interview and, thus, the story you get. You can see that the reporter here has great natural "people skills." Marjorie Daughtridge's direct eye contact and engaging smile makes people comfortable talking to the staff writer for the Southern Pines (N.C.) *Pilot. Remember*: Access + Rapport = Success.

rects her to stand against a blank wall. He adjusts the camera and flash, then looks up and shoots a quick shot without warning. Then, checking the picture on the back of the digital camera, Tuttlemaus says to himself, "OK, I guess that's good enough."

The pianist nods, and leaves with a growing sense of dread at how the story and picture will turn out in tomorrow's *Bugle*.

Is it any wonder that the 20-inch story turned out shallow and weak, and that the photograph looked like a glorified passport mugshot? What could Tuttlemaus have done differently at the front end to have strengthened his story and photo?

The Importance of Being Earnest

Great newswriting can be divided into three functions: gathering, writing and editing.

Let's take it from the top, with the gathering. In our business, we're only as good

as our raw material. That comes from the interview, a critical stage that many
beginners tend to gloss over, thinking that the true art lies in the writing. However, we are only as good as we are curious. A great interview almost always results in a strong story, while a weak interview invariably produces a weak story. Almost never does a great story grow out of a weak interview.

So first things first. Give credit, importance and dignity to this vital initial step. It cannot be overemphasized. We are journalists. We are not novelists. We do not write fiction. We do not invent people and conjure up quotes. We are completely at the mercy of our people, and they are only going to reveal themselves to us in truth, giving us stunning quotes and shimmering insights into their lives if we conduct skilled interviews. This comes with work, dedication and time. With apologies to Neil Young, I advise you to be "a miner for a quote of gold."

Especially in community journalism, it all boils down to this:

Access + Rapport = Success.

Close Encounters of the Fourth Estate: Tone and Direction

Psychologists who study a discipline called Transactional Analysis (TA) tell us that every encounter between two people can be broken down in terms of the relative positioning of each person. From the most simple to the most complex encounter, all our dealings with others are "transactions." Listen to two college buddies passing each other on the way to class:

A: Hi, how are you?
B: Fine, how 'bout you?
A: Great. See ya'.
B: Yeh, bye.

Seems simple, but look again. A opens with a friendly greeting and a non-ego inquiry about the health and happiness of B, who responds with a report of his condition, and then returns the question in kind. A reciprocates and gives an appropriate farewell, which B accepts and returns. In short, the transaction went A-B, A-B, in a complete circle. A nice tight little interview.

Now, consider for a second what might have happened if the first guy had said only "Hi." It's very likely B would have responded in kind with just "Hello."

The point of all this: If A doesn't *initiate*, B isn't required to answer. *From the very first question*, A is the interviewer and sets the tone for the entire encounter.

Consider poor Bob Tuttlemaus' botched interview. When he asked "So, where were you born?," that sent a clear message to our musician. Privately, she was thinking, "Oh brother, Wunderkind here doesn't know the first thing about me and is asking for my life story. He doesn't even have the common sense to flip open the program I gave him and find out simple facts for himself. At this rate I'm going to be here all afternoon with this puppy."

Control: Carpe De Interview

From the very start, Bob Tuttlemaus had lost control of the interview.

Like it or not, recognize it or not, an interview is a control situation. Either you the reporter will control it, or your subject will control the encounter—or possibly if neither takes charge, the situation and events driving the interview will dictate where it goes, usually resulting in a story that wanders in a muddle or spirals aimlessly outward to la-la land.

The skillful community journalist knows how to steer an interview subtly yet surely. It's a lot like riding a horse. You impose your will over your steed with your attitude and your gentle yet firm touch on the reins. Relinquish control of the reins, and your horse or your interview will run away from you.

Bottom line: It's yours to control. So don't just carpe diem. Carpe de interview!

The Interview as an Inner-View

Remember the old newspaper axiom that says the purpose of an interview is to provide an "inner-view." And you'll get the clearest, quickest and most accurate picture of someone when they're surrounded by their *stuff*.

Therefore, the first rule of interviewing is: Go to your subject's home or workplace. You want to meet the person on his or her turf, lair, habitat or environment—the author in his study, the dancer in his studio, the mayor in her office, the cop on the street, the musician at her piano.

In community journalism, where distances are shorter between office and interview site, and you have more time generally to do your interview, there are fewer excuses for doing interviews in the office or—heaven forbid—over the phone or by e-mail. (The exception here is if your person knows you well and is a continuing source, a public official, etc.) What is there to learn about someone by talking to him in the newsroom or a vacant office?—except how flexible and well he handles himself in a strange situation.

Not only will the home turf reveal your person to you, but it will also make the subject more comfortable, allowing you to go deeper and get more details. Again, if you can get Access and establish Rapport, then Success likely will follow.

Is it any wonder that Tuttlemaus, who sought access only to a spare office, and who never established rapport, ended up with a story that just sort of lay there flopping weakly?

Perhaps Tuttlemaus forgot Lauterer's Law of Interviewing. "Warning: Shallow In, Shallow Out." If you go in weak and just wade around in the kiddie pool area, you'll never get to the deep end, where the fun is.

By placing the interview in a neutral, no-person's land of a vacant office, Tuttlemaus lost even more control over the transaction. People kept walking in and out, and the phone kept ringing. To make matters worse, the intercom constantly interrupted them and Tuttlemaus couldn't figure out how to turn it off, further embar-

rassing the musician who felt sorry for the cub reporter. Tuttlemaus' ineptness and
attitude inadvertently signaled to the pianist loud and clear: "I don't have a clue how
to run an interview, so don't expect much out of this story. After all, a musician
story is a musician story is a . . ."

Helpful Hints for the Meteors: This Is Not *Larry King Live*

A great interview is not so much a science or technique as it is an acquired and
subtle art. And as such there are few models or formulas we can use. However, there
are some time-honored guidelines for interviewing in the community journalism
context, where the last thing you want to do is the I-sit-here-you-sit-there-and-
I-bark-these-10-questions technique. Leave the formalities to Larry King.

One very good question can sometimes do it all. Ethnographer Roxanne Newton
of Mitchell Community College likes to use what she calls "the kitchen sink" type of
question, where she might start out with, "You know I'm interested in women
in the labor movement. Tell me the story of your life." Newton says, "And then just
let 'em talk."

BE SENSITIVE

As you will quickly discover, if you already haven't, many if not most of the people
you interview in community journalism aren't "media savvy." Your story subjects,
whether in news, sports and features, have preconceived ideas about us newspaper
types—most of which they got from TV! They are likely to be intimidated by the
encounter, and for many, this will be their first and perhaps only face-to-face
experience with what one old mountain man in all seriousness called "the meteors."
What seems normal for you as a reporter is to them like a visit from an alien. The
more you appreciate the novelty of your interview, the better will be your success in
community journalism. (Also see Notetaking, below.)

BACKGROUND

Writers and photographers at the *National Geographic* magazine spend *weeks* doing
background research for each story. Of course, we in community journalism don't
have that kind of time, but there's no excuse for going in cold. For anyone you
interview, you should do background research—especially in a smaller community
where so many people know each other. If nothing previously has been written
about your subject, ask community members about the person you're to interview.
(If you're lucky, there will be some old salt in your newsroom who's been there
forever and knows everybody.) Nothing will establish your reputation as a light-
weight quicker than a vapid, shallow story on someone who is well-known around

town. Also, if you do your research, you won't have to waste time covering the basic biographical and professional info that any vita, bio, résumé, book jacket or program notes would contain. It will save you from truly stupid questions such as "So, what kind of music do you play, anyway?" which only signals your amateur standing. And ultimately, truly stupid questions further distance you from the very person to whom you're trying to get close. At all costs avoid the "cold interview." If circumstances beyond your control force you to go in totally unprepared, apologize and acknowledge it up front—and then do research after the interview, and follow up with e-mail or a phone call.

VISIT

Be a person first. A reporter second. Visit first. Chat. Strike up a conversation. Leave your pen and your pad, your tape recorder and camera on the floor in the camera bag. Talk about what's in front of you. The pictures on the wall, the family, the decor, the garden. Comment favorably about what you see. Be politely inquisitive. The first question should flow out of that conversation, not leap off your notepad like a barb thrown by Mike Wallace from *60 Minutes* (unless, of course, it is a confrontational interview). Give it time. Then, when your subject is comfortable with you, ease into the reporter role. Omaha *World-Herald* photographer Jeff Carney, who started taking pictures in high school for his parents' 4,000-circulation weekly Wahoo (Neb.) *Newspaper*, says, "I use humor, and then . . . there's an element of trust . . . and I assure them that I'm not going to embarrass them. I try visiting with them, get people talking, leave the cameras in the bag at first, assuring them I won't put them in a bad light. I'm up front and honest. I tell people who I am and what I'm up to. *Access is everything.* Once they know you and like your work, it seems to open doors."

DON'T UPSTAGE

While the conversation should be the vehicle, beware of what former radio commentator Earl Nightingale used to call the "dynamic monologue." In other words, don't talk about yourself too much, and never lose sight that this is an interview.

SPACES

Study body language. Putting some thing between you and your person, such as a desk, represents a philosophical, emotional barrier. It's a power statement. Bosses use it when they want you to feel small. If you're in an interview where you're going for that inner-view, try to keep the space free between the two of you so the information can flow in a lively, informal way. Tuttlemaus should have come out from behind that desk, or invited the pianist to sit in a position in which she would feel more valued. Of course, the canny reporter would have insisted they drive over to the pianist's studio, where Tuttlemaus would have seen her collection of 43

Beethoven busts of all sizes arranged like a menagerie on top of the pianist's polished black enamel Steinway grand. There's your lede. And what an image. Where's that camera?

CATALOG THE DETAILS

Literally, take notes about all the stuff your person has around—on her desk, on the walls, the kind of room it is, the decor. Each thing is a little window into your person's personality.

Picture this: You go to interview the distinguished old professor, and there in his study you see three clocks side by side on the bookshelf over his computer. Remember: You're only as good as your questions. So it may sound dumb, but you've got to ask about those three clocks. Maybe you'll get a wonderfully revealing answer like "Because I'm so busy. It's how I budget my time. One clock is for my teaching time, the second is for my research time, and the third is for my writing time."

Whoa! There's your lede. And you'd never have gotten that priceless insight from a phone or e-mail interview.

BE PROMPT

"Well begun is half done," says the proverb quoted by Aristotle. Being prompt shows a measure of your respect and gets things off on the right footing. This is especially true if your subject has never been interviewed before. On the other hand, the quickest way to discount your person is to be late. That's inconsiderate and sends a message: "I don't care about you; my time is more important than yours." Being late will poison the friendly atmosphere you're attempting to establish, and you'll spend the bulk of the interview trying to play catch-up.

BE GOOD TO YOURSELF

Speaking of time, give yourself the luxury of time. A good single-source interview takes one to two hours, depending on the subject, the situation, the novelty of that situation, how it unfolds and flows. And you may want to go back and visit again after your first draft. You may want to call on other people to expand the piece. That can be done over the phone if you're well-known, but nothing is better than face to face—the personal approach style of community journalism.

EASY DOES IT

Give your person the dignity of time. Don't rush it, no matter how rushed you are. You want to kill an interview? Just tell your subject something like, "OK, I'm in a hurry. I've only got 20 minutes. Now—where were you born?" On the other hand, respect your subject's time. Find out how much time she can devote to the interview and stick to it. Important people usually have tight schedules.

QUOTES, QUOTES, QUOTES

An interview should be loaded with quotes. Nothing beats complete direct quotes used in context for bringing veracity, legitimacy and life to a story. A balanced use of paraphrasing and partial quotes is pleasing, so long as you let the direct quotes (on your journalist's honor: accurate, word-for-word) carry the load. Of course it's hard work. That's why beginners cop out and paraphrase too much. It comes down to knowing when to use which type of attribution. John Neibergall of Bethel University offers these guidelines: "Quote the quoteworthy. Paraphrase when the subject's words do not reveal something of the subject's personality or address the subject in an especially clear or bright manner."

DRESS APPROPRIATELY; BECOME INVISIBLE

Dress to suit the occasion. Use common sense. An interview with the mayor requires shirt and tie or a dress or a nice business suit, whereas an interview with a country family making their fall run of molasses calls for jeans, T-shirt and boots. The rule of thumb here is to blend. Dressing inappropriately will make your subject feel uncomfortable and call attention to yourself. You'll have a more difficult time establishing all-important rapport. Wearing heels or wingtips to a corn-shucking will have your people wondering about you. The same goes for ratty jeans at city council meeting. When it comes to being neighborly and talking the language of the people he's covering, Ohio University assistant professor of journalism Bill Reader has a technique. For instance, if he's doing a local farming story: "You just hook your thumbs in your jeans and talk farmer."

NOTETAKING

Since it's likely your subject is a first-timer in an interview situation, he brings preconceived notions about what newspeople are really like. Think about how reporters are portrayed or seen by popular American culture on TV and in film. We are mostly gruff, aggressive, loud, insensitive, messy, self-serving, puffed-out, egotistical, impossible to live with (read: divorced), irascible curmudgeons who care nothing about people but only the story and our professional advancement—and that's just for starters. You've got your work cut out for you simply earning your subject's trust.

When you sit down to do a community journalism interview, the first step in notetaking is to not take any. You read right. That means, you must show your person that the image he has of the stereotyped reporter just isn't true in your case. You must earn his trust. You can gain access by showing him that you care, that you're a person first. Don't interview. Visit. How long you "visit" before you start taking notes is up to you and how quickly you establish rapport. But generally, with a first-timer, the rule of thumb is: Don't rush it. Then, when you can't stand it a minute longer, slip out the notepad while you are in conversation, but don't make a production out of it.

Alecia Swasy, a fine *Wall Street Journal* reporter at the time, was doing a story on poverty in the Kentucky hill country. She found a poor woman who consented to be interviewed. But instead of sitting down with her, flipping open the notepad and firing pointed questions, our wise reporter spent one whole morning doing the wash and folding the laundry with the woman. Didn't take a single note. The reporter was being a person first. She spent one whole day just establishing trust. And because she had gained access and established rapport, the following day she got an interview that sizzled. Swasy is now the deputy managing editor of the Norfolk *Virginian-Pilot* and the author of several books.

So it's a given that most folks have never had a camera lens or a mic thrust in their face before, and they're likely to never have the experience again. Knowing this should affect your style, whether you use notepad or tape or both, and how and when you go about taking photographs.

Even the simplest act of taking notes is likely to unnerve the first-timer. Your subject will likely lose her train of thought as you start taking notes. "Are you writin' down ever'thang I'm sayin'?" one old woman asked incredulously of a young reporter. "Why law, child," she said with an embarrassed laugh, "I'm jus' an old-timey country woman a-rattlin' on. Jus' as old-timey as I can be. Why would you wanna' write down what I say?"

Why, indeed?

Although you will develop your own style with time, it will be obvious to most that the situation described above negated the use of a tape recorder. Why? Because the notepad itself was intrusive enough. The rule of thumb, the more primitive the setting, the more basic your technology should be. Remember, we are *writers* first. Even with all our technological wizardry back at the office, we're still writers, and we'll always *be* writers. We don't need electronic brouhaha. That means we can write anywhere on anything. Take notes on café receipts, match covers, old envelopes, napkins, brown paper bags, your own hand if need be. But never, and this means never, be caught without a pen.

That's rule number one: Find a pen you love and carry it (or several of them) everywhere you go. It should be a fast, dependable, long-lasting rolling-ball ink pen. Avoid pencils and fountain pens and ballpoints. They fade or run or won't write on some surfaces (such as the palm of your hand). Pilot Precise Rolling Ball V5 and Uni-Ball Micro by Faber-Castell are favorites of many.

Next, equally simple and just as important: Find a type of notebook that fits in your hand and with which you feel comfortable. It doesn't matter if they're the traditional reporters' notebooks, or steno-sized flip-top pads or little notebooks, just so long as you're consistent and keep your notes in order over the years, when such a system of sourcebooks will prove their worth to you. Not unlike the oak and the acorn, big books grow from little (note)books. And you never know, you may someday have a book in you.

In high school journalism classes, they taught us to write down 10 questions before the interview. That's not a bad idea, but if you take such a list to an interview, keep it out of sight. Who wants to feel like his life is a fill-in-the-blank quiz? Better to memorize the questions and ask yourself before the interview: What's this story really about and who cares?

Before we go another second, we've got to address the issue of tape recorders.

Testing One Two Three . . . : Are There Batteries in This Thing?

You can safely assume in community journalism that you won't be doing many inside-the-beltway-style interviews. That's the running, hand-held tape recorder thrust in a politician's face and shouting-questions-style interview popularized by the "pack journalism" of the Washington press corps.

Under certain circumstances, however, the tape recorder can be an invaluable tool for the community journalist: When the subject is media savvy, doesn't mind being taped or even wants to be taped for accuracy's sake, when it's someone who talks a blue streak, or someone with a dialect or colorful speech pattern you want to get down to perfection—and *if your subject doesn't mind*—then it's appropriate.

But there are no two ways about it, a tape recorder is not usually present in the course of a normal conversation. So to place a tape recorder on the table beside you and someone else and to try to have a conversation is unnatural. Normal conversation becomes theater. Face it, a tape recorder is an intrusion. (So too is taking notes, but at least notetaking is less threatening and doesn't take electricity.) Many people will simply freeze up on you if you stick a recorder in their face. It says in effect: "Everything you say can and probably will be used to embarrass you in front of your family, friends and neighbors." To the uninitiated, the very act of recording every single "uh" and "er" will petrify them into yes and no answers.

Be wary of becoming too dependent on gadgetry. A tape recorder can be your pal, but it can (and will) turn on you. Anyone who's ever relied completely on a recorder during an interview knows about Murphy's First Law of Journalism: A tape recorder getting vital information will have dead batteries. Or, put another way: Tape recorders tend to fail in direct proportion to the extent you depend on them.

Lauterer's Law of Tape Recorders: If you have to use one, pretend it isn't there. Take notes like a wild thing. Not only does that intimidate the tape recorder, thereby negating Murphy, but it also guarantees you will get the data, possibly twice.

The wonderful thing about notes is they provide you with a visual picture, a map almost, of the interview. You can see repeating themes in your notes. If it's only on a tape, then you can't ever look at the interview and see what the person was saying. A tape recorder, used in conjunction with good notes, can be useful. However, be forewarned, this is time-consuming. If you use this technique, use your notes to organize and outline; use your tape to get precise quotes and nuances. Other pros and cons of tapes:

- Some reporters maintain that the presence of a tape recorder puts people on notice of the reporter's dedication to accuracy. It may even help guard against people being tempted to go "off the record" because the tape recorder is still running.
- Another plus for the tape recorder is that it can provide you with an ironclad defense against people who later claim they were misquoted (as long as you did get it right).
- One busy editor likes tape recorders because he simply can't get around to writing most stories right after he does the interview. However, he says the tape recorder keeps the story fresh for him. If he had used notes alone, he would have forgotten much of the interview.
- Tape recorders take batteries; pens don't. Notetaking exclusively satisfies the KISS rule and means you have less to lug around and less to worry about. Do I have fresh batteries? A fresh tape? Do I have enough tape? There's nothing worse than a tape running out before the interview is over, clunk, right in the middle of a sentence—and the reporter shutting down the interview apologetically.

Notetaking Hints—Part Two

In the course of a normal conversation, people look at each other a lot. Granted, it's hard to take notes and maintain constant eye contact, but that should be your goal. Especially early in the interview, you should look at your subject as much as possible. The more you hunch over your notepad, eyes locked on your notes, the more you're expecting your subject to do all the work.

So how to do? Forget about Mrs. Fudnucker, your second-grade teacher. Take big loopy notes. Ignore those lines. Notebooks are cheap. A lost quote is priceless. So let 'er rip. By the way, when you learn to do this, it will enable you to take notes in the dark, a most helpful skill for any reporter—for instance, covering a speech in a darkened auditorium. Other stuff:

- Write in code. Come up with your own reporter's shorthand. Abbreviate as much as you can. If you're doing a story about sexual harassment, write SH every time your person says it in a quote. Come up with specific abbreviations for each story to speed you along.
- Learn the fine art of creative listening—also called deep or eloquent listening. Go for exact words and colorful, vital quotes. Write down key phrases, leaving out the articles, pronouns and prepositions if you have to. Fill in later.
- Avoid yes/no questions ("Did you learn to play the piano here?") unless you intend to follow up. ("Oh really? Who was your piano teacher? Have you been in

contact with her? What'd she say when she heard you were going to debut at Carnegie Hall?")

- Don't cheat your reader. Remember, this is not TV. When you can sneak it into your notes, or when your subject is off on a tangent you don't think you need, get down the descriptions and imagery of the person and setting. His bow tie, the beach shorts and shiny penny loafers, her hair parted in the middle, faded Pointer overalls, Gucci shirt—the details make the picture.

- Learn to end an interview, not stop it. When the interview is over, and when you've got enough material, go out as gently as you came in. Be friendly and supportive. If you're taking your own photo, this is the time to do it, unless you did it already during the interview. (See Chapter 14.) Tell your subject when and where the story will appear. Make sure your subject is amenable to any needed follow-up e-mails or phone calls you might have to make. If you have a business card, handing one out is a nice way of showing you are an accountable, accessible professional. And, finally, thank your subject for the interview and for the time given you. An interview can be exhausting.

   If your subject asks to see the story before it goes to press, politely explain that it's against your newspaper's policy, and that it's a matter of trust. The exception will be the technical story in which you or your editor may opt to let the subject review the story for content errors only—but never style or substantive editing.

- Right after the interview, go back over your notes and fill in blanks and abbreviations. The longer you wait to do this, the harder it will be.

   If you've got something that looks like gibberish in your notes, read all around it, and read the sentence aloud and see if the mystery word comes clear. Remember, it was your code. You knew what it meant when you wrote it. Go run. Take a shower. Come back and look at it again. Hold it up to a mirror. Really, sometimes that unlikely trick will shake it loose. Ask somebody else in the newsroom, or a friend, to attempt to read the whole sentence (without telling them that part of it is gibberish to you).

- Organize your notes with color-coded highlighters, circling repetitive themes so you can find them quickly when you start writing. This is also the way an outline will appear.

- Write the story as soon after the interview as possible. A story is perishable. The longer you wait, the weaker the story will be. Notes are meant to jog your memory, not serve as a substitute.

Words from the Pros

Kirk Ross and Woody Marshall are two community journalists who have honed the craft of interviewing to a fine art. Both will tell you that learning to interview well takes time. Perhaps their advice will help you improve more quickly.

Kirk Ross, managing editor of the N.C. *Independent Weekly*, is a past master of interviewing. The secret of a great interview, according to Ross sounds deceptively simple: "The thing is to get people talking."

Ross warns, "The first 12 seconds are the most important. It's almost like a sales call. You tell 'em who you are, what you're doing, why you're there and what's in it for them.

"You have to build trust" and show them you respect them and what they do. . . . And don't be afraid to "humanize yourself," he says.

Your interview will only be as good as the questions you ask. Ross employs both "open probe" and "closed probe" type questions.

Closed probe elicits either a yes/no answer or a specific response to a direct question:

Did you enjoy the trip?
What year did you graduate?
How old are you?
What was the name of the school?

—whereas an open probe question, gets people talking, what Ross calls "mining the details."

An open probe question might go like this:

So, when you got to the accident scene what was going through your mind when you saw the car . . . ?
Tell me what it was like to be there . . .
Describe the scene . . .
Walk me through what it was like . . .
Help me connect the dots . . .

Ross says, "Your job (as interviewer) is to wind 'em up, get people talking, to focus the conversation." To mine the details Ross uses the following type of non-invasive questions:

Tell me a little bit more about . . .
Let's focus on . . .
I want to try and nail this down, so can you share with me . . .

WOODY'S WONDERFUL WAYS

Watching Woody Marshall work an interview is a privilege. A veteran newspaper-man, Woody is far more than just chief photographer and picture editor—he is also a consummate, committed and total community journalist. He understands his people and what they need, and he knows how to treat real people. Long before a camera ever comes out of his bag, Woody is talking, being neighborly, asking questions, telling the curious who he is and why he is here—but mostly asking questions and making new friends at every turn.

Covering a tobacco auction in rural North Carolina, photographer Woody Marshall sits close and listens carefully and with respect as 80-year-old tobacco farmer Russell Simpson talks about his life.

Today the assignment is to capture the mood and color of a fall tobacco auction in the small North Carolina Piedmont town of Reidsville, just up the highway from the Burlington *Times-News*, where Woody worked at the time. He has found out who's in charge of the morning auction at the Smothers Auction Warehouse and is establishing himself on a human level with the management, the buyers and the farmers alike.

"How long you been growing tobacco?" "Where's your farm?" "How's the crop?" "What do you expect to get this year?" "Really? That much?" "That's pretty good, isn't it?"

Woody scribbles notes quickly on a traditional, narrow reporter's notepad, while maintaining eye contact much of the time. Then, 20 minutes into the event, he sees something he can't not shoot, and out comes the Nikon. Yet with this, Woody doesn't abandon his role as reporter, as human—just to take pictures.

It's difficult to say what he's doing at any given time, for Woody is shooting, talking and writing so fluidly that the three activities appear to be the same physical act. In a word, his work is seamless.

Woody possesses, or has refined, the rare gift of being everywhere at once, while being virtually invisible. He is clearly a man in his element—now here, throwing himself on a tobacco bale for a low-angle shot—now there, dashing up a pile of tobacco bales for a high-angle shot.

Not surprisingly, he has worked himself into a towering sweat. His wet shirt flops open in front and clings to his back. Even the svelte, imperturbable auctioneer appears awed by Woody's efforts.

"Man's workin' his ass off," he comments with genuine admiration.

Woody, whose sweat-soaked hair is standing as stubble straight as a new-mown hayfield, confides with a rueful grin, "I'm having too good a time."

Two hours later, Woody has a notepad full of notes and a camera full of images. Is it any wonder that the final result is rich and fulfilling, for journalist and subjects alike? His photos accompany a story that starts like this:

> It might be the last days of a dying weed, but you'd never know it at Smothers Warehouse on auction day.
>
> Tobacco, which has taken its lumps, is still king at this family run operation in Reidsville. Each fall the old steel-sided warehouse resounds with the musical chant of the auctioneer as the season's tobacco is graded, sold, baled and shipped.
>
> Everybody at Smothers seems to be either chewing, smoking, breathing, buying or selling tobacco, the golden weed which today seems anything but deadly. Indeed, here, it feels life-sustaining. Across the brick front of the warehouse, the nickname speaks volumes, "The Money Box."
>
> Inside the cavernous building, illuminated only by open doors, dusty skylights and a lone, frail incandescent bulb far in the back, a ritual as old as the Old North State is played out. It is a feast for the senses. . . .

The Tough Ones

The school board chairman accused of plagiarizing a commencement address. The grieving mother of a 17-year-old all-American boy killed in a car accident when alcohol was ruled a factor. How does the conscientious community journalist handle these difficult or at times contentious interviews?

- Be There in Person: Unless you know the person you're interviewing pretty well, the first rule for the difficult interview is to do it in person. Do not use the phone, and above all, do not expect an e-mail interview to work. You need to suck it up and show your face. Eye contact, the personal approach and the fact that you took the trouble to physically come to your subject for the interview— all are critical dynamics of getting a decent interview out of a difficult situation. Of course it's easier to hide behind your phone, but this is how we do it in community journalism.
- Be Honest: Kirk Ross suggests leveling with the interviewee with something like this: "Look, I know this isn't easy, and it's not going to be fun for either of us, but if we could just go through this step by step, it'll be over soon. Now if you could just help me reconstruct how . . ."
- Be Observant: In the contentious interview, watch for what Ross calls the "Urk Response," as in when he asks a tough question and the subject breaks eye contact and gulps before answering. That's when Ross says he knows he's on to something; the subject is probably hedging, lying or covering up.

- Be a Human: Find out about the case before you go blundering in asking insensitive questions for which the media are universally reviled: "How do you feel about the death of your son," etc.

Winthrop University journalism professor Larry Timbs tells of the reporter at a 34,000-circulation chain-owned paper who phoned the mother of the "17-year-old, all-American boy from a good home with the million-dollar smile" who had just been killed when thrown from his vehicle. The highway patrol said alcohol had been a factor in the accident, and the boy was underage.

Timbs says the mother was not aware of the alcohol factor until the reporter who called her for her reaction told her over the phone. Of course the distraught mother was too upset to continue the interview.

Timbs says readers were irate when the paper published the story about the alcohol connection. Even the preacher who did the funeral bashed the paper from the pulpit for predatory reporting that re-victimized the victims.

Timbs notes that it is a disturbing fact of human nature that "bodies stacked like cordwood in Rwanda don't elicit cries of protest, but [a case like this] closer to home does."

In response, Timbs says the paper's editor tried explaining in a column that they were just trying to do their job, that the problem of underage drinking and teen traffic deaths is a real one; also that the paper had waited 20 hours before phoning the family—and that the reporter had *not* known that the family was unaware of the alcohol factor.

Should the reporter have had more background? Should the reporter have asked for a face-to-face interview? Should the paper have published the alcohol connection? Yes to all three.

An in-person interview by an informed and compassionate reporter would have conveyed the human side of the newspaper to the grieving family—what media ethicist Donald Shriver calls "being human to other humans." And perhaps an on-site personal interview would have tipped the reporter off to the mother's ignorance, thus entirely avoiding the insensitive blunder.

However, publishing the facts surrounding the case is another matter. The newspaper of record is bound to print the full story in this case. But even this could have been softened by a community journalist's personal touch during that interview. The family deserved to know before the story went to print. In the words of South Dakota weekly publisher Tim Waltner, "We have to be hard-nosed but softhearted."

Hey, Kid, This Is Off the Record

It's happened to every reporter. You're in an interview with someone; you've worked so hard to get access and establish rapport; and now you're really rolling. Suddenly, your interview subject says the dreaded "this is off the record," and proceeds to tell you the greatest story before you can think of something creative to say to stop him. And if you did stop him, wouldn't that anger him and derail the interview? And by just sitting there listening, haven't you implicitly agreed to the conditions of nonuse?

In a community journalism setting, you have.

At many large papers, the reporter might use the off-the-record material without a second thought. So what if the subject feels betrayed? He said it, didn't he? Besides, in a city of half a million, you'll never see him again. And just let him try to get past security downstairs.

But the whole issue of "off the record" in the community journalism context is made more complex by the inherent just-us-folks-good-ol'-boy nature of small-town life, where word is bond.

Be forewarned. Just because you may be buddies with your subject doesn't give him the right to jerk you around journalistically. The great danger is that you will let yourself be used because of your ongoing friendship with many of the people you interview.

If you sit there and let Bubba tell his great story, which he thinks is off the record, and then you print it, you'll risk destroying not only a friendship, but also that source, that link to the community. And remember, in the community setting, there are just so many people you can alienate before you've got the whole place angry at you. You can bet he'll tell everybody you broke a confidence and that the *Bugle* can't be trusted. Worse yet, he'll claim he never said any of what you've reported and that you made it all up.

The recommended time-honored practice in community journalism is this: Respectfully stop your subject the moment he utters the expression "off the record," and tell him politely you respect his right to ask for that status. However, if it's controversial, you'd just as soon he didn't tell you anything at all, because if it's a big deal, you're bound to find out about it from some other source soon enough anyway. In many cases, that independent stance will prompt the source to go on the record after all. Because here's the bottom line: Your subject really wants to tell the story.

Next, if the off-the-record segment is simply going to be something the source perceives as slightly embarrassing, you can try for the conditional off-the-record approach. You can say this—again, before the story's been told—"Now, I'll listen to this story, but if it's so great and colorful and contributes to the overall picture of what I think this whole story is about, I may try to convince you to let me use it. OK?" And then let him tell the story. If he still insists on nonuse afterward, you should comply.

For example, a reporter was interviewing an old man from the class of '47 celebrating its 50th anniversary at the local college. The gentleman wanted to go off the record when telling about the wild night he and his college buddies set squealing pigs loose in the hall of the women's dorm and later hauled a World War II jeep up on the library steps. Using the above technique, the reporter was able to convince the old grad to let him use the story. "You're right," the old man replied, laughing. "That was a long time ago. I reckon we're not going to get in trouble now!"

Another way to handle the dilemma is the cop-out technique. In this approach, you stop the person before they go off the record and say you're sorry, but it's against your newspaper's policy to do that, or that you'll have to ask your editor. Sometimes, people want to tell the story so badly that at this point they'll tell it on the record.

And finally, there's "not for attribution," or "deep background" off the record. We usually encounter this situation when dealing with volatile data typical of investigative journalism. "Deep background" means you get your subject to agree that you can use the information so long as you don't reveal the source. However, you must substantiate the information from other sources. Needless to say, this is a dangerous game and should be approached with care and full knowledge and consent of your editor.

From the Trenches

In 1965 I was a green cub reporter, working on my first internship at the *Transylvania Times* in Brevard, N.C. The editor, Johnny Anderson, was using me that summer to do mostly features, which had been my strength on the college newspaper. Fact is, I was the features editor/photo editor at the *Daily Tar Heel* and thought myself a Big Man on Campus at the University of North Carolina at Chapel Hill.

My editor assigned me to go interview some famous out-of-town newspaperman vacationing at a nearby mountain resort. Guy with the odd name of Vermont Connecticut Royster. My editor told me Royster was the editor of the *Wall Street Journal*. Oh yeah, I thought to myself, that's the paper with no pictures.

I drove up to the Sapphire Inn, found a chair in the lobby where we were to meet, and presently a short, white-haired, no-nonsense man in a gray tweed suit strode in, shook my hand, and sat down. I started asking questions, but he stopped me quickly.

"Son," he asked, "have you ever read my paper?"

"Well—no," I admitted weakly.

"Interview terminated," he said, looking me right in the eye, and then he got up and strode back out of the room. I returned to the newspaper office in shame.

Twenty years later, teaching journalism at UNC–Chapel Hill, I found myself in the cap-and-gown line at commencement beside a short, white-haired, no-nonsense man whom fate had put there also as a visiting lecturer.

"You don't remember me, do you, Mr. Royster," I said.

"Ohhh, yes I do," he said, winking up at me.

You see, no matter how vaunted my career had been since that time, to him I would always be the boy who didn't do his homework before the interview.

Have you ever noticed how many people read their favorite news magazine backward? After glancing at the front page or cover, they automatically flip right to the back page—thus negating all that neat, well-thought-out graphic design packaging.

Are people being just plain perverse, or might not such a skewed reading practice reveal something deeper about the reading public?

What's going on here if it's not the readers trying to find a trace of something human and personal before they're ready to take on the burden of hard news in the front? Designers at *Time* and *Newsweek* got the message, and the current design features lighter, more accessible human interest packaging at the front of the magazine. Perhaps the publishers have even hired consultants and pollsters to ascertain whether this reformatting has converted the backward-reading subscribers.

You can count on it—people thirst for the human touch. That touch has made people their careers. If the great American humorist and humanist Will Rogers had published a newspaper, you can bet it would have been a community newspaper, one with the common touch.

The late CBS newsman Charles Kuralt, who raised the news feature–gathering-by-wandering technique to a fine art with his celebrated *On the Road* series in the '60s, was one of the few people in the national media who proved to be a community journalist at heart. In fact, he was doing "his people" features at the Charlotte *News* in the mid-'50s, well before he achieved national recognition. What he called "innocent little features," vignettes of real people we'd never heard of but who were out there living decent, honest, productive and authentic lives along the back roads of America, ultimately said positive things about a nation and a people in need of an encouraging word. Are we not in such times now?

What Kuralt called simply "neighborliness" informed his journalist's knowledge that there were no taxpayers, no consumers, no homeowners, no homeless, no voters—but only people. Kuralt's secret for success—his sheer love of people, his faith in the essential dignity of every person—is central to what makes community journalism viable.

The enlightened community journalist embraces Kuralt's philosophy, and takes it a step further, concluding that there are no readers but only people, that *people* are what matter.

And people love a rattling good yarn.

THE POWER OF THE ANECDOTE

The weekly editor had been asked to give an after-dinner speech to a year-end awards banquet honoring the high school yearbook, newspaper and literary magazine staffs and their parents.

Driving to the high school, he sighed, thinking about the cafeteria rubber chicken and dutiful but probably bored parents and what he'd say about his assigned topic:

Celebrating the ordinary: The everyday rituals of small-town and family life need never be boring. These are the enduring themes. A great-grandmother recites "This little piggy . . ." as the enthralled toddler listens in rapt attention, a drool forming on his chin. You too are in the storytelling business. And if you get to take the photo, remember, the best ones are unposed and unstaged.

What Journalism Has Meant To Me. It was like having to pick your own form of execution—no way to cram all that in 20 minutes. What could he say that would make any difference to these budding writers?

Stopping at the Boone's Convenience Corner, the editor went in for a cold soft drink—what old-timers in that region still called "a sodey-dope." Standing there wondering if he should get a pack of Nabs as well, he could not help but overhear a local fisherman telling the patient clerk "how to cook a carp."

"You go out in th' spring-uh-th'-year and you catch you a carp," the old gentleman delivered the formula with a straight face. "Then you go home, roll him in cornmeal and butter and you fry him up good till he's nice and brown." The fisherman looked up from his story to see if the clerk and the journalist were paying proper attention to the fine details of his recipe.

"Then you throw away the carp—and eat the cornbread!" he finished with a flourish, while his audience groaned with appreciation.

That's when it hit the editor: What's the basic unit of exchange for the human race? Is it dollars, yen or the euro? No, it's *words*. And writing is the word made permanent. People who know how to skillfully mold and string words together effectively—they are the wordwrights, the wordsmiths, the real power brokers in our society.

And what had he just witnessed at the little country store? A basic transaction as old as humankind itself, the simple yet pervasive act of storytelling.

Everybody who writes at all for newspapers, magazines, the electronic media—be they obituary writers, beat reporters, advertising copy writers, creative feature writers or artistic poets—their basic unit of measure is the story. How well they choose their words and paint their pictures determines how effectively they communicate.

SHOW, DON'T TELL

Gene Roberts, the former managing editor of the *New York Times*, likes to tell how Henry Belk, his mentor and the former editor of the then 8,000-circulation daily Goldsboro (N.C.) *News-Argus*, used to edit copy. Because Belk was blind, Roberts would have to read his stories out loud to the old editor.

Blind Henry Belk would sit there in his big oak armchair, head titled back, the warm humid air blowing in off the city square, and Gene would read his pieces aloud. Gene wrote the farm column, "Rambling in Rural Wayne." And if a story didn't work or didn't suit old Henry Belk, he'd cry out loud, "Make me see it, Gene! Make me see it!"

Too often, beginning writers assume the reader knows all about the story and can see the people in the story just as clearly as does the writer. But this is not the case. Pretend you're writing for old blind Henry Belk, our visiting speaker told those kids at the awards banquet. He said if you want your writing to come alive, assume your readers are blind and you have describe the whole scene from scratch—foreground, background, atmosphere, mood, lighting, as well as the characters with all their details and differences. Don't talk *about* the subject; immerse the reader in the experience. Consider the old Spanish proverb: *To talk about bulls is not the same thing as being in the bullring.*

What other writing tips had our editor and after-dinner speaker gleaned from over two decades in the trenches of community journalism?

DON'T FORGET FOR WHOM YOU'RE WRITING

In journalism the term "human interest" has become so overworked that it's all but lost its meaning. To some, the term has a definite pejorative ring to it—connoting a soft filler story or a feature denigrated as "fluff." These same folks would never suppose that human interest had any place in a news story. But in community journalism, if a news story, a feature, even a commentary or an editorial doesn't have some element of human interest, then it's missing the key to connecting with the reader.

High-paid consultants who help business, industry and education leaders with "strategic long-range planning sessions" take executives into brainstorming think tanks where they engage in hours of corporate soul-searching. The consultants challenge the leaders to identify deceptively simple elements of their businesses such as "Who are our customers?"

That's a useful question for community newspapers writers to ponder.

What are we writing about and for whom—if not human interest and people?

Perhaps next to cats and chimpanzees, humans are the most curious species out there. We have an insatiable curiosity about each other. Dennis Gildea, a journalism professor at Springfield College in Massachusetts, says that the *Weekly World News* has a lot to teach mainstream American journalists about human interest.

To paraphrase Gildea, just watch the eyes and face of any supermarket shopper waiting in the checkout line. Confronted with racks of baby-making aliens, re-appearing dead Elvises and gay Wild Bill Hickocks, the shoppers who might never dream of buying a *National Enquirer*, *Star* or *Weekly World News* still stare trans-fixed at the silly covers. Gildea wonders, why is that, if not sheer curiosity about our own humankind?

OTHER WRITING TIPS

The KISS rule: Write to inform, not to impress. Remember Fozz E. Bear. Get on the stage, do your bit, and get off. There's nothing worse than being held captive by a meandering after-dinner speaker enamored by the sound of his own voice. The old curmudgeons in the balcony are likely to start yammering insults at you. Get off the stage, Fozz E. Bear.

And since readers aren't held captive at all, you have nothing with which to hold them except the power of your words. You can't assume they're going to stay with you from line to line; they're free to bolt at the first hint of boredom. After all, there's always *Dilbert*.

Use imagery; appeal to the five senses. Show, don't tell. An apple that is bright red, taut-skinned and juicy is an apple that fairly leaps off the page.

Quest for brevity. Eschew obfuscation. Don't be very very redundant. Get a copy of Strunk and White's *The Elements of Style*. That's the writer's bible.

Use it or lose it. A good writer is like an athlete. A runner who runs regularly, a tennis player who practices three times a week, or a basketball player who is constantly shooting hoops steadily improves. The same with a writer. Work out. Write often. Do windsprints on paper. Work on your serve and delivery. No one ever said writing was easy. Folks who pump iron say, "No pain, no gain." Folks who pump keys agree.

Good writing is hard work, says nationally syndicated columnist Leonard Pitts Jr. Speaking to a gathering of journalists, the 2004 Pulitzer Prize winner for commentary quipped, "Now on some days, the ceiling parts, there's shaft of white light and the voice of God says, 'You type; I'll dictate.' Those are the best, but they don't happen often enough." Most of the time, Pitt asserts, "You apply the seat of the pants to the seat of the chair and you hammer at it." And he adds, "Writing well is hard. I have come to respect sweat."

WE AIN'T GOT TIME FOR WRITER'S BLOCK

So you don't know where to begin? You think you've got a case of writer's block?

Years ago, Mark West worked as a summer intern at the Asheville, N.C., *Citizen*. West remembers having trouble on a story with the deadline close at hand. He was just sitting there gazing at his computer when veteran city editor Jay Hensley approached and asked what was the problem. West explained that he had writer's block—to which Hensley announced to the entire newsroom with a mocking, piteous wail: "*Oh my goodness gracious! Mr. West has writer's block!*"

"Mr. West," now a respected journalism professor (and author!) in his own right, says that that experience cured him instantly and forever. Since then, mysteriously, he has never had a reoccurrence of the fashionable writers' ailment.

Which is to say, if the beginning has you stumped, just start where it seems logical and forge ahead. The point is to get started. What will almost always happen is that once you get going, without even knowing it, you will write the beginning somewhere else in the story. This is something you can count on; the beginning will reveal itself to you. It's called the Eureka Factor. Cut and paste the lead at the top. Et voilà!

Get tight with your dictionary (not just Spellcheck). And by the way, as wonderful as Google is, don't ever count on Google as a source for accurate spelling. Beware homonyms: "site," "cite" and "sight" are all perfectly good words; but which is which? Learn your "its" and "it's" and "theirs" and "there's." Learn to spell. Expand your vocabulary. Read voraciously. Learn to listen well and pay attention. Very little happens in the course of the day that is not somehow significant to or fodder for a writer.

It's just like the old J-school admonitions said: *Your Copy Ain't Holy* and *Good Writing Is Rewriting*. Read your stuff out loud. If your writing sounds stilted or pontifical, then it's awk. And that's not a nearly extinct species of New Zealand bird. An awk is that little red squiggle English teachers and editors scrawl in the margin when your writing goes clunk. The fact that awkward sentences are almost always the result of a passive verb formation is something about which you can do. See? Wasn't that terrible? Try this: Passive verb formations create awkward sentences.

The fix: write in the active voice. Avoid the "to be" verb in its many forms. Instead, use action verbs.

Give yourself permission—permission to be bold, to be creative, to have fun with words, and to make mistakes. You can always go back later and clean it up. Write fearlessly. Writing that sings won't come if you're filled with anxiety and fear of rejection and failure. Forgive yourself in advance. Get jacked up. Football teams aren't the only ones who need cheering. Instead of *Go! Fight! Win!*, how about *Go!*

Fight! Write! Say to yourself, "Hey, I may be only human, and I'm gonna goof up occasionally. But not right now. Right now, I'm gonna knock their socks off. I'm gonna make old Henry Belk see it."

And that's exactly what the editor told the young writers. He told them to go out there and knock the socks off their readers. As he finished and looked out at his audience of a hundred or so people, he saw in some of those fresh young faces that they had listened, and amid the sea of dull faces wanting to get home to Gameboy or *South Park*, some eyes were shining.

Other Voices; Other Newsrooms: The Lesson of Hue

Remember Gene Roberts, the young reporter who wrote the farm column, "Rambling in Rural Wayne," for blind Henry Belk's Goldsboro *News-Argus*?

Roberts had a couple of other lessons to learn—about reader loyalty and the power of community journalism—though he had to go to the Vietnam War to learn them.

In 1968, more than 10 years after leaving the *News-Argus*, Roberts was sent to Vietnam as a war correspondent for the *New York Times*. During the height of the Tet offensive, he found his way to the embattled city of Hue, the scene of the most intense, street-to-street fighting. One day, he went to interview beleaguered U.S. troops dug deep in an underground bunker. He introduced himself, "My name is Gene Roberts. I'm with the *New York Times*..."

But out of the gloom Roberts heard a soldier's voice with a distinctive twang.

"Hey!" the soldier exclaimed. "Did you ever write the 'Rambling in Rural Wayne' in the Goldsboro *News-Argus*?"

Looking back on that experience, Roberts chuckles. He may have been a big-time war correspondent for the vaunted *New York Times*, but what impressed that soldier in the bunker in Hue was Roberts' farm column in an 8,000-circulation community newspaper in the rural South. No matter the size, it was the soldier's hometown paper, a thing of inestimable value.

"I learned valuable lessons from the *News-Argus* and my tobacco farmer readers," says Roberts, who now teaches journalism at the University of Maryland. "Because I was linked closely to events that were important to farm families, I—and what I wrote—became important to readers in a way that I never was, before or since."

Your Town; Your Turn

1. Go to the local greasy spoon, the town's favorite café or coffee shop. Find a story with human interest there. You have 90 minutes.

2. Pick a person at random right now. Be like Yogi Berra, who said: "You can

observe a lot just by watching." Study her eyes, hands, mouth, hair, walk, clothes, how she "looks out of her face." Take notes and write about it.

3. Pick an impersonal prune of a story from the last front page of your newspaper and find a new human interest angle.

4. Reconstruct the scene of your last interview. Where did you stage it? How did location affect the outcome?

5. Arrange to do a feature story interview "on location." After determining that the source has ample time available, make a point to just visit at first; don't take any notes or photos for at least 30 minutes. See how it feels.

6. Remember your worst interview experience, the Interview from Hell. How could you have strengthened the interview or saved the situation?

ELEVEN

It Used to Be Called the Women's Page

Vital Ingredients

So you're thinking of starting a community paper, or buying one, or taking one over. You go over your inventory of expertise and equipment: business manager, ad reps, news editor, reporters, computers, cameras, a press or someone to print the paper . . . what else?

But wait, your paper is missing a vital ingredient. Without one of these you might as well not even turn on the press.

You need a Virginia.

Forgive the first person, but it would be impossible to talk about the growth, development and success of any community paper with which I've ever been involved without saying up front that the old-fashioned "women's editor" can make all the difference.

When my partners and I started our first paper in 1969, we were blessed by great kind fortune to have secured the services of Virginia Rucker, the former "society editor" of our competition, the cross-town Forest City (N.C.) *Courier*. I was a mere 24, and Virginia, at 55, seemed to me a virtual ancient. Looking at the situation 37 years later, I can only imagine what she thought of the still wet-behind-the-ears kid trying desperately to act

like a co-editor (and for the duration of this chapter I simply refuse to call her just "Rucker").

Virginia never let on. She gently guided me, celebrated my little creative triumphs, discussed spelling and grammar in a nonjudgmental fashion, and shared in the paper's dynamic growth. I can see now that much of the reason for *THIS WEEK*'s success was due to this wise woman's fine touch. Her grace under pressure provided us all with the lesson of her example. In short, she brought continuity and class to our paper. By the sheer dint of good work over time, she endeared herself—and by extension, the paper—to the community.

Until 1998 she was still at that old golden oak desk, pecking away at a typewriter (never a computer) with that ever-present and never-ending sheaf of AP paper feeding up from a box on the floor. To my eye, Virginia didn't look a day older than she did in March 1969. The only thing different was her current Atlanta Braves poster and season schedule tacked to the wall behind her. Though *THIS WEEK* had become the *Daily Courier* (now owned by the Paxton Media Group, Inc.) and Virginia was called an associate editor, the old society editor was still a die-hard Braves fan.

They don't call women like Virginia "steel magnolias" for nothing. Her influence in the newsroom was subtle but pervasive.

Virginia is famous for her gracious nature, but she also knows how to get the best out of the photographer who may accompany her on assignment. I should know; when I was shooting something for Virginia, she used to give me kindly but very specific directions, which I had to grudgingly admit resulted in better photos and a better package.

But for some young hotshots right out of J-school, it's not easy learning to take directions from what may appear to be a little old gray-haired lady.

Case in point: A former U.S. Navy commander had retired to his home village, and in the process of helping restore the tiny community, he had uncovered an old monument of historic importance. Virginia wanted a photo of the man with the monument. But what she got from her photographer was a mugshot. Just a shot of the man. No monument.

"That's not the way I wanted it," she told the photographer, and she proceeded to read him the riot act: "Now, you're there to help me tell the story, and you've got to put in the picture what I tell you. With my other photographers, I could get what I wanted."

"Well," the photographer retorted, "they weren't *artistic*."

Virginia recalls, "I said, 'Ho-ho-HO! That won't do at all!'"

And she marched the young photographer into the editor's office where they had a word of prayer.

After that, the quality of the photography improved noticeably.

But This Is the 21st Century, Isn't It?

You'll find places in these United States where they still call her that—the women's editor or the society editor (as if men weren't members of that august body we deem "society")—and the page might be called something anachronistic such as the "Distaff Side."

Somewhere along in the '70s, most papers caught up with society and retooled these pages or sections under thinly disguised monikers, such as "Lifestyle," "Style" or "Family."

Stories about weddings, engagements, anniversaries, fashion, births, child raising, women's health, home, food and cooking used to be the staples in an age that seems quaint and sexist to us now. While that lineup may still be found at many newspapers, others have expanded the vision to include stories on societal trends, the changing role of the sexes in general and women in particular, and issues in family life such as child abuse, father absenteeism, and aging and health care.

Example: Virginia did a series of stories and photos depicting how local elderly on fixed incomes in a modest retirement community had gone about making their homes reflect their individual tastes and values. The overall effect of the series

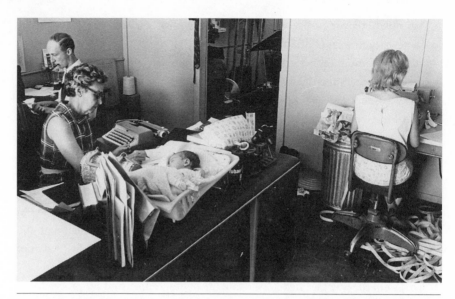

Handling the weddings, engagements and society news, Virginia Rucker works in the tiny newsroom of *THIS WEEK* in 1969, sharing the space with the typesetter, co-editor Ron Paris and the sleeping infant daughter of the other co-editor.

convincingly showed readers that they could do quite a lot at a minimal expenditure using mostly imagination and flair.

Also, you'll still find papers that haven't figured out what to do with community arts coverage, and so by default have given this beat to the "women's page," because historically manly men weren't supposed to be sensitive and artistic; that was a girl thing. So such coverage traditionally was relegated to women's editors. It wasn't until the late '60s that many community newspapers woke up to the silly imbalance. The resulting expansion of coverage has changed the face of community newspapers. However, weddings, club news, engagements and "society" still need and deserve coverage in community newspapers.

So how did the women's movement affect community journalism?

Ask Virginia. She's been in the business for 60-plus years.

Other Voices; Other Newsrooms

When Virginia started at the old Forest City Courier *in March 1945, it wasn't even called "Women's News." Her page was called "Society." Here she recalls what her job entailed.*

Before It Was Women's News It Was Society

Large papers didn't use all the stuff (I use the word advisedly) that I did: circle meetings, bridge club meetings, and personals—I phoned various women I knew and they told me of people from their neighborhood, or their relatives, who had been on trips—even to Charlotte or Spartanburg (30 to 50 miles away). A trip abroad was outstanding.

And the Society Editor was a person to respect back in those days. It would be nice to have a little bit of that nowadays.

Women phoned me, any day or time, to ask my advice. Usually, the caller did not identify herself, but society was so much more structured in those days she did not want—heaven forbid—to arrive at a party and find she was the only woman in the room wearing a hat.

Whether to wear a hat or carry gloves was the burning issue of the day. Where to seat guests for a wedding rehearsal dinner was another. One of my favorites was the woman (anonymous) who phoned to inquire if her daughter should be allowed to wear eye make-up to high school.

I skirted that diplomatically until she finally asked: Would you? I told her I wouldn't (back then it was worn only to dances or night parties), but if her friends were wearing it, she (the mother) might as well acquiesce. In a triumphant voice, she said: "I told her you wouldn't wear it." Which gave another disgruntled young girl reason to dislike that Society Editor.

Gradually times changed and women changed. The cleanest house, the highest risen cake on the block became unimportant, and the word Society fell into disrepute. And, in this area at least, old families, proper manners gave way to Money and show of same.

And at age 80, I have reached the point in life where I can sit back and observe the foibles and changes with amusement, acceptance and, finally, have gotten off my charger ready to change the world. It's been a relief but a lot less fun.

Writing in 1992, Virginia contemplated how the changing times had impacted on the society editor. Here are her observations:

If you read many newspapers you're sure to notice the change in reporting over the years. Nowhere does it show up more vividly than in wedding write-ups.

Forty years ago we described the potted palms in great detail, what music was played and what the bride's and groom's mothers wore.

Somebody must have decided back then that no wedding was legal unless "O Promise Me" was sung. I welcomed the day when that changed, but surely using "We've Only Just Begun" in a religious ceremony was no improvement.

Some papers (not ours) wrote about the "radiant" bride and every detail of the ceremony—anything the bride's mother wanted, even if it included saying the wedding dress was trimmed in one thousand pearls. And mothers threatened the "society editor" with disaster if she didn't use the picture above the fold of the newspaper.

Enterprise at 85

One of my favorite "Virginia stories" comes from some years back when she was a mere 85, and still writing one or two large features each month for the B—or second—front. She was so well networked in the county and her nose for a story is so sharp that finding stories was no problem.

For instance, through a conversation with a friend she discovered that the local bookstore owner had built a whimsical tree house for himself and his expectant wife. The tree house perched up there in the tree, all gingerbread, glass and gables, looked fit for a spread in *Better Homes and Gardens*. At 85, Virginia clambered up a ladder because she had to see inside that tree house to get the story.

After 50 years of covering the same patch of ground in Rutherford County, you have to wonder, how on earth can she keep coming up with fresh story ideas?

"Well they *jump* at you, honey," Virginia declared with a merry smile. "Of *course* they do!"

Time to Go

In the fall of 1998, when it became clear that the new owners of her newspaper were requiring that she make the transition from typewriter to computer, Virginia decided it was time to step down—at least in part. She was not about to put herself through the nearly vertical learning curve of grappling with a computer for the first time at age 85.

In her final column she reflected:

Today I officially leave a job I've had for 50 years—50 years of learning, of challenge, and rewards. It was the only job I ever wanted and it was even more fulfilling than I could possibly imagine.

It has been the best of both worlds,—meeting people whom I would never have met otherwise: from governors to the jobless—both of which had fascinating stories of how they arrived there; seeing the interior of homes that ranged from starkly modern to those filled with century-old family treasures; being impressed at the range of local talent in the fields of arts, crafts, music, writing. . . .

I learned the operation of various government agencies while attending city council, school board and county commission meetings, and occasionally was so bored I resorted to knitting sweaters during these sessions, which prompted a spectator to comment at the close of one that I was the only person who had accomplished anything all day.

And there was the fun of feeling free, as a reporter, to ask questions I might otherwise not have asked and sometimes acquiring information I could never divulge.

But when it comes down to the crux, the really important thing, it was

She may not be climbing treehouses at 92, but Virginia Rucker still writes for the paper from home. And yes, she still uses her faithful old typewriter.

the people. Regardless of their status—the wealthy, the poor, the educated, the illiterate—they were what made my job a joy. . . .

So why am I quitting? Age—mine and the technological. I haven't the skill to use a computer and this is an age when virtually everything in our business is done on them, and here I am, pounding away on my Royal typewriter. I know I often slow the process and I am unwilling to work unless I can do my share. . . .

After a rest . . . I will take [the new publisher] up on his gracious offer to write an occasional article.

So this is not a total goodbye. I'll still be around to misspell your name, incorrectly report the color of your draperies and ask you impertinent questions.

Not So Fast . . .

More than sixty years. That's got to be some kind of record. Virginia, 92 as this edition goes to press, started to work at the Forest City *Courier* in March 1945, and she's still at it.

In a recent column, titled "Salmagundi" (i.e., a mixture), she reflected on her 50-plus years behind the typewriter, noting that when the newspaper was sold to the Paxton Media Group in 1998, the former owners "probably told the news owners that I went with the building—along with the Goss press . . .

"These years have been what everyone needs in their job: fun, exciting, challenging, only occasionally discouraging and an enormous help through some painful personal times in my life.

"I continue to love my work though my ability has decreased considerably . . ." Maybe she's not climbing into tree houses anymore; nevertheless, her Sunday "Spotlight" features still take the pulse of Rutherford County: a local couple who went to China to adopt a baby; a new priest and first woman rector of the local Episcopal church; a local author who opened an Irish pub downtown; the 30th anniversary celebration of a local church for mentally and physically handicapped people.

You Gotta Have Lifestyle

The reporting of some lifestyle stories may not seem to vary so much between large metropolitan dailies and community papers. But when it comes to old-fashioned women's news, there is a vast difference in the two types of newspapers.

In community journalism, reporting of weddings and the like, though, as Virginia observes, pared down over the years, is still vital and given ample spread. The two-column photo and 14-inch story is common. By contrast, many major big-city papers, if they even run weddings at all, either give them short shrift (a three-inch story wrapped around a photo not much larger than some postage stamps) or charge money for running the couple's photo.

Virginia notes, "Now, city papers often have a standard report, using only the couple's name, when and where the ceremony was held and parents' names. And some metropolitan papers, surprisingly, report on the parents' occupations."

From a sheer commonsense standpoint, there's the paper's reason for supporting a strong lifestyle section. The enlightened publisher will realize that a great lifestyle section is another way the community paper can distinguish itself and thus distance itself from any big-city dailies trying to compete—either directly or indirectly (with "Neighbors" editions). If your paper doesn't already have such an editor, it ought to be looking for someone like Virginia Rucker, who can provide the community paper with a valuable perspective, years of continuity and quality reporting with the personal touch.

Paid or Free?

OBITS, WEDDINGS, ENGAGEMENTS, ANNIVERSARIES ARE NEWS TOO

Twenty years ago most community newspapers would never have considered requiring a payment from the reader for publication of obituaries, weddings, engagements and anniversaries (and accompanying photos); that was just a part of the community news that a good community paper covered.

That was then, and this is now. The trend nowadays (which some critics would call "disturbing") is away from the free obituary, wedding announcement, or other notice toward what media managers call "a new revenue stream."

It's reasonable to ask: Why group obituaries with "Lifestyle" items when they're usually handled editorially by different departments? Because anecdotal research suggests that if there's a charge for one, there's a charge for all others. So it's a top-down decision made by management to increase the bottom line. Or not. Some editors and publishers say leaving those items free is a public service and simply "the right thing to do."

Whether charging for what was traditionally free is a result of increased chain ownership or just plain hard times in a post-9/11 world is difficult to say. In a poll done in 2004 by my students, several editor-publishers justified the practice with a thinly disguised rationale: "Well, we charge less than the big guys [the nearby major metro daily]." Others contended it's just a matter of pure business: "Whatever the market will bear," and, "These are hard times; we'll do whatever it takes to float the boat . . ."

Indeed, one daily editor who only months earlier had vehemently vowed to keep the practice free reported to his chagrin that his publisher had changed his tune. And, indeed, the trend toward charging for these previously free services seems to be growing.

However, there are notable holdouts who say they recognize their duty to remain true to what they consider a veritable community covenant: that charging money for such stories and photos amounts to price gouging. After all, a typical mother, regardless of her ability to pay, will do practically anything to get her daughter's engagement and/or wedding photo and write-up in the paper.

CHARGING FOR NEWS

Virginia Rucker makes no bones about her views. "I don't think they should charge for that because that's news too. You don't think a wedding is news?! Yeah! And an obituary? Certainly! It *is* news when people die or get married!"

However, Virginia fears a "creeping charge" tactic in which newspapers start inching toward charging for more information while printing less for free. But the rate increase is implemented at such an incremental pace that the public at large doesn't notice. Virginia's *Daily Courier*, a 10,000-circulation Paxton Media Group paper, has a largely free policy.

Editor Neal Rattican of the Roxboro (N.C.) *Courier=Times* told community journalism student S. B. Miller: "People ought to have their names in the paper three times: when they're born, when they get married, and when the die—and they shouldn't have to pay for it." Rattican says that death is news, and charging for obits is "real close to selling the news." The *Courier=Times* is an 8,500-circulation family-owned semiweekly.

"Free—the dress and all," says Whiteville *News Reporter* editor Les High of the policy used by the family-owned 10,213-circulation semiweekly. "We don't let them take up the whole page—but whatever they want to put in (within reason) is fine." And his father, publisher Jim High, adds, "And the same goes for obits, too."

Forest City, N.C., town planner Danielle Withrow says the stakes are even higher than some publishers might realize. "It's civic responsibility," she asserts. There's a moral imperative for printing obituaries for free as a matter of public record, she says, noting that obituaries are critical for those doing genealogical research. Withrow, an advisory board member of the Carolina Community Media Project, says she was able to trace her family line by going through old obituaries that gave her the vital clues to finding her birth mother.

Several editors and publishers expressed the fear that their bosses higher up, especially in a chain ownership setting, will someday mandate a fee-based policy. Owner Scott Hinkle of the Lake Norman *Times*, a weekly in partnership with the Womack group of Virginia, told journalism student Laura Webb, "I'm going to fight that as long as I can. I believe the passing of a human life is news, no matter what they did."

THE SURVEY

When in the spring of 2004 my journalism students at the University of North Carolina at Chapel Hill polled 53 (29 percent) of the state's 182 community newspapers on the fee issue, they divided respondents into "free," "paid" or "mixed" policies. The survey revealed that 68 percent of the papers surveyed had had a "free, within reason" policy (including free photos). Here's how the results broke down:

Free: Of the "free" category, 83 percent were weeklies, with ownership split almost evenly between the chain-owned and independents. Of the six "free" dailies, only one was an indy while five were chain-owned (but note that four of those five dailies belong to "small group" chains).

Paid: Out of the papers polled, 10 (19 percent) were classified as "paid" and were made up overwhelmingly (80 percent) by chain-owned papers, of which 75 percent were dailies.

Mixed: Of the papers surveyed, seven (13 percent) had a "mixed" policy. For example, they might have free obituaries but use a complex pricing structure for stories and photos related to weddings, engagements and anniversaries. Significantly, the papers with a mixed policy were 100 percent chain-owned, four of them being dailies and three weeklies.

Conclusion: Predictably, papers are more apt to charge for obituaries, weddings, engagements and anniversaries if they are chain-owned dailies.

However, the majority (68 percent) of papers surveyed still offer free coverage—with weeklies, regardless of their ownership status, leading the stats.

Maybe it seems like a small thing—charging for items that used to be considered bread-and-butter local news. But this author thinks the trend, like putting ads on the front page, is a marker for the entire community journalism industry—sort of a core sample—and one not to be taken lightly.

Gay Wedding Announcement

You almost have to look twice: The "Lifestyles" page of the *News Leader* of Staunton, Va., Sept. 2, 2001, looks like any other—and then you see the wedding photo. Two guys standing together.

Wagner -Childress

John Franklin Rennie Wagner and Brian Edward Childress

WILLIAMSBURG — John Franklin Rennie Wagner and Brian Edward Childers exchanged vows Aug. 11 in the chapel of the Sir Christopher Wren Building on the campus of the College of William and Mary. A civil union ceremony was conducted March 17 in Manchester, Vt., by Cynthia A. Kilburn, justice of the peace.

Wagner is the son of Jody Wagner of Staunton and the late Franklin Wagner.

Childers is the son of Mr. and Mrs. Steven Childers of Goose Creek, S.C.

The ceremony was officiated by the Rev. Peter Gray. A program of nuptial music was performed by harpist Annie Heckel; organist Tom Marshall; octet, Steven Meeks, Rhonda Miller, Michael Jessup, Andrew Dyer, Rebecca Howell, Scott A. Hearn, Rachel Purver and Virginia MacNemar; and soloists Joel Furtick and Amy Carpenter.

Best men were Mark Childers of Arlington, Childers' brother; and Michael Cole of Gloucester. Maid of honor was Amanda Adair Brown of Brooklyn, N.Y. Attendants included Annie Lorie Wagner of Harrisonburg and Alexis Rennie Sabados of Staunton, Wagner's sisters, and Louis J.

Timmons of Arlington.

Flower girl was Grace Huddleston of Vienna.

A luncheon reception was given by the couple at the Radisson Fort Magruder Hotel in Williamsburg followed by an evening celebration at the same location.

A wedding trip is planned for March to Austria. The couple reside in Arlington.

Wagner is a graduate of Robert E. Lee High School and the College of William and Mary. He is a certified teacher.

Childers is a graduate of Irmo High School in Charleston, S.C. and Tennessee Tech University in Cookeville, Tenn. He is a teacher in Vienna.

The M.E. of the Staunton (Va.) *News Leader* decided the gay wedding announcement should be treated the same as any other wedding story and photo.

After a civil union ceremony in Vermont, the couple wanted a local commitment ceremony back home, complete with story and photo in the paper. Just like any other couple.

David Fritz, managing editor of the *News Leader*, a 20,000-circulation Gannett daily, says that he knew he'd hear from some irate readers in his relatively conservative Shenandoah Valley community, but that he also knew that printing the story and photo was the right thing to do.

Under the headline "Lifestyles pages reflect evolving culture," Fritz explained his reasoning the following week in his "From the Editor" column: "I've had a few discussions with readers this week about our choice to publish an announcement of a gay commitment ceremony in our Lifestyles section last Sunday. While a few were supportive of our decision, more were critical.

"That's not a surprise, really, given the emotions, beliefs and rhetoric that surround homosexuality.

"But when we first received the announcement—the first one like it we've received in my tenure, by the way—we resisted looking at in such cosmic political terms. Instead we approached it as we do most things, by considering it in light of our community role. And we thought in terms of the men in the picture as human beings, not icons.

"Lifestyles pages long have been places were people turned for news of personal milestones. . . . Such announcements aren't Page One news, but I know I would include my engagement, our marriage and the birth of a child on the front page of my life. These are the milestones that bring individual joy, and the types of things we want to share.

"I suspect that same sentiment was behind last Sunday's announcement, but many readers saw only a political element. It's a sign of our polarized times, I suppose.

"Similarly, some folks probably saw politics rather than people when an African-American couple first used our pages to announce a wedding, or when an unmarried parent first used our pages to announce the birth of a child, or when someone submitted the first interracial engagement. Expecting us to keep such personal stories off our pages would be asking us to participate in a deception. . . .

". . . So while the debate no doubt will smolder and occasionally flare up here on the Opinions page, we'll continue to leave the milestones portion of the Lifestyles page open to people who simply want to share their joy. After all, we all need it in our lives."

The following week was 9/11, and Fritz reflects, "The *only* good thing about 9/11 was it gave folks who were griping about [the gay wedding notice] some perspective. The letters and calls dropped off quickly."

And by way of follow-up, Fritz adds, "I had a really nice note from the mother of one of the guys. . . . She was really thankful that we ran it and stood our ground. She also was amazed that my folks took the information and photo without a sideways glance. She came [to the *News Leader*'s office] armed with all sorts of proof of the commitment ceremony, etc., expecting to have to argue her case.

"Never happened. We try to be the entire community's newspaper."

Your Town; Your Turn

1. Examine the lifestyle section in your community newspaper. Does your paper have a Virginia? In your estimation, how could that section be improved?
2. Compare its style of wedding coverage (size of picture, length of story, etc.) with that of the nearby large metropolitan daily. Does your community newspaper charge for this coverage? Why? If it's free, why don't they charge?
3. Talk to the lifestyle editor at your community paper about the changes in that field. If there are men working on the lifestyle section, ask them how they feel about the content and the approach that they have to deal with.

TWELVE

Community Sports
It's Only a Game, Right?

Out at Home

The venue was not exactly what Joe, the new photographer at the *Bugle*, had had in mind. Not exactly Camden Yards or Yankee Stadium.

The grass in center field at the Sandy Run School baseball field was over ankle-deep. The scorekeeper sat on a folding metal chair using a collapsible card table to keep track of the game.

There were no lights. No dugout. No concessions. The field could only be described as marginal for sandlot. The bleachers, if you could call them that, consisted of a grassy hillside, now dotted with parents on quilts and blankets, cheering for a game between the Sandy Run Pirates and the Pleasant Gardens Phillies.

Joe was there on his first assignment with the *Bugle* after graduating from a major university school of communications. He'd even won a Hearst Award his senior year. He was good. He knew it. His professors knew it. The Hearst people knew it. So why was he here today shooting Little League? Didn't they know who he was? And the final insult—his editor even expected him to write the game story. Imagine!

Joe wasn't at all convinced he'd done the right thing settling for this first job with this 8,000-circulation

twice-weekly. He told himself it was the best job he could find at the time. Joe figured he'd put in his time doing what he called "a rural gig," and make his jump as soon as possible to a big, impressive-sounding metro daily. Then he could forget he'd done time in Podunk, U.S.A.

Meanwhile, the game had started. The first batter had walked and was now attempting to steal second. Joe, bored already, watched with his state-of-the-art digital camera hanging listlessly around his neck as the runner arrived safely at second—only to have the looping throw from the catcher strike the boy directly on the top of the head and bounce off comically.

Joe had to keep from laughing out loud as he thought to himself, "These kids don't even know how to play baseball. If I was at a real ball game, I could get some great sports shots."

Soon, a summer shower passed over the little ballpark, halting the game for the duration of the brief downpour, which prompted the scorekeeper to find shelter beneath the card table as he phoned the Rec Department to tell them the game was temporarily delayed. Joe was too busy packing up his cameras to notice. "Man! What a waste of my time," he grumbled to himself as he headed for his car.

Great photos are everywhere, even at a "rural gig." In the community setting, where high school major sports tend to dominate, it's easy to overlook the events that occur off the beaten track. Of course you have to cover the big three: football, basketball and baseball. But don't forget the so-called lesser sports, such as swimming, soccer, cross country, track, rodeo (the list goes on)—all involving hundreds of local young people. What better way to appeal to the kids, reach parents and attract new readers?

Work Where You Work

The ancients have a wise saying that goes something like this: "Eat when you eat; breathe when you breathe; die when you die." Jon Kabat-Zinn's book title catches that Zen essence: *Wherever You Go, There You Are.* It means life is now, in the present, not in the recalled past or the imagined future. You might even condense the above sentiments into "Work where you work."

Right before his very eyes, Joe had the makings of great human interest photos and an entertaining, worthwhile story. But his own attitude blinded him just as surely as if he had his personal lens cap on. And so long as that "baditude" persisted, no fancy equipment made by Nikon, Canon or any other manufacturer could have opened his vision to the value of sports coverage on the community journalism level.

What a waste indeed.

We'll say it once more: Before you go to *Sports Illustrated* or the *Sporting News*, you've got to show your stuff at the Butler *Eagle* or the Cary *News*—"little" papers you may think no one has ever heard of. But ask any great reporter or photographer with *SI*, and they'll tell you they paid their dues and earned their stripes covering community sports.

Learning to work at the community level, learning to deal with people as people, learning to frame stories in terms of community issues—these are all skills you will acquire working at a community newspaper—whether you're covering sports or taking pictures or writing obituaries.

"I credit my weekly reporting and editing roots as being responsible for getting me where I am today," says award-winning Omaha *World-Herald* photographer Jeff Carney who started shooting in high school for his parents' 4,000-circulation weekly, the *Newspaper* of Wahoo, Neb.

"A lot of success I've had at the daily level I attribute to my community background. At the big dailies we whirl into peoples' lives and out again," Jeff says. But because of growing up at a community paper, he says he's "learned to treat people with a little dignity."

Let's go to the top of the heap, to every photographer's dream: *National Geographic* magazine. Not long ago, your author had a dream come true when he was selected for the *National Geographic* faculty fellowship, which is awarded each summer to a photojournalism professor. During my conversation with the great photographer O. Louis Mazzatenta (who had the cover photo of the *Geographic* that month!), he traced his career trajectory from a wonderful internship at a community newspaper.

"It's where I started—the 8,000 circulation Peru *Daily Tribune* in PEE-roo, Indiana," Mazzatenta said with a grin, pronouncing the town the way the locals say it. And then, "I got to do everything. I loved it! I look back very fondly on those days. I got to shoot the pictures, write the captions, write the story, do the layout. And I was important; when I'd walk in to that school board meeting, they'd treat me like Somebody." And he added with a laugh, "Why, I must have been all of 21."

So—heads up! In this journalistic ballpark you will be expected to be a utility infielder—able to hit, run and field at many positions. In other words, the team needs a generalist. Young reporters or photographers on the community journalism scene will find out one of the major differences between the community paper and our big-city cousins on their first assignment.

It may happen when the managing editor sends you to your first high school game and expects you to take photos as well. Or if you're a shooter, you'll be expected to bring back a game story along with your photos. What may boggle your mind and infuriate you is that the people at the paper will act as if this is normal.

So hear it right now. It is normal.

Why It's Important

Few things can ignite, divide, excite or unite a community more than the issues surrounding church, school and local sports.

And perhaps nowhere is the reciprocal relationship between the paper and the community more strongly evident than in the arena of sports. This is because sports coverage on the community level is so personal and immediate. It reaches into households that otherwise might not be touched by the paper.

The late Ken Byerly, a longtime community newspaper publisher and former professor, was fond of saying that successful newspapering had everything to do with printing lots of names and faces. He even went so far as to advocate the use of photos of large groups of people staring into the camera. "Trees full of owls," he jokingly called them. But there was a publisher's shrewd judgment behind this practice. To Byerly's way of thinking, for every name or face in his paper, there'd be at least eight people who were directly impacted—mom, dad, sisters and brothers, grandparents, aunts and uncles—not to mention friends.

Community sports coverage affords the paper a unique opportunity to get ample names and faces in the paper. And the more people in the paper, the more personal and vital the paper is to the community.

Think about your own childhood scrapbook. If you were raised in a small town with a community paper, you should have clips of yourself as a kid growing up, photos of you winning a Cub Scout birdhouse-building contest or getting an award in high school for civics, and surely a picture of you and your Little League team. Think about how you felt when you saw your picture in the paper for the first time, and you'll see that old Ken Byerly was right on target.

Your newspaper's mission statement should be to cover everything in your neighborhood—from Little League to area civic and church league teams to high school and college sports. This sort of highly inclusive community sports coverage provides "points of entry" for the community, and ultimately translates into more papers sold, which can be only a win-win situation for everyone.

It Just Takes Commitment, Commitment, Commitment

Great local sports coverage can and should be one of your paper's greatest strengths. It doesn't even take particularly gifted writing or photography; it just takes a commitment to comprehensive, exhaustive and consistent coverage.

"Commitment to me means going in early and staying late to work on projects I care about," says Suzanne Carr of the Fredericksburg (Va.) *Free Lance–Star*. "But I don't mind, because I'm doing what I love."

This is your turf. Nobody should be beating you here. Television can't give the Friday night high school football game much more than a 20-second blip on the 11 P.M. news. You should be running circles around the big-city dailies (if they chose to cover that high school game) because you've got fewer schools to deal with. Plus, big-city shooters typically have to leave after the first quarter because of their assignment load and stringent deadlines.

You, on the other hand, can stay for the whole game and get the complete story with all its subtleties and personal nuances, plus photos of crucial plays and of the winners and losers.

Working at his parents' weekly, Jeff Carney loved "doing the community thing." High school sports is honest, he says—no player strikes, no walkouts or salary disputes. For the reporter or photographer, it's a delight. "You're the insider. There's not as many [media] people there; you can experiment, you can get unique positions. At big college games, you usually get pushed off the floor or field by other people. And at the high school level," Carney emphasizes, "the access is there."

You, because you are known and trusted, can wander around behind the bench, and go to halftime locker rooms and postgame coaches' offices to get the details of the story. If you have friends working at big papers, they will tell you that that is a great luxury for which they envy you mightily. Imagine that: They envy you.

Then, after you've taken the necessary time to get the story and pictures, the great community paper can give them all the space they need and deserve. So what if the Nitwitness News scoops you on the score? When your paper comes out, you can give the story 30 inches and a slew of photos. And remember: Somebody's mama will be clipping that game story and sticking it on the fridge, between the pages of the family scrapbook or even in the family Bible.

The Digital Bulldog

How can a community paper exploit its inherent strengths and take advantage of technology too?

Larry Haulk, editor-publisher of the twice-weekly *Leader-Press* of Copperas Cove, Texas, realized that his Tuesday and Friday publication dates didn't give his football-crazy readers enough of what they wanted.

After all, Friday nights are what it's all about in high school football.

So Haulk and his staff created a Saturday A.M., 12-page football edition called *The Bulldog* (named after the local high school's mascot) that they put together Friday night after the game. What really makes the football extra possible, says Haulk, is digital photo technology. Do his football-loving readers love *The Bulldog*? What do you think?

Balance, Tone and Emphasis

The local junior college soccer team was getting beaten very badly by a clearly superior visiting team. Suddenly, the home team's coach, Don Scarborough, leapt off the bench and began racing up and down the sidelines, cupping his hands over his mouth and shouting at each of his players—first one and then the other:

"George! I believe in you!"

"Billy! I believe in you!"

"David! I believe in you!"

Each individual affirmation floated faintly but distinctly across the field, as intimate and personal as a sweet memory.

The fans in the bleachers on the opposite side of the field couldn't help but hear Coach Don's rallying call to his players, and many were moved. It wasn't grandstanding; it wasn't intended for the crowd to hear; it wasn't a ploy or a gimmick; the coach meant it.

The home team lost anyway, but in the long run the score didn't matter. After the numbers would be forgotten, the unconditional testimony of the coach would be remembered and live on. Coach Don had put things in perspective—win or lose, he believed in his boys.

If a community newspaper has a mission statement for sports coverage, this is it. The underlying motivation, tone and perspective of the paper should be predominately a positive, benevolent, supportive voice for the efforts of local sports participants.

Put-down coverage of area teams, regardless of how inspired the writing is, can only result in justifiable community outrage. Does the depiction of a weeping high school athlete, in an unguarded moment after a major loss, serve the public's right to know?

On the other hand, solid yet positive coverage can benefit both the community and the paper in many ways. For one thing, the paper has a real chance to help build community pride. But maybe even more important, a paper can help teach undergirding core values that can help young athletes throughout life—values such as the sanctity of personkind and the intrinsic worth of participating—not so much winning at all costs. Coach Don used to tell his teams (some of which were extremely successful) that "more human growth occurs and you learn more ultimately in defeat than you do from victory."

In sports especially, American society tends to reward only winning. How the media handles losing is fundamentally formative for our youth. When we subject kids to the false paradigm of winning at all costs, a very destructive set of dynamics can be set in motion, and people become secondary to winning. Consider the two true scenarios from a community newspaper reporter's notebook:

The Little League coach watched as the opposition's batter hit a fly ball to the left fielder, who happened to be the coach's son. The little boy dropped the ball. The coach, in a towering rage, shrieked like a madman at his son, the left fielder. Everybody in the stands heard him bellow: "WHAT'S WRONG WITH YOU?"

At a Special Olympics 100-meter race, there were six contestants. When the race was over, the last runner cavorted from the field shouting gleefully, "I came in sixth! I came in sixth!"

"The good thing about community journalism is that it gives people something they can't get anywhere else—names and faces," says Summerville, S.C., editor Bill Collins. The shot of the two happy marathon runners at the end of the race will get clipped from the paper and hang on somebody's fridge door until it turns yellow. That would be the highest compliment we could receive.

Which one makes you want to lose your lunch and which one makes you want to cheer? Which one is constructive and which one is destructive? We are not in the business of tearing people down for the sake of clip contests and our own advancement; we're about building community through balanced, fair and positive coverage.

This does not mean you have to sell out when writing community sports, that everything has to be, in the words of media observer L. K. Redmond, "all sunshine, Care Bears and rainbows," or that you must be a shill or a flack for local teams. It does mean that the emphasis is different from that at the major metro daily; in a word—it's *personal*.

The personal approach means you apply this yardstick to every judgment call: How would I feel about this story or picture if it were about me, my kid, someone in my family, my best friend?

Our approach toward sports means we have to be more concerned, conscientious, precise, discerning and balanced. In short, just because they play sports doesn't mean we can chew people up and spit them out for the sake of a great story or picture. And, yes, it does make it harder—especially when your home team loses badly.

There's a fine line between balanced reporting and giddy boosterism. The rule of thumb: You should know it when you see it.

Consider the lede from one community newspaper reporter, who, after his home team took a drubbing, wrote this piece of puffery: "It's possible that the 60-0 loss to South Point was a blessing in disguise for the East High Cavaliers."

If it sounds more like shameless PR than reporting, then you've probably crossed the line.

Critical or Not? How Much to Say?

How judgmental or critical should community sports coverage be? A tried-and-true yardstick: The higher up a team or an athlete is on the ladder of sports hierarchy, from T-ball to the NFL, the more critical a paper can be. Once a sporting event gets into the professional arena, then media scrutiny is more appropriate; the rationale is that people being paid to play must expect to be held accountable for their performance. A grayer area is how to handle coverage of college players on athletic scholarships. Aren't they receiving remuneration for their services? The generally accepted practice: the bigger the school, the more intense the coverage. But even here, the community paper should exercise judgment.

When in doubt, better to err on the side of restraint. Especially in the area of nonprofessional sports coverage. Remember, the kid you blast in the paper on Wednesday may be bagging your groceries that weekend. Could you look him or her in the eye?

By this set of guidelines, critical, judgmental coverage of individuals from the high school level on down is off limits. At the extreme end of the spectrum, some community papers have an iron-clad "my town right or wrong" policy that will strike some energetic young sports reporters as unnecessarily restrictive.

However, you can tell the truth and give a fair and balanced account of the event without reducing to roadkill the hapless kid who dropped the pass. The key here is balance. Of course this isn't easy because on the surface sports seems to be about winning and losing. Amateurs tend always to lead with the score. But the seasoned community sports reporter is wise to search for other angles and de-emphasize the culpability of a single young athlete. Pointing a journalistic finger after the fact can only be destructive for athletes at that age and stage. For one thing, print is so permanent. Besides, overly critical coverage can make the paper look insensitive and even mean spirited.

If there's to be a critical voice, which is appropriate, it should be one of authority, and that's the coach's, not the reporter's.

Situational Ethics and a Judgment Call

A couple of years back, when Andrea Hurley was news editor of the 2,700-circulation weekly Mercersburg (Pa.) *Journal*, she was covering the Friday night football game of the local team, camera in hand, as the following scenario unfolded unexpectedly before her. Put yourself in her shoes (she was the only reporter-photographer to witness this.) In her own words:

Friday night was senior parents' night. Before the game, one kid (a junior) comes onto the field with the parents and the brother of a kid killed in a car accident this summer. They present this boy (who was the best friend of the dead kid) with their son's jersey . . . then they all walk back to the bench with his friend's parents. He's still holding the jersey . . . then he removes his own jersey, and puts on his buddy's jersey.

He starts to sob uncontrollably, and little by little almost every kid on the team comes over, hugs him and they're all just crying and hugging. A very emotional scene. Do you take the picture or let these kids have their moment? It would have been an awesome photo.

If Hurley did shoot the picture, wouldn't she be intruding on what was essentially a private moment? If the *Journal* published the picture, wouldn't it needlessly embarrass those high school boys, whom everybody would see crying like babies? And again, the press would be seen as a bunch of insensitive ghouls just trying to sell papers.

On the other hand, if she decides *not* to take the picture, then isn't Hurley crossing the line of objectivity? After all, why couldn't she take an honorable, humanistic photo from a great distance with a telephoto lens (sans flash) . . . and then write something empathetic in a commentary about the event?

A third option is to *not* take the picture, but to write the empathetic commentary and let the words paint the picture.

A fourth option is to do nothing.

What do you think Hurley should have done?

And by the way, what's the difference between reporting with photos versus writing about an event without using pictures? Does one have more impact than another? You betcha. And lastly, what difference would it have made, if any, if TV had been at the game filming the whole thing for the 11 P.M. news?

Andrea Hurley didn't bury the coverage of the football players boo-hoo'ing, but says she was just too uncomfortable to run out on the field and make that intrusive flash-in-your-face photo. Instead, she chose to write about the incident tastefully within her regular game story. (We'll meet Hurley again in Chapter 20, on the subject of best practices.)

Favoritism and Who's on First

If you've got multiple teams, especially at schools, and they are intense rivals within your coverage area, how do you handle fair and balanced coverage leavened with the personal approach?

One upstart community newspaper with three rival high schools in its county solved the problem (and astounded the competition paper) by assigning one editor to each school and giving each school a full page of sports every week. No more. No less. It was a massive amount of coverage. People were bowled over; they'd never seen anything like it. And yet, after the newness of it wore off, they watched jealously to see that the other schools weren't getting more space. The paper even rotated the page order of the three schools' sports pages to prevent any claims of unfair emphasis and favoritism.

The equation *Access + Rapport = Success* is particularly true in the area of sports coverage. Master teacher and author Michael C. L. Thompson says, "Success is a function of accretion." On the sports beat that would mean the same editor, reporter or photographer covering the same sports area, team or beat. Coaches, players and parents, seeing the same reporter week in and week out, get to know that reporter on a deeper, more personal level, and are certain to give him or her stories, angles, tips and photos that a hit-and-run itinerant sports reporter will find continually elusive.

Tips for the Community Sports Journalist

- If you're a newcomer to sports reporting, learn as much about each sport before you attempt to cover an actual game. To do otherwise would be about as foolhardy as walking into a county commissioners' meeting without knowing the local politics, the names or the issues.
- If you have a college or university in your neighborhood, their SID (sports information director) should be feeding you with stories, photos and ideas. On a low budget, the trick here is to figure out how to look different from the handouts and the competition: localize, personalize, visualize.
- Because they are often the major sports venue in many communities, high schools usually receive major attention from community papers. Popular sports vary from region to region. In some places it's football, in some it's wrestling, in other places it's basketball. Whatever—your paper ought to be outhustling everyone else for the story, the local angle, the color piece, the personality portrait, the athlete of the week, the play of the week, the scholar-athlete of the week, the coach's talk story, the pre-game and postgame stories, as well as every sort of human interest sidebar you can create.
- If one of your town's teams goes big time, your paper ought to go ballistic right along with the fans. Here's a unique opportunity for the community paper to outshine everyone else, regardless of publication frequency. When one community's Little League all-stars went to the nationals, the innovative semiweekly paper sent the sports editor halfway across the country to get the story and pictures. The resulting double truck in the next paper created immense community goodwill, high reader interest and record single-copy sales. In addition, the exhaustive coverage stunned the competition, which hadn't even bothered to send a reporter.

- To perform at their best, the athletes we cover have to get psyched up for each game. If that's true of them, why isn't it of us as well? The best sports reporters and photographers get pumped for each game. Everyone has his or her own method. There's one reporter who prior to each game does push-ups in the press box. The simpler, less physical method is to get to the ballpark early and soak in the atmosphere to get you in the mood.

- "Luck is the residue of design," said Branch Rickey, late great visionary manager of the then Brooklyn Dodgers. With apologies to the Boy Scouts, that means "Be Prepared." Before the game, get a team roster from the game program. Underline the numbers of key players. Take extra pens. Can you work in the rain? Carry a plastic grocery bag for your cameras, just in case. Do you have your duct tape?

- Take copious notes. In sports as in any other reporting, you live or die by your notes. If you're shooting and reporting, shoot the play, then write down what you saw on a reporter's notepad you keep stuffed in your belt. You'll soon develop your own personal shorthand. "45 OLT 4/50" means number 45 went off left tackle for four yards to the 50-yard line.

- Or better yet, train a volunteer high school kid to take the play-by-play for you. Many aspiring young journalists will be only too happy to help you for free— and for the experience and the thrill of being close to the action on the sidelines. It's a great deal for both of you.

- Want to increase your paper's sports coverage but can't afford another reporter? Form a network of community sports correspondents and stringers to feed your paper results and box scores. Enlist coaches, parents, wives, husbands. At the end of the year, take them to the steak house. Or give them a free subscription.

- Think divergently. You don't always have to do it the same old way. One young sports editor, facing yet another preseason high school football story, chose to take the George Plimpton approach. The journalist, who had never played a day of high school football in his life, convinced the local high school football coach to let him dress out and practice with the team for a couple of days. After one of the paper's photographers showed up to document the nonsense, the resulting first-person story, "Pssst, the Linebacker Is the Sports Editor," ran as a full-page spread, creating tremendous goodwill and community response, as well as winning first place in the state press association's feature-writing contest.

- Don't let the competition get you down. One weekly paper had its photos of the Friday night high school football games ready late that same night, but with a traditional Wednesday publication date found itself regularly scooped by the competition, a tri-weekly that came out on Monday-Wednesday-Friday. To get the jump, the weekly sports editor decided he wouldn't wait until Wednesday to show his best stuff. He found a local drugstore owner who was willing to exhibit, in his main street storefront, the paper's photos from the previous night's game. It turned into a win-win situation. The drugstore owner was delighted by the increased business the pictures generated; the high school kids loved it; and the paper created a great public relations coup while confounding the competition.

From the Trenches

"There's a fragile relationship between the reader and the paper," says the University of New Mexico's Bob Gassaway.

Butch, the *Bugle*'s sports editor, found out just how fragile that relationship can be. He was famous for saying, "You can't make everybody happy all the time," followed by, "So why even try?"

One Friday, swamped with at-home football games and short on reporter-photographers, Butch elected to skip the game coverage of East, one of the smaller of the five high schools the *Bugle* covered regularly. The other four were bigger and more important, right?

Butch was a busy guy. He reasoned that with five high schools to report on every Friday night, he could afford to think that the folks at East would understand, forgive and forget. Yeah, that was it.

Until the following Friday night rolled around, and Butch elected to go cover the East game in person. Sort of to make up.

But as he walked down through the crowded football bleachers, and headed out onto the field to his usual spot on the sidelines, he heard the PA system announcer say in not very pleasant tone of voice over the speaker, "Weeeeeeelllll, if it isn't ol' Buuuuu-uuutch from the *Bugle*. Glad you could make it tonight, Butch."

And that was followed by a loud, sustained booing from the crowd in the home stands, the likes of which Butch from the *Bugle* would never forget.

He had learned the hard way that readers expect—and on occasion even de-mand—consistent coverage of *their* team by *their* newspaper.

Other Voices; Other Newsrooms

The following account of coverage of the 1999 U.S. Open first appeared, in a some-what different form, in Publishers' Auxiliary *in July 1999, and is used by permission.*

Twice-weekly goes daily for U.S. Open; "whups" the competition

How does a community newspaper respond when a major international sport-ing event (accompanied by the international media) comes to town?

When the U.S. Open Golf Championship chose the fabled Pinehurst #2 golf course for its 1999 site, the Southern Pines (N.C.) *Pilot*, at that time a hefty, healthy 15,000-circulation twice-weekly, refused to be intimidated by the event or the other media.

The local paper went daily in style.

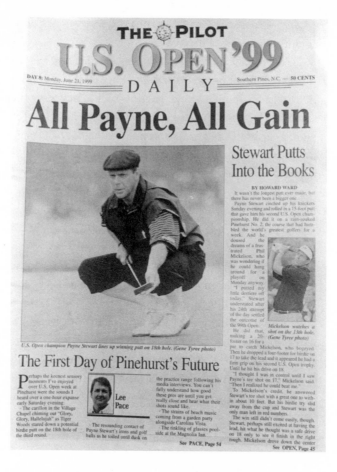

The tabloid-format front page of the final edition of *The Pilot U.S. Open '99 Daily*.

Moreover, the U.S. Open's coming to Pinehurst served as a focal point for the "new" *Pilot*, which was under different, younger ownership in 1996 after years of honored leadership by the highly respected editor-publisher Sam Ragan, "Mr. Sam," a figure of almost mythic proportions and the state's poet laureate as well.

Planning for two years paid off. *The Pilot*'s dynamic young publisher, David Woronoff (34 at the time of the Open)—along with four other partners—used the occasion to take the paper to another level. Not only did they completely renovate their downtown offices and install a new Goss nine-unit (including one stacked) Community press, but they also went daily for the duration of the 1999 U.S. Open, June 14–20, complete with full color on section fronts and peppered throughout the paper.

"We'll always be small-town," Woronoff explains, "but we'll never be small-time," adding, "We can put out just as sophisticated, cosmopolitan and journalistically excellent a paper as any place in the country."

Indeed. In normal times, *The Pilot* publishes Monday and Thursday, with the early week paper running from 40 pages broadsheet upwards, and the Thursday behemoth usually 80 pages and above. "We're like a Sunday paper twice a week, because we're so big. Five press runs and six sections," observes *Pilot* features assistant editor Melissa Breedlove.

For the U.S. Open, Woronoff's crew, ably led by *The Pilot*'s indefatigable editor, Steve Bouser, produced eight, 56-page tabloid format daily editions, *in addition* to the big mother paper. The guts of the daily was a preprinted 32-page section created back in May; it contained ads and "evergreen" stories and photos. And this can't be said strongly enough: *The Pilot* is an all-local community paper; all copy and photos are generated by either the staff or the community. There is absolutely no canned or wire copy. To pull off the daily, Woronoff recruited what he called "an all-star cast of ringers"—two "hired guns" in each of *The Pilot*'s sports, photo and circulation areas to bolster *The Pilot* for the U.S. Open coverage.

Interestingly, *The Pilot*'s roughly 20,000 a day *U.S. Open '99 Daily* was not mailed or delivered but rather sold by local kids (on practically every street corner) dressed in old-time "newsboy" garb. The proceeds from the daily sales went to the Boys and Girls Clubs. Also, the *Daily* was delivered to every hotel room and rental home in Moore County, as well as to selected hotels in the nearby cities of Raleigh and Greensboro.

In addition, *The Pilot*'s Web site, manned by online editor John Chappell (<www.thepilot.com>), which, in an ordinary week gets 6,000–7,000 hits, received a whopping 637,000 hits during U.S. Open week, according to Woronoff. "And we didn't crash!" he adds happily.

THE SETTING

Moore County, in the Sandhills region of south-central North Carolina, is a study in contrasts. It is home to 72,000 residents ranging from some of the most affluent in posh Pinehurst Village and the upscale but more middle-class residents of Southern Pines to the very poor in hardscrabble trailers in pine barrens.

THE PAPER

In 1998–99, the old office of *The Pilot* on Pennsylvania Avenue in Southern Pines was renovated and expanded with open accessibility as the key design element. News, prepress and advertising departments each have their own areas, but are in plain view of one another. There are no open-and-shut doors between departments. Rather, the visitor gets the positive impression of light, space and flow. The walls between each department are interrupted by large block-shaped openings. This was on purpose, says the publisher. "It's what makes a community newspaper great. We see each other, holler at each other, throw things at each other. We can't go to the bathroom without walking through each other's area . . . it keeps it open and vibrant."

One gets the early and distinct impression that folks at *The Pilot* genuinely

In the newsroom, staffers at the Southern Pines *Pilot* huddle informally to discuss a coverage issue with editor Steve Bouser, seated at right.

appreciate and respect what other people in other areas are doing. On the wall over the light table in the ad department, where editors and photographers huddle over negatives, a quote by former Raleigh *News & Observer* editor (and Woronoff's great-uncle) Jonathan Daniels is prominently displayed: "Advertising makes possible the free press."

The new offices, especially in the front, beckon to the readers or advertisers when they drop in. Refinished heart pine tongue-and-groove flooring glows invitingly under Oriental carpets and throw rugs. The original 14-foot-tall pressed-tin ceiling adds a homey feel. In a second front entrance, a counter resembles more a kitchen bar than an office partition. The publisher points out proudly that the visiting reader or advertiser at that counter can see the new press right through a window in the adjacent pressroom.

Woronoff, himself a relative newcomer to a community that appreciates continuity, put his office in the very space inhabited by the revered former editor-publisher. Dodging the temptation of hiding in the back, Woronoff established his office in a quaint wrap-around bay window that literally sticks out into the sidewalk on Pennsylvania Avenue, prompting him to joke about himself as the "boy in the bubble."

Just to make sure everyone keeps their priorities in order, Woronoff installed a basketball goal outside the pressroom loading dock in back of *The Pilot* building.

"Welcome to hell week," an editor quipped with a rueful grin to the newcomers before they huddled Sunday night in preparation for the following day's first daily edition. The budget session led by editor Bouser was sort of a war council: 14 editors, reporters, photographers and designers who would make *The Pilot* daily.

Introducing Howard Ward, the golf writer who would coordinate *The Pilot*'s coverage at the U.S. Open, Bouser explained the roles, "Howard is like Schwarzkopf in the field; I'm like Colin Powell back at the Pentagon . . ." This prompted visiting publisher and volunteer circulation worker Ashley "Brownie" Futrell Jr. of the Washington (N.C.) *Daily News* to joke, ". . . so I guess Woronoff would be Bill Clinton."

Good humor like that would permeate the week—in the field, at the media tent and back at *The Pilot*. It's a happy shop, and Bouser and Woronoff have worked hard to make it that way. The spirit of *The Pilot* appears to be spontaneous; its people—all the way from the guy catching the papers coming off the press to the publisher—take palpable pride in working there.

The new people brought in for the week fit right in too: a pair of photographers, a couple of golf writers and two circulation experts to help deliver papers. When it came to inserting the humongous five-section Monday–Thursday 156-pager, everybody pitched in. *Everybody*—publisher Woronoff included.

Throughout the week, women from accounting, the front office and classifieds cooked breakfast for all who were putting in extra hours. The fridge was kept stocked with sandwich makings, and food seemed to materialize daily in the company kitchen like a country Sunday church supper on the grounds.

The thrill of going daily became contagious: During the excitement of the second day, editor Steve Bouser exclaimed, pounding his desk with glee, "This is where it's at! We're not gonna be able to stand it when we're just foolin' around with *The Pilot*"—by which he meant the twice-weekly edition.

That might have been adrenaline talking, for by midweek, the staff was dragging from exhilarating but draining 14-hour days.

And the week was not without its trials and tribulations:

- The warehouse contracted to store preprinted tab sections had set the papers loaded on pallets *outside*, resulting in yellowed inserts. Publisher Woronoff was apoplectic.
- Arriving at the media tent on a rainy day, golf writer Steve Williams and sports editor Hunter Chase found a sizable leak dripping right where their laptops would have to go.
- *The Pilot*'s valued news editor, Clark Cox, came down with a serious illness and was forced to miss the entire experience. Bouser picked up the slack but admitted it was like losing his right arm.

Multiple sections of the mid-week *Pilot* (including the *U.S. Open Daily*) created a 156-page behemoth, prompting publisher David Woronoff to help out with the inserting operation.

- For some inexplicable reason, the paper ran out of blue ink.
- Just when it was needed the most, the drive chain in the inserting machine broke.

But *The Pilot* staff met all the challenges and soldiered on. Then, an exceptionally fine Wednesday daily got everybody psyched back up again.

Also by midweek, Bouser's highly organized system of deadlines was proving its worth. Additionally, the team in the field learned to shoot feature photos and shuttle the film back for processing by early afternoon, so that when the action film came in later in the day, feature photo pages would already be filled, allowing chief photographer Glenn Sides time and space to scan the late deadline action.

By the last day, everybody at *The Pilot* was pretty much wiped out: writers from cranking out multiple stories every day; photographers from lugging cameras over the 4-mile course in the rain; editors, designers, pressmen, inserters—everybody had been stretched to their limits and done exceptional work. But remarkably, there was little or no grousing from staffers. The papers looked great and readers had noticed. Photographers in the field at the U.S. Open were told to "tell Woronoff he's doing a great job."

On Sunday, the last day of the U.S. Open, two golfers, Payne Stewart and Phil Mickelson, were tied going into the final hole. Among the journalists at the U.S. Open and the staff of *The Pilot*, there came the awful realization that an 18-hole play-off might be required, stretching *The Pilot*'s marathon publishing effort into another whole day. When late in the day the news arrived that Payne Stewart had drained a do-or-die putt on the 18th hole to win the championship outright, *The Pilot* staff literally danced in the newsroom. They didn't care who won so much as that *somebody* had won.

Pilot golf writer Howard Ward reported later that when Stewart sunk that putt to break the tie Sunday evening, the press tent erupted in cheers. "Yes sir," Ward reported to a laughing newsroom, "right now Payne Stewart is the most popular player on the PGA circuit!"

VIGNETTE AT WEEK'S END

It's 9:15 P.M. on the last day. The final paper is about to go to bed. One of the volunteer photographers is sitting at staff writer Marjorie Daughtridge's desk, eating three-day-old moo goo gai pan. He has been at work since 7:30 A.M. The desk contains, in addition to a phone, a reporter's notebook, pens, sticky notes, a dictionary and the AP *Stylebook*, also photos of Daughtridge's husband and dogs, a droopy house plant, a tin of chocolate-covered cashews and a bag of half-eaten animal crackers. The flotsam and jetsam of one reporter's day.

Next to the photographer, design coordinator Brenda Berger, who has been working on a detailed scorecard page for hours, sees the page crash on the screen. "At least it was just one page and not both of them," she says philosophically. She does it all over. Editor Bouser comments, "She's a jewel."

She *is* a jewel. And the wonder of it is, she's not the only one. Bouser is surrounded by a newsroom full of jewels. They're the ones who made this whole crazy daily thing work. Remember what publisher Woronoff said at that war council meeting a long week ago: "We're small-town, but we're not small-time."

"Man, guys," Bouser emerges from his office and congratulates the newsroom folks putting out the final page, "what an accomplishment!"

CONCLUSION

When it was over Bouser said something that captured the essence of *The Pilot* experience at the U.S. Open. "I don't think this newspaper will ever be the same," he said. "We may go back to our old twice-weekly *Pilot*, but we're forever altered. Sort of like we went to war together . . . because we were on a crisis footing together. We went through some things [a week of dailies] as a newsroom team that has made a difference in how we think about each other, *The Pilot* and what we're doing."

What they did was fun, exhilarating, exhausting, confounding, frustrating, wonderful—extremes of great and grueling . . . It was like a stage production. And now the run was over. However, it would be a mistake for anyone to assume that the success of *The Pilot* during Open week meant that the paper could blithely convert to daily. Such an announcement would probably cause a mutiny, or at least a mass exodus. As staffer Melissa Breedlove said half-jokingly, "It would not be pretty."

As this book goes to press, the folks at *The Pilot* (joined by your author) will be trying to outdo their 1999 efforts as the U.S. Open Men's Golf Championship returns to their community. Here's a piece of their promotion material.

Several days later, after the dust had settled, publisher David Woronoff took stock. "We put out more pages last week on the U.S. Open than [the big dailies in] Greensboro, Fayetteville, Charlotte and Raleigh *combined*," he concluded happily. "It showed that a community newspaper can compete with the dailies—and we whupped 'em!"

And the bottom line? In addition to considerable goodwill, *The Pilot* made money, and Woronoff was generous, using 15 percent of the gross earned that week to pay out bonuses to his 65-member staff based on their roles in the project.

One Good Thing Leads to Another, and Another, and . . .

The success of the men's championship led to Pinehurst's hosting the U.S. Women's Open Championship in 2001—and that in turn led to the decision to bring the women's championship back to Pinehurst in '07.

And, as this book goes to press, the U.S. Men's Open Championship returns to Pinehurst in June 2005. Not ones to rest of their laurels, publisher Woronoff and his staff have geared up for another eight 72-page, tabloid-size daily editions of *The Pilot*—in addition to the regular three broadsheet editions of that week! (*The Pilot* went tri-weekly shortly after the 1999 Open.)

In a slick, four-color media kit produced a whole year before the '05 event, Woronoff writes, "We want to recapture the magic of the 1999 Open. So we will publish—once again—a morning daily publication devoted exclusively to the events of the Championship. . . . In the 105-year history of the Championship, no newspaper besides *The Pilot* has attempted that feat. . . . We at *The Pilot* plan to achieve the same level of excellence with our coverage, as we did with our critically acclaimed reporting on the Open's first visit. . . . We will endeavor to put a Moore County face on all eight editions with feature stories about the local folks involved with this community event."

Your author, digital Nikon in hand, will be greenside to help cover the U.S. Open again.

Your Town; Your Turn

1. Rate your paper on its local sports coverage. What are its strong points? How could it improve?
2. Did your hometown paper cover your youth sports when you were a kid? Cite examples, good or bad.
3. Within your newspaper's coverage area, are there high schools that are sports rivals? How does your paper attempt to balance its coverage?

THIRTEEN

Graphics, Design and the Community Paper

Design Should Enhance Communication, Not Defeat It

Good design makes us feel good. When we look at a well-designed page, we are drawn into the page, and find ourselves reading everything, almost effortlessly. But when we look at an ugly newspaper page, our reaction will be to bolt, and head off for the predictable. That usually means the comics or TV.

Kenny Irby of the Poynter Institute for Media Studies in St. Petersburg, Fla., says that the ultimate function of design is to solve a problem or meet a challenge. For the newspaper designer, that challenge deals with arranging three elements—words, pictures and space—in a meaningful and attractive package. And packaging takes planning.

A wonderfully written story on a page without photos looks drab. A gorgeous photo illustrating a poorly written story is as sad as a rose on a streetwalker. A fabulous and inventive design that is forced to use weak photos and a poorly written story is as transparent as a flashy used-car salesman trying to hawk junkers with nothing but hype and shouting.

Since the advent of *USA Today* in 1982, larger newspapers across the country have been jumping on the color bandwagon (even the—gasp—*New York Times* and *Washington Post* in 1998–'99), converting to the use of more color photographs, "spot color" for headlines and color bars, and colorful informational graphics such as explanatory maps, charts and graphs. Many community dailies have followed suit, as new technology has made color more economically feasible.

This can be expensive stuff. Smaller community papers, particularly weeklies with small budgets, may think that what has been called "the new graphics" is out of their league. But it ain't necessarily so. There are plenty of things a paper can do to look better without breaking the bank. Smaller community papers, many of which are competing with area metro dailies, can have a sharp and savvy presentation too, without hiring an expensive outside design firm. But it takes someone who cares or a flexible management courageous enough to take risks.

Not Just Ugly, but Really Ugly

Graphically speaking, there are a lot of worthwhile but poorly designed newspapers out there—papers that are doing good work otherwise—relaying vital information obtainable by the community in perhaps no other form. They win no beauty contests, but they are vital to the public life and social fabric of their community. Consider the *Bugle* . . .

Matt was bummed; there was no other word for it. After a tough first year as managing editor of the *Bugle*, what had he got to show for it? Oh sure, a whole raft of second-place awards from the state press association. But he couldn't get one judge's comments out of his mind.

"If only the *Bugle* looked as good as it reads," the judge had written on the runner-up award for General Excellence. And in the Typography/ Design division Matt's paper hadn't even placed.

Stung by the realization that appearances are important, Matt resolved to redesign the *Bugle*. But where to start? At college it had never occurred to him that a course in newspaper graphic design might someday be vital. Too late he recalled the words of John Neibergall: "No matter where you get the education, you're gonna pay the tuition."

The young editor decided to do a little informal market research on his own. For his "focus group" on graphics and design, he decided to approach the most opinionated bunch of old coots in town, the 9 A.M. coffee club down at the Village Cafe, where caffeine was in and tact was out. This crew may not have been experts in newspaper graphic design, but—as with everything from high school football to national foreign policy—they knew what they liked and didn't like; moreover, they weren't afraid to say it.

"Why sure, son," said the retired mayor, "the *Bugle* is ugly. But then it's *always* been like that." And with a laugh: "We wouldn't recognize the *Bugle* if it wasn't ugly."

When Matt approached the paper's publisher about the subject, Mrs. Hinson told him he could do as he wanted—within reason. She said she would be especially pleased if the proposed design changes resulted in more readership and increased ad revenues. Matt replied that he had no idea if there was any such correlation, but that he'd look into it. They ended the meeting agreeing that a better-looking paper should attract more readers, and hence more advertisers. At least the idea was worth a shot.

But Mrs. Hinson cautioned Matt to phase in his changes slowly. "Remember, people don't like change," she said, adding with a chuckle, "people think of the *Bugle* as *their* paper, not our paper, and certainly not Mrs. Hinson's paper."

Moreover, the publisher told Matt, the *Bugle* couldn't afford an outside design consultant, but Mrs. Hinson said she would be supportive of sending him to state and regional press workshops on newspaper design. She further counseled him simply to look at the better community papers in the region and try to absorb what the winners were doing. And finally, did Matt have any informal contacts whose expertise he could draw upon?

That's when Matt remembered Gloria.

Matt's next move was to contact his old college buddy who had become a graphic design editor for an out-of-state newspaper. After hearing Matt's situation, Gloria agreed to critique the paper's existing design and offer simple alternatives. Two weeks after sending her a packet of papers, Matt received them back, covered with Post-it Notes and accompanied by a long letter that started like this:

Dear Matt,
You were right. The *Bugle* isn't just ugly, it's really ugly . . .

The graphic designer's comments were divided into three areas: type, photos and space. Gloria's recommendations follow.

TYPE

The Flag—Let's take it from the top. Your nameplate is so archaic it's almost comical. That *Bugle* you've got there looks like the Old English Gothic typeface came off the front of some hymnal.

But I also realize that changing a newspaper's nameplate can be tricky business. So consider this: Many people in town will be very upset if you summarily trash your old flag and go with a new, more modern typeface.

When my paper was considering a redesign last year, we ran a poll of our readers, and actually put the choice for a new flag design up for a readers vote. We published our top five choices, and the readers wrote and called in their responses. When we finally incorporated those changes into our final new nameplate, the readers felt they'd been a part of the process. Oh sure, some people were still miffed, but many more said they appreciated being included in the decision-making process.

Headlines—Honestly, Matt, what is that stuff you're using, Futura Bold Condensed? Anyway, it's too black and dense. I'd suggest lightening up by converting to a more friendly looking and airy Roman-style font, perhaps a nice Bodoni, Times or Garamond. If you must use sans serif, find a lighter, less-condensed Helvetica or Avant Garde. And let me warn you about going type-happy; don't go into fontasia. Feature fonts can be useful, but beware "wearing all your jewelry to the ball," as the Poynter Institute's Ron Reason calls it.

Body Type—Typeface choice is critical. Most newspapers including the *Bugle* use Times Roman for their body type. Nine point is average. Make sure the spacing between the lines (the leading) is not so crammed. The *Bugle*'s body type looks like boilerplate. I suggest airing it out by increasing the leading at least one point.

Column Width—In addition, you need to convert from eight to six or fewer columns. An eight-column format causes too many strange hyphenations in justified copy. If you go to a six-column layout, your copy will become far more inviting, accessible and readable. Right now, frankly, it hurts my eyes even to look at your paper. Sorry, but you asked.

Just a thought, but try setting your commentary (on the edit, lifestyle and sports pages) ragged right instead of justified. That style signals the reader that this is a more informal piece, and it's a good way of airing out the pages, thus introducing pleasing whitespace.

PHOTOS

The quickest and easiest way to dress up your paper and boost readership is with good local photos displayed well.

Photos First—Did you know that readers look at photos first? Not only that, but the presence of a photo doubles the likelihood of readership. A lot of "word people" hate to acknowledge what's been proven in reader research, but it's true.

Photos Bigger—The *Bugle* needs to run its photos bigger. That means you've got to be bolder with your layouts. The photos I saw weren't that bad; you just ran them like postage stamps. In my experience, if photographers realize beforehand that their photos will be running large, they produce far better work. Try and see.

Color vs. B&W—I would advise using all the color you can afford; but this is not nearly as critical as the quality of the photos. A great black-and-white shot is extremely powerful. Other suggestions:

Dominant Image—Make sure every page is anchored by a Dominant Image Above the Fold.

Dominant Image First—Lay out your page around that dominant image. In other words, start with the photo as your main building block and then make the copy and heads work around the photo. Not only will this result in a more pleasingly designed page, but your readers will like it, and your photographers will love you.

Crop Carefully—Don't crop photos without conferring with the photographer first. Slash-and-burn cropping is the surest way to discourage any future creativity from your shooters.

Use Photo Pages—What about a photo page? I didn't see any photo essays in the papers you sent me. You need to showcase your photographers more. Turn your people loose on the county fair, the Boy Scout field day, a barn raising, a farm auction, the local fire department at a practice burn. You get the idea. Occasionally devote B-1 to some creative visual space. Your readers will like it, and your photographers will blossom.

Use Headshots—Is there some reason you're not using headshots for your editorial columns? I recommend good mugshots for all columns, including commentary on lifestyle and sports pages, and even your community correspondents and the lady who writes the community college news roundup. Good headshots personalize the paper by connecting faces with the commentary. It's also an easy way to dress up the page by breaking up the gray of copy.

Informational Graphics—The *Bugle* probably can't afford a full-time graphics editor now, but I hope that someday your publisher starts thinking along those lines. One of the things a great graphics person could do for the paper is to bring informational graphics to your pages. These infographics include charts, graphs, maps and simple computer-generated illustrations that enhance stories and make them not only more readily understandable but visually appealing as well. Matt, I'd suggest you might start by taking a computer course at the local community college. Also, I've noticed from time to time that the state press association offers hands-on computer graphics workshops.

SPACE

If you'll follow some of the above suggestions, I think you will be introducing whitespace into the paper in a pleasing way. Whitespace refers to the creative use of what artists call "negative space," in other words, anywhere that there appears to be nothing. Think of the paper like an art gallery. For the pictures to have the desired impact at an exhibition, there's got to be enough wall space between each hanging; otherwise the effect is crammed and difficult to look at. The same goes for your newspaper. Give each story its due by providing enough whitespace between different stories, and between heads and copy, photos and story and so forth.

PACKAGING

Some thought needs to be given to packaging. That is, the consistent grouping of like stories. The *Bugle* appears to have a mysterious organizational concept known only to its editors; I couldn't figure it out. For your size paper, I'd suggest devoting the front page to almost exclusively local coverage, then group state, national and international news on Page 2 under a clearly marked section header.

Use Section Headers—I'd recommend that formula throughout the paper: 48–72-pt. headers, such as sports, editorial and lifestyle, denoting each page or section.

Strive for Consistency—In addition, try to keep pages in consistent positions. For instance, editorial should always be found in the same position. I like 2B.

Start a Page-One Briefs Box—Finally, I found little news announcements scattered all through the paper like filler stories. What about compiling all those bulletin board-type community announcement stories into a front-page, left-hand briefs column?

Gloria ended her recommendations with a wrap-up set of comments that addressed the overall feel she got from looking at the paper.

OVERALL FEEL

With just a little work, the overall feel of the *Bugle* could be so much more visually reader-friendly. Recommendations:

Sky Boxes—Create a space above the nameplate to highlight what's inside the paper. This is also a great opportunity for spot color.

Indexes—You need a clear table of contents on the front to help out the reader.

Captions—If the photo is the first thing the reader looks at, the caption is often the second thing. Call this a point of entry. Think of captions as little ledes. They should be written as if the reader were not going to read the story the photo accompanies. Captions also offer opportunities for "refers," flagging an inside story that relates to the photo.

Phone Numbers and E-mail—On the *Bugle*'s editorial-page masthead, you don't list any way of getting in touch with the editors. A listing of phone numbers and e-mail addresses would make the paper more reader-friendly and accessible.

Letters Policy—If the *Bugle* has a "Letters to the Editor" policy box, I couldn't find it. A regularly published and clearly stated policy box not only serves to encourage letters, but it also establishes your guidelines, prevents potential confusion about unsigned letters, etc., while graphically breaking up what tends to be a gray page.

Good luck, Matt. Let me know what you decide to do. I'll be especially interested in the community reaction to any changes in the paper's design.

Design Wrap-Up

Matt studied and then incorporated many of Gloria's suggestions for enhancing the graphic design of the *Bugle*. And as Mrs. Hinson advised, he introduced the changes gradually over a period of three months. In fact some readers didn't even realize the paper was changing before their very eyes. Circulation and advertising did increase that quarter, but it was difficult to determine whether the new design changes were solely responsible. Most gratifying to Matt was the comment from the former mayor down at the coffee club. "Well son, I couldn't help but notice," he opined. "The ol' *Bugle* doesn't look nearly as ugly as it used to."

Matt was betting that the judges at the coming year's state press association contest would notice too.

Words from a Winner

In 1995, the *Centre Daily Times*, a 29,400-circulation Knight Ridder daily in State College, Pa., undertook a comprehensive redesign. Since then the paper has continued to make gradual improvements. And it has paid off for the *CDT*. In all three years since the initial redesign, the paper has made the list of the World's Best Designed Newspapers in the 49,000 circulation and under category, accorded by

Examples of a successful redesign: The *Centre Daily Times* of State College, Pa., spent many months on a comprehensive self-study before unveiling its dramatic redesign. The old look is on the left, the new look on the right. The newspaper (a 29,400-circulation Knight Ridder morning daily) wanted a graphic presentation that enhanced their new local coverage emphasis and community-intensive initiative. Reactions from readers were mixed; people seemed to either love or hate the fresh, airy look. Regardless, the redesign process itself, while exhausting, energized the newspaper from within. It paid off: after the redesign, the *CDT* made the list of the World's Best Designed Newspapers for three years running. (Pages courtesy of the *Centre Daily Times*.)

the Society of News Design. In 1999, the *CDT* was one of three winners in this international division; only 17 papers were on the international list.

John Winn Miller, *CDT* executive editor and vice president at the time, told *Press*, published by the Pennsylvania Newspaper Association, "It honors not only our overall design but also the newspaper's *usefulness* and how well our stories and photos reflect the community."

Here are, in his own words, some of Miller's design and layout tips:

Heads Up: The tops of the Sports and Features front always list the themes and the columnists for the week. At the bottom of the front we have an index of stories inside the section and a headline for what we think will be the best story for the next day. We frequently use the bottom part of 1A to promote stories coming later in the week.

Reader Access: In Features we run a short box on how to get items included in the paper. We also run a calendar of standing features every day telling readers what day such things as Student Achievers or weddings appear in the paper. At the bottom of every day's themed calendar, we tell readers how to submit material for publication in it and which editor to contact with questions.

In addition, we have added features to help readers plan their entertainment. This includes the Just Go grid on Thursdays previewing new movies, performances, concerts and other happenings. And we do a daily Movie Grid so readers don't have to look through the itty-bitty type in some of our ads for movie times.

Short Cuts: Because we have such a large coverage area, including 36 municipalities and five school districts, we use a variety of short cuts to help readers. We run a "what's on the agenda" section to alert readers about government meetings.

On Saturdays we run a government meetings roundup. The format is almost like box scores with who attended, how they voted, what was discussed and when they will meet again.

Quick Hits: Every story possible has a breakout box for more information or useful phone numbers or interesting Web sites. All bylined stories end with the reporters' e-mail and phone number to help readers communicate directly with us.

Efficient Use of Space: Our primary focus is local news. But to serve as one-stop shopping for our readers, we use a "Breakfast Briefing" on 2A. This serves not only as an index of the top national and international stories in the paper, but also as a briefs package.

Some of the items do not refer to inside stories (as one finds in the *Wall Street Journal*). This allows us to increase our national-international story count while saving space. We also include the top business indicators, the lottery numbers, the People column, our Out and About column and *Dilbert*.

Although this is designed to save readers time, many readers have told us that this makes them spend even more time with the paper.

Judicious In-Depth Coverage: To balance the short, snappy items, we have a facing Spotlight page on 3A. The page is devoted to one subject in depth. It can be one story or multiple stories with photos and graphics. We occasionally will use a local story there, but it's purpose is to anchor an island of reading on national or international issues.

More Guideposts: Local news that doesn't fit on 1A is packaged together with clearly marked briefs packages for police, courts, university news or around the state.

Fun for Readers: Probably the crowning achievement of our philosophy of utility and time savings for readers is the redesign of our Friday entertainment magazine, *Weekender & More*. The focus is on information and functional design. That means using lots of grids, Top 10 lists, easy to follow calendars, phone numbers, standing features, breakouts, Internet links and, most importantly, very short formatted stories. The only traditional narrative is our Spotlight feature.

Update: John Winn Miller has moved on at Knight Ridder to help lead the larger 57,000-circulation *Tallahassee Democrat* as senior vice president for news and circulation. Meanwhile, under executive editor Bob Heisse, the *CDT* has continued to flourish, winning the coveted state Newspaper of the Year Award in 2002. And for the last seven years running, the paper has garnered the most state press awards of any paper in its category.

Nine Tips for Designing at Small Newspapers

Foster's Daily Democrat of Dover, N.H., is a 131-year-old independent daily with a circulation of 24,000. When Molly Hartle was the assistant editor of *Foster's Sunday Citizen*, she created this handy tip list, which can be found on the Society for Newspaper Design site <http://www.newspagedesigner.com>. (Reprinted here by permission of the publisher.)

1. *Keep it simple.* You don't have time to deal with complicated designing requiring three different software programs. Try pushing the envelope in one program, and avoid time-consuming tasks such as doing a cut-out on a porcupine.
2. *Define your parameters early.* Knowing your limits is essential to creating a design quickly. Decide on things like grid structure, art elements and font early on in the process and avoid looking back. Good design doesn't require hours of contemplation.
3. *Stick to one font.* You don't have time to browse font foundry catalogs or to experiment with 100 different fonts. Try to be as creative as possible within your paper's font family. Experiment with different sizes, weights, and color (if appropriate).
4. *Avoid spending money.* Most small newspapers don't have the budget to buy outside photography, graphics and font. Look for inexpensive art elements such as leaves for a fall foliage splash, file photos for a look-back story and clip art for logos.
5. *Make friends.* Never forget if it weren't for reporters, photographers and copy editors, designers would be out of a job. You don't have time for senseless, ego-driven arguments. If the managing editor is bent on using indigo instead of blue for a feature headline, go with indigo!
6. *Ask for help.* One of the biggest drawbacks of designing for a small newspaper is the lack of people to bounce ideas off of. Get to know designers (preferably

good ones) at other papers, and solicit their input whenever possible on pages you've already created or pages you're working on.

7. *Look at other publications.* Look at as many other papers, magazines, books and other publications that you can get your hands on. Just because you're not *The Boston Globe* doesn't mean you can't look at *The Boston Globe*. Post your favorite designs on the wall and look at them daily.

8. *Read.* Many small newspapers don't have the budget to send their designers to workshops and short courses. If this is the case, read up on design yourself. Do a search of "newspaper design" on Amazon.com for the latest books on design or browse through the classics at your local library.

9. *Pray to the God of Small Newspaper Design.* Good design at small newspapers is just short of a miracle. You don't have to be religious or even spiritual to get some help from the Universe. It might be as simple as putting a little statue of Buddha on your computer terminal or wearing a lucky pair of socks. Know that you're not alone. Even if you're the only designer for 50 miles, the God of Small Newspaper Design is looking over you.

Resources: <http://www.newspaperdesigner.com>

Whaddaya Lookin' At?!

When the folks at the Wilson (N.C.) *Daily Times* decided to do a redesign, they had no idea what they were getting into.

Editor Hal Tarleton, a 24-year veteran at the *Times* (a family-owned, 17,000-circulation Monday–Friday P.M. and Saturday A.M. daily), says publisher Morgan Dickerman "wanted people to pick up the paper and say, 'Wow!'"

After an eight-month reassessment and a total makeover that included scrapping the body type for a new font and replacing the old-fashioned flag with a modern stacked nameplate, the new Wilson *Daily Times* hit the stands Oct. 25, 2003—and readers said "Wow!" and more.

On the first day of the redesign, over 300 readers called in to complain that the body type was unreadable, Tarleton says with a wry grin. The typical comment was an unvarnished "Why are you messing with my paper?"

Chastened by the unprecedented negative reaction, Tarleton says he and his staff got a summary lesson in newspaper ownership: "If you start messing around with their paper, they don't like it."

Within a week after the redesign, the *Times* responded, changing the body type to a more legible font, and carrying two front-page stories, according to Tarleton, "saying, 'Yes, we hear you.'"

In the long run, the redesign has turned out to be a very good thing, sparking a comprehensive self-study at the *Times* that has resulted in a superior community paper. Even the old-timers have accepted the new look—albeit grudgingly.

If It Ain't Broke, Etc.

And the argument for leaving well enough alone? Editor-publisher Dwight Sparks of the Clemmons (N.C.) *Courier*, a 2,400-circulation weekly, owned by the *Evening Post* Publishing Co. of Charleston, S.C., told community journalism student Vicky Bouloubasis:

> When I came here, the *Courier* looked like an old paper. And I re-did everything. And I thought, "Man, people are going to love this." But I think I may have run some people off. I think you can tweak a paper too much, and you can worry about design and layout and prettiness too much. The only thing that really matters is content. And as long as it's well-written, or it's a good picture. Style is nice, but it doesn't sell papers. After the layout changes I made then, I've been very reluctant to change anymore. When you're comfortable with what you've got, it's like a kid with its blankie; another blankie won't do.

Your Town; Your Turn

1. You have been put in charge of redesigning your paper. What changes would you put into effect? Remember, you need to be able to justify each proposed change.
2. Does your newspaper have a reader-friendly design? Find some examples of design features that help readers through the paper. If you think your paper could do a better job in a particular area, make specific suggestions.
3. Evaluate the typography and graphics of the paper's flag, or nameplate. Find out something about its history. Who designed it, and how has the flag evolved through time and use?

FOURTEEN

Photojournalism
Put That Camera Down and Dance, Boy!

The Power of the Image

One should use the camera as though tomorrow he would be stricken blind. Then the camera becomes a beautiful instrument for the purpose of saying to the world in general: "This is the way it is. Look at it, look at it."
—DOROTHEA LANGE

Look at your paper's front page—or the front of your hometown newspaper. Examine the covers of this week's *Time* magazine, a copy of *Rolling Stone* or the *National Enquirer*. What is the common denominator that links all of these fronts?

That the cover is to the publication what the lede is to a story.

It should beckon; it should entice; it should seduce; it should grab; it should make you stay. It should make you read. It should make you turn the page.

The eye is a lusty hunter and also a fickle one.

Bored, our eyes leap for new game.

A drab front page tells our eyes, "Bummer. Gotta split. Go find something to entertain us. How 'bout the funnies?"

If it was your job to shoot the lead picture or to design the front page, you just failed. You lost a reader.

A reader?

What are readers?

Before we were readers, we were lookers. What do we look at?

Pictures.

From the dawn of time, from the cave drawings of early humankind through the span of civilization, men and women have been lookers first. Lookers at pictures.

It is a particularly human trait that other animals lack. Our eyes quest for more than just functional information, as in, Where's that gazelle I'm going to have for dinner?

Our eyes quest for entertainment, relief from boredom. But deeper still is the quest for new information. The human mind is not content to remain static; it needs and wants fresh images to scan and process.

And finally, and most excitingly, our kind are gregarious. *People* magazine is not so different from a busybody lead dog in the prairie dog village. Who's Hot and Who's Not. Arf Arf. Sexy Hunks of Daytime TV. Bow-wow.

You may laugh, but why is *People* so terrifically popular? It's because we love ourselves. We love to find out about other prairie dogs—people with two-headed babies and too many wives and people who want to be buried with their Cadillac and people who want to go to the jungles of Africa to work with AIDS patients. *Homo sapiens* is the only species so intensely curious about and utterly fascinated with itself.

Back to the cave drawings. Recall the little stick figures running beside the huge prehistoric bison? People. People talking to people.

The earliest way we had to talk to each other—over time and over physical space, even before there was the word—was by pictures.

We don't know the language of the ancients, but we know their brushstrokes. We have no written tablets from the caves, but we see their bravery and their fearless stature in their artists' hands.

Pictures were the earliest form of impersonal communications, an exchange of information that didn't have to rely on Thag's grunts and hand-waving to Grog.

Pictures were our earliest basic language and have endured as a universally understood form of communication. Take your photographs seriously. Run the good ones big. People love pictures; always have; always will.

We Do It All

We no longer question whether a photo will make a story or a page more appealing. The evidence is in. Readership soars when a photo accompanies a story. Enlightened editors and publishers now demand visually exciting pages. For the community paper, photography is the simplest and most inexpensive way to make any story or page more appealing.

In spite of this increased emphasis on visual communications, many, if not most, journalism school graduates emerge into the real world with no working knowledge of cameras or graphics.

See if this scenario doesn't ring true: The new hire from State U is told to interview the new police chief and bring back a headshot to dress up the story. When handed a digital point-and-shoot camera, the new reporter is struck dumb with terror. The managing editor might has well have handed a snake to the new recruit. All she's ever photographed is vacation and party pictures.

But many if not most community papers have always expected and required reporters to be able to shoot. Community papers traditionally have not been able to afford the luxury of specialization. And because editors and publishers historically have been "word people" who put more emphasis on reporting than visuals, it is usually the photos that suffer—as a cursory glance at many community newspapers will reveal.

On the other end of the spectrum, at the better large dailies, more emphasis is being put on newspaper graphics and design. Therefore, photography is receiving nationwide attention from savvy publishers who regard pictures as a new marketing tool—a way to hustle papers. Here is where community newspapers should be paying attention to their big cousins. Rich Clarkson, *National Geographic*'s former photo chief, told photographers at the Southern Shortcourse in News Photography,

Every face tells a story: guitarmaker J. D. McCormick guffaws after finishing a song on his front porch. The Southern Appalachian craftsman was so conscientious about his instruments that if one didn't sound just right to him, he would burn it in his trash fire. Now *that's* a story—and a photo.

"One of the trends I see is the nationwide growing awareness in the importance of graphics and intelligence in packaging . . . that means planning the shoots and tying the photos well to text. But of course, that requires committed editors committed to visual reporting." Clarkson said that "the thoughtful use of thoughtful pictures" is what wins Pulitzers these days.

What It's All About

"The mission of a newspaper is to provide a written and visual record of what makes our community special," says Michael Sellett, publisher of the 5,000-circulation weekly Jackson Hole (Wyo.) *News and Guide*. "We believe an arresting image looks beyond the obvious, transporting our readers into the lives of ordinary people. In a sense, we use our lenses to find the soul of Jackson Hole. And that's really what community journalism is all about."

"It's that time of year again," begins the all-purpose cliché lede. Good editors say you get to use that lede one time in your career, and even then it should be rewritten because whatever is happening, it's *always* that time of year again.

Nevertheless, community journalists must cover annual events, year in and year out; and frankly that is a huge challenge. How to cover the annual county fair, the local festival, the high school graduation and the Christmas parade differently? After a couple of years, these events all start to look alike because unimaginative or burned-out journalists fail to see their novelty.

Here are some tips: Try seeing the event from a human angle; follow one person through the event with an in-depth feature with pictures, in the fashion of an "A Day in the Life of . . ." series. So, for instance, for a county fair, you might follow a little girl who has groomed her pet lamb for competition; or the behind-the-scenes people like a groundskeeper, a tent-erector or a cook; or a farmer who has planned all year to enter the tractor-pull competition.

Ted Richardson, a photojournalist in North Carolina, says he finds novelty in these events by "going at different times of day, early morning, evening." He says, "It's going to look totally different" from what one sees during standard office hours, when most journalists would rather be working.

Why is all this important? Beyond keeping you fresh, creative and sane, the search for novelty will take you where you want to go.

Kent Kobersteen, director of photography at *National Geographic* magazine, likes to say, "Before you come to us [*National Geographic*], you've got to be able to shoot the pig races." (For more on this subject, see the best practices discussion in Chapter 20.)

Bloom Where You're Planted

Someone who definitely knows how to shoot the pig races, award-winning weekly newspaper photographer Jeremy Waltner of the Freeman (S.D.) *Courier*, says, "It doesn't matter where you are—Alaska, Ireland, Brazil (or Freeman, South Dakota)—photography is photography and language is language. Use it wisely and do it well. And by all means, have fun doing it!"

Community Newspaper Photographers: Be a Person First

As anybody who's ever shot for a small paper knows, equipment isn't nearly as important as gaining access and then building trust quickly.

"You've got about a five-minute window to make yourself that person's best friend," says veteran Pennsylvania photojournalist Greg Grieco. And he explains, "If you can win their confidence, you've won yourself a good photograph."

Pulitzer Prize–winner Bill Strode, whose credits include many national news-magazine covers, says, "Access is all important. Be a person first; then a journalist; then a photographer."

Strode speaks as if he came from a community newspaper background. He says, "I am so tired of hearing national press photographers complaining and whining all the time. It's time for photographers to dig up good pictures within ourselves. It's time for us to try to do good in a grander sense . . . even in small ways. If you can help your local United Way by taking a better photograph . . . then if we have this attitude . . . that your photo just might help . . . then that will change your entire attitude about your work."

The late great combat photographer Robert Capa had a motto that fits community photojournalism too. He said, "If your pictures aren't good enough, you're not close enough."

The Thirst for Community

Globe-trotting freelance photographer Charles "Stretch" Ledford of Richmond, Va., certainly knows how to get close enough. "Making photographs is what I'm about," he says.

"Stretch" got his start in high school with a photograph published by the Asheville (N.C.) *Citizen*. He went on to become the National Press Photographers Association Student Photographer of the Year, eventually photographing all over the world for the much-respected *Commission* magazine. One of his most memorable shooting experiences occurred in Tampa, Fla., when he decided to become immersed in the Cuban community of Ybor City.

"The two years I spent living and working in Ybor City were without doubt the most intensely creative period in my life," he says. During a Southern Shortcourse, he shared these insights about that experience:

"The world is simultaneously a very beautiful and a terribly ugly place. Such is also true, I believe, for each of us as individuals. We each have within us the capacity for extraordinary mercy, grace and compassion. Yet somehow we each inevitably find ourselves at times acting in ways that prove us to be little more than selfish, spoiled children. Sometimes we act much worse than that.

"This is the dichotomy of human nature: Our ignoble self-interest is in opposition to our innate and more truly human desire for Community. Note that I use Community as a proper noun. In this form, to me at least, this desire for Community expresses a need for 'connectedness' or 'belonging.'

"Looking back, I realize that it was the way the people of Ybor City expressed and met this human need for community that made that particular place so remarkable.

"While photographing this personal project, I was also working a full-time Wednesday through Saturday 2–11 shift for the newspaper. While working on this project I moved into the community, and lived there for two years. It was a time of great personal, spiritual transformation.

"It was during my short stay in Ybor City that I began to realize what Edward Steichen was talking about when he said, 'The role of Photography is to explain man to man, and to explain each man to himself.'

"I believe this to be true. It is continually proven to me through my work—through both the photographs that are successful and the countless ones that are not.

"I firmly believe that when we photograph, we do so both 'in' and 'from' a particular place. We may be 'in' Africa, or Asia, or Tampa, Fla., but the place that we inevitably photograph 'from' is our own interior spiritual landscape.

"Clearly, what drew me to the people of Ybor City was, within myself, my own profound inner need for Community."

Digital-Schmidgital

One can't talk about the spiritual/creative side of photojournalism these days without addressing how technology has impacted the craft. Better-quality digital cameras coupled with lower prices have contributed to the broad acceptance of digital photography at even the smallest of weeklies.

The advantages of ease of use, speed and cost-savings are obvious: digital cameras don't use film, don't require processing and have electronic images that can be downloaded from the camera quickly. And they are essentially "point-and-shoot" cameras, also known as "Ph.D. cameras" (Push Here, Dummy).

And therein lies the main disadvantage.

Because most digital cameras being used by most community newspapers are in the relatively inexpensive "pro-sumer" area, they are limited in what they can do.

First, what they can do: The megapixel digital point-and-shoot is perfect for Grip 'n' Grins, check presentations, ribbon cuttings, static subject matter, stand 'em up and shoot 'em's.

But the beginner should realize what "automatic" means: that the camera is doing the thinking for you. If the light is low, the camera is going to flash the subject glaringly; if the subject is moving, the camera won't "know" this—and the resulting image will be blurred.

And most infuriating, since you've ceded the function of focus to the automatic camera, it has to "think" about focus for you, taking a millisecond after you press the shutter release button to perform this function—hence, you've lost that magic split second of peak action, what the late great Henri Cartier-Bresson called "the decisive moment."

Pressing the shutter release button on a P&S camera does two things: first it tries to focus the lens, and *then* the shutter opens and shuts.

The only way to avoid this "shutter lag" is to purchase a full-blown professional-level 35mm-size digital camera. And the good news here is that as time goes by, the prices on these cameras are steadily dropping, coupled with a rise in quality. So the longer you wait to go high-quality digital, the cheaper and better the camera will be.

For instance, when the full-size professional digital 35mm equivalent was introduced in 1994, it cost over $17,000. As this book goes to press, you can get a state-of-the-art professional 6 megapixel digital camera (body, dedicated auto-focus zoom lens, software and required accessories) for under $3,000. Watch that price continue to drop.

A few more things you need to know about digital cameras. They don't like temperature extremes or moisture. They require batteries. Oh, and don't dare go on assignment without back-up batteries. And unlike the old manual Pentax K-1000, they don't bounce.

But on the plus side again, the high-end digitals have two other advantages: They are quiet. When the picture is taken, no more attention-getting ka-CHUNK of the old film camera. Photographers, who prize their invisibility, love this feature of digital. Secondly, you can change the film speed, the ISO, on the fly. That is to say, if you're in a low-light situation and don't want to use flash, you can simply ramp up the ISO (the light sensitivity) to get the shot.

And finally, digital has changed the editing dynamic of photojournalism. With film, the photographer didn't know what he or she had gotten in the camera until the film had been developed, printed or scanned. Now, with the instant replay on all digital cameras, the photographer can take one photo, stop and check it for content and quality.

Though this feature is a terrific safety device, guaranteeing the photographer success, it interrupts the creative process of the interview or the shoot. The photographer essentially changes roles from shooter to editor, right there in front of the subject. Also, if the photographer is satisfied with the result, he or she might stop shooting right there. After all, you've got the shot don't you?

The fact that real photojournalists call this practice "chimping" should tell you something—as in, "Even a monkey could get a picture doing it like this." So, don't stop shooting just because you think you've already captured a passable shot; the decisive moment may be yet to come. And to capture it, you've got to be patient.

It could be argued that the broad acceptance of point-and-shoot digital photography has dumbed down the art of photojournalism. But you can't argue with the ease, cost-savings and speed offered by these wonderful devices.

By the way, your author still shoots film. But, yes, he also delights in his state-of-the-art digital Nikon. Because in the words of Poynter Institute photo guru Kenny Irby, they are both "tools for storytelling."

In this pre-digital era vignette, we meet Bill and his editor. Though some of the editor's rules will are now dated, much of his crusty wisdom is still valuable for the aspiring novice reporter-photographer.

Bill was a good reporter; he prided himself in that. But he was not prepared for what he ran into at his first job out of college. They wanted him to take pictures. "But I'm not a photojournalist!" he tried explaining to the editor. "You are now," came the reply.

It wasn't fair. The editor had started out as a photographer and grown into writing. Somehow that struck Bill as an easier progression.

Bill had to admit that he didn't know diddly about photography, and his early work showed it. Every time he'd turn a photo in, it was so bad that it invariably resulted in the editor hollering something like "This isn't just bad—it's really bad!" or "You call this a photograph?" Such outbursts were usually followed with an admonition about how Bill should have shot the picture.

Gradually the editor noticed that Bill seemed to be improving. One day, while talking to the young reporter in his office, the editor caught a glimpse of something strange taped to the back of Bill's door. At the top, the large lettering caught his eye: *How Any Idiot Can Take Good Pichers*. And scrawled on a four-foot long sheaf of AP paper were the preachments. Every time the editor had hollered, Bill had gone back to his office and written it down.

They may not have been the community photojournalism version of Strunk and White's *Elements of Style*, but all of the editor's hollerings had been therein recorded almost verbatim:

1. Is there film in the camera? Are you sure it's loaded correctly, dummy?
2. You can tell if there's film in the camera like this: Shoot a picture, wind the film, and see if the rewind knob turns. That's the knob at top left. If it's not moving, you're taking fantasy pictures. Pay no attention to the frame counter on the top right. It turns even if film isn't going through the camera.
3. Don't shoot into the light. Instead, get the light behind you, for the most part, so the subject is illuminated.
4. Don't bring me any Dead Snake Pictures. That's a photo taken of a dead snake made by a photographer who wants to put as much distance between himself and the snake as possible. See 'em every summer in the *Bugle* on slow news days. What—are you terrified of your subject? You gonna catch something from him?
5. The most valuable and inexpensive attachments you have for your camera are your two feet. Step closer to the subject. Also, you have knees? They do bend, don't they?

6. Fill the frame with significant matter. Look what's really in the viewfinder. I don't want tennis players with power poles growing out of their heads.

7. Remember Peter Pan? Watch your shadow. Keep it out of the photo. The photographer's shadow in a photo is a sure sign of a rank beginner—which you are, but you don't have to broadcast it.

8. Speaking of shadows, avoid direct flash. It makes people look either guilty or nuked. For softer, more humane lighting, bounce your flash off the ceiling. Open up two stops to compensate for the light falling off. Oh, for God's sake Bill, that means 1/60th at f/5.6 instead of f/11.

9. People look at pictures to see people. Put people in your pictures. This campus scene you just brought me looks like somebody dropped a neutron bomb on the place. All the buildings are intact, but not a living soul in sight. How'd you do that?

10. No butts. Give me people's faces. Not their behinds or their backs or their butts. Their faces. And I want to see their eyes.

11. Whoever said Ansel Adams got the shot with a single try? Take lots of pictures each time you shoot a single subject. Three frames per assignment is the bare minimum. Film is cheap compared to the lost shot or your having to drive back to do a reshoot, because the guy blinked and you'd only shot one frame.

12. Be paranoid about focus. A fuzzy picture is acceptable only in combat photography or pictures taken during an earthquake.

13. Don't trust your light meter. What do they know? You've got eyes, don't you? Bracket. That means, after shooting the picture like your light meter tells you, open up one stop above that setting, shoot some and then reset one stop below the advised setting, and shoot some more. It's called life insurance, 'cause I'm gonna kill you if you screw up again.

14. Take lots of pictures. If you want to get better, do it like a sport. Practice. And Bill, let me tell you, when it comes to photography, you need to practice bad.

15. Bill, you screwed up again. But lemme tell you something, son, that's all right. Because infinitely more can be learned through defeat than from victory. Take advantage of the lessons afforded by a really good screw-up like this one. Figure out what went wrong. The picture is blurry; it's gotta be one of only four things: You shot it out of focus, you shook the camera, your shutter speed was set too slow for the action, or your enlarger slipped out of focus in the darkroom.

16. Bill! These pictures look like they were taken by the Doughnut Man. You remember that little fat bald guy that used to be on the TV doughnut commer6cials. You'd see him stumbling around blearily before dawn, repeating to himself automatically, "Time to make da' doughnuts . . ." Don't take pictures like a half-awake robot. Nothing is automatic. Every situation is different. Novelty is everywhere. Any picture could be your best.

17. Hey Bill! This photo actually isn't too bad. Keep clickin' and windin', son, and we'll see what develops.

It was at that point that Bill recalled a quote he had read long ago in *Night Lights* by writer Phyllis Theroux: "Mistakes are the usual bridge between inexperience and wisdom."

Caption Writing 101

Here's a short course in what the AP's Mike Putzel (a former small-town newspaper guy) calls "the fine art of effective caption writing." Some guidelines:

- Don't assume that just because captions or cutlines (the latter name derived from a block or "cut" of wood on which the metal photoengraving used to be mounted) are so short that they don't deserve our attention.
- Don't give short shrift to this highly compact journalistic form. The cutline is a mighty mite, a vital byte of data, a veritable nugget of information. Consider the caption like the piccolo of the paper; it may be tiny, but yet it can be heard over the blaring trumpets of a 60-point headline. Done right, a caption can justify and enhance a good or even a fair photo. Done poorly or sloppily, it can ruin a great one. When writing the caption, give it the full weight of your attention.
- Consider the caption a little lede. Provide the 5W's in three to four accurate, cogent, concise, pithy lines.
- About names: Be paranoid about accuracy and spelling. Nothing kills a photo deader than a misspelled or wrong name.
- For starters, try the Subject–Verb–Direct Object sentence construction.
- Write in the present tense unless your paper dictates a different style.
- The caption not only must provide vital information on the photo's content; it must also set the picture in the correct context—not only what is happening in the image, but also perhaps what happened to lead up to the event portrayed, and maybe what happened just following the making of the photo. Write as if the reader will not read any story accompanying the photo.
- The caption is a potential point of entry. Be aware of its power to draw the reader into a story and, hence, into the entire paper in a way that even headlines sometimes can't do.
- If there's an inside story to which the photo refers, make the caption user-friendly by providing the reader with a refer (pronounced "reefer" by pros)—as in "See related story on A-12."

Photo credits are important too. They're not so much about ego-stroking as they are about assigning responsibility and accountability. Local photo credits serve a subtle but profound function in community journalism. Photos credited to local photographers signal to the community that the paper is on the job; that it didn't rely on AP to do its work. Maybe the local credits are only in tiny agate type, but they provide another way for a paper to tell the community that it cares.

Who writes the caption? At many large metro dailies, shooters only shoot and turn in assignment sheets with caption information. Someone else—whom the photographer may never see or even meet—will write the caption. This strikes some photographers as an odd division of labor. Who else is more qualified to comment on the subtleties of the scene or event depicted than the person who was there in person? At the larger community paper, if captions aren't written by the photographer, then the caption writer should at least secure data from the photographer and ideally check out the final version of that cutline with the shooter. At the smaller community papers, the photographer, who might be a reporter or editor as well, enjoys the luxury of writing her or his own cutlines.

Story Ideas Can Be Photo-Driven

In 1995 when a relatively unknown photographer from a 13,000-circulation community daily in rural Indiana won the prestigious Photographer of the Year prize awarded by the National Press Photographers Association, some people, who had not seen his work, sniffed . . . He's not from the *Washington Post* or the *LA Times* . . . He just shoots for a "little" paper.

But Torsten Kjellstrand's work speaks for itself—and of the creative support and quality leadership of the Jasper (Ind.) *Herald*, edited by John Rumbach, himself a much-honored newspaperman.

Kjellstrand's black-and-white, documentary-style photojournalism "celebrates the ordinary," and comes from his backyard, a 25-square-mile area surrounding Jasper (pop. 10,000), where the *Herald* enjoys a remarkable 84 percent penetration.

Most notably, each Saturday, the *Herald* turns over its entire tabloid format front page and the double-truck inside to a single photo project, which is always enriched by a well-written, sensitive, in-depth story.

During a photojournalism workshop on "reconnecting with your community," held at the Poynter Institute, Kjellstrand shared some of his insights.

Kjellstrand says story ideas can be "photo-driven." That is, a story can grow out of a single photo or an idea for a visual project. Indeed, the entire paper is so lovely that it, too, seems to be "photo-driven."

Kjellstrand recommends that photographers "pick your own reporter early in the process," someone with whom you know you can work well. Then sit down with that reporter and "do your homework, do research, outline your story, project with the writer. Have a plan, and a point of view."

Most often, he and a reporter go on story assignments together, and he likes that. Kjellstrand finds that "I do consistently better work when I work with a writer. It's like having another set of eyes and ears."

And when the photo story is over, Kjellstrand often finds it is not over. Pay attention, he advises. "One story leads to another . . ."

Fame has not gone to this young photographer's head. "I can't imagine turning my ego over to this profession entirely—otherwise it'll kill you."

A devoted family man, Kjellstrand has his priorities in order. On taking time off, and being with his family and kids, he says, "Short of Godzilla and Elvis showing up—along with an earthquake—I'll be at home!" In 1998 Torsten took a huge leap to the 128,500-circulation *Spokesman-Review* of Spokane, Wash. He moved in part because his wife had a better job opportunity there.

Not Just Learning to Work Together, but Flourishing

Mario Garcia's w.e.d. concept, in which Writer, Editor and Designer work together on a story from start to finish, is an excellent idea—especially for big-city dailies where interaction between staffers from other areas is limited because departments are often highly segregated.

Happily, at many community papers, Garcia's w.e.d. creative give-and-take interaction—including the photographer—occurs naturally because of smaller staffs and smaller newsrooms. In short, the intensely personal work environment of most community papers promotes a creative interaction. However, that depends on the corporate culture of the newsroom and the individuals working there.

With apologies to Mario Garcia, we'll call it the w.p.e.d. concept because really without the input of the photographer, the project will fall flat. And while we're on the subject, don't be treating photographers like pizza delivery boys. ("Hey boy! I wanna extra large veggie, hold the anchovies, and *I want it now!*"). And don't be calling him or her "your" photographer. Many photographers find the constant use of the possessive to be demeaning. If you're the writer, how would you like it if the photographer constantly introduced you as "my reporter"?

In the best cases, there is a creative synergy in writer-photographer-editor-designer teams that occurs because you like what you're doing and you like with whom you're working. For instance, at the Southern Pines *Pilot* here's how staff writer Marjorie Daughtridge worked with the photographer and the editor (who served as the designer) when the U.S. Open Golf Championship came to town during the summer of 1999.

Daughtridge knew well in advance that she had a major feature story due for each day's daily edition. She knew her story size, placement and deadlines because editor Steve Bouser kept her in the loop from the beginning. Bouser also *showed* Daughtridge, prior to each day's work, what the story placement would look like. For instance, today she would have 24 inches on a full tab page. The story would be located on page six, and it would be a black-and-white page.

Why is that important? Because, the photographer is standing right there beside Daughtridge at the editor's shoulder. The photographer is looking at the layout on the screen and thinking . . . "OK, today's story is on bicycle-riding paramedics at the U.S. Open . . . I've got to keep in mind this photo has to work in black and white."

Also, the photographer sees in advance if the photo is going to be vertical or

U.S. Open cycling paramedics Greg Biggs (foreground) and Angel Cartagena Flash past on their mountain bikes. (Jock Lauterer photo)

Ambulances With Handlebars

Biking Medics Kept Busy by (Mostly Minor) Emergencies at Open

BY MARJORIE DAUGHTRIDGE

Lots of people have been saved by an ambulance, but few can claim they've been rescued by a bike.

At this year's U.S. Open, that is one of the fastest, most efficient ways to get to an injured person, typically within one or two minutes.

Barry Britt, one of the organizers of the event's emergency services and director of emergency services for Moore County, is pleased with the efficiency of the ambulance-bikes.

"They're very mobile," he says. "They can go right out into the woods and ride between fairways." The bikes are equipped, in moderation, with much of the equipment that is on an ambulance, except for large items such as stretchers.

The bikes have heart monitors with defibrillators, IV fluids, equipment to perform tracheotomies and a full array of medications for cardiac, diabetic or other emergencies. Greg Biggs is one of the paramedics selected to work on the bikes.

"The treatment we are able to render off these bikes is the equivalent to what they can do off an ambulance," Biggs says.

Perhaps the greatest advantage of the bikes over ambulances is that they can get there quicker, especially in situations like the Open, and the first few minutes can be the most critical.

But riding around an ambulance-bike is not as easy as it may sound. The down side of the bike rescue squad is that all that equipment gets heavy, adding some 30-35 pounds of additional weight to the mountain bikes that can make them difficult to pedal and maneuver.

"It makes it rather heavy," Biggs says. "It gets a little top-heavy and it gets a little squirrelly at times." Biggs seems undaunted by this drawback and enjoys the work.

"It's pretty fun," he says. "It's great. It keeps you in shape."

Other paramedics who have joined the team have subsequently lost up to 40 pounds and even quit smoking. There is a team of 10 altogether here in Moore County, and they work in pairs. Two bikes

together make a complete set of equipment.

Biggs and his partner for the day, Angel Cartagena, have been busy this week. Many of the reported injuries are minor cuts and scrapes or blisters, but a few have been more serious. A few cardiac calls resulted in trips to the hospital, and one bicycle rider on his way to the Open fell and hit his head. He was not wearing a helmet.

Perhaps the most interesting injuries are spectators getting hit by golf balls, at least five of them this week. The two laugh as they describe how delighted individuals are after they've been struck by a ball from some illustrious player.

"They're just as happy as they can be that they've been hit by a golf ball," says Biggs.

He recalls one man who was whacked in the leg.

"He wasn't about to get up from his seat where he was sitting to watch," he says. Biggs was tending to the man's injury when two more balls landed only a few feet away in the gallery, making Biggs a little nervous about even being there.

The man was undaunted.

Cartagena went on a call for a man who was bopped in the head by Greg Norman's golf ball.

"This guy was really happy. 'Norman's ball hit me!'" Cartagena says. The injury was slightly serious, though. "He needed a couple of stitches on that one."

This year's Open was well-prepared for medical emergencies. There were eight paramedics, four emergency room nurses, four EMT's and two physicians. Together they have treated over 1,000 people, including the golfers and their caddies.

One caddie even needed emergency medical treatment between holes for a migraine.

Most of the staff, including the physicians, are volunteers, and a lot of the equipment was donated as well.

Organizer Britt feels his time was worth it and feels lucky to have been a part of it.

"We've had the pleasure of coordinating this Open," he says, "because this is a once-in-a-lifetime event."

"Go loaded for bear," the old expression says. Carrying your camera with you at all times will result in great shots. "f/8 and Be There" goes another old photographer's maxim. There's no substitute for being in the right place at the right time with the right lens—as demonstrated by this wide-angle "panned" shot of biking paramedics.

---

horizontal. This is critical because it allows the photographer and the writer to brainstorm confidently on the photo's content and composition. In this case, the photographer suggested a panned photo (perfect for the horizontal 10″ × 6″ photo hole) in which the paramedics would be shot with a creative blur effect to suggest motion on the page.

A happy shop is the result, in part, of editors and publishers clearly articulating their expectations, and staffers knowing and trusting what those expectations are. Doesn't this all sound like common sense?

But just imagine the effect on goodwill, newsroom morale and working relationships, if, when Daughtridge and the photographer return from the assignment all psyched about the cool story and the killer horizontal photo, the editor tells them he's changed the layout and he needs a big strong *vertical* shot instead and he's *cut the story* to only 10 inches . . .

"Sorry, there was this late ad we had to get in," he tells them.

What happens then? A line from Meredith Willson's *The Music Man* comes to mind: **239**
"We got trouble, I say trouble, right here in River City."

Photojournalism

Of course, the latter scenario did *not* happen at *The Pilot*. Instead, the writer and photographer got such a charge out of working together that they generated their own story ideas, excited about sharing their discoveries and getting to work together again. Daughtridge had stumbled across the biking paramedics story; the day before the photographer found a human interest story at the lost-and-found booth (lost cars, credit cards, husbands, etc.).

However, the ultimate responsibility for making the system work lies with the editor, and not enough emphasis can be put on this point. Each day at *The Pilot*, editor Steve Bouser got just as excited about what this team was generating as the writer and the photographer themselves.

Talk about non-ego-state interaction: Several times during the week's coverage, *photographers* suggested the best headlines, and editor Bouser was only too glad for the creative input.

From the Trenches

So you wanna be a photojournalist . . . ?
Can you eat a taco and drive a car at the same time?
—WOODY MARSHALL, chief photographer, Macon (Ga.) *Telegraph*

The great five-string banjo picker Snuffy Jenkins was coming home to Harris, N.C. I couldn't believe my luck. Snuffy, a famous figure in old-time and bluegrass history, had his roots in my county. I had been invited to interview him at his ancestral home in Harris, not more than seven miles from the paper's office.

Arriving at the Jenkins home, I was directed to a wicker chair on the front porch, where I began taking photos and conducting my interview without much preamble. I admit it: I was young and didn't understand the subtleties of interviewing country folk.

Snuffy, however, had his own agenda.

The music began with his daddy, Roy Jenkins, striking up a clawhammer tune on the banjo. Then one of the brothers got out of his chair and began buckdancing around in the red clay of the front yard. Snuffy joined in with his banjo. The front door opened and out came Ma Jenkins. Now there were several more dancers afoot. I was going nuts taking pictures.

But Snuffy would have none of it; maybe he knew I was missing the real essence of the moment. Or maybe spoiling it. Wagging his head at me as he flailed the banjo, Snuffy grinned at me and hollered something that almost sounded like a square dance call: "*Put that camera down and dance, boy!*"

And I did.

The Jenkins family takes to dancing in the yard. What's a photographer to do? Make a quick shot and then join in as Snuffy commands: "Put that camera down and dance, boy!"

Other Voices; Other Newsrooms

When photojournalist Michael Palmieri graduated from Penn State, the last place he thought he'd start his career would be Iowa. But the Heartland had something to teach this self-confessed "Jersey boy," as we learn in the following reminiscence.

Growing up in coastal New Jersey, I had long dreamed of taking my cameras and traveling to distant and exotic lands. I visualized documenting these foreign territories—connecting with their people and their cultures.

Shortly after my graduation from the Pennsylvania State University in 1998, I did just that. Packing my bags, I headed west to a land unlike any I had ever seen. I moved to Iowa.

And, while it may not be the other side of the world, Iowa is, after all, a world as distinct from New Jersey as China.

I moved 1,300 miles from home, mere light-years from my friends and family, to the Heartland of America to become the final member of a three-man pho-

tography staff in Ames. The Ames *Daily Tribune* officially became my first professional journalism job as a J-school graduate—and Iowa my adopted home.

The issues facing me were myriad. In addition to the typical first job, new
job jitters, there were the challenges of traveling around an unfamiliar town,
county and state. But perhaps the most formidable task of all was the over-
whelming reality of being immersed in an entirely different culture.

I experienced true "culture shock," encountering so much that was so new so
fast. It was just yesterday that I rolled into the state of Iowa, fresh off the Jersey
Turnpike, entering a strange place full of 45-degree parking spaces and friendly
faces. It was indeed foreign territory.

Before too long, I was able to burrow through the simple things like the parking and the language barrier. No, I never could refer to soda as "pop" or my grocery bag as a "sack." But, in due time, I did come to understand most of what
the locals were talking about. But, could they understand me?

However, it was far more important that I understood not the words but the
people behind them. It was critical that I experience the community that I was
serving. And, as I soon discovered, the only way to accomplish this was to get
out there and do it.

It was wonderful from day one when I rode into Slater, Iowa, to make a portrait of Howard Hammond. The 68-year-old former mayor had been a resident
in the town of approximately 1,500 people since 1944. Slater, a quaint little town
with notable landmarks that include the *Tri-County Times* newspaper office, the
Town & Country Grocery and the Good Times Saloon, is the home of Hammond's Housing mobile-home park—owned and operated by Howard.

Mr. Hammond is the classic small-town celebrity, the kind of fellow whom
everyone just seems to know. And, he's well-known for cruising around in his
fully functional 1950 Ford 8N tractor. Could I have asked for a better portrait prop?

Not bad for day one.

There were so many others. As I sit back and thumb through my Iowa portfolio, I am reminded that each image had its own story, each subject had his
own tale.

Here is another classic community newspaper vignette: the returning letter
winners for the local girl's high school basketball team. Nothing too amazing,
just a shot of the three standout players for the Ames High Little Cyclones.
While setting up my lights, I was conducting my usual routine of chitchatting
with the subjects. We kibitzed about the upcoming season, the Iowa State
women's team and whatnot—it was pleasant conversation. Finally, the lights
were set and the shooting was about to commence when one of the girls looked
at me with a cocked head and asked, "*Where* are you from?"

Was it that obvious that I wasn't from Iowa?

Perhaps my most memorable assignment was covering a baseball afternoon
at the home of the AAA Iowa Cubs, Sec Taylor Stadium. There two local high

schools had squared off in a midsummer classic at this wonderful minor league park. That afternoon I made what is probably my favorite image, a picture that summed up the importance of the entire event.

It was a simple photograph, but one that begged to be made. The outfield walls at Sec Taylor Stadium, like at many minor league yards, are true works of art. Painted corner to corner with advertisements from locals, the perimeter is wonderfully rich with color and life. As an I-Cubs regular, I had been well aware of the dental ad painted in right field. It was the image of a girl showing her teeth as only a child could. All it needed was a player in the foreground to make a great image—an image that would capture the feel of that warm afternoon. For in the end, it wasn't the final outcome or the box score that mattered to most readers, it was the fun of the event itself. There they were, 15-, 16-, 17-year-old students playing ball on a professional field in the state's capital—a great way to spend a summer's day.

The *Tribune* proved to be a remarkable place to begin my life as a community photojournalist. There I was, working as a staff shooter at a 50,000-circulation paper trapped within the body of a 10,000-circulation publication. The *Tribune* offered a "big" paper feel without sacrificing local coverage or forfeiting newsroom access for our readers.

The readership was comprised of folks who staked a claim into that newspaper—*their* newspaper. They felt as comfortable calling the *Tribune* as they did phoning any other neighbor. And believe me, they called.

They called to question why a certain photograph had appeared in that day's issue. They called to ask why we covered one event and not another. They called to remind the photo staff that we needed to create "scrapbook memories" for *all* of the high school students. Funny thing is, I even had a student athlete e-mail me and suggest that the picture we ran of him turning over the basketball ball really didn't happen.

And yet, at the end of the day, there was nothing more rewarding than feedback from readers—real comments from real people. I suppose that at the very least, it showed that what I was doing mattered to someone.

Some two years had passed and the goals that I set for myself after graduation were achieved. The time spent in Ames was indeed rewarding, but a new adventure called.

Returning to my alma mater in State College, Pa., I was to again hold a position at the student newspaper, not as a shooter this time, but serving as the inaugural photography adviser at *The Daily Collegian*.

However, in spite of the familiar surroundings, I have again found myself in strange waters. Perhaps equally as shocking as Iowa was to a Jersey guy are the feelings of being on the other side of the desk. The act of being not a student but a teacher is certainly new and different. The current task is not to produce images but rather to help produce the future participants of journalism. It is a labor of love wherein the passion for photojournalism is passed from one to another.

It has been six months since I accepted this post, and I can honestly say that each day has been enjoyable. That is not to say that there aren't moments of frustration. Believe me, there are. However, at the end of the day, the rewards typically outweigh the effort. I suppose that is what journalism is all about—making a connection. The elbow grease and the long hours, the struggle and the frustrations seem so unimportant once that connection is made, albeit with a reader or a student.

And, it is only in the real world that this lesson can be learned, as it is one that must be experienced not taught in a classroom. I was fortunate enough to have experienced this lesson in one of the distant and exotic lands I long dreamed of documenting after J-school.

Thanks, Iowa. I needed that.

To check out Palmieri's Iowa photos, go to <www.palmieriphoto.com>. As this edition goes to press, Palmieri has returned to his native New Jersey, where he teaches middle school math and is a freelance sports photojournalist. In the future he hopes to teach high school journalism and photography.

Ten Things That Make a Good Photograph

- Capturing a "decisive moment." Peak action—even in a seemingly static moment like a check presentation, a ribbon-cutting or a ground-breaking.
- People in the picture. No matter what you're photographing, make sure there are identifiable people in the photo.
- Faces that can be seen clearly, especially eyes.
- FTFWSM: "Fill the Frame With Significant Matter." Dominant foreground; contributing background. And no detracting clutter! In other words, make everything in the picture count.
- Getting close. No "Dead Snake Pictures."
- "Here, look at this!" A clear visual statement by the photographer so that the viewer knows what the photographer is trying to say and wants the viewer to see.
- It should either contribute new information to its accompanying written story or, if it's a stand-alone image, raise the reader/viewer's level of understanding of and appreciation for the subject.
- It should be graphically and compositionally pleasing.
- It should entice, beckon, make us curious, make the reader want to read the caption, read the story—and hence, serve as a "point of entry" for the entire newspaper.
- Technical quality: It should have acceptable sharp focus and tonal values. But remember: There's still no substitute for "f/8 and Be There." In other words, get the image, get the moment—we can correct for technical problems later. But you can never go back and capture a lost moment.

1. Pick a newspaper at random, your hometown newspaper, or the paper where you work. Identify the lead photo on the front page. Is it a "grabber"? Is it the dominant graphic image on the page? How could it have been strengthened? Would color have made any difference. Would black and white have made any difference?

2. Look at that same photo. Do the photo and page appear harmonious? Can you tell if the page was laid out around the photo or was the photo made to work within the confines of the page layout? Does the photo appear oddly cropped?

3. Again, the same photo. If it relates to an accompanying story, was it taken by the reporter? If it wasn't, does it relate well to the story? How could the photographer have done a better job coordinating with the reporter in tying the photo to the story?

FIFTEEN

Technology and Community Newspapers

First, a "Caviar"

There is in our society an almost visceral need for currency in technology, the newest, the latest, the fastest—hence, the coolest—as if we gauge our worth by how many megapixels our snazzy new digital camera has. Six? Ooooooh. That's big! Admittedly it is easy to feel smug in an airport when you pop out your sleek new silver X-6 laptop as heads turn admiringly.

But wait, haven't you heard? The X-6 is out and the X-7 is in research and development. So today's tech toy is tomorrow's relic.

If dogs age seven years for every human one, tech ages more like 50 to one. Within one year the gadget that was new becomes middle aged or downright "old"—what the techies kindly call "legacy" hardware.

So too with authors brazen enough to include in their books sections on technology. Future shock indeed.

With that caveat (or "caviar" as one of my students put it), we soldier on.

Hello, Generation D

(Would you please take off your headphones so I can talk to you about technology!)

Many college students of today are so bound to technology that if the campus e-mail server goes down, they are at a complete loss. They would rather have e-mail than food, and many don't wear wristwatches because the time is right there on their cell phones—and of course Gen-D'ers wouldn't be caught dead without their cell phones.

Those old poops attempting to teach or manage this generation should remember this cohort was born *after* the creation of MTV and *USA Today* in 1982, while their elders talk about Watergate as if it were last week.

The instructor can see students' eyes begin to glaze over when mention is made of some event that preceded their world-altering entry into this life. Yes, there is such a thing as a "dated cultural reference," but there is also the "classic cultural reference." Watergate is one of them, and so is John Belushi's "Killer Bees" skit from *Saturday Night Live*. Knowing about and understanding both are important to fully understanding our culture today.

Ever See a Press Run?

Similarly, there is a disconnect between many college journalism students and the technology that will support their careers. Many, if not most, have never witnessed an actual newspaper press in action.

Newspapers by their very nature are technology-driven. From the Gutenberg press to the typewriter to the invention of photography and the development of the halftone reproduction method, to offset printing, the digital revolution and satellite transmission, newspapers historically have adapted and improved production methods as new technology emerges.

So while the newspaper of today may not *appear* that dramatically different from one dating from the '70s, *how* a newspaper is produced has changed by light-years. Yet ironically, no matter how digitally dazzling their newsrooms and prepress areas, many community newspapers still print on the faithful Goss Community press, the veritable flagship of the industry, state of the art circa 1975.

We are in an age of technological ambivalence. You can go into many a modern community newspaper and find some pages being laid out completely by computer, but then go into the backshop production area and still encounter folks pasting up other pages using X-Acto knives and waxers.

Meanwhile the real change has occurred in what are called the "front-end capture systems." Reporters at even the smallest papers usually have access to tools that yesterday were considered "Star Wars" emerging technology: the laptop with its portability, the e-mail with its typesetting savings, the digital camera with its speed and ease of downloading, the cell phone with its connectedness. Then you get in the newsroom where reporters can Google facts, pages can be laid out on computer (pagination) and sent via e-mail as a PDF file to a distant printing operation that has an FTP site. (Of course, the irony is, with all that cool tech, some poor guy has still got to physically truck those printed newspapers back to town.) Still, it's a brave new world.

Blog On

Perhaps someone at your paper is keeping a blog, an online journal, usually with a theme—as when community newspaper editor Andrea Hurley blogged her 1,500-mile Appalachian Trail hike. Editor Kerry Sipe of Norfolk says blogs can "bring back the lost sense of urgency" that newspaper journalists once had about their work and have ceded to TV. He ought to know. As Sipe was blogging the trial of John Allen Muhammad (the D.C. sniper), he scooped the world when Muhammad unexpectedly announced to the court that he intended to defend himself. While scores of reporters dashed from the courtroom to make their calls or write their stories, Sipe hit the send key. Pretty cool stuff.

Does your paper have an online edition? It better.

Is it interactive? It should be.

Fact: Over half the people in the country—150 million users—went online in September 2003, according to one study cited by the Project for Excellence in Journalism's *The State of the News Media 2004*.

That's up from one-third, or 67 million, only five years ago, according to *Time* magazine.

And, the report notes, up to two-thirds of those current users are looking for news, and over 50 percent are young readers, ages 18 to 34, the very group print publishers have been losing for so long. According to the Project for Excellence in Journalism's report, "The Internet is also having success attracting young people to news, something older media were having trouble with before the Internet existed."

This is good news for the more than 2,300 U.S. daily and weekly papers with Web sites, according figures from the Newspaper Association of America. Now 83 percent of newspaper Web users cite their local paper's online site as their top Internet source for local news and information.

An Online Snapshot of One State

How people use and perceive newspaper Web sites is of intense interest to newspaper publishers—especially at smaller newspapers, which have the vast majority of Web sites. For instance, of the 189 newspapers in North Carolina, 135 have Web sites, of which 127, or 94 percent, belong to "small" newspapers.

But what do readers think about online newspapers? The 2000 N.C. Statewide Readership Study by Belden Associates, done for the N.C. Press Association, revealed the following:

- Readers know their newspaper has a site (40 percent said they were aware). But newspaper sites are underutilized: only 14 percent said they had accessed their newspaper's Web site in the last week; 7 percent in the last 30 days.
- Of those readers who did access their paper's Web site, most (60 percent) used the site in addition to the paper. And good news for publishers: 92 percent said they had no plans to discontinue subscribing to the ink-on-paper version. However, 38 percent said sometimes they used the paper's Web site instead of reading the paper.
- Nearly half of the adults surveyed, 46 percent, said the Internet could provide them with information "I can't get anywhere else." Newspapers came in second, with 26 percent responding positively to that same question, beating out TV and radio.

"The most important thing a Web site does is include the stuff left on the cutting room floor," says Gene Roberts. Because there are no spatial limits on the Web, depth of content is one of the great advantages of a Web site, says the former *New York Times* managing editor. For instance, a paper could cover the high school commencement in traditional fashion in the print version and then on the online site provide the full transcript of the commencement speeches.

"Every single twist and turn," Roberts says, "even the most minute thing, should find its way into your Web site. Details can be very important."

Embrace the Internet

Now is the time for forward-thinking community newspaper editors and publishers to embrace online technology, according to one national expert.

Tony Marsella, corporate director of classified advertising for Morris Communications, told the Texas Press Association, "We're in the communication business. Don't make the mistake made by the 19th-century railroadmen, who said they were in the 'railroad business,' when they should have realized they were in the 'transportation business.' So now it should be the B&O Airline, the Great Northern Airline, the Chesapeake Airline. But they were mature, rich and fat—*like us!*"

"We are a mature business," said Marsella. "We've been here since the start of this country. But that doesn't guarantee we'll be around in another 50 years. You must embrace the Internet. Stake out your turf, get your name plate/flag out there on a site."

As to the future, Marsella told the newspaper people: "So right now 99 cents of every dollar you earn comes from the newspaper and 1 cent comes from the Internet. Some day it may be 99 cents from the Internet and 1 cent from the paper. It doesn't matter."

Why Small Is Beautiful When It Comes to Tech

Canny community publishers have not lost sight of what got them to the dance in the first place: the ink-on-paper, hold-and-fold newspaper. Publishers profess faith in the newspaper as the "core product" while online services augment, enhance and strengthen the newspaper.

Community newspapers, with more forgiving deadlines, smaller overhead, tighter territories, more dedicated and loyal readers, can afford to look at technology quite differently from the major big-city dailies, which are always competing with television. First of all, remember, we're not faced with that sort of competition.

Until TV can air the equivalent of a 24-page broadsheet of local news, we've got the on-air broadcasters beat cold—especially if we have an online edition.

Before a publisher gives the green light to a technology upgrade, he or she needs to ask: What does it do for my paper?

In the case of offset in the 1960s, the change that swept the community publishing business was so pervasive because offset papers looked great compared to the smudgy images we had been getting from the old hot-type presses. The investment in new technology was tangible: The paper flat out looked better—better than it had in the past and better than the competition. Again, the bottom line is what our readers want.

And here's the good news: Because community newspapers are small, they can invest in new technology incrementally and not break the bank. The *Bugle* doesn't need to spend millions for a whole newsroom full of Bigothings; it may need only one Lilothing.

For this very reason, the community newspapers quietly led the offset revolution of the '60s in the publishing industry, whereas the large metro dailies embraced it wholesale only after decades of competing with terrific-looking outlying and suburban community papers. For years, big-city newspaper management had maintained that replacing those immense stereotype presses would be just too expensive. Some people say the advent of *USA Today* in the early '80s changed those publishers' minds. But many community newspaper folks think it was another thing.

High Tech Pioneered at Community Papers

When it came to computerization, community newspapers, with their intrinsically smaller economic base, turned to the free-standing PC out of need. Here was an affordable technology that didn't require a huge, complex and expensive mother computer and a sophisticated network system. If you had one Mac, a scanner, the right software (QuarkXPress and Photoshop) and a laser printer, you could put out a paper. Pagination? No problem. You think that drove the big boys nuts? You bet. Little publications have sprung up like dandelions all over the country—right in the front yard of the big-city dailies—spunky alternative weeklies, gonzo little 'zines, arts and leisure tabs, newsletters of every ilk. As this book goes to press, the ethnic and alternative weekly press continues to be an area of solid growth, one that attracts young readers.

It only stands to reason that community newspapers would latch on so quickly to this relatively inexpensive, simple and fun way to turn out type on paper. Both the technology (the Mac) and the product (community journalism) are user-friendly. It was a marriage made in heaven. Or at least Silicon Valley.

Tom Terry, a Ph.D. student at the University of North Carolina at Chapel Hill, formerly owned three state and national award-winning weekly newspapers in Illinois. According to Terry, community papers pioneered the use of emerging technology. In the early 1960s, his offset press was one of the first in the state of Illinois.

"While it was a huge expense for a small newspaper, it was nothing like the expense necessary for a daily newspaper to undertake when it abandons hot metal production in favor of offset," Terry says.

"So many technological advances in newspapers began at the weekly level and filtered *up*. Cold type took over from Linotypes at weeklies first. Weekly newspapers were paginating with personal computers—Macs mainly—perhaps a decade before it became the norm at dailies."

Terry's newspapers had one of the first Web sites in Illinois and were the first in the state to convert completely from petroleum-based ink to soybean ink, colors as well as black.

Terry credits this nimbleness on the part of weeklies to the absence of layers of bureaucrats who can get in the way and actually work to curtail innovation.

"I only had to convince myself it was a good idea and then find a way to pay for it," he says.

He also notes he never instituted a technological advance that did not pay for itself. "You just can't afford pretty toys at the weekly level. I know publishers who don't carry libel insurance because the premium is enough to push them from the black into the red. Presses and computers and digital cameras have to first and foremost pay for themselves," he stresses.

Relentlessly Local Online

During the technologically tumultuous '90s, weeklies were not asleep at the switch, either. Editor Ed Harper of the Southport (N.C.) *State Port Pilot* cranked up a Web site in 1996, and it's been a huge success for his 9,000-circulation award-winning weekly. The genius of the plan lies in its configuration. Harper linked the *Pilot's* Web site with that of the local Chamber of Commerce on a single home page—and, most significantly, became a local Internet service provider (ISP).

But the impetus for the site originated in a nonjournalistic source.

Harper started "looking around to see what was out there [online] about my town, and what I saw was embarrassing; I was offended. So I started exploring ways we could create a proper representation of our community. The object was to present a good front door for Southport and Oak Island. . . . We did not set out to make it a money-making venture.

"In all honesty, I was reluctant at first, but then there was the Chamber of Commerce impetus."

Success in both print and online: editor Ed Harper of the *State Port Pilot* in Southport, N.C., throws an affectionate arm around the online edition of the award-winning weekly.

When the *Pilot* became an ISP, Harper says, "we never expected to make a lot of money, but we have made a little." Harper adds that "being an ISP means that, in addition to making (not a whole lot of) money, we are provided with superior access for our own in-office needs."

Initially, Harper hired an outside source to provide them lines, and then the *Pilot* staff rose to the occasion with strong weekly content. "All the creation was done in-house from the beginning," he says. Harper thinks that the link to the Chamber of Commerce works because of a balance between PR and honest reporting. People calling up the Chamber site will "see pretty pictures and read nice things about the town," and then on the *Pilot* site, they may read about a local crime. Harper says, "The theory is that that truthfulness in the *Pilot* makes each [site] more credible."

But the single best thing that has come out of the online venture was a total surprise to the publisher. Complaints about late delivery of the ink-on-paper *Pilot* from out-of-county subscribers have dropped substantially. At first Harper couldn't figure it out. Was the U.S. Postal Service getting better? Then he realized many of the *Pilot*'s 2,900 nonresident subscribers were going online to check out the *Pilot* days before the actual paper arrived. It turns out that the online *Pilot* fills a critical time gap in the weekly's publication cycle.

For instance, Harper offers a scenario for an out-of-town reader without access to the online *Pilot*: "It's a shame if you're in California and you find out the next week that someone's mama has died. . . . So, we give [readers] the news to tide them over until their paper arrives."

Because the *Pilot* is so dense with local news, the online edition does not detract from the ink-on-paper product. "If we were [only] a front-page newspaper, we would have a problem, but nobody has canceled." In fact, Harper suspects that the online edition heightens interest in the print version.

Harper concludes: "A lot of nonresident subscribers makes it work for us. And any small-town newspaper ought to be able to do this. But if you're going to do this and think you're going to make a lot of money, you can forget it. But if you do it the way we did, you won't lose anything, and you might just make a little."

For a great-looking weekly online site, go to <stateportpilot.com>.

Online and Out-of-Town Readers

Ed Harper has touched on a vital feature that online editions provide: that of connecting quickly to what one of my students refers to as the paper's "far-flung hometown readers."

On the other side of Brunswick County from Southport, Ben Carlson edits another excellent weekly, the 17,000-circulation Brunswick *Beacon* in Shallotte, N.C.; almost one-third of its run is mailed out of town or county.

According to Carlson, online has given his paper a new competitive tool; he says, if need be, the weekly *Beacon* can become a daily.

Another trend that is beginning to become noticeable: more paid online sites. The *Beacon*'s ink-on-paper subscribers get the complete *Beacon* online at <www.brunswickbeacon.com> by keying in their subscription number as their password; nonsubscribing online browsers get only a highly abbreviated version of the paper.

The Best of All Media Worlds

"Newspapers have a bright future if they're willing to look up," says Priscilla M. Brown, the Web/print content coordinator for the Cox community newspaper group in eastern North Carolina. "Your Web site is not an appendage—it's part and parcel of the brand."

Online, she says, "doesn't supplant the newspaper; it's an extension of the newspaper."

When Brown is proselytizing for online journalism, she likes to create a flip chart evaluating the various media and their respective characteristics. She breaks down the differences in print, TV, radio and online relative to the following factors: portability or "hold and fold," pictures, sound, depth of content and immediacy.

- Print supplies depth, still pictures (albeit from yesterday), something to hold and fold, but no immediacy or sound.

- TV provides immediacy, sound and moving pictures, but no hold and fold (meaning that if you missed a story, you can't go back and reread it), and generally very little depth.
- Radio has immediacy, sound and more depth than TV, but no pictures or hold and fold.

"But online?" Brown announces with genuine enthusiasm, "Online can do it all! It brings everybody on the same playing field." And what's the chief difference not present in the other forms of media? she asks. "Interactivity!"

And because online newspaper sites can be accessed by anyone anywhere, even the smallest, most out-of-the-way places can have a site that will make a difference.

When in February 2003 the space shuttle *Columbia* came apart over Texas, the Nacogdoches *Daily Sentinel*, a 10,000-circulation Cox community newspaper, had an online site that "became the eyes and ears of the world," Brown notes.

She is fond of saying, "Think of your readers as 'users.'" And . . . "We have an obligation to serve our users. They want polls, discussion groups and forums. There's no end to their imagination if we just think beyond the printed page."

Brown scorns the Luddite editor who says, 'We don't want our Web site to scoop our newspaper,' by responding, "No, no, no . . . if it's online, it *is* you. You can't scoop yourself."

"Don't sit on online stories" for the sake of the print version, she urges. "TV can't do it—they're entertainment. Radio can't do it—they're music."

Community paper sites should do more than just shovel the paper onto the Web. "A lot of community newspapers move print and photos to online, ignoring sound, immediacy and interactivity," she laments.

Newspapers should also take advantage of cross-promotion, Brown says. The Web promotes print and print promotes the Web, because online has its advantages and portability has its advantages.

"I'm on a crusade with small newspapers to get them to understand the opportunities [offered by online]." Many companies, when faced with new technology, recoil as if tech is a threat rather than an opportunity, she says. At Cox, they realize it's both—a threat and an opportunity.

Convergence

Many media futurists think that convergence not only is the key to newspaper survival, but also is in fact the inevitable and almost organic direction the industry is taking. However, that is a contested notion.

Defined loosely as the sharing of news-gathering resources between associated media, convergence partners newspapers with radio, TV and the Web to create more complete coverage and richer, more layered content, proponents claim.

Community newspapers, with their relentlessly local focus, are uniquely positioned to thrive into the future if they work hard to provide quality local news and advertising content, stay creative and take advantage of new technology, according to the chair of the NAA (Newspaper Association of America).

Speaking to a Kansas Press Association convention, Dean Singleton of the Denver-based MediaNews Group was quoted by reporter Amy Bauer of the Topeka *Capital-Journal* as saying, "We have something that no other medium has or can build or can buy at any price—our connection to the community."

And speaking of partnering between newspapers, television, radio and the Internet, the NAA chair is quoted by Bauer as saying that newspapers are "in a position to drive the content that's found across media in convergence."

Obviously, this is going to take management freeing up more resources. Already overworked newspaper reporters and editors can't be expected to do double duty as on-air broadcast personalities. So it comes as no surprise that in many newsrooms where those additional resources have not been allocated, convergence, the C-word, is a bad word—a gimmick some bright bulb in the front office dreamed up to make the paper sexier.

On the other hand, when it works, it really works.

When a citywide manhunt for an escaped murder suspect forced the lockdown of three schools and the evacuation of two others in Chapel Hill, N.C., the community radio station, WCHL-AM, which had partnered with the Chapel Hill *Herald* for two years, produced wonderfully up-to-the-second coverage of the breaking news. While announcer Ron Stutts anchored the mic at the station, he was taking calls from WCHL reporter Eleanor Murray in the field, from all manner of local law enforcement and school officials, and also, via cell phone, from Chapel Hill *Herald* editor Neil Offen, who even put his high school–age daughter on to give a personal account of what the lockdown was like.

The WCHL-*Herald* coverage provided vital information for thousands of worried parents as to how and when—and even where—to pick up their kids. Students from two schools had been bussed to schools outside the police dragnet. If parents weren't tuned in to WCHL, all they had to go on was word-of-mouth and rumors. Predictably, the traffic tie-ups were horrendous, and the WCHL-*Herald* team was on top of that too.

To say that the WCHL-*Herald* partnership scooped all the other media outlets in town is putting it mildly.

Learning to Blend

In spite of all the evidence, many print editors are still leery of their own online sites. At a national technology conference, a weekly editor voiced that very fear, saying, "We're afraid of scooping ourselves . . . or alerting the nearby daily and giving away the scoop." But former Pottsville (Pa.) *Republican* Editor Jim Kevlin responded, "We never found that to be a competitive problem. Blending is something we'll be doing more and more. We own our own radio station that scoops us all the time. There's no point in holding back information. We're flexible in the way we assess stories. It's not an us versus them thing—but communication and service to the people—and that gets us out of the box."

Jim Van Nostrand, online manager at the 57,000-circulation Wilkes-Barre (Pa.) *Times Leader*, said that now more than ever, newspaper sites must be devoted to quality, accurate journalism. "Trust is essential," he observed. "There are so many sites out there with garbage. Newspaper sites should be a bastion, an island, where people can come to get information they can trust. And that has to be us."

Van Nostrand, who comes from a weekly newspaper background, added: "When I was at a weekly we made hay covering the things they [the big dailies] could not or would not do." He advised, "Do the same thing in your online weekly. When people know they can find chicken suppers, school menus, team photos, school bus routes, grip and grins . . . it will bring some of the *stickiness*, we talk about." For example, the *Times Leader*'s site, <www.timesleader.com>, carries a page of free obits, which Van Nostrand claimed is the "third most heavily trafficked thing on our Web site, fueling interest in the hometown newspaper."

As community papers go online, we must remain true to "journalism's core values," asserted York (Pa.) *Daily Record* editor and publisher Dennis Hetzel, including

- balance/fairness and wholeness: going beyond conflict and not dwelling on the he-said/she-said
- accuracy and authenticity: getting not just the facts right but the tone of the event and the quotes right too
- leadership: stimulating discussion and offering solutions
- accessibility: providing a window on the world, and thus connections, via both print and online
- credibility: demonstrating a consistent practice of and a devotion to high journalistic standards and values, and taking responsibility for our actions
- news judgment: understanding our community/ies and helping readers decide on issues for themselves.

New Tech, New Problem

Every new technology has always carried with it the threat of misuse. It's no different in the digital age. On the one hand, it's so fast and easy to simply scan in or download photographs. But tampering with the content of of an image is equally easy.

The real demon in the box here is the computerized abuse of authentic news photos. Using the sophisticated software Photoshop, the computer operator can fundamentally alter the content of any given picture, thus compromising the photo's veracity. Because present imaging technology has the capacity for altering photographs drastically (moving people around, interchanging body parts, excluding objects from the image entirely), this alarming trend raises questions of fundamental photojournalistic authenticity and credibility.

Community newspaper folk need to realize the depth and inherent dangers of digital-imaging manipulation. At smaller papers, where visual decisions may rest with a single person who may not have to answer to anyone until the paper hits the streets, there's a real potential for someone abusing the new technology of digital imaging. While Photoshop is a fabulous deadline tool, it is also a Pandora's box. And the box has already been opened.

Across the top of every newsroom computer in the land, from the weekly *Bugle* to mighty *Time* magazine, editors should tape a copy of the National Press Photographers Association's Statement on Manipulation of Photographs in its code of ethics. It reads in part: "As journalists we believe the guiding principle of our profession is accuracy; therefore, we believe it is wrong to alter the content of a photograph in any way that deceives the public. . . . Altering the content of a photograph, in any degree, is a breach of the ethical standards recognized by the NPPA."

You could hardly have been an American during the summer of 1994 and not known about the *Time* magazine cover with the computer-darkened face of O. J. Simpson.

No matter whether *Time* tried to justify the modification by calling it a "photo illustration" or a "computer-altered photo-montage," to you and me as readers it was a fake. The police mug shot was characterized as "computer enhanced"—as if that made everything OK—with eyes and face darkened, stubble emphasized, the image out of focus and a dark, sinister pall thrown over the brooding face. Though *Time*'s cover "photo illustration" was derived from the same police mug shot, the image looked completely different from the untampered version published by *Newsweek*. It boggles the mind that it never occurred to *Time*'s computer artist or managing editor that darkening the photo would be construed as racist.

The next week, even after a firestorm of protest from readers, the editors were unrepentant. In a letter almost as insensitive and infuriating as the doctored photo, they said they considered the cover an illustration, or "art," and as such that justified the darkening and altering.

No, they were wrong. The Associated Press and NPPA are clear on the guidelines. No tampering with news images. Nothing beyond what we've always been able to do in the wet darkroom: cropping and minor adjustment of tones and contrast. No moving trees, no moving the moon, no moving a Diet Coke can. If you shot it like that, you run it like that. Period.

In the words of then–NPPA President Joe Traver of Buffalo: "If the cover is an 'illustration,' it had better look like one. Great documentary photos derive their power . . . from their content. Their power is in their truth. No one has the right to distort this truth. If a photo looks real and is used in a context where the viewer expects to see actual photos, then the photo had better be real."

That's it then. If a news photo isn't real, then it's a lie. When photographers, artists or editors distort photos for the sake of a scoop, art, sales, layout—whatever reason—they are striking a death blow at the very heart of what makes authentic photojournalism so valuable.

I'll Just Photoshop It Outta There, Right?

You'd think we would have learned by now. After all, the landmark O.J. example is getting pretty old. But you can always count on people to keep on providing fresh examples of photo-abuse. In the Iraq war, *Los Angeles Times* photographer Brian Walser was fired after it was discovered that he'd faked a photo, combining parts of two images to create a scene that never happened. Even as this book goes to press, the *New York Times* has just had to issue an apology over a digitally faked photo in its pages. The photographer, on assignment in Alaska to illustrate the 5:1 male-to-female ratio, shot a bunch of guys surrounding one lone woman at a bar. No problem so far . . . until the photographer got back to his computer and realized he'd inadvertently photographed himself in the bar mirror. Then, his thinking must have gone something like this: "What the heck, I'll just Photoshop myself outta there. Nobody'll ever know."

Wrong.

If the media keep creating fantasy images where readers expect to see unfettered objectivity, our readers will begin suspecting the integrity of every photograph they see. Once we've lost our credibility, we've put ourselves out of business.

High Tech—Community Spin

What's so new about what we're going to be shooting and recording with our amazing new equipment? We're still going to be dealing with living, breathing flesh-and-blood people. Young journalists enamored of All the Very Latest should consider Virginia Wesleyan College President William T. Greer's approach to the future.

He calls it "high tech with heart."

No computerized notepad or digital camera is going to help you get your foot in the door with prime sources if they don't like you as a person. In community journalism, if we lose sight of the fact that we are in the people business, then all the computers in the world won't save us. It's one thing to have state-of-the-art tools, but the reporter-photographer still has to have soul and an eye with heart when using that digital camera or liquid crystal notepad.

This, the human element, must still be modeled by great editors and teachers.

1. Look in your own newsroom and backshop and catalog the technology, old and new.
2. How has the newest piece of equipment altered the dynamics of your workplace?
3. In what direction is your paper moving with regard to technology? Ask your publisher what he or she thinks about the future of print.
4. How well is your paper's online edition integrated into the ink-on-paper version?

SIXTEEN

Ethics and Community Newspapers
A Different Way of Looking at Things

Ethics and the Community Newspaper

Most community newspapers orient themselves ethically toward their communities in a fundamentally different way than their big-city cousins, according to a former Maine weekly newspaper editor and now professor and editor of the book *The Journalist's Moral Compass*.

While the community paper, like the large metro paper, serves in the vital role of public watchdog of governmental affairs, Steven R. Knowlton of Hofstra University says the similarities end there.

"At many large metro papers, when a bad guy is caught with his hand in the public till, they report it almost with a sense of triumphant glee," Knowlton says. "But at the community paper, when the bad guy is caught," he notes, "it is still reported, but with a certain sense of sadness."

The very nature of a community's shared physical geography and common social landscape makes it highly likely that people at the paper will know the accused or guilty party in more than just an abstract, detached manner. The accused will be a neighbor, someone from church, the Lions Club, the elementary school PTA.

When a top college basketball prospect got busted for selling drugs along with 46 other classmates at the local high school, Algernon Primm, editor of the Mebane (N.C.) *Enterprise*, a small chain weekly, reflected candidly, "It's one of those days you don't like being a journalist. But you've got to do what you've got to do."

Community newspapers do not enjoy the luxury of issuing detached, abstract editorial and news judgments. When it comes down to making tough ethical decisions, the community newspaper editor better have a moral compass that is locked unswervingly on magnetic north, because his or her reasons concerning whether and how to publish will be tested and questioned with almost every issue that comes along and every issue of the paper that comes out.

In plain Texas talk, here's how Charles "Mac" McClure, editor of the weekly Wimberley *View* puts it: "There's going to come a time when you have *the* story—and your town won't want you to publish it. They'll say it would be bad for business. And your publisher might not want you to write it. He might even threaten to fire you. But you know you've got to write it. Besides, you're no good in community journalism unless you've been fired for taking an unpopular stand at least once."

Community journalism has been around for a long time. Even before this country was a country, our first papers were concerned with intensely local political coverage. It's nothing new. It's just what works because it suits the way we're made.

Call it whatever you will—community journalism, civic or public journalism, relentlessly local coverage—it's not a new idea; it's just an idea whose time has come again. In the 1990s, largely in response to cities out of control, we finally started to embrace the concept of the human scale, neighborhoods in the truest sense, and the realization that people can only relate to so many other people at any given time. Communities only work to the extent that they're personal. Large aggregates come unglued because they never adhered to start with.

And yet, there are a lot of people who don't get it. Witness the following real conversation that occurred between two friends, one a self-proclaimed enlightened but openly cynical media critic, and the other a young but dedicated community journalist:

> "News is news. It's all the same, isn't it?" demands the devil's advocate. "What differentiates what happens in Harrisburg [the state's capital] and what happens in Danville?"
>
> Comes the quick reply from the journalist, who, just a couple of years out of college, often subs as managing editor: "About 50 freakin' miles."
>
> "Are you a Democrat or a Republican?" the critic demands.
>
> The reply comes quickly and with surety. "I'm a reporter."
>
> Rejoins the skeptic: "Why would I believe and trust the story in your paper as opposed to [the one in] the other paper?"
>
> "Because you can trust me," says the reporter.
>
> "And why is that?" laughs the critic, who has seen too much tabloid television and not enough of great community papers like the Dixon (Ill.) *Telegraph* or the *N'West Iowa REVIEW*.
>
> The community man doesn't even pause to think before saying, "Because I've got a track record. Because of accretion. Because you know me."

Because They Know You

The gemstone of accountability is perhaps the heaviest burden for a community journalist to carry, yet it is the most precious lode one can possess. If invested wisely, it can earn you a lifetime of satisfaction.

In short, if people know you (you shop at Food Mart, you attend the Methodist church, your kid plays for the West High Comets, and yet your coverage seems balanced and fair), they will trust and believe your word in print and the images you present on your pages. And why shouldn't they? You know this is a trusteeship, not to be entered into lightly. Think of your reader as a good neighbor or a best friend, someone you would never knowingly deceive. And if you erred, you would make it right quickly, wouldn't you? You bet you would.

That is the kernel—the "nut graf"—of community journalism ethics: Never deceive knowingly. And when a mistake is made, correct it promptly, and with equal weight. In other words, front-page errors should be corrected in the same space. After a blaring P-1 story that was flat wrong, the readers will pick up on how grudging and mean-spirited the paper was to bury the correction among the classifieds.

Public Service / The Public Interest

What is the role of the community newspaper in serving its community?

First off, you must accept—no, that verb is not a strong enough—you must *commit* to the first law of community journalism: that there exists a fundamental and reciprocal relationship between the paper and its town. It's a perspective as possessive and affectionate and all-seeing as that of Thornton Wilder's *Our Town*.

A community newspaper cares about its community in a supportive, positive, nurturing way. The paper's own birth, history, development, welfare and future are inextricably bound up with the history and future of its community.

How could it be otherwise? The community paper, by its very name and description, is a creature of service. It's not called just a newspaper; it's a *community* newspaper. That's why knowing what you are and staying on message, as the politicians say, is so vital.

The role of the enlightened community newspaper is far more demanding and complex than that of the big-city paper, which can afford to be detached, remote, critical, aloof, cynical and (sadly enough) at times elitist.

On the other hand, the work of the great community newspaper is made more complex by its difficult multiple and *conflicting* roles as fair and balanced reporter of the news while also serving as advocate for all that it finds good and worthwhile in the community—a consistently positive force for community building and appropriate growth.

We are also adviser, booster, supporter, advocate and—above all—mirror to the community, one that is accurate, unflinching yet benevolent. At times the paper must function as a "tough love" counselor and say things the community may not want to hear but needs to be exposed to. This is where, as they say, the rubber meets the road. Without putting down our brothers and sisters at the big-city papers, theirs is a relatively simple role when it comes to public service—report the news fairly and completely, and don't get involved.

Dave Marcus says, "There's a real nobility to community journalism that a lot of people don't or rarely understand." The editor of the 38,000-circulation Salem (Mass.) *Evening News*, Marcus explains, "The big difference between big-city journalism and community journalism is that the big city newspapers don't have a chance to see each reader as an individual. They see demographic groups. They see big issues and great questions. But in a community, we get to see individual people, with individual problems, problems with the neighborhood. And we get to help them. We get to understand their joy; we get to understand how they feel about their children. We get to understand the problems and the uncertainty of raising children. We get to understand exactly what it means when the tax rate goes up. We get to see these things. In a big city, if the editor doesn't want to, he'll never have to talk to the reader. We [in community journalism] all answer our own phones. We want to know: Who are our readers? What do they want from us? How can we help?"

For us in community journalism, it's much more likely to be a matter of intense involvement on many levels of the community. Your pressman may belong to the American Legion. The sports editor may play on a church softball team. The news editor may coach a Little League team. The m.e. may be active in the local arts council. The executive editor may be on the board of trustees of the community college. The publisher may be in the Rotary Club or on the county's economic development task force.

So—I hear you thinking—what about conflict of interest? What happens when Joe, the m.e.'s rival Little League coach, complains that the paper's coverage of the big game was slanted in favor of the m.e.'s team? Is it improper for the staff to have outside involvement in the coverage area? Doesn't that set you up for charges of favoritism and biased coverage?

But what are you going to do? Restrict your staff to live in a biosphere called "The Newsroom"? If you live in a small town, you can't help but get involved with community life. It's one of the things that makes community life so rich, fulfilling and worthwhile.

The question begs to be answered. And that's what this book is all about, and that's why the study of community newspapering is so enduring. There are no simple answers, friends. The newspaper's role in a community setting is complex, ever-changing and downright difficult. When it comes to the ethics of how you serve your community, how you handle news judgment and community involvement, you take each issue on a case-by-case basis. There are no formulas in community journalism, except that people are what really matter. And that you are there to serve your community. And *that* is "on message."

Stick to Your Ground Rules

Having a set policy in place can aid ethical decision making in times of high stress. Community journalism student Christina Rexrode reports that the Asheboro (N.C.) *Courier-Tribune* (a 16,300-circulation Stephens Media Group–owned daily) has a policy to not run photos of "uncovered or disfigured dead bodies." Says news editor Annette Jordan, "It takes away the dignity of human life." That policy came into play recently when a local deputy sheriff was shot and killed in the line of duty, and both the *Courier-Tribune* and the big-city daily had a photographer on the scene. Rexrode reports that the local paper opted not to run the photo focused on the body, even though it was covered by a sheet, because, as former editor and columnist Bob Williams says, "It goes back to the idea that we live here. . . . We shouldn't just show things because we can." Instead, the local paper ran a photo of an arresting officer handcuffing the shooting suspect, with the dead officer's body in the corner of the frame. Williams told Rexrode, "Here is a picture of the risk that a law enforcement officer takes any time he goes out." In spite of the paper's sensitivity, they still got a complaint from an irate reader. Jordan told Rexrode she responded to the reader with a pointed comparison: "Did you happen to see [the big city paper's] picture? *That* will give you a reason to be upset."

Thorny Problems

Too many newspapers rely on a *Recovered Forward-Fumble Policy*. That is to say, they dropped the ball and miraculously got it back—and maybe even picked up a little bit of ground—but everybody saw them lose it in public.

Then the paper has to come clean in public, making excuses with lots of "wuz-gonna's" and "ifs and buts." Theologian and author C. S. Lewis says, "An explanation of cause is not a justification of reason." Veteran Penn State sportscaster Fran Fisher puts that sentiment in folksy terms: "If 'ifs and buts' were nuts and candy, we'd all have a Merry Christmas."

If schools can have fire drills, why don't newspapers have ethics drills? Then when the real thing comes along, you'll be better prepared.

What are some of the ethical dilemmas a community paper editor is likely to encounter in the course of an average week?

Accusations of conflict of interest, whether to depict dead bodies and human suffering, how to handle obscenity and poor taste in relation to community standards, to name a few.

DEAD BODIES OR NOT?

The scanner went off in the newsroom two hours before the final photo deadline for the twice-weekly paper. It sounded bad; a tractor had overturned on someone out plowing. According to the emergency broadcast over the scanner in the newsroom, a man was pinned beneath the tractor and presumed in critical condition at best. Ed, the news editor, grabbed his camera and raced out of the main street office, heading toward the site, just north of town. Who is it? he wondered. When he got there, he was greeted by a most unsettling scene. No one was rushing around, as they would do ordinarily. The emergency workers were milling about despondently or standing around the tractor in a circle, looking down. The news editor suspected the worst. The poor tractor driver was dead. Approaching the scene slowly and with decorum, Ed quietly inquired of an EMS worker he knew, Who was the victim? The reply came back as a shock. It was the chairman of the county commissioners.

Just then, as the news editor was formulating his decisions about what to shoot and how to deal with the story, there appeared on the scene a reporter from the competition, a tri-weekly. Without any preamble, the reporter pushed his way through the emergency workers to the crushed body beneath the tractor and began shooting pictures, obviously very close up and very graphic. After a few quick questions, he left the scene, headed back for the paper's office and the scoop—but not before he was overheard saying, "Wow, this is great stuff."

This is not a parable about a small community paper gutting it out heroically against a giant metro daily. This is about two community papers with diametrically opposed ethical standards. One reporter thought the gore was "great stuff," while the other found it tragic—and yet was also aware of the long-range significance of the unexpected death of the community's most important political leader. Ed's pictures showed no mangled corpse, in keeping with his paper's policy of no dead bodies, but rather just the overturned tractor and the workers standing around, looking down helplessly. The strength of Ed's coverage lay in its in-depth reporting and backgrounding, explanatory journalism that tried to make some sense of the tragedy as it related to both the affected family and the county's political dynamics.

The competition predictably concentrated on depicting the death scene in multiple, large, lurid photos beneath shrieking headlines. It doesn't take a rocket scientist to know whose papers sold out quickest on the newsstands.

WHAT IF IT WERE YOUR FAMILY?

Dewaine Gahan and his wife, Bobbie, own and run the Oakland *Independent*, a 1,800-circulation weekly in Nebraska. He's the editor-publisher and she's publisher too. For years they had been shooting and running photographs of car wrecks. Dewaine said they never gave it too much thought when people complained that such pictures were invasive, intrusive or offensive.

Then one day, they ran a photo of a particularly bad wreck. You couldn't see the unidentified victim trapped in the car, but the blood on the pavement showed clearly in the color photo.

It wasn't until the next day, when the paper was on the streets, that the identity of the victim was learned. It was Bobbie's brother.

Dewaine said, "That was it. But we learned the hard way. Since that day we've never run another wreck photo, and we never will. It just hurts too much, and it does more harm than good."

Torsten Kjellstrand, the 1995 National Press Photographers Association Photographer of the Year, agrees. At the 13,000-circulation Jasper (Ind.) *Herald*, the publisher and staff made a conscious decision to stop running photos depicting

people in car accidents, regardless of what that decision might do to newspaper
sales. Says the soft-spoken Kjellstrand, "We don't do much in the way of covering car accidents because we don't think our readers need to be reminded that car accidents are bad for you."

TO COVER OR TO AID?

Kenny Irby, an associate at the Poynter Institute for Media Studies, recalls a pivotal event early in his career. Working at a community paper in Michigan, he raced to cover a "Ten-50 with PI," the scanner alarm for a traffic accident with personal injury. Arriving on the scene before anyone else, Irby found a woman pinned in the crushed wreckage of her car and, without thinking, got a blanket out of his car and comforted the woman, preventing her from going into shock until the ambulance arrived.

Only then did Irby go to work as a photojournalist, taking photos of the emergency workers getting the woman out of her mangled car. By then, other photographers had arrived to shoot the scene too.

Back at the newsroom, Irby was confronted by an editor who demanded to see the exclusive photos of the wreck in its earliest stages. He wasn't interested in shots of the rescue. "But you had the scoop! You were the first one there!" the irate editor exclaimed, "*Where are those photos?*"

Irby replied, "There aren't any, because I didn't take any."

Later, Irby realized, "I did what I had to do, and I made up my mind right there, that was the right thing to do."

Hartford (Conn.) *Courant* chief photographer John Long agrees. Addressing a National Press Photographers Association session on ethics, he said, "After a day's shooting, you've got to be able to go home and sleep with yourself."

SLEAZY TACTICS TO GET THE STORY?

At some point in your career you may be asked to do something or cover some story that pushes you too far. Consider the story of "Becky," a reporter for a community daily paper in central Pennsylvania.

During the summer of 1996, when TWA flight 800 went down in flames off Long Island, Montoursville, Pa., lost 16 kids from the high school French club, a teacher and four chaperones. Twenty-one people from a small town (pop. 4,937). Imagine the impact on that community. The national media descended on little Montoursville to record the scenes of grieving, raising the ire of the locals, and justifiably so in some cases.

Becky was there too, but she was an insider, since Montoursville was within her paper's coverage area and folks in the town knew her. She didn't particularly like the assignment, but she did what she was told to do. Still, after four or five days, the story assignment remained: Montoursville grieves . . . and then . . . Montoursville is still grieving. Becky began to object, wondering aloud, "How many days [are] we going to run pictures of people sobbing and stories that say essentially, yes, Montoursville is still grieving?"

The final straw came when she was assigned to cover another funeral. She refused. She had witnessed reporters from larger papers disguising themselves as mourners in order to get inside the churches.

"I went up there [to Montoursville] and just sat in my car," she recalled. She came back to the office and wrote a personal commentary that said, in effect, enough is enough; let Montoursville grieve in private.

Her editors were not happy; they docked her pay for one day.

Did Becky do the right thing?

"Oh yes, I'd do it again," she said emphatically.

CORRECTIONS POLICY

When it comes to trust and credibility, the importance of making forthright and prompt corrections cannot be overstated. Here's a well-crafted corrections policy, published weekly on the masthead of the 5,000-circulation Barrington (R.I.) *Times*:

> "We adhere to the highest standards of accuracy, fairness and ethical responsibility. If you feel we have not met those standards, please notify us. We will correct all errors brought to our attention or that we discover ourselves. They will always appear on this page."

Editor-publisher Ken Ripley of the weekly Spring Hope (N.C.) *Enterprise* tells the story of a new hotshot young reporter working in the front office on a story when an understandably upset bride-to-be came in to complain about an egregious error in that week's paper: The wrong caption was run under her wedding photo.

And hotshot said this to the reader: "*Buzz off!*"

Ripley can laugh about it now, but he recalls, "It took me *two hours* to get her off the ceiling."

WHEN DO YOU PRINT FOUL LANGUAGE?

The assignment had been to do a color story on the outdoor fish market down by the wharf. Marge, a reporter-photographer for the *Bugle*, returned to the newsroom excited about the contents of her notebook and her camera bag. This was going to be a neat story.

Once the photos had been downloaded and edited, the photo page started to take shape. "Hey, got something we can use for a pull quote?" asked the young layout editor.

"Well," Marge said, laughing, pointing to a fishing boat captain in one of her photos, "this guy told me, '*They're selling the shit out of them fish this morning.*' "

"Hey, that's a killer quote!" the layout editor said. "It really catches the excitement of the event." And she put the quote right beside the photo of the fisherman.

Marge wasn't so sure: "Well now, wait a minute, do you really think we ought have this guy cussing in the paper?"

"Aw, it's OK," the layout editor responded. "He said it, didn't he? And besides, he knew you worked for the *Bugle*, right?"

"Yeah, but I'd still feel better if we asked the M.E.," Marge said.

"OK by me," shrugged the layout editor. "But it's still a cool quote."

It didn't take Brenda, the M.E., long to give them her answer. "Do you really want to do that to this guy?" she asked Marge and the layout editor. "In this community that man would never live down that quote. If we print him cursing in the paper, he's going to catch it at church, his kids will be teased at school, his wife will be the object of ridicule, and he himself will be publicly embarrassed. Unless there's a compelling reason for this newspaper to print a curse word in a direct quote, we shouldn't do it."

"Yeah, but the quote makes the page and the story so much better," the layout editor urged.

But the M.E. had the final word. "Look, I'm sure that's true. But this is community journalism and not a stage play. We're dealing with living, breathing people here, not a bunch of fictitious characters we've dreamed up. These people have to live their lives in the context of this community's standards. If we go around quoting their every verbal indiscretion for the sake of a zingy or lively quote, not only will we wound our sources by wrecking their standing in the community, but we'll also offend many readers, and eventually no one will be willing to talk to us on the record."

COMMUNITY STANDARDS

When it comes to issues of taste, every community has a shared sense of what is acceptable and what is over the line. Nudity, expletives, cursing and bathroom humor may have their place in some publications, but less so in community journalism— unless there is a compelling reason to use something objectionable.

While the fishing captain story provides an example of an offensive quote that the paper has no compelling reason to print, what about the following? At a volatile public hearing, the chairman of the county commissioners shouts at a long-winded citizen, "*Sit down sir, you're starting to piss me off.*"

So we have in this instance an elected official cursing at a member of his constituency at a public meeting. Now *there's* a compelling reason to print. How can the paper not use the quote?

Still, this isn't an easy call for a community newspaper. It's not just a matter of whether to print or not, but also how to handle the fallout. With the county commissioner's gaffe, a community-savvy editor might take the occasion to write an explanatory editorial outlining the paper's guidelines for printing offensive language in direct quotes, and why in this instance the paper chose to print it verbatim.

When it comes to matters of good taste and community standards, most community papers think of themselves, broadly speaking, as "family newspapers." That old term means that the newspaper will be "safe" for everyone to read, from innocent children right on up to granny. But different communities have different standards, and the papers that serve those places reflect those different community standards.

When an art student at "Yaleanova College" staged an exhibit that included his AIDS awareness posters employing used condoms, it made the news. The story was politically topical, the art was unique, and people all over campus were talking about it.

After publication, the newspaper serving the large, culturally sophisticated northeastern college community received a blistering letter to the editor from a parent living in a rural area of the state. The older woman said she was highly offended by the material both in the photos and in the story.

Writing back, the editor responded in part:

> Thank you for your frank and candid letter regarding "Grad Student Creates Art with Used Condoms." I agree with you, the story did contain some objectionable material. However, I think it was well within the tolerance level of our readers. Our editorial news judgment was based on the matter of audience. That audience, a college town at a major university, is mainly students. The community's standards are different at a college town than they are elsewhere. More tolerant, certainly less apt to be shocked and offended by what they see, hear and read. Even so, we carefully weighed whether or not to run the story. We decided our main audience, while finding some of the material distasteful, would want to know about the story. Also, our paper merely covered the story of this controversial public exhibition—a story which other area papers covered as well—we didn't create the art you found distasteful.
>
> Finally, had this same story broken in a different kind of community with different standards, and if I were editor of that paper, I would have handled it otherwise. Perhaps a simple announcement of the show's opening without any photos.

What to Do When You Blow It . . . Literally

We've all done it. Written a cutesy, off-color or vulgar headline just for newsroom staffers' enjoyment, meaning of course to substitute the joke headline with the real headline before the paper goes to press . . .

But it ain't exactly cute when that playful head accidentally gets in the paper, as Bill Horner III will tell you. The publisher of the Sanford (N.C.) *Herald* is all too familiar with that kind of worst-case scenario. On the bright side, Horner has become such an expert in crisis management that he leads workshops titled "What to Do When You Blow It . . . Literally." Here's how the whole thing started:

On the top of the *Herald*'s front page, Jan. 22, 2003, a sports promo headline above the nameplate read in all caps:

"JACKETS BLOW IT OUT THE ASS."

When Horner saw the headline, he phoned his editor and said, "Have you seen the paper this morning?"

"Oh God," was the reaction.

Horner says they decided their response would be to "meet it head on and own up to our mistake; no excuses." Horner and the editor immediately wrote apologies on the paper's Web site, returned every phone call and issued the apology again, for distribution the following day via the paper's "total market coverage" product. The publisher's apology:

> It's always been the aim of the Sanford *Herald* to be a great local newspaper and to be family oriented. We were neither on Wednesday. The promotional head-line on the top of the front page in Wednesday's edition, referring to the results of a Lee Senior–Western Harnett High School basketball game, contained pro-fanity. It was the result of a foolish mistake by an editor and an incredible lack of oversight by others responsible for the production of the paper. That kind of language has no place in our newspaper. I'm horribly embarrassed. It was offen-sive, inappropriate and inexcusable, and should never have happened. We're better than that, and this community deserves better.

Horner went on to apologize to the readers and the students, faculty and admin-istration of both high schools, and he closed with "We've taken appropriate steps to make sure this kind of appalling mistake doesn't happen again."

And the editor's apology:

> I wish to apologize to each and every reader of the Sanford *Herald* for the ter-rible error on the front page off Wednesday's edition. Many callers have asked how such a thing could happen. As editor of the front page, I wanted to "pro-mote" the Lee County–Western Harnett basketball game because it's an impor-tant rivalry to our readers. On most nights, including Tuesday, the front page is completed before the sports pages. I'll leave the front page with the sports department to "fill in" the "promo" at the top of the page after they get the game results. Normally, I would write something like "Jackets promo here" as a reminder for the sports editor to fill in the headline. On Tuesday evening, as an inside joke with the sports staff, I wrote something that was quite offensive and was never intended for print. I deeply apologize to our readers as well as the Lee and Western Harnett school districts. I promise it will never happen again. For the many readers who called, I appreciate your good humor and understanding about this mistake and the support you gave me with your kind words. It has helped me weather the worst day in my career.

Horner says readers' reaction ranged from "They hate us . . . to they love us . . . to they forgave us . . . to they didn't forgive us."

After the predictable "shocked and appalled" and ". . . have you lost your minds?" calls, letters and e-mails, including demands for the firing of the editor, Horner says he was surprised by the supportive tone of many readers' responses:

"Mr. Horner, I hope you weren't too hard on [the editor] . . . I laughed so hard I saw stars."

"Hang in there . . . this too shall pass."

"I can only imagine what a tough time you're going through right now."

"I hope Sanford is not so stuffy that we can't accept this little oversight. Laughter is good, and anyone who really thought the headline was serious ought to lighten up a little. The Sanford *Herald* is no less of a quality newspaper today than it was yesterday (or the day before). No apology needed. Quite frankly, here at work we were hoping it would make the Jay Leno show."

"Dude, as soon as I saw the mistake I knew someone somewhere dropped the ball. . . . I'm sure you've been rotated over a slow fire enough by now, probably more so of your own doing than others. Things happen. You gave an apology. For me that's enough."

LEMONADE OUT OF A LEMON

One particular letter writer was not so forgiving. The reader challenged Horner to take this public gaffe and "use it as an opportunity to begin the improvement process and to return the *Herald* to its place as a quality newspaper." And the letter writer threw down the gauntlet to the publisher: "If any individual or corporation allowed its business to perform as the *Herald* has for the past two years, they would surely have to close their doors. The responsibility for making the improvements required start at the very top."

Instead of brushing this comment off, Horner went into action, the two net results being a "Newsroom Quality and Excellence Project" (similar to long-range strategic planning) and a series of meetings with community leaders to discuss Sanford's future and the role of the *Herald*.

Plagiarism: From Latin for "Kidnapping"

Lucy was totally psyched about her new in-depth story; she had researched it fully and just knew the long piece about the hiring of the new football coach, Bubba Flushwater, would win her accolades at the next state press association competition.

For her background on the story, Lucy had waded painstakingly through back issues of *Sports Illustrated*, where the legendary coach had been profiled several times during his long career. Lucy even went so far as to call the sports information director at the local college to check the veracity of those anecdotes printed about the new coach in *SI*.

But as her deadline loomed, and the busy coach still hadn't returned her calls, Lucy grew increasingly uneasy. She had no direct quotes from the coach, except what she'd gotten from his first press conference. She'd have to rely more heavily than she had planned on those *SI* anecdotes, she reasoned.

It wasn't until after her story had appeared in the *Bugle*, and her editor, Tom, approached her desk with a level, "Hey Luc', we need to talk—in my office," that she sensed something was terribly wrong.

"Listen, this may be nothing . . . ," Tom began, "but I just got a call from Ralph over at the *News*. He's accusing us of lifting stuff right out of *SI* on that coach piece in today's paper. Is that true?

Lucy felt her face suddenly flush crimson. "I . . . uh . . . checked 'em out thoroughly," she stammered.

Her editor leaned across his desk. "But all those stories about the coach's past. And the direct quotes. Did you get them on your own?" Tom was looking at her without blinking.

"No . . ." Lucy's voice sounded small and hollow. Then she rallied, "But the SID said they all checked out."

"So you *did* lift them from *SI* . . ." Tom blew out a long sigh, leaned back in his chair and addressed the ceiling. "Good grief, Lucy, what did they teach you over at the college? Don't you know that's plagiarism, and around here that's a firing offense?" Tom paused, and then added, as if to himself, "Ralph says I oughta fire you outright; said he would if he were me."

"But I didn't know . . ." Lucy protested as the hot tears sprang.

"Didn't know what?" Tom demanded. "That it's unethical to steal the work of someone else? That any time you use the work of another writer you give them credit. That the best way to avoid plagiarism is to cite cite cite?

"Look, maybe you can chalk it up to inexperience, but regardless, you've broken the first law of the journalism fraternity: that we don't steal from each other. That if we use anything we ourselves did not independently research and report, then we cite and attribute the source, completely. In the interest of full disclosure."

Tom paused, and then appeared to be speaking to himself again: ". . . of course I fault myself for not reading everybody's copy before we go to press—but you know how it is around here . . . some days I just can't."

Tom steepled his fingers in front of his face, his lips pursed in thought. Then he said, "So here's what we're going to do: You're going to go back to your desk and with a highlighter underline everything you 'borrowed' from *SI*. Then you're going to write that reporter at *SI* a personal letter of apology. And when you're done, I want to see both. Now, while you're doing that, I'm going to write an apology for tomorrow's paper which you're not going to like because it's going to embarrass you in public, but that's just the way it's got to be if you want to stay at this paper—and incidentally *I do* want you to stay—but you screwed up, and now you've got to take your lumps, you got that?"

Lucy nodded and gulped. "Thank you," she heard herself say, as she pulled herself to her feet and headed for the door. "This will never happen again."

Tom managed a rueful grin: "Well, they don't call community newspapers the real journalism graduate school for nothing."

Here's what appeared in the *Bugle* the next day:

An Apology

In our last issue, the *Bugle* published sports writer Lucy Fudnucker's profile on Bubba Flushwater, titled "Tough as Nails," in which several anecdotes about Flushwater's life were first published by *Sports Illustrated* in 1995. Even though those anecdotes were rewritten for the *Bugle* story, we should have acknowledged *Sports Illustrated* as their original source. The *Bugle* regrets the error, and we apologize to our readers. We recognize the vital importance of verification, full disclosure and proper citation of outside sources.

Grip 'n' Grins—Just Say No?

We've all seen this photo: one person handing another a check while they shake hands. Such a static picture of a staged check presentation and deadpan handshake is called a "Grip 'n' Grin." They are the community journalism equivalent of the "Photo Opportunity" or "Photo Op," in which a political person stages an event designed to make him or her look good, and then invites the press to witness this supposedly heartfelt and touching moment. Photographers loathe such assignments; editors hate running these pictures. So it's not surprising that the larger the paper, the less it runs "check presentations." Many larger community dailies simply refuse to shoot or print Grip 'n' Grins at all.

Good riddance. They're a bunch of hooey.

Or are they?

If the local Lions Club has raised $5,000 with their pancake suppers to help inner-city kids have eye checkups and new glasses, don't they deserve a photo of that check presentation?

If a women's church group has held bake sales to raise money for Habitat for Humanity, don't they get a check presentation photo in the *Bugle* too?

How can you say no to these and other worthy causes that deserve coverage? You don't have to say no, but you do have to do some creative thinking. Try coming at the story from a different angle. You cover the event or the result, and thus avoid the eye-glazing Grip 'n' Grin.

For instance, send a photographer to the Lions pancake supper or the church group's bake sale. That way, you can encourage the worthy works as they are

occurring, and the caption can give credit while there's still time to help the groups
raise more money.

Another tack: Do an in-depth, follow-up story on one of the inner-city kids who was actually helped by your local Lions Club money. Do a photo spread on Habitat for Humanity and find the connection between the women's church group and that worthy effort. Maybe one of the women is on the construction team. Bingo, there's your angle.

For every potential Grip 'n' Grin, there's a creative solution and a good story behind the boring check presentation. It just takes work on the paper's part. The problem (or challenge) is the same year in and year out. Whether it's the annual Girl Scout cookie sales or Red Cross blood drive, the *Bugle* will be called upon to supply deserved coverage. The trick is to find new and fresh angles on repetitive stories.

Yet another solution used by some papers: Buy some cheap point-and-shoot film cameras and pass them around the community to civic clubs and businesses and let them take their own Grip 'n' Grins, which you run on a community salute page or business round-up page once a month, or in a quarterly business publication loaded with ads they've bought.

Perhaps the simplest way to handle these photos is to collect them and every so often run them on a page titled something appropriate like "Scrapbook," as the Sunbury (Pa.) *Daily Item* does. It's a perfect venue for images of school reunions, five generations and award winners as well as your Grip 'n' Grins. Instead of fleeing from static celebratory pictures, the *Daily Item* solicits such photos from its community. Good thinking.

GRIP 'N' GRINS AND THE BIGGO MART

The manager of the local Biggo Mart phones and says she wants you to start running photos of her Employees of the Month, and that means one for each of the six separate departments in your hometown store.

When you tell her it's against your paper's policy to run employee-of-the-month (or of-the-week or -day) photos, she grows belligerent and threatens, "Do you know how much advertising we place in the *Bugle*?"

Is this fight worth a fight? What do you do?

Here are some creative solutions offered by other community newspaper folk under the gun.

- Tell the manager you'll do a story on her honored employees, simply listing their names. Then at the end of the year, say you'll do a photo and feature on the winner of the store's annual employee-of-the-year contest.
- Suggest to the manager a group shot of all the honored employees and limit it to once a month. Explain to her that whatever the *Bugle* does for Biggo Mart, the people down at Bleck's Department Store will demand the same coverage. Point out to her that the paper's photographer can do only so much.
- Run the photos on that "Scrapbook" page as space permits.

How Can You Not Report Suicides?

When someone in your community dies by his or her own hand, how do you go about reporting it? Many newspapers have policies guarding against what seems to be glorifying suicide by giving it news play. Here are several options:

- Don't print the cause of death at all, in either a news story or an obituary.
- Print the cause of death as listed by the funeral home or the police (in the case of a news story) with attribution to the law enforcement agency. Example: ". . . died of a self-inflicted gunshot wound" instead of using the word "suicide."
- Print a "clean obituary," one that does not list cause of death. This way the bereaved family has a clip they can keep.

Loren Ghiglione, the former editor of the Southbridge (Mass.) *News*, is currently the dean of Northwestern University's Medill School of Journalism. While still an editor in 1992, Ghiglione addressed this issue as it pertains to community newspapers. He wrote in his paper:

> However hard-nosed the self-image that journalists wish to perpetuate, they need to recognize that emotion—the anger, even terror—that surrounds suicide. It symbolizes society's failure. Parents, ministers, counselors and other safety nets have not worked. That "frightens the horses in the street," as Virginia Woolf wrote before killing herself. Painful for survivors, suicide, nevertheless, remains newsworthy. It should not be allowed to disappear, slipping silently back into the community's closet. It may be most usefully as well as most sensitively reported but not in a details-and-drama profile about a victim. And not in a medical examiner's one-sentence finding or in an obituary code-phrased like "died suddenly." It may be best reported in an annual review of the region's suicides that, without identifying victims by name, draws attention to patterns and issues that should concern us. So this scribbler will add one item to his list of New Year's resolutions: to report at the end of each year on those in the area who killed themselves. Perhaps those who died can provide a lesson or two for those who live.

Other Voices; Other Newsrooms

The following is adapted from an article by the author that was originally published in the NPPA's News Photographer *magazine, April 1998, and is reprinted with permission.*

Wrestling with the Bear

Though it may seem like a long time ago, the tragic death of Princess Diana in 1997 remains a benchmark event for photojournalism because of the involvement of paparazzi.

Even community journalists, including community *photo*journalists—are not immune to the sort of rapacious, scoop-driven, insensitive behavior that typifies the paparazzi, the metro tabloids and the celebrity press.

It is worth asking the seemingly humorous question seriously: Paparazzi in Peoria? Could it happen in Our Town? To many, what happened in Paris in 1997 is antithetical to how we think of community journalism. Although the event happened in Europe, the paparazzi behavior is all too often typical of the worst of American major metro journalism. Such media and its practitioners can be adversarial, possessing little or no regard for the people involved because these journalists are scoop-hungry. They lack a sense of responsibility and accountability, operating on a hit-and-run, shoot-and-scoot mode, having little care, concern, human compassion or sense of community, and few if any shared values with the subjects (RPS), so-called Real People.

But I wonder if what happened in that Paris tunnel would or could have happened in my town, at my paper—in your town, at your paper? Would your photographer have taunted the driver? Jumped on the back of a motorcycle and chased the subject? And then run away without helping?

It does little good to defensively distance ourselves from "them bad guys," the paparazzi or those insensitive "shooters" from the major metro papers—for the public largely views us all as members of the same mad family—celeb tabs and all. So we in the community press had better be able to articulate Who We Are and What We Do—especially regarding the issue of human suffering and "revictimizing the victim."

How does the community photographer know how to act in the face of a breaking news event? Who teaches him or her the community journalism Way? Does your paper have a stylebook for news coverage protocol? Who tells whom what when? Do your photogs get any in-house training before the fact, or are lessons learned the hard way, reactively, after the fact, after the disaster, after the poor journalistic behavior and the resulting very public stumble?

Enlightened community newspapers don't wait for disaster to set their moral agenda. They are proactive. They have in place and practice guidelines or at least a set of accepted (albeit perhaps unwritten but nonetheless articulated) values of newsroom culture based on fairness, balance, compassion, journalistic integrity and community standards.

Perhaps a case study of one newspaper's struggle will illustrate these points.

If you are going to write about a bear—bring on the bear!
—PHILLIPS RUSSELL, late UNC–Chapel Hill professor of journalism

Friday afternoon at the Macon (Ga.) *Telegraph*, I was lecturing *about* photojournalism ethics. By Friday night we were wrestling with the bear.

The Macon *Telegraph*, an 85,000-circulation Knight Ridder morning daily, strives to be a regional newspaper, covering a staggering 39-county spread of what the staff calls "middle Georgia," while, in the words of one long-time editor, "still keeping in touch with the folks."

I was there at the behest of two old chums, Cecil Bentley, the relatively new executive editor, and Woody Marshall, the even newer photo chief. The idea was sound enough: bring in Lauterer, the author of that book on community journalism, and talk about ethics, case studies and community framing.

About a dozen photographers, designers and editors huddled in the conference room where I showed my portfolio of photographs from my 15 years of co-running two community newspapers in western North Carolina. I talked about the compassionate photojournalist, about how the "shooter" could and should also be a person, an active member of the community.

Then I brought out my tray of ethical-dilemma slides, examples of the Good, the Bad and the Ugly of photojournalism. For two solid hours, we talked about whether hypothetical Paper X should have used theoretical Photo Y.

We covered community standards. We haggled about the old breakfast rule (Can your readers look at the front page without losing their Cheerios?) We debated proximity versus detachment. We grappled with objectivity versus point of view. We discussed charges of the media's insensitivity in portraying minorities in scenes of grief and suffering. We vented over privacy versus the public's need to know. We examined the handling of suicide. We condemned paparazzi and rushing to print without thinking.

From a 1994 *Time* magazine, I read them a letter to the editor that framed our discussion perfectly. An Illinois reader had objected: "Is it necessary to print photographs like those of the Sarajevo shelling showing blood-soaked snow and dead children? I'm tired of being shocked and depressed every time I turn a page. The same results could be accomplished through words."

We all agreed. The same result could *not* be accomplished through words. Photography hits the reader far more forcefully.

And we also agreed that while a newspaper might have policies governing the use of problem photographs that will certainly offend some readers, in the end it gets down to ethical decision making on a case-by-case basis.

I told them about what author Steven Knowlton calls "the journalist's moral compass"—a sort of personal guidance system that keeps us on an even keel in a storm. How we behave at a disaster scene and what we will show visually in the next day's paper depends on where our own personal "true north" lies.

Whatever you print, I told them, after you've made the decision to use a problem photograph, you've got to be able to articulate to yourself and the readers why you did it. What are the overriding compelling issues that prompted you to go with that photo? Are you being sensitive to potential racial issues? Is your reasoning sound? Who are the stakeholders? How would *you* feel if the roles were reversed? What are the consequences, both in the short and the long term? I told them that Bob Steele of the Poynter Institute says that this is not talking *about*

By 4 P.M. I am out of time, and there are assignments to shoot. A press conference, a mug, a ballet troupe, a local bed and breakfast that had made the four-
star rating, a basketball game. The P-1 photo from the state legislature has already been decided upon. Would I like to go along on a shoot?

Bouncing along Macon's cherry tree-lined streets in Beau Cabell's pickup
truck on the way to the ballet troupe shoot, I hear the photographer say, "You
know, all that stuff we were talking about today . . . that was cool, but in Macon
we hardly ever have to deal with anything like that."

By 6 P.M. Beau and I are back at the paper, souping the film, when Woody
rushes into the room. "We got big news happening, a murder-suicide." And he
adds grimly, "Nick was there. He's coming in."

Nick Oza, the slim, bespectacled 30-something photographer from India who
looks more like a professor than I do, had sat thoughtfully through my ethics
lecture before slipping out discreetly for an assignment.

He had been at Macon's Baconsfield Plaza getting early supper from a fast
food place when he heard a commotion outside, realized it was a shooting, and
ran back to his car. Having calmly loaded his Nikon as all hell broke loose
around him, Nick had 40 exposures shot before the yellow police tape went up.

In the newsroom now, the usually garrulous Oza was uncharacteristically
quiet.

"You OK, buddy?" Woody wants to know.

"Yes, I am fine," Nick replies stiffly. Clearly, he is shaken by what he saw and
photographed. He'll feel better when he goes to shoot that basketball game.

Woody processes the film, and over the light table looking through the loupe
he makes an exclamation of approval and alarm. The color negative below his
Rodenstock loupe shows a police officer with a concerned look on his face,
bending over the prostrate body of a young woman. He is checking for a pulse.
Blood is spattered on a nearby car door.

Woody, the front page designer, a copy editor and I begin the debate:

"What a great shot!"

"We can't use that . . ."

"But we've *gotta* use that."

"Is she alive?"

"What if she's dead?"

"What difference does that make?"

"It makes a big difference!"

"What if she's alive now and we decide we want that picture and she dies before we go to press?"

"What difference does that make?"

All eyes glued on the disturbing image on the photo desk Mac, an ad-hoc team of editors, photographers and designers from the Macon (Ga.) *Telegraph* help photo chief Woody Marshall (seated, center) make the tough call; from left to right, Beau Cabell, photographer; Nancy Badertscher, deputy news editor; Phil Dodson, copy desk chief; Kerry Griggs, page designer (and in charge of P-1 layout that night); Barbara Stinson, presentation editor; and John Parnell, page designer.

"It makes a big difference!"

"But there's no sense in sending photographers out there to make a great shot like this if we're not gonna use it."

"Hey, isn't this what we were talking about all afternoon?"

Fresh news arrives: the victim is alive. The assailant, who then killed himself with the shotgun, was an estranged boyfriend, one day out of jail on domestic violence charges. He had stalked her to the beauty college she attended at night and shot her in the chest as she got out of the car.

At the scanning station in the middle of the newsroom, the debate becomes even more democratic. The presentation editor, the police beat reporter, the news editor and other photographers huddle around Woody at the Mac, all eyes on the photo.

Woody wraps both arms around himself in thought. "You can't see her face. You really can't see much of anything bad. But some people are gonna have trouble with that blood on the car door." We all agree.

But the shooting happened at a peak rush time, in a very busy, public place in Macon, right there in Baconsfield Plaza between the Kroger and Subway, where so many people witnessed it, where so many people could have been killed or wounded by stray fire. Those considerations make it a very different sort of news story.

The crew around the computer wonders aloud: Are we being fair to the victim and her family? Would we run this picture if the victim were white? Are we re-

The Macon Telegraph

SATURDAY

Macon, Ga., January 31, 1998 ■ Our 173rd year — Number 31 ■ Home edition ■ 6 sections — 48 pages — 50¢ Daily/$1.50 Sunday
www.maconsentinel.com

House OKs no parole for some crimes

Senate, voters still must approve measure

By Tony Heffernan
The Macon Telegraph

ATLANTA - The Georgia House overwhelmingly approved legislation Friday that would abolish parole for most major crimes by July 1999.

Under the measure, adopted 141-30, a referendum would be held in November and, if voters approved, the General Assembly would define the crimes for which there would be no parole.

The legislation, billed as one of the most controversial and significant bills of the session, has already passed the Senate. But it has to go back because of changes made in the House.

Two changes made in the House were key to defusing Republican opposition and preventing potential defections by conservative Democrats from southwest Georgia.

Those changes came in a crucial bipartisan amendment, sponsored by House Majority Leader Larry Walker, D-Perry and Rep. Mack Crawford, R-Zebulon.

An amendment co-sponsored by House Majority Leader Larry Walker was designed to make it certain that the General Assembly next year would define the crimes for which there would be no parole.

Macon police officer Steven Draper renders aid to [ ] who was shot in the chest by her ex-boyfriend, in the parking lot at Baconsfield plaza Friday. Dean was on her way to class at a beauty school in the shopping center.

Nick Oza/The Macon Telegraph

Man kills ex-girlfriend, self at North Ave. plaza

The *Telegraph*'s front page, above the fold, with photographer Nick Oza's controversial and much-discussed photograph. (Page courtesy of the Macon *Telegraph*)

---

victimizing the victim? Is this gratuitous gore? Will we come off like vultures? After "doing ethics," they agree: Go with Photo A.

They also come up with a Plan B. If the victim dies, use a less offensive image of the body on a gurney. Scan in this back-up photo the same size as the first photo, and build the page from there. Then, they'll show both photos to editor Bentley and let him make the final call just before presstime.

We run the photos over to Cecil at his home, where we learn that Cecil had himself been at Baconsfield at the time of the shooting. He was heading for a phone when he saw Nick taking photographs.

By 9 P.M. Woody arrives at Cecil's with bad news. The kitchen where we have gathered grows quiet as Woody tells us the young woman has died.

One of Cecil's teen-aged daughters comes into the kitchen, looks at the blood-spattered car door and the woman dying in the parking lot. "Oooh, I don't know if I want to have to look at that in the morning," she says.

Still, Woody wants to use it. Photo A. Barbara, the presentation editor, sighs, yes. Cecil suggests that someone get a mugshot of the killer to "put a face on the crime."

Photo A. "Is that what everybody wants to do?" Cecil asks. Slow nods around the kitchen. Nobody looks especially happy about the decision. They know it will offend some readers, but all agree that the event is too unusual and too important to the community.

"I'll take the heat for it," the editor says with confidence to his kitchen cabinet.

Woody offers a story to break the intensity. "Nick phoned from the basketball game and wanted to know: 'Woody, are the photographs in focus?'" Woody replicates Nick's formal but endearing delivery, "'because I was shaking.'"

The kitchen cabinet is glad for an excuse to laugh. In the space of two short hours, the *Telegraph*'s staff had made a quantum leap from dry speculation over theoretical photos to the in-your-face reality of tomorrow's front page. It has been a long day of wrestling with the bear.

FOLLOW-UP

Public response to the photograph was "mild, very mild," says photo chief Woody Marshall. There were three calls on the *Telegraph*'s "Straight Talk" phone line that expressed objections. One caller said, "If that had been a white woman . . . you never would have put her there on the front page like that." A second caller was incensed: "Don't you people care about anybody? Is all you care about selling newspapers? The picture . . . is just too much. What about kids looking at the paper? I can't believe you did that."

The *Telegraph* received only one letter to the editor, but it was very strong, coming from a nurse who worked at the local hospital emergency room where the shooting victim died. The nurse wrote in part: "It truly sickened me to see a large picture with the dead girl's crumpled body below a car dripping with her blood. I feel that the *Telegraph* should consider the fact that not everyone, especially a grieving family, would like to see the horrific detail of a dying child's last breath on this earth. I do understand that this type of journalism sells more papers. I only wish you, the editors, could have witnessed the sadness of the child's family in the Emergency Center, then maybe you would have used more tact in reporting the details of her death."

From the *Telegraph*'s advisory board, the response was mixed but overall very positive, according to Marshall. Only one person was completely against the photo's use, saying it would have been OK if the blood on the car door had been airbrushed off. Marshall comments: "I explained very politely why we couldn't do that." And he continues, "Most everyone else thought it was good . . . because it showed what happened. . . . After the meeting one of the board members told me she didn't realize how serious we were about how we choose photos. I think she may have a new respect for the *Telegraph* photo department." And finally, Marshall thinks that learning how to "do ethics" enabled him to better articulate his reasoning for running that difficult photo.

In the week following the murder-suicide, the *Telegraph* ran three related follow-up stories that shed more light on the social context of the tragedy as it related to their community.

Editor-photographer Jeremy Waltner wrote this commentary for the Freeman (S.D.)
Courier, *a 2,000-circulation independent weekly owned by his father, Tim Waltner.*

On page three of last week's issue of the *Courier* appeared two photos of a fire
that destroyed a machine shed southeast of Freeman. There were no fatalities,
but the damage was significant.

Three weeks ago a photo appeared on page three of an overturned grain
truck. A firefighter is standing on its side, reaching in to help a victim. The pas-
senger sustained a fractured collarbone.

In the Oct. 3 issue of the *Courier*, a photo appeared on page three that showed
Freeman firefighters and EMTs working on rescuing a trapped victim from his
car after a head-on collision on the eastern edge of Freeman.

The man died that evening.

You could go back over the years: the Freeman *Courier*—like most
newspapers—has traditionally published photos of fires, accidents and other
tragedies that occur in and around our communities.

And therein lies the conflict.

One of the biggest complaints about the "media" from audiences nationwide
is that they dwell on the bad and re-victimize those involved in tragedy through
pictures.

Angry phone calls are placed. Threats are made. Subscriptions are canceled.
Advertising is pulled.

Nothing cuts to the core of ethics more, it seems, than perceived insensitivity
by journalists. . . .

. . . Other journalists and myself struggle with the issue of photo ethics all the
time. We wring our palms with sweat when we talk about it.

We question ourselves. Our motives. Our ethics.

For the issue is very gray.

Perhaps our motives for publishing pictures depicting tragedy are misunderstood. Contrary to what some believe, we don't slap a picture down on the
paste-up and send it to press, cackling in our triumph:

Ah, ha! Another newspaper sold.

For most journalists at most publications around the world, that is far from
the case.

In reality, we ask a lot of questions and find the answers frustratingly vague.

When do we and when do we not publish a photo?

Does it make a difference if there's a fatality?

Does it make a difference if blood is visible in the picture?

What if we can see the victim's face?

What's too graphic?

What's too intrusive?

When are photographers invading somebody's right to privacy?

Are we there to document history?

Are we there to sell newspapers?

Are we there to show the truth?

Why is it when the fire whistle blows and the ambulance goes, we're right behind?

Are we glorified ambulance chasers?

Is that all we are?

If so, how come?

And should we change?

What if (from when the camera was first invented until now) there were a written code of ethics that pictures of fires and accidents (could) never be documented on film?

We wouldn't have pictures of World War II, the *Challenger* explosion, the plane crash that killed South Dakota Governor George Mickelson, the fire that destroyed the South Church east of Freeman, the accident earlier this month that claimed the life of a young Sioux Falls man. . . .

When do we start taking pictures, and when do we stop?

There's no code.

But everybody seems to have an answer.

The issue of accident photos in newspapers is an ongoing debate that will continue long into the future.

And my hope is that readers will understand that most newspapers struggle long and hard with the issue, trying to strike a balance between sensitivity and documenting history.

Your Town; Your Turn

1. Does your newspaper have guidelines for ethically challenging dilemmas? Are they written down or just implied? What's the paper's policy on reporting suicides?
2. Does your paper have a "dead body" rule? What would you have done in the case of the tractor wreck?
3. The local Ruritan Club has raised $500 for new playground equipment at the town park. The members of the club want the *Bugle* to take a photo of the check presentation. What do you tell them?

SEVENTEEN

We Mean Business, Too

Super Mario versus Reality

Mario had always wanted his own paper. At eight, he'd put out a neighborhood newsletter. In high school, he started an underground 'zine of his own; he'd never gotten over the thrill.

Now he was in his mid-20s and had a couple of years under his belt at a mediocre chain-owned afternoon daily with a circulation of about 14,000. Mario told himself he wasn't totally miserable at the paper, but he wasn't inspired either. Nobody cared much about quality journalism or community growth. It was time to do one of two things: Find a job at a better paper where he could get expert editorial guidance—or look into getting a paper of his own.

The very thought of his own paper left him sleepless with excitement for several nights. Then one day, making his rounds in a neighboring town, he got his break. A local commercial printer had recently bought a thriving print-shop business that included the *Sun*, an old, white-elephant sort of community newspaper. The paper had been started by the former owner's grandfather, and for sentimental reasons, the old rag had been kept afloat by the commercial printing part of the business.

Now, the new owner wanted to unload the white elephant and keep the cash cow. He quoted a price that sounded unbelievable to Mario. For less than a new car, he would have his own paper.

But something kept nibbling at the edges of his consciousness. A question begged to be answered: If the old *Sun* hadn't been a success in this town, would it be a success just because of Mario's presence? Mario had to admit, although he was a newsie, when it came down to the business of running a paper, he was a newbie. Back at the J-school at State U., he hadn't thought of taking advertising, business or media management courses. Now he realized, he could have used that background.

But he did have a name. His old college newspaper's faculty adviser was a former community newspaperman who'd had his own paper. Mario decided to call Professor Bolton.

"I was about your age when I helped start my first paper," Bolton told Mario when the young man phoned. Mario's spirits soared, and then plummeted when Bolton warned, "You've got to realize two things: A newspaper is a business first. And, secondly, if there's not enough advertising in your area, it doesn't matter what a hotshot writer you are, the paper won't make it."

Mario responded, "But Professor Bolton, the *Sun* has lots of ads."

"Yes, Mario," Bolton replied, "But who are they from, how big are they? And what percentage of the paper generates income?"

Mario had to admit he'd been mainly concerned with that nice big juicy news hole. He didn't know about the ads, just that it seemed like there were ads on most pages.

Bolton advised Mario to select four random issues of the *Sun*, and catalog the ads: the name of each business, the size of each ad, and the reappearance of the ad or that business in subsequent issues. Mario was to compile the total column inches (multiply columns times vertical inches) of the entire paper, compute the ad inches in the same way, and figure out the percentage of ads.

Finally, Bolton told Mario to multiply the number of ad inches in each paper times the paper's open-column inch rate. That way, Mario could tell fairly accurately just how much money each issue of the *Sun* generated. Doing that would give Mario a fair idea of how much advertising revenue each issue generated. Using that number as a benchmark, Mario needed only simple math to figure out the *Sun*'s monthly advertising income.

Mario's research revealed that an average issue of the *Sun* carried 24 ads, all local, ranging in size from one column by one inch to the largest at three columns by 10 inches deep. The average size was a two by four (two columns wide by four inches deep). There were no full-page ads, no big department stores, and not a single large grocery-store chain in town. The *Sun* was under 20 percent ads. In addition, Mario discovered that the full page of classifieds the *Sun* carried all turned out to be freebies.

When Mario compared his projected ad-generated income to his projected expenses, he was shocked. The *Sun* would be lucky just to come close to breaking even every month—and that was if Mario did it all himself. He'd have to get a day job to support his newspaper habit. And hiring a staff was out of the question.

Not surprisingly, Mario didn't need Bolton's advice to save him from crashing into the *Sun*. Mario could see for himself: Little wonder the paper had been carried by the print shop all these years. Mario conceded that Bolton had been right when he'd said, "If your ad base is nothing but mom 'n' pop places (unless you're independently wealthy), your paper is going to be a mom 'n' pop weekly."

Sadder but wiser, Mario resolved to hunker down at his old job, keep his counsel, and bide his time until another opportunity presented itself. He knew that it was just a matter of time.

Ripley's Believe It or Not

Veteran editor-publisher Ken Ripley says a community newspaper has four separate functions. And to be as successful as Ripley, a publisher must balance the four:

1. It's a business first. It must make money not just to survive, but also to support the other three functions.
2. It's a creative shop. It produces writing, photography and design.
3. It's a factory. The paper has a production cycle that must be met without fail.
4. It's a community institution. They don't call it the fourth estate without good reason. Ripley says, "We not just printers; we're editors."

It's None of Your Business?

When Joan spotted the movie ad on the paste-up board in the backshop, she felt her temperature rise; how could Buzz, the *Bugle*'s veteran advertising director, let such a piece of trash get in the paper? The ad for the Bijou theater displayed a mostly naked young woman on her knees, hands tied behind her, about to be abused by a leering male standing over her. It didn't help that the submissive figure in the ad was about Joan's age.

As the young M.E. glared at the lurid Bijou ad, she tried to reason beyond her growing indignation: Buzz is on vacation this week; we're about to go to press; what harm can come if I jerk this ad? It's clearly prurient, designed to titillate; and furthermore, it's way beyond the acceptable limit of taste according to our community's standards.

Without telling anyone, Joan removed the 2 × 10 movie ad from the paste-up, replacing it with a standing house ad, one that urged readers to use the *Bugle* classifieds. Then she promptly put the incident out of her mind and went about the business of running the news department.

"How could you do that?!" Buzz was practically shouting.

"Do what?" Joan barely looked up from her computer. She was concentrating on the end of a really complex zoning ordinance story for that day's deadline. She didn't usually have to talk to people from the business side.

"You know very well what I'm talking about!" Buzz said hotly. Then the ad director, trying to keep his anger in check, lowered his voice with visible effort, "Look Joan, I know you're the M.E., but I get back from my vacation only to find that last week's Bijou ad got pulled. Did anyone ask me first? Did anyone even bother to warn the Bijou manager? No! And now he's pulled all his ads from us, and he's going to the competition. Can't you see where that puts me?"

Joan was fully engaged now. "Yes, Buzz, but that movie ad was soft porn—downright obscene," she said.

"It may have been," Buzz responded reasonably. "But it was *my* call. What you did was the same as if I came over and jerked a story off the front page without telling you—just because the subject matter offended me."

"Well, you're right about that," she said. "That would light my fuse."

"And not only that," Buzz went on, "but the Bijou manager is so mad he's talking it up with all his business buddies, and the whole incident has damaged my and the *Bugle*'s credibility in the advertising community."

"But it's just one little ad," Joan said without thinking.

Buzz had to sit down and take a deep breath before telling his young M.E. the facts of community journalism business life.

"You just don't get it, do you? Look Joan, the entire paper is built on such little ads. One little ad after another; each one the result of a carefully crafted relationship between me and the store owner. From the mom 'n' pop fruit stand that runs a one-column by two-inch ad to the big supermarket with its full-page ad . . . to me, to you, and to the *Bugle*, they're all equally important.

"At the risk of sounding like I'm preaching, let me remind you what pays the bills around here and what makes your paycheck possible. In my years I've seen editors and reporters come and go, and you newsies are all alike. You think you're so almighty powerful and important. You look down your noses at us ad people as mercenary bean counters. But let me tell you—without us, without the ads, you'd have nothing to print your news on. News doesn't make money; advertising does." Buzz was clearly on a tear.

Joan held up both hands and laughed, "OK, Buzz, OK, down boy, I'm starting to get it. I admit it—I've never thought about the newspaper business like that. But hey, what about subscriptions? What about street sales, news racks and circulation? I thought that made money. People buy papers for the news more than for the ads."

Buzz took another deep breath. "Welcome to Community Journalism Business 101," he began. "First of all, you'd be surprised at how many people buy the paper mainly for the ads, and just give the news a glance. Secondly, yes, circulation does bring in revenue, but only about 10 percent of our gross comes from subscriptions and street sales. In other words, *circulation about pays for itself*. Remember, the postal rates aren't cheap, and we pay our route carriers to deliver those *Bugles* all over the county every afternoon. It's advertising—local advertising—that carries the freight."

Joan sat there a minute thinking, and then said: "You know Buzz, in one sense I'm sorry I pulled that ad; you're right, I shouldn't have done that, and I see your point. On the other hand, I don't think the *Bugle* has any business portraying women the way that ad did. That ad was disgusting, and this is a family newspaper. And I'm just as serious as I can be about that.

"But I also think I owe the Bijou manager an apology and an explanation. What do you think about my going out to the mall and speaking with him? Maybe I can get your ads back and at the same time get him to start running ads that are more in keeping with this community's standards. How does all that sit with you?" Joan finished.

Buzz exhaled in relief, "Joan, that'd be great. And you're right, I admit, that ad was over the line; I really didn't even look at it when it came in, I was in such a hurry to get things done and go on vacation."

Then an idea struck Buzz. "Say, Joan, maybe you and I could sit down some time with the publisher and think about this notion of community standards as it relates to advertising. It would help me and my staff, as well as the advertisers, if we had a written set of guidelines."

About That Bottom Line

The narratives about Joan and Mario are based on true stories. They both underscore a critical fact of community journalism that most young, dewy-eyed reporters don't want to hear.

"I loved advertising," says former editor-publisher Bob Hillard of Washington State University. "*I never met a news story that paid the rent.*"

No matter how altruistic our values, we on the news side can't escape the fact: A newspaper is a business. It is a business first, and it is a business in the end. When a newspaper folds, it fails because the advertising didn't happen. When a paper succeeds, though the news side may want to take all the credit, it is a business success. Advertising—local display advertising—makes the news possible. If you want to survive in this arena, give the folks on the business side the respect and support they deserve.

Remember the quote on the wall from the Southern Pines *Pilot*: "Advertising makes possible the free press."

If a newspaper is skating on thin ice financially, creativity and journalistic fervor can be hard to come by. Editor-publisher Bob Buckel of the very successful 4,880-circulation Azle (Texas) *News* learned a terrible lesson back in the 1980s when he lost an earlier paper. Buckel puts it bluntly, "It's difficult to be fearless when you're one advertiser away from extinction."

A community newspaper must be prospering financially in order for it to fulfill its destiny as a positive and effective factor in community growth. Frank E. Gannett, the founder of the immensely successful Gannett chain, realized that when in 1948 he said, "The independent community newspaper has two incentives: To promote the general welfare and to make money. Like the physician, it must be more concerned with the good that it does."

Wealthy Enough to Be Honest?

Mark, a dedicated journalism student, was mystified when he heard community journalism professor Ken Byerly say, "You've got to be wealthy enough to be honest."

Only two years later, Mark found himself with the title of news editor of the *Bugle*, a struggling but quality 5,000-circulation weekly. It wasn't long before he would hear Byerly's words resonate. The son of the manager of Bleck's department store had been arrested for suspected DUI and marijuana possession. The father called the paper, threatening, "If you run that story, I'll pull my ad. And as you know, I'm your biggest advertiser."

Mark now realized just how right his old professor had been. He'd have to stand up to the manager of Bleck's. Do it politely and with respect. To do otherwise—to kill the story to keep the advertising—would be reprehensible. The *Bugle* had to be wealthy enough to allow Mark to be honest.

That meant that the *Bugle* had to be able to ride out the storm of lost revenues. Yes, it would hurt everybody on the paper, but to cave in to the demands of the big advertiser would be to sacrifice his and his paper's integrity and credibility on the altar of just staying alive financially.

What the father really feared was a front-page banner-headline story of his son's arrest, a fear that was evident when he dropped in at the *Bugle*'s offices. So the editor calmly explained how the *Bugle* handled such stories: It would receive no special treatment and be placed inside the paper, down among the police blotter stories in small type. Mark tried to help the distraught father realize the *Bugle*'s obligation to provide complete, fair and accurate coverage. "If my son was busted," Mark explained, "I'd have to report that, just the same."

The Bleck's manager would not be placated. As he left Mark's office, he made good on his threat and pulled his full-page ad from that week's *Bugle*.

For a whole month, nothing changed. Mark held his breath while the Bugle's ad director went about the office ashen faced. He supported Mark's decision, and on the streets put on an air of courage. But all the same he was privately shaken by the course of events.

And then, miraculously, Bleck's came back, along with a note from the manager. In it, the father wrote: "I was surprised by two things: How many people told me they respected the *Bugle* for doing what it had to do, and how many people told me, 'We missed your ad in the *Bugle*.'"

Mark breathed a silent thanks to his old journalism professor.

When Too Much Advertising Is Too Much

If a publisher is interested in only making money, then that publisher might as well be putting out a "shopper," of which there are plenty. The shopper carries nothing but ads—or if there is a news hole, it's tiny, or filled with canned copy and superfluous filler. This type of paper makes no pretense at covering the news; its sole reason for being is to make money. Typically, you'll find the shopper as a freebie tabloid in supermarket racks. Such a publication makes no claims to being a true newspaper; the owners are in it for the bucks.

More insidious is the mock community paper disguised as a shopper. These papers claim "total market coverage" (TMC) and so, armed with the impressive circulation numbers, are able to convince local advertisers of their market penetration. By itself there's nothing ethically wrong with that. However, some such closet shoppers fill their news hole with retrofitted "news" from other papers, or, worse, replate a local front page, and fill most of the rest of the news hole with canned stuffing they get by subscribing to the feature services. Such publications do a vast disservice to the name of quality community journalism. (For that reason, when crunching the numbers for this edition, your author deleted the shoppers from the statistical totals provided by the *Editor & Publisher Year Book*.) Finally, it must be noted that many high-quality community newspapers fight fire with fire by creating their own TMC shoppers just to keep out the competition.

What Really Matters

When newspaper consultant Bill Fuller says that for a paper to succeed it must be vital, he means more than just vital to the community as a source of news. He means business, too.

A community newspaper must be vital to the reader as a source for business information, sales, product reinforcement, business identity—in other words, advertising.

Just as clearly, Fuller stresses that the paper must be vital to its advertisers, providing a platform for timely messages, significant circulation, and market penetration.

The publisher of the Dixon (Ill.) *Telegraph*, William Shaw, understands that reciprocal relationship between advertiser and newspaper. In a unique, award-winning publication called the *Owner's Manual of The Telegraph*, Shaw says, "The readers are the real owners of this newspaper. . . . It is not enough for us to convince people to buy the newspaper. They must buy into it. Only then can we claim to have a healthy partnership with our owners."

The *Owner's Manual* further underscores the paper's vital role in the community: "From the publisher's desk to the mail room, there is one overriding philosophy *The Telegraph* subscribes to. Give the readers a full-service newspaper, one that is filled with information which will make their lives more meaningful, more rewarding and more interesting."

The ad staff's stated goal is "to help businesses prosper." The *Owner's Manual* explains: "Calvin Coolidge once said, 'The chief business of America is business.' That's something *The Telegraph*'s Display Advertising Department can relate to. Because, to paraphrase the 30th president, the chief business of the Display Advertising Department is to help businesses."

After emphasizing that the six sales reps "are all LOCAL and have a good insight into the communities we cover," the *Owner's Manual* demonstrates just how vital *The Telegraph*'s advertising is with the following blurb: "If you were to mail a 3 × 5 postcard to each one of *The Telegraph*'s nearly 11,000 subscribers, it would cost you

$2,090. But if you were to place a FULL PAGE AD in *The Telegraph* and cover the same number of people, that would cost you $737. A full page ad would have a much larger impact than the postcard, and look at the cost savings."

An Advertising Snapshot of One State

Newspaper advertising works. Just as people read their community newspaper to get local information, so—polls have revealed—readers value newspapers for advertising content.

"Two-thirds of adults say newspapers have the best shopping information," compared to TV, radio and the Internet, according to the 2000 North Carolina Statewide Readership Survey created by Belden Associates for the N.C. Press Association. Other statistics:

Three-quarters of those polled said the paper is the best place to get information on where to shop for special sales. Sixty percent said newspapers have the most helpful ads. Sixty percent said they looked at grocery store ads. And 71–73 percent said they relied on their newspaper when shopping for a new or previously owned house or vehicle.

And you can take that to the bank.

You Scratch Here, and I'll Scratch There

Bob and Peg Allen spent almost 50 years building their high-quality family-owned newspaper, the *Wake Weekly* of Wake Forest, N.C. Over the years, all four of their sons have worked at the paper at some time or other. The Allens sold the *WW* in 1998, but it didn't go far from home. (See Chapter 18 for the story.)

While they were still running the paper, they reflected on the topic of the business of community journalism.

Peg observed, "Bob says advertising now has become a science. It is no longer enough to say you have a good paper with strong readership. Advertisers want demographics. They need cold hard facts."

Bob's advice was to consult good books on newspaper advertising, attend area seminars on advertising and seek outside help. Peg said, "Bob found it particularly useful to organize an all-day Saturday advertising seminar with an expert from Georgia. Area weeklies attended, and it proved to be a helpful event."

Peg explained that all community newspapers "are struggling with direct-mail, big dailies who want to move back into the communities they have been ignoring. Some [big metro dailies] publish free tabs to squeeze into the markets traditionally held by community papers.

"Perhaps the biggest competition is the circular ads in the big dailies. In our county, chains [stores] think they don't need to be in the local papers." Peg said this was occurring despite a survey that showed the *Wake Weekly* had more circulation in the local zip code area than the major metro daily from the nearby city.

To counter this, the Allens stressed local advertising. "Bob tries to get his ad people to realize they must know their advertisers," Peg observed. The Allens know shopping at home helps. On one Saturday jaunt to a local strawberry farm, Bob picked up an ad, took photos of the owner for a future feature, and then proceeded to purchase armloads of strawberries, which he distributed to his staff back at the paper.

Bob may not have needed those strawberries, but in this business, if we don't shop at home, how can we expect our advertisers to do the same when it comes to us?

One Publisher's Puzzle

It's one thing to shop at home in hopes that they'll remember you when it comes time to advertise. It's entirely another thing to make local news content dependent on advertising.

Consider the following dilemma. The weekly *Bugle* is faced with competition from a new shopper, called the *Merchant*. The latter carries no news whatsoever, only classifieds and display ads. In the words of the *Bugle*'s news editor, Mark, here's the situation:

> Very often different local groups that have something going on will contact us about the *Bugle* doing an article or something, or maybe they'll submit a photo. Then we'll do a little piece on it. And when we pick up the *Merchant* that week, the same group has bought a full page ad to advertise it! Of course, they haven't run an ad with us! My publisher thinks that if groups like this spend money with the *Merchant*, they should spend money with the *Bugle* too. The result is my publisher doesn't want to include *any info on the event* as a news item unless the group buys an ad. For example, an area golf course sent us a press release about an upcoming job fair. The golf course also ran a full page ad with the *Merchant* but none with us. My publisher decided not to run anything about the job fair in the *Bugle*.

So what do you think the *Bugle* should do? Should they stonewall groups such as the golf course that buy an ad in the competition but not in the *Bugle*? After all, a newspaper is a business. Or doesn't the *Bugle* have a higher calling? Don't they owe it to their readers to let them know about the event? Put yourself in Mark's shoes.

On the Separation of Church and State

While advertising may float the financial boat, news content (including features, sports, lifestyle and editorial) must remain independent of financial influence, unfettered by advertisers' lobbying. To do otherwise is to suggest that there is a relationship between money and news content, that the paper's news content can be bought.

For us, it's as sacred as the separation of church and state: There should be absolutely no relationship between advertising and news content. It is morally corrupt for a publisher to say or imply: "If you advertise, I'll do a story on you."

Remember, advertising sells influence and what they call "eyeballs on pages." All the news side has going for it is credibility. Once trust is lost, news is devalued. If your readers come to believe that news content in their paper is dictated by various businesses buying advertising, then your paper is in serious trouble.

According to Irene Van Winkle, staff reporter for the Kerrville (Texas) *Mountain Sun*, a 5,000-circulation weekly, that's why her paper has two signs posted in the lobby: "THEM" and "US," with arrows pointing in opposite directions, one toward the advertising and business offices and the other toward the newsroom.

Your Town; Your Turn

1. How would you characterize the relationship at your paper between the business people and the newsroom? If you see resentment and bad feelings, see if you can determine where they come from.
2. Determine to the best of your ability who really "owns" your paper.
3. Does your newspaper have business competition? What is the nature of that competition and what is your paper doing about it?
4. Ask your publisher what the biggest business problem or challenge facing your newspaper is right now. What is he or she doing about it?
5. Does your paper have "good taste" rules for the advertising it will accept or reject? If so, what are the guidelines? If the paper doesn't have such standards, why doesn't it?

EIGHTEEN

Newsroom Management
The *Personnel* Approach

Why This Matters To You

David Day, a Penn State associate professor of psychology who studies businesses, describes the challenge like this: "Dealing with personnel is probably the toughest thing managers have to do—yet it's the thing for which they're the least prepared."

If you are a college student or a newcomer to the field contemplating a career in community journalism, you may think you're years away from becoming an editor or publisher. But in community journalism, things can happen quickly and without much warning. Sooner than you might imagine you could find yourself in a management position in which your personnel abilities will be tested. Some come by their people skills naturally; others must learn the hard way. Usually, it's an acquired skill. At a community newspaper, where in many cases the newsroom resembles a goldfish bowl, personnel work can be a demanding and time-consuming task. Many papers can't afford the luxury of personnel managers; it's just part of the editors' many duties.

So how does a successful editor inspire the paper's staff to reach consistent levels of quality work while dealing with an individual's problems?

One key is to look at and understand the various relationships that exist under one roof. Consider the following single relationship in microcosm, and then how it relates to the big picture.

Our Relt Is in Trble

Kathy loved her work, no question about that. As the chief photographer for the *Bugle*, she found personal fulfillment, professional rewards and enough creative satisfaction to keep her going eight days a week and far into the nights.

Never turning down an assignment opportunity and gladly taking on weekend darkroom duties, Kathy was the model employee—cheerful and bright at work. People wondered how she did it.

Her husband, Brian, thought he knew. She brought it all home—what little time she was home. She'd come in from another 12-hour day, fall on the bed and inevitably start complaining about whatever had ticked her off that day. Or she'd unload on him—or even worse—on their 5-year-old, Seth, for some trivial misdeed.

Brian, a quiet, thoughtful accountant, was trying to make this relationship work. After all, he reasoned,

Space is tight and so are relationships at community papers. When you think about our newsrooms, remember the old Beatles classic, "All Together Now," because that's the way it is. Above, some of the news staff of the 10,000-circulation Bedford (Pa.) *Gazette* gather in the morning to hash out the day's events, including, from left to right, executive editor Chris Frear, feature editor Vicki Henry, Lee Frear from the accounting office, copy editor Paul Rowan, and acting feature editor and reporter Leslie Lauer.

hadn't Kathy supported him by working at the local paper while he'd finished college? Now he was keeping his part of the silent bargain, helping with Seth while Kathy was out shooting evening sports, city council meetings, Boy Scout field days, farmers' markets, Special Olympics, the arts festival, the college's theater group in rehearsal . . . There seemed to be no end to the events that took Kathy away from her family.

In short, Brian was starting to feel as if he were raising the kindergartner by himself while Kathy was out covering what he was coming to regard as petty events. It was a good thing he could cook, too, he told himself with growing bitterness, or else he and Seth would have starved long ago. He tried to remember, when was the last time the three of them had sat down at the dinner table together?

Brian realized he was starting to openly resent Kathy's work schedule. But every time he mentioned the problem to Kathy, she either blew up or dissolved in tears. He'd even hinted at their going to a marriage counselor. But Kathy had dismissed that notion with the typical statement: "You know how busy I am." He never mentioned it again.

And the worst part of it, little Seth could feel the tension between them.

It all blew up on the day of Seth's class play. Brian had even made the little boy's costume (the program listed Seth as a Rock in the environmental play). But when Kathy failed to show up for the play—and hours later explained in a hurried phone call that there'd been a bad wreck out on the four-lane, the patient, loyal Brian knew his long fuse had about burned down.

He decided he'd try writing it all out for Kathy. But once Brian started, he found he couldn't write fast enough to record the flood of pent-up anger spewing out on the page. In his haste, he began condensing words and leaving out letters.

One sentence read: "Our relt is in trble." And from then on in the letter, every time Brian wanted to use the word "relationship," he simply scrawled the abbreviation "relt."

When Kathy read the letter, she couldn't understand, first of all, why he was mad at her and, second, what was this goofy word "relt"?

"It's short for relationship!" Brian exploded at last, "and short is what our relationship is! Don't you see? What kind of relationship is this? We don't even see each other enough to have a relationship. All we've got is a—*relt*."

We're All in This Together, Again

That story could have been written about a journalist and her spouse on a large metro daily as well, but when the above scenario occurs at a community paper the fallout is much more widespread.

The theorem goes like this: Because everything on a community paper is more concentrated—fewer people to do the job all packed in a smaller space—relationships can't help but be intensely personal. It's all the same, whether it's between colleagues, editors and staffers, business and news, word people and picture people, backshop and newsroom.

It boils down to a basic nut graf: We're all in this together. If that sounds familiar, it's because the same statement has been made about the paper's relationship with the community. That philosophy applies equally to the internal workings of the paper, too. Contrary to the situation at many large metro daily papers, where some reporters don't even know each other, on the community paper it's like the old country expression: If Mama ain't happy, ain't nobody happy. In this line of work, everything touches everybody.

For instance, it's not unusual for a publisher like award-winner Gene Johnson of the 6,327-circulation weekly White Bear Lake (Minn.) *Press* to refer to his staff and employees as "our family"—and mean it.

Community journalism, which has been called "the journalism of inclusion," may be the only form of American newspapering in which its practitioners still embrace the concept of being neighborly in the professional context.

Small newspaper staffs resemble families much more than their counterparts at the big-city dailies, where journalists can live in the luxury of anonymity if they so choose. As with a family, community newspaper staffers are thrown together in close proximity with people they did not chose to be with, and basically they have to live with each other's faults, foibles and bad habits. The extent to which a newspaper staff thrives is a function of how well they have come to terms with each other's individualities.

When it works well, it can be a lot of fun. "We're close outside of work, and we're close inside of work," graphic designer Richard Holladay of the Asheboro (N.C.) *Courier-Tribune* told community journalism student Christina Rexrode.

Whether you want to or not, you will come to know each other's weaknesses, strengths, personal lives, husbands, wives, kids, significant others, histories, hopes, dreams, hobbies, fetishes, phobias, pets, pet peeves, drinking habits and whether you like your coffee black and your hot dogs with relish. You may not even like each other, but you must learn to work and survive together.

Then, consider the nature of the beast. We're not talking about running a shoe store here. Take this goulash of egos mixed together and throw it into a high-stress, deadline-driven, high-profile, production-oriented enterprise that never seems to take a holiday—and what do you expect?

There are going to be fireworks.

When personnel problems ignite, the most common problem areas are conflicts between the community newspaper staffer and a spouse or significant other not in the business; between staffers themselves, in and across department lines; and between labor and management.

It's another truism of our business: Every facet of our work is more personal, even personnel work.

If a community paper's chief photographer is having marital problems, it's going to be felt in the newsroom. Once Brian confronted Kathy about their non-relt, it was bound to show up in her work. Not only is the conflict going to impact Kathy and her attitude when she's in the newsroom or darkroom, but it could also start to have a negative impact on the look of the entire newspaper as well.

Can This Marriage Be Saved?

How do you stay married to a non-media partner (or have a real relationship) and still be a good community newsperson? What do you do about a non-media spouse who doesn't understand your devotion to your craft and your calling, and who resents the time it takes for you to do the job?

Work comes first, doesn't it?

Not . . . exactly.

Every couple has to work out for themselves what matters. It comes down to balancing a constellation of priorities. Perhaps the bright spots in one couple's constellation might be work/career, family, lifestyle, location—not necessarily in that order. Depending on individual needs and situations, the priorities are always shifting among elements in the constellation.

The media spouse, however, must make it plain to the non-media partner that because this work is time-driven, the professional life may seem all-enveloping. Understandably, this is a business that is rough on marriages. You can make it work, but you have to be aware of and understand the speed bumps.

A couple of common sense guidelines for relts:

"Newsies" tend to be big egos. It's a common mistake to assume your mate automatically thinks of your work as a divine calling; more likely your partner will not share your enthusiasm for your coverage of the city council or the Little League. Share, don't preach. Try to get your significant other involved with your work. Explain the issues and your perspectives on each story you're working on.

Give equal time; what's going on in your partner's world? Listen well, and don't swing the conversation back around to you and your work. Establish time for creative conversations when there's no talking shop allowed, times when you both agree that talking about work is off limits.

On the topic of relts in the newsroom—you've heard that old expression, "Don't get your honey where you get your money." But it's no accident there are so many media relationships, simply because of proximity, common interest and just plain chemistry. Still, such a relationship has no guarantee of working out any better than the media/non-media mix. There are pitfalls aplenty for the couple who work together, including natural competition for headlines and bylines; conflicts over career direction, salary, and promotion; conflict of interest; and possibly even who works for whom. Some papers have strict guidelines about spouses working together; some forbid it outright, whereas others not only allow it but actually encourage it, figuring such a union guarantees staff permanence.

Other Voices; Other Newsrooms

FAMILY-OWNED PAPERS

The declining number of family-owned newspapers and the rise of the chain-owned community papers has been well documented. No other single change has so dominated the American community journalism landscape over the last quarter century. But it would be a mistake to read the eulogy for the family-owned paper— far from it. There are thriving, quality family-owned papers out there. In fact, in my home state *52 percent of the "non-dailies" are still independent*—and many of them are family-owned. The question for now is, how do they do it? How do they get along, brothers and sisters, wives and husbands, moms and dads working together? Do they bring it home each night? Are they happy? How do they keep winning press contests? What's their secret for success? Let's visit two such high-quality weeklies, both located in North Carolina.

The *Wake Weekly*—a Look Back

In the following section, written in 1993, we meet again the remarkable Allens of Wake Forest, N.C. Bob and Peggy Allen have put out the *Wake Weekly* since the early '50s. The paper has been regularly ranked among the very best of the state's weekly newspapers. But it took a long haul for Bob and Peg to get the *WW* to the coveted first place in the general excellence category.

It's been a family operation from the get-go. Bob, only 22, bought into the paper with his older brother in the early '50s, and by 1956 Bob and Peg owned the *Wake Weekly* outright. For years, Bob was in charge of selling ads and Peg managed the news side. Peg recalls, "Bob was the only ad salesman until Greg, [our] second son, was old enough to help out. News coverage, including meetings, was shared by the two [parents], with the one not attending a meeting tending to the kids."

When asked if they took the business home, you could almost hear Peg chuckle as she responded: "Through the years [we] didn't take the business home as much as the business kept [us] at the office. As the boys grew—there are four—they helped out around the office, cleaning . . . pulling proofs. Mostly, they did homework in the spare office and slept on the floor (4 A.M. Tuesdays not being unusual) until it was time to go home. That was one way to keep them away from TV."

The Allens considered themselves fortunate to have four sons who are or have been involved in the business. Jimmy was news editor for years. His wife, Ginger, a bright University of North Carolina at Chapel Hill intern from a few summers ago, covered school and county government and did features. Bobby, the oldest son, worked in the front office and helped with proofing and classifieds. Son Greg, after graduating from the University of North Carolina at Chapel Hill, became the *Weekly*'s ad manager, a position he held for several years, until he decided to sell for an Ohio-based graphics company supplying newspaper-related copiers. Todd, the youngest, also finished at UNC-CH, and took up the reins as ad manager for a time.

The Allens, as they contemplated thoughts of retirement, realized they had a rare thing in a family newspaper. Peg said, "Everyone will help out when another is in a bind. Family is more apt to volunteer than employees, it seems. The family is also a good sounding board about all kinds of problems from editorials to ads." And, she noted, no matter how far the four boys may roam from Wake Forest, "You can take the boys out of the paper, but you can't take the paper out of the boys."

She conceded there is a certain prestige—"whether the family would admit it or not—to being the town newspaper folks." But that status has not come without its own demands. Through the years the family has been highly active in the community. Peg observed that "Bob and two of the boys served on the Chamber

All in the family: During the summer of 1984, the Allen family and staff toil on the next edition of the *Wake Weekly*.

[of Commerce] board, Fourth of July committee and about everything that comes along." But the Allens made sure their boys knew the light of justice and print shone equally on all. They believed raising the boys in the community news business "has helped the boys become good citizens. A family newspaper business is a good one for bringing up children as law-abiding, involved citizens. They always knew if they got in trouble, they would see their names in the paper."

The Allens built the *Wake Weekly* from a struggling paper with barely 700 subscribers (many of whom, back in '52, didn't even pay to receive the paper) to a prosperous, successful, respected home-owned weekly.

Peg asked herself, "Would [we] do it again? Of course. In fact [we] are having a hard time thinking of retirement." The Allens said they would like nothing better than to have the sons or some of them continue running the paper.

PASSING THE BATON

By 1998 big changes had taken place at the *Wake Weekly*.

Who says, "You can't go home again"?

Thomas Wolfe must not have envisioned Greg Allen when he wrote the novel titled with that classic line about homecoming.

Greg, who had worked on the paper from the third grade through high school and then after college as well, is the second oldest of the four Allen boys. He left the paper in 1991, in part because "there were too many Allens," he says with a wry grin.

For seven years Greg sold newspaper graphics systems, and admits now he never dreamed of coming back home—much less taking over the family paper.

But in 1997, with Bob and Peg pushing their late 60s, the *Wake Weekly* came a hairsbreadth from being sold. Greg says he had something of an epiphany. His younger brother Jimmy (the paper's news editor for 11 years) pitched to him the idea that they could and should team up and buy the paper from their parents.

But even after they figured out the financing, the issue of leadership had them baffled.

After weeks of going back and forth, the two brothers came to an unusual conclusion. Greg was reluctant to go 50-50, afraid that in a crunch only one person should have to make the tough call. And Greg wanted to be that person. Then Jimmy bowled everybody over by announcing that he wanted to go into the ministry.

Jimmy says, "We were darned close" to an agreement," but then "I sensed this call . . ."

So Greg did the newspaper deal by himself, assuming the position as publisher on Jan. 1, 1998.

And after a transition period in which the brothers worked together, Jimmy went off that summer to Campbell University to earn his master's degree in divinity. As irony would have it, Jimmy then became the assistant editor of the *Biblical Recorder*, the 48,000-circulation weekly tabloid-format journal of the Baptist State Convention of North Carolina. So while he was going to school, Jimmy was still doing community journalism. "It's like a big community newspaper," he maintained at the time, because "you're still dealing with a community, only in a more nurturing fashion." In addition, he served part time in a youth ministry, and he and Ginger had three little girls under the age of 5.

In Wake Forest, walking around town with the new publisher, observing how people interacted with Greg, one couldn't help but get the feeling that folks were delighted with Greg and pleased that the *Weekly* had stayed an independent, locally owned community paper.

He said, "Because we own it, we're fortunate that we don't have a board of directors telling us what the profit margin has got to be."

FAST FORWARD FIVE YEARS

If you had to choose one word to describe the *Wake Weekly* and the town of Wake Forest in the five years following the change in ownership, it would be "growth."

Greg Allen's paper has grown in multiple ways in addition to circulation, up by 1,000. The paper is larger (42–52 pages) and has more color. But other changes are not so apparent to readers: an increase in staff, new advances in technology and, most recently, a long-range strategic business organization plan that has given structure to everything they do now, Greg says.

His coverage area has changed dramatically too. The population has doubled, most of that coming in Wake Forest alone. Then add the influx of thousands of new

residents in two nearby planned golf course communities (complete with their own schools)—"Wakefield" and "Heritage," each encompassing a couple of thousand homes. In addition, nearby towns in their coverage area, like Rolesville with 1,500 new housing starts this year, are "exploding."

It's a classic example of urban sprawl: folks who work in the burgeoning region of Raleigh, Durham, and the Research Triangle Park being willing to drive an hour to and from their jobs daily so they can have the amenities of small-town life (albeit with golf courses).

Of concern: Because his circulation of 8,500 has not kept pace with the population growth, Greg plans to aggressively court these new citizens with a subdivision by subdivision circulation campaign.

Realizing they needed a solid organizational structure as the paper and its staff grew, Greg and wife Janet Rose (vice president and co-publisher) brought in a team of business consultants. "It was like getting an MBA in five weeks," Greg vows. Now, each staffer is a part of one of four management teams with a clear chain of command. The heads of the management teams meet with Greg and Janet Rose weekly for planning sessions; and once a month two departments have lunch together.

"Here's what [the reorganization] did," Greg says. "It's allowed people to have control over their departments. Al, who has been with us for 50 years [in charge of production], is now officially a manager with a staff under him; he takes it very seriously—and he looks out for his people."

There's a solid team feeling at the *Wake Weekly* these days. Greg puts it like this: "I'm a firm believer that we're all like a flock of geese. One goose is out there leading in the head of the V—and all the rest behind are squawking like hell until someone else can move up and give that guy a break."

As a result of the reorganization plan, Greg says that communications, efficiency and output are up. And so are revenues. That's critical, because since 2001 and the recession that followed, Greg says, making a go of a newspaper got a lot tougher, requiring that managers of community papers be more sophisticated in their business practices. But for the folks at the *Wake Weekly*, it's working. "I never knew planning ahead could be so much fun," Greg grins.

ALL IN THE FAMILY SOME MORE

Bringing Janet Rose into the management team has made the paper much stronger, according to Greg, which he credits to her business and management skills. "She's a fireball," in his opinion, and so he has handed to his wife the must-do burdens of accounting, human relations and past due accounts.

Bob and Peg turn 75 the summer of this visit. They look terrific. She works out at "Curves," and Bob swims. Of course, he still goes to the weekly pressrun to tinker with the press. Same as it ever was.

They've come a long way since 1947 when the *Wake Weekly* was housed in a tin building with a potbellied stove for heat. The staff of the award-winning weekly assembles in front of their office (a renovated old house) in downtown Wake Forest, N.C. Publisher Greg Allen, joined by wife Janet Rose and son Davis, is front right. Former publisher Bob Allen and editor Peg Allen are right behind them.

And who's that kid answering the front office phone with the aplomb of an adult? It would have to be Davis, Greg and Janet Rose's personable 14-year-old son, already an accomplished photojournalist as well. The heir apparent? Lucky lad. And what about Jimmy, the former editor-turned-seminarian? He's back home too, the preacher at the local Heritage Baptist Church. He and Ginger now have four kids.

Not one to rest on his laurels, Greg says, "There's a lot of good stuff going on here . . . but in the world we're living in today, you can't sit back."

THE EVOLUTION OF TECH

At the *Wake Weekly*, they've been entirely digital since 2003, using two professional state-of-the-art Nikon digital cameras and about six other assorted less expensive digital point-and-shoot cameras for routine photos. The advantages of digital are myriad, Greg says, with time being the most saving. No darkroom time; no runs to the one-hour-photomart. Just download and slap it in the paper.

Greg says, "It took me longer to lay out the four pages of July 4th pictures than it did me to [adjust the photos from the digital files]." When his parents ran the paper, such a spread would have taken many, many hours just to produce the *photos*, much less the layout.

Another time-saving dynamic of the new tech: most civic, governmental, church and school news now arrives at the paper via e-mail, saving enormous amounts of work that would otherwise have to be done by laborious typesetting. Greg says, "It's amazing when you can take something [a press release] and do a little rewriting, reformat it and send it on."

GREG ON THE FUTURE

"I still believe the community newspaper has an infinite life—as long as you can get people's names and faces and the news you can't get anywhere else."

As an example, the paper's coverage of the town's annual gala July 4th celebration featured four consecutive photo pages, including 45 photos containing no less than 221 identifiable faces. Of course, there were several crowd shots with far too many folks in the picture to be identified. But many more photos had complete identifications. At the *Wake Weekly* they make a point of ID'ing every photo. Greg slaps open the pages and exclaims matter-of-factly, "There ain't a damn name missing!"

Now that's relentlessly local coverage.

Is There a Formula for a Great Community Paper?

Ed Harper "bleeds ink." That's an editor's way of saying that he lives, breathes, eats and sleeps newspapers.

Sitting at his favorite waterfront café in the undeniably charming seaside town of Southport, N.C., Harper is talking about his twin interlocking passions: his town and the family-owned paper he publishes. "I love it!" he says emphatically. (During the conversation, Harper will say this at least three times.)

But now ask yourself: How cool would it be to have the same job for 32 years and to be able to wake up each morning saying what Harper says, "I love it!"?

Harper will be the first to tell you, when it comes to the success of the 9,103-circulation weekly *State Port Pilot*, he owes it "primarily to my family." In 1972, a couple of years out of college, he walked into a great situation. His father, the late James Harper, had acquired an interest in the paper back in 1935, and along with his wife, Margaret, built up the *Pilot* over the years into a profitable weekly. But in securing the operation's finances, the Harpers created something just as critical: a newspaper that is a beloved institution within the community itself.

"He established a wonderful relationship with this community," says the son. "The reason the paper works so well is that *he* loved this place so much . . . and *I* honestly and truly love Southport."

Ed Harper, 50-something, built like a former college football running back, sounds a lot like a great coach when he talks about his staff at the *Pilot*. He doesn't take much credit for all the awards won by the paper (36 from the state's press

At the height of the recent recession, Ed Harper's weekly *State Port Pilot* made a bold statement by constructing a glorious new building right in the heart of Southport, N.C. Harper says, "Downtown is not downtown unless it has three things. There must be a bank, a church and a newspaper." And when asked why he didn't build outside of town, where it would have been cheaper, Harper responds, "History demands it, and my father would have it no other way." Here, the staff gathers in the lobby atrium for a group portrait. That's Ed leaning on the rail on the crosswalk. The photo was made by the *Pilot*'s award-winning photographer (and Ed's brother), Jim Harper.

association this year alone). "We've got a great and talented staff," he says. "Everybody thinks of it as a joint venture in putting out a great product."

That product would be the *State Port Pilot* (this week a 56-page broadsheet), so named for the town's location at the mouth of the heavily navigated Cape Fear River leading to the port city of Wilmington.

The *Pilot*'s formula for success seems to be based on several critical factors:

- A history of positive publishing
- Location, location, location
- Good people who revel in their work and who, in turn, are rewarded by an ownership dedicated to quality journalism and community building
- A willingness to take risks for the good of the community regardless of financial gain
- Visionary leadership that is willing to work longer hours than anybody, while keeping its eye on the big picture

The Harpers have poured themselves into the *State Port Pilot* and into Southport. Harper says, "My father did public relations for my first 22 years . . . he was a tremendous asset to me . . . as a protector and as a mentor. He taught me so much—not so much the ethics of journalism, but the ethics of how you treat people."

Ed's dad also taught him something invaluable about the subtle joys of community journalism lifestyle. Once heavily courted by the *Washington Post*, the elder Harper turned them down politely, telling the *Post* that after the paper was published that week, he intended to spend the afternoon engaged in his favorite weekly ritual of bird hunting . . . and according to Harper, his father said something like this: " 'With all due respect to the *Washington Post*, but what I'll be doing this afternoon is what you'll work 30 years to do.' "

The bird-hunting editor's son sits at the picturesque waterfront café, a leisurely five-minute stroll from the *Pilot* office, and grins with understanding and satisfaction. "This is hard to beat."

Given their financial success, Harper's parents were able to to hand him a healthy publishing interest. The paper is co-owned by publisher Jim High of the nearby Whiteville *News Reporter* in a 50-50 arrangement, which Ed considers "an extended family in more than just a business sense. Jim is also my best friend." Harper is president of the State Port Pilot Inc. as well as editor. To be sure, he has enlarged on the base his parents started. Location is also key to the paper's success lately, Harper says.

LOCATION

Located in a booming golf, resort and beach area along North Carolina's burgeoning coast, Brunswick County and Southport are becoming increasingly attractive to tourists, retirees and golfers. Real estate and car ads are the paper's bread and butter. The town's economy is fueled by antique and specialty shops, restaurants and tourists. Harper maintains that even an impending Wal-Mart opening doesn't really threaten the downtown's stability. "In the last five years, the *Pilot* has become a very prosperous paper—and that's due to the real estate market," says Harper. "Last year was quite a good year. And that follows a good year . . . and we had a pretty good year before that."

But it was not always so. Back in the '30s and '40s, Harper's parents made do with a profit margin based largely on a single annual tobacco warehouse edition. Then for a time it was car ads; then it was grocery store ads. Perseverance paid off, along with linking the town's development to that of the paper. "For many years," Harper asserts, "the paper *was* the Chamber of Commerce. Now, in the last 15 to 20 years, golf [golf course and retirement communities] has begun to make the difference. Until then, it really *was* a sleepy little town."

When he was recently president of the state press association, Harper told community journalism student Lauren Rippey: "We know our place, and we cannot touch the job of the big daily . . . but they also cannot come close to touching ours. Practically everything that is in the *Pilot* each week concerns Brunswick County. And 'practically' means near 100 percent." This local imperative keeps the community newspaper booming while big dailies are at best holding their own.

And he's keenly aware of who his readers are—both in and out of town. "Although our average reader is a local retiree or second-home owner, our nonresident circulation is equally important," Harper told Rippey. Of the *State Port Pilot*'s 9,103 weekly circulation, 2,800 go out of county.

GOOD PEOPLE

In addition to talent, his staff shares three characteristics, says Harper. They like each other, they like what they do, and they like the community in which they work. "It makes it easy to keep good people," he explains, adding that "everybody on staff is an award winner."

Also, Harper makes a point of providing the staff with "good equipment and good cameras." Importantly, reporters' salaries at the *Pilot* are comparable and in some cases better than those at the nearby 60,615-circulation daily owned by the *New York Times*.

News editor Terry Calhoun told Rippey the paper's recipe for success: Take "a premium, full-bodied mix of hard news and community journalism, ground weekly for freshness, topped with a choice of cinnamon or chocolate-flavored features . . ."

WILLINGNESS TO TAKE RISKS

In 1996 the *Pilot* linked its own Web site with that of the local Chamber of Commerce on a single home page (<stateportpilot.com>)—and, most significantly, became a local Internet service provider.

In addition, the pure profit motive comes second to quality community journalism. "We are driven by pride, and not consciously by [the need to produce] profits. But we believe if we do a good job, we will be rewarded with readership and advertising." Harper told Rippey.

HARD-WORKING, VISIONARY LEADERSHIP

"I don't expect anyone to work my hours," says the editor, "but I've got a couple of people who do anyway . . ."

He estimates that he works until about 11 P.M. every Monday night and till 1 to 2 A.M. every Tuesday night/Wednesday morning. "I could find somebody to do that, but I don't want to . . . it's too self-satisfying."

"And," he says with conviction, "I have *not* put out my best newspaper yet."

Wednesday he had spent the day riding the routes with a new man in circulation, delivering the newspapers. "It's great. I love it," Harper says with a grin. "There's nothing like standing in line behind people buying your own paper."

Welcome to the Orchestra

A newspaper is like an orchestra, and every orchestra is different.

The publisher or perhaps the executive editor or even the managing editor is the conductor contending with the fractious sections. The subtle woodwinds look down on the ego-driven high brass, who look down on the plodding lower brass, who resent the flashy percussionists, who wonder why people would want to waste their time in the string section—and so it goes.

The effective conductor must take all this potential personal and professional cacophony and make music. In the end, if an orchestra is to succeed, various sections must lay aside technical and philosophical differences for the sake of the product, which in their case is sound.

If you could be a fly on the wall at almost any newspaper, you'd see that the business side doesn't get along with—much less like—the news side. Their attitude will be that the "news hole" is a waste of space better spent on ads that produce money. Additionally, they are resentful that the news side gets all the romance and glory. (When was the last time you saw a TV show or a movie about a newspaper ad person?)

But even within the news department, traditional divisions run deep. Word people versus picture people. News versus editorial. Sports versus everybody.

Following this very extended orchestra metaphor—why do people become flute players versus tuba players, drummers versus clarinetists? Or for that matter, reporters versus ad reps, editorial writers versus circulation managers, copy editors versus sports writers?

Most people tend to self-select, that is, gravitate toward the type of work that suits their personality, meaning that you've got an orchestra or staff in which people find themselves where they are best-suited to play their part, so to speak.

Bossing 101

> Great newspapers are published by great people.
> —BILL HAUPT, editor-publisher, Lodi (Wis.) *Enterprise*

For a newspaper to work well, something has got to be there that makes all the diverse factions play the same tune with such harmony, fluidity and clarity that the audience gets the message without experiencing any communication disorders.

Sometimes it's a great editor. Sometimes it's a great tradition of excellence. Other times it's the influence of editor and tradition plus a great community where readers demand high quality. But make no mistake about it—ultimately for a newspaper to work well it takes an editor-publisher with a vision far beyond merely the bottom line. The wise editor-publisher recognizes and yet cherishes the natural differences in his or her orchestra and knows how to draw the finest out of each player, each section.

In community journalism, where turnover is typically high, and newsrooms tend to be made up mostly of young people starting their careers, the editor is often the first real-world teacher. To know that is to recognize the fundamentally different nature of newspaper management at the community level.

If you are that editor, your role is far larger and more demanding than that of your big-city counterparts; you are model and mentor for young reporters who will never forget you. For better or for worse, the impression that you make will be indelible.

But to be fair here, sometimes green, overzealous reporters deserve the upbraiding they never got in college. "Community newspapers serve as grad school for kids right out of J-school, hotshot cub reporters who haven't yet learned the rules of the road," says one battle-hardened photo chief of a 30,000-circulation daily, "so it's up to us to 'educate' them."

Sometimes that finishing education is conducted with a hands-on approach. "These kids rush right in at a spot news event and begin firing questions without surveying or scoping out the hard news scene," says the community newspaper veteran. If the young reporter gets in the way of emergency personnel at the scene, they might get off with a mild warning. But heaven help the reporter who gets in the way of our grizzled chief photog at a hard news event. It's called upstaging, and it can result in your early demise.

"I grab 'em by the back of the neck," he allows with a fatherly grin, "and tell 'em calmly, 'If you ever get between me and a person I'm shooting—*ever*—I'll kill you.' "

Coming from the crusty old shooter with an inside as gooey as a melted marshmallow, that is a message of "tough love."

Community Papers as Grassroots Grad Schools

In this business, every year or so editors are going to get new people in the newsroom, perhaps right out of J-school. The novices are going to make mistakes; that's a given. Since we learn and grow most substantively not through our successes but rather our mistakes, what matters is how the editor handles a gaffe. It can make all the difference between a hell hole and a happy shop.

As Pulitzer Prize–winning Bronx, N.Y., co-publisher Bernard Stein of the Riverdale *Press* quips, "I'm the dean of the best J-school in New York City."

Contrast that example with the editor-publisher who marches into the newsroom and summarily begins shouting abuse at the offending reporter right in front of the entire staff.

Whoa. Instead of motivating the newsroom, such "leadership" makes odd things happen. Work ceases. Staffers get their résumés updated. If the editor-publisher goes on tirades regularly, the word gets out. Furthermore, he will have destroyed the staff's sense of drive and purpose. If there is any unity, it will be against the Psychoboss. There will be little possibility for quality work on the paper, except by accident. Staffers will plod through their daily work as if in prison.

This "Newspaper from Hell" scenario takes place all too often. Employees don't just leave such papers; they evacuate. And afterward, when they laugh about it, they speak of themselves as refugees or survivors.

As the expression goes: Is that any way to run a railroad?

While we're in Code Red mode, here's another warning. Sometimes the baddie ain't the boss at all. It's been said that in every institution (including newspapers) there is likely to be lurking in some corner someone who is *a giant sucking black hole of negativity*, feeding on the tender cheery souls of unsuspecting newcomers through stealth, cunning and treachery. Even gullible old-timers can fall prey to power-eating Mr. Black Hole, who often is a wolf disguised in sheep's skin. Consider yourself warned.

Management Styles

Every newspaper has a "corporate culture," resulting in a management style, whether it's stated or only implied.

At smaller papers, the management style is usually reflected in the highly personal style of one or two individuals. At larger community papers, defining and identifying the management style becomes more complex. The most successful papers are the ones that have taken the initiative and time to craft a coherent credo or mission statement of management style. To be effective, guidelines must be written down, shared, and practiced as a model for management behavior.

If a newspaper doesn't have a mission statement for its management style, then that very nonstyle becomes its style. The newspaper lurches forward, propelled by the inertia of nothing more than its own production schedule and publication frequency—without direction, guidance, or any sense of self, calling, purpose or mission.

You will find a variety of management styles in various newsrooms. Listing just a sampling will sound suspiciously like Matt Groening's "Nine Types of Bosses" cartoon essay from the *Work Is Hell* cartoon book; however, management styles do tend to be easy to type.

You've already met the Psychoboss several pages ago. She's the one whom you know better than to even approach because she's like Khrushchev with his shoe; you know she's going to try to bury you. Other types:

- *The Unapproachables.* The upper-level people keep their doors closed. They're sending a message: Don't bother me; I'm too busy and important.

- *Zombies on the March.* Not really a living thing at all. The paper has no effective leadership. It just muddles on without a clue. Of course, the reading public is aware they're getting the Chronicles of the Dead.
- *Bottom Feeders.* The paper is dominated by a leadership dedicated only to the bottom line. The result is a tiny news hole, an unhappy newsroom and a predictably uninspired news product. The paper, in fact, is a closet shopper.
- *Cutthroats.* Where everybody is watching out for their own necks and advancing only their own careers. See *Zombies on the March.*
- *Fiefdoms.* When a paper has ineffective leadership, individual clan chiefs arise and lead tiny insurrections. As in an orchestra without a conductor, the result is corporate cacophony. See *Zombies on the March* and *Cutthroats.*
- *Mom 'n' Pop.* A family-owned operation dominated by a single family or patriarchal/matriarchal figure. Going to work here can be like marrying into the family, which can be wonderful if you like the family and they like you. However, if you fall out of favor, you can fall very quickly.
- *The "10."* The enlightened, quality journalism–conscious community paper with a benevolent, nurturing management style. A young reporter who finds him- or herself at such a paper is blessed indeed. Working there is like going to journalism graduate school tuition free. This paper likely has a heightened sense of internal corporate community. Employees feel more like team members than just numbers. Everyone knows about and shares in the paper's mission, core values, load and rewards.

The One-Minute Editor

So, what are community newspaper management tactics that have been proven effective in dealing with employees, especially young ones? To borrow from the title of a highly successful management book, let's look at how to better "boss." Points to ponder:

- *Zen and the Art of Newspaper Management.* As far back as the sixth century B.C., the wise men of China have studied the qualities of great leadership. Lao-tzu advises, "No fight; no blame." In other words, never angrily confront a young reporter and denounce him publicly.
- *The Aretha Franklin Factor.* Lessons are best taught one on one. When a reporter stumbles, give her R-E-S-P-E-C-T. If you have guidance to give, talk to the offending reporter in private to preserve her dignity. Craft your constructive comments so that reporters come away from the discussion with something they can use. If they've screwed up, they're liable to already feel bad enough as is. Your firm but nurturing treatment reinforces the community journalism mantra within your own staff, "People are what really matter."

- *The No-Fault Policy.* Let's take a cue from the automotive insurance industry and try this policy. There are no mistakes, only lessons.

- *High Tech with the Human Touch.* Just because your shop has gone digital and sprouted candy-colored computers like dandelions, don't let high tech override the personal nature that has been one of the traditional strengths of our business. E-mail does not replace eye-to-eye contact or a pat on the back.

- *The Gospel According to the Boy Scout Patrol Leader's Handbook.* Instead of ordering your staff around, you might follow the dictum from an old *Boy Scout Patrol Leader's Handbook*: "Let's go do it!" That beats "You better do it or else" every time. An involved, active editor gets far better results by participating in projects as opposed to issuing flat orders. In fact, the editor who demonstrates that he is enthusiastic about sharing the load generates respect and loyalty, which in turn motivates the staff to produce quality work far beyond anything you could order from them.

- *The Ben Franklin Dictum.* "We must all hang together, or assuredly we shall all hang separately," this nation's great revolutionary publisher told his Continental Congress brethren. The same goes for community papers, where the product is infinitely improved when reporters and photographers and editors talk to each other about projects and stories beforehand. At the larger metro papers this is being treated as a novel concept. Admittedly, it is a welcome change for the large daily, one that requires quite a bit of logistical reorganization and long-range planning. At the smaller papers, where editors, reporters and photographers should have easy access to each other on an informal daily basis, if we aren't already talking to each other a lot, then something is dreadfully wrong with the newsroom.

- *No Mo' Memos.* Does anybody out there actually like memos? If you have a small shop, the overuse of the memo is the quickest way to alienate someone who you could otherwise talk to like a human being. Memos—those terse little impersonal statements issued to save time in large institutions—are officious and demeaning in a small setting. Here, the subtext of the boss's memo may be this message: I'm so big and important and busy that I don't have the time to walk down the hall to speak with lowly little you.

- *Netiquette.* The same goes for e-mail. If you have a small shop, avoid the overuse of in-house e-mail. Nothing beats eye-to-eye verbal communication. Just ask anyone who's ever had an e-mail message taken wrong or misunderstood. Have you ever been accidentally "flamed" by a colleague? It's tough to be creative when you're a crispy critter.

- *The Peripatetic Editor.* The "management by wandering" technique has proven highly effective. If you're an editor, take a moment, just walk the halls, chat with whomever you run into. Or, if you have something to say to someone, do it by visiting the reporter in her office or at his desk. Talk about something else first— like how their kids are doing in Little League—then slide into the issue that you really want to address. Studies of leadership show that the least effective bosses are those who never leave their offices and issue all their decrees through e-mail and memos. If you're in community journalism, get out of your office, mix it up. And you should do the same vis-à-vis the entire community. Wander down main street. Drop in at the local greasy spoon, hit the back roads with a clear mind, your camera and a notepad. You don't have time? Make time. It will add years to your life and zest to your paper.

Recruitment and Retention

How do you effectively recruit and retain a high-quality newsroom staff? Again, the answer is local, local, local.

According to community journalism student Christina Rexrode, in the mid-1990s the staff of the Asheboro (N.C.) *Courier-Tribune* was turning over every two years. New editor Ray Criscoe came on board in 1994 at the 16,300-circulation Stephens Media Group–owned daily. Rexrode notes that after Criscoe got his sea legs, he began hiring reporters from within the community. Rexrode reports, "The strategy worked. The current staff members, almost without exception, have lived in Randolph County for some time, and many of them grew up there. Turnover is almost nonexistent."

Grievance Procedures

At large corporations and institutions, the employee with a gripe knows what to do. There's usually a personnel officer to go to, or a formal grievance procedure through which the employee can state his or her case without fear of job reprisal.

However, at many smaller papers no such grievance procedure exists, and in many cases it would be somewhat silly. Ideally, with the open-door access typical of many community papers, if you've got a beef, you go see the editor or the publisher and have your say. The downside of this informality lies in the absolute authority of that manager. If the management thinks your concern is trivial, the editor or publisher can deep-six it as if it had never been mentioned. And then what is your recourse? To bring it up again might make you appear to be a whiner, a constant complainer.

Two young women reporters, one white and the other African-American, approached the executive editor about what they perceived as unconscious bias on the part of the managing editor, an older white male. According to the women reporters, the M.E. gave all the good story assignments to the male reporters. They were also convinced that the M.E. wasn't doing this maliciously, that he was just behaving along the good-old-boy lines of traditional male management styles. After the conference with the exec. ed., the two women said they felt better, but after six months the situation in the newsroom hadn't improved one bit. They became convinced the exec. ed. "just didn't get it." Within a year both had found better jobs at more enlightened community papers.

On the other hand, if you are that manager, you should listen patiently to the concern of the employee, make note of the nature of the complaint, and then either do something about it or explain and clarify why the situation is the way it is.

For a paper to have a happy shop, employees must feel that the management is accessible, supportive, sympathetic, eager to listen and, most importantly, flexible enough to change policy when it's needed. Such a creative and dynamic atmosphere can be achieved by taking the personal approach to personnel work.

Get Out of Your Comfort Zone

It is pure human nature for people to stay within their comfort zones. And in an ethnically non-diverse newsroom, this can lead to unconscious bias in reporting.

Frank Fee, associate professor at the University of North Carolina at Chapel Hill, was working for a chain-owned major metro paper in the Northeast where management mandated a newsroom assignment they called "Roaming Days," or "Walking 'n' Talking." Over a three- to four-week period, reporters were to get out of the newsroom and into the community, not so much for stories per se, but just to get a feel for the community, to "get out there and know real people." At the end of the project, the staffers assembled to evaluate their experiences. But when they put pushpins on the city map to show where they'd gone, Fee reports that not a single reporter had ventured into the black part of town.

And what was the racial makeup of that newsroom? It was overwhelmingly white, of course. Fee notes with some irony that the newsroom included several black reporters who also avoided the perceived "dangerous" part of town.

Diversity in the Newsroom

A sad fact of our business: Newsrooms, large and small, fail to accurately mirror the racial and ethnic makeup of the communities they purport to cover.

According to the U.S. Census, between 1990 and 2000 the Latino population increased 62 percent, from 17.3 million to 28.1 million. But how many mainstream community newspaper newsrooms even have a single Spanish-speaking reporter?

The typical daily newspaper*man* is "still a liberal college-educated white-male baby boomer," writes Indiana University's Paul S. Voakes in *The Newspaper Journalists of the '90s*, a 1997 publication of the American Society of Newspaper Editors. According to 2005 figures from ASNE, the percentage of women in the daily newsroom is only 37 percent. The percentage of minorities (blacks, Hispanics, Asian Americans and American Indians) is far worse: only 13.42 percent in the daily newsroom compared to 31.7 percent in the national population.

How can we adequately endeavor to accurately cover and fairly reflect our multiple constituencies without a broader gender-racial-ethnic representation in our own newsrooms? According to Voakes's study, 42 percent of newspapers have no nonwhite reporters, leading author and ABC News correspondent Farai Chideya to conclude in a 1999 *Media Studies Journal* article, "An all-white newsroom is not incompetent. It is, however, incomplete." For instance, a newsroom without a Spanish-speaking reporter really can't penetrate, much less understand, the Hispanic community. "Diversity in journalism is not a feel-good exercise," writes Chideya. "It is essential if reporters are to achieve the accuracy that journalism demands."

Not surprisingly, the Hispanic press in the United States is burgeoning, according to 2004 figures from the National Association of Hispanic Publishers. Since 1990 the number of dailies has doubled, and their circulation has tripled. *And that's not even counting the weeklies!*

Journalism professor Tommy Thomason of Texas Christian University recently urged members of the Texas Press Association to broaden their coverage of the local ethnic minorities, especially the Hispanic population. Pam Fikes of the Idalou *Beacon* attended that workshop and realized she had been culturally blind. "Our town is about 50 percent Hispanic and 50 percent white, and we discovered that out of all the feature stories and events that we cover, besides school, we never had done a feature story on a Hispanic or at the Catholic Church." In the first week that the *Beacon* began covering local Hispanic issues, single-copy rack sales of the paper shot up dramatically, she reports. Covering diversity issues is not only good business; it's the right thing to do.

During the '40s, legendary university President Frank Porter Graham gave an early lesson on the importance of multiculturism to a troop of Boy Scouts in Chapel Hill, N.C., saying, "Boys, always remember this: When you sit down to play the *Star Spangled Banner*, it takes the black keys as well as the white keys." (Thanks to 70-something old scouter John Earnhardt for that gem.)

As we retool our industry for a new age, and try to include new multi-ethnic neighbors into our communities, we in community journalism need to reappraise how we think about place, interest and ethnicity and thus how we can best serve our conceptually enlarged communities.

"America as the melting pot is a myth. The 'salad bowl' is a better model," says Stephen Byers of the Urban Studies program at the University of Wisconsin–Milwaukee. Byers, a former editor, says when foreigners move to the United States they are not subsumed into a homogeneous mass; they create or find their own indigenous cultural cohorts. This is more true now than in the past. Byers asserts that "*a sense of community becomes more important in uncertain times.*"

Your Town; Your Turn

1. What are the orchestra sections at your paper? How do they get along? What is the glue that cements them? Or are they unglued?
2. Does your paper's leadership appear to have a coherent and consistent management style? Can you identify it? In your opinion, does it work?
3. Does your newspaper have a grievance procedure? What are the steps involved? If there's not a formal process, what options exist for an employee with a concern about management policies and practices?

NINETEEN

¿Hablamos Español? (Do We Speak Spanish?)

How Seven Mainstream Community Newspapers Have Started Covering Their New Latino Communities

While the American Southwest has a long history of Latino presence and acculturation, in the East this demographic is a relatively new phenomenon.

In North Carolina, where the Latino population increased a dramatic 400 percent during the 1990s, several mainstream (read: mostly white newsroom) community newspapers have begun experimenting with coverage of Latino issues. Some of these traditional community papers have started bilingual columns in their core product. Others have introduced special bilingual pages. And still others have created entirely new and separate Spanish-language publications. But for every enlightened community newspaper that has addressed this issue, there are a dozen others that, for whatever reasons, have done little or nothing. Publishers of such passive papers often cite a fear of reader or advertiser backlash, yet pioneering publishers of proactive Latino coverage papers say there's a moral imperative at work in their decision-making process: It's the right thing to do. And

the new demographic, they say, is just too large to ignore.

While the growth of the Latino press itself is important, a more pressing issue for existing traditional community newspapers is how they deal (or don't deal) with the stunning influx of Latinos into their communities.

This set of case studies examines seven examples of "best practices" across the spectrum of community newspapers in North Carolina, including a 4,500-circulation family-owned weekly in a conservative rural farm community; an 8,450-circulation chain-owned semiweekly in a rural mountain town; a 9,000-circulation chain-owned six-day-a-week daily in a farming market town; a 12,500-circulation chain-owned daily in a bustling county seat; a free 22,000-circulation chain-owned semiweekly in a liberal university town; a chain-owned 30,000-circulation daily in the media-rich Piedmont; and a 57,000-circulation family-owned daily in a blue-collar city.

Editors and publishers were asked to candidly address the following issues: What prompted them to do initiate the change? Who at the paper was the driving force? How did they arrive at their format decision? Who is helping out? Volunteers? Has it been worth the effort? Examples of challenges, "speedbumps" and "war stories" were requested. Those surveyed were also asked to weigh the pros and cons, as well as the financial and distribution considerations. How would they assess feedback from readers, advertisers and the Latino community?

Six of the seven case studies were done during summer of 2003, but we will revisit them to get an update on changes. The seventh is current, and we'll begin there.

High Hopes in High Places

Deep in the heart of the Southern Appalachians, the bustling river valley town of Franklin seems like an unlikely place for a Latino influx; it has a population of 3,500 in a rural mountain county of 30,000. But editor Barbara McRae of the Franklin *Press*, in her day-to-day work with the local health department, library, department of social services, schools and law enforcement agencies "started noticing the names and the numbers." There might be as many as 4,000 Latinos in Macon County, McRae estimates, prompting her to conclude, "Gosh, we need to do something."

When the *Press* did a story about Edda Bennett, a Puerto Rican teacher fast-tracking local Latino schoolchildren (of whom there were at least 135 in the local schools), McRae said she knew she had stumbled across the person who could be the driving force for positive change. McRae and Bennett pulled together a local committee of concerned Anglos and Latinos who helped create a bilingual newspaper. The first edition of *El Noticiero* (the News Items) was published in May 2004 by the *Press*, a semiweekly owned by Community Newspapers Inc., a small chain out of Athens, Ga.

On the front page Edda Bennett clearly states the newspaper's public service mission:

> Our objective is to work together to enrich and strengthen our community. This will help us to obtain the best for our families, such as education, employment, adequate housing and access to medical service. The first step toward this goal is to break language barriers and share differences in traditions and cultural customs. By sharing our lives with our community, we can show that we have more in common than we think. Our thanks to Ralph Morris, the publisher, and Barbara McRae, the editor of the Franklin *Press*. They have given us the opportunity to have a voice in our community and enabled us to reach our goal. We need the help and cooperation of all of you to be able to maintain and continue this newspaper. We ask that you contribute information and communicate your ideas to Tomas Marquez at Garibaldi's Restaurant.

Though that first 12-page, tabloid-format paper contained no advertisements, McRae said they wanted to get the premier edition out so the sales reps would have something to sell in the future. *El Noticiero* was inserted in the *Press* and also dropped at strategic locations around the county where Latinos would find them.

The first edition contained the results of a local Latino soccer tournament with photos of the teams; general and contact information about local educational, governmental, medical, emergency and social services; in-depth pieces about immigration reform and the proposed temporary worker program; a story about ESL classes at the local community college; and brief wedding, birth and death announcements—all presented with the English version beside the Spanish.

"This is the most exciting thing we've done," says editor McRae. "We've received a lot of good feedback and only three or four negative comments. Most of those are people saying, 'Well, they [Latinos] should be learning English.' " McRae responds pointedly, "Well, that's why we're doing this. It's bilingual!"

On the masthead of *El Noticiero*, bilingual contact information steers the reader: "To speak to someone in Spanish, please call Edda Bennett (828) 369-9955, or email her at <latinooutreachprogram@dnet.net>."

Just a Weekly, Just Doing Great Things

Robert Dickson is publisher of the Raeford *News-Journal* of Hoke County, an independent 4,500-circulation weekly published in a rural town of 3,386; the county's population is 35,000.

Part of the reason for the start-up was economic. Dickson explains, "Hoke County is typically number 100 out of 100 counties in per capita income in North Carolina. So we have to always look out for ways to generate new sources of income. We have to scratch out a living any way we can."

Dickson said they decided to launch *Acento Latino* "on a shoestring" in September 1999 after he began noticing changes in the labor force spilling out of the poultry processing plant in town.

"We saw them changing," says Dickson, "from predominately African-American to Hispanic, and we wanted to reach this market to serve our readers—and we hope they're our readers . . ." Dickson explains, "[because] I think the Hispanic community has just become part of the fabric of our community."

Describing how he found his first Hispanic editor, Dickson gladly concedes that he "got lucky." He found Elena Askey when she approached him about running a Latino column in his paper. Dickson says "Hispanic Corner" began appearing in the *News-Journal* and the *Fayetteville Observer* in 1999. Later that year, Elena Askey would become editor of *Acento Latino*. (The current editor is Liliana Parker.)

Acento Latino began as a free 5,000-circulation 12-page tabloid-format monthly covering Hoke and the three adjoining counties of Cumberland, Moore and Robeson.

Dickson chose to locate *Acento Latino* 22 miles away from Raeford in the city of Fayetteville, which he describes as "a tremendous market," in part because of the "Army post [Fort Bragg] and its traditionally high number of Spanish-speaking people."

Dickson explains, "We operate [*Acento Latino*] as a completely separate operation. It has its own separate office; it has its own separate staff. I won't let our [*News-Journal*] staff sell Spanish paper ads, and I won't let our Spanish paper staff sell weekly ads; they don't cross. And we consider [income generated by *Acento Latino*] to be new dollars to us that we wouldn't get any other way."

The new Spanish-language paper was a success from the outset. "And we immediately started getting calls from all over requesting papers," Dickson says.

Four years later, *Acento Latino* has more than doubled in size to 32 pages, with a circulation of 15,000, published twice-monthly and distributed to "a couple of hundred sites in eight counties," Dickson says.

The publication's success seems to be a result of Dickson's commitment as well as aggressive partnering with a variety of agencies including chambers of commerce, public libraries and Latino centers. No less important was the publisher's holistic approach to involvement with the Latino community.

Dickson's paper has sponsored events such as fiestas and Hispanic Day at the Cumberland County Fair, and has held forums and government fairs.

One session at the public library in Fayetteville attracted 600 people, Dickson says. It was such an eye-opener, according to Dickson, that the librarian described the audience's reaction like this: "Their eyes were on stalks."

Acento Latino's content is almost all local, Dickson says. "We have tried to use our knowledge of community newspapers to our advantage. We don't know how to do anything but a community newspaper." So *Acento Latino* runs items such as birthday pictures, social notices, employment opportunities, immigrant information and stories helpful to the Latino community that might not appear in any other publication. "We try to highlight things going on in our area; we're trying to be the hometown newspaper. Most of what we do is local," he asserts.

Reaction from his community has been relatively good. "We've run into very little resistance from our community," says Dickson. "I think maybe that's because our paper has been around for a hundred years. We don't hear anything but positive stuff." And besides, he adds, "it's hard to bad-mouth people who are supporting your economy."

From the business angle, *Acento Latino* is evidently holding its own through some tough economic times. The publisher notes, "We're going not as strong as we'd like with our ad sales. . . . We were doing better a year ago. . . . It's been a little flat lately." (Most publishers would agree it was that way across the board as of the summer of 2003.)

Dickson adds optimistically, "But we continue to add new advertisers which I think is a great sign for a new publication."

"It's a very interesting mix," he muses with a grin, ". . . the redneck newspaper and the Hispanic newspaper."

Dickson says he recently saw a local T-shirt that summed it all up for him. The shirt read, "¿Como esta, y'all?"

Update: Proving how fluid the newspaper market is these days, Robert Dickson has sold his *Acento Latino* to the *Fayetteville Observer*, an independently owned 75,865-circulation daily. Publisher Charles Broadwell reports that *Acento Latino*, with a biweekly eight-county circulation of about 15,000 and an average page count of 32 pages, has improved due to a redesign that employs more color and added education and entertainment features. The paper's Web site is <www.acentolatino. com>.

El Heraldo Hispano de North Carolina

Ironically, one of the counties that *Acento Latino* covers is Sampson County, where two years ago the local community paper, the *Sampson Independent*, started its own regional Latino tab.

El Heraldo Hispano de North Carolina is overseen by Sherry Matthews, editor, and Andy Rackley, marketing director of the *Sampson Independent*. The parent paper is a 9,000-circulation six-day-a-week daily, chain-owned by CNHI (Community Newspaper Holdings Inc.). It is published in Clinton, a rural farming and market town of 5,000; Sampson County has a population of 47,400.

Rackley says that the 2000 Census report was their wake-up call. "The birth of the publication came from a marketing study our staff was completing for Sampson and neighboring counties in southeastern North Carolina," he explains. "As the publisher and I began researching the 2000 Census report, we learned that our main coverage area now included a rapidly growing Hispanic community. We were shocked to see the 890 percent growth of our Hispanic base."

Early in 2001 the *Sampson Independent* ran some Spanish-language articles in the main newspaper, Rackley says, "just to test the response we would get from both the Hispanic and the English sectors of our community." They got very few complaints from their traditional readers, but then again they "found the Spanish articles didn't attract any new readers from the Spanish-speaking sector."

From further research, Rackley notes, they learned that Latinos accounted for 10 percent of their county's population, and 15 percent of neighboring Duplin County's. "We knew we had to address this sector of our community," he says. The catalyst came in the form of Enrique Coello, a former Honduran doctor and current Hispanic local business owner, who approached Matthews and Rackley about starting a Spanish-language paper.

Partnering with Coello, who was put in charge of editorial content, the *Sampson Independent* launched in September 2001 *El Heraldo Hispano*, a free 8,000-

circulation 32-page tabloid monthly going to eight counties in southeastern North Carolina. Rackley estimates that the area is home to 100,000 Latinos.

The arrangement between Coello and the *Sampson Independent* works because Coello is a "well-educated gentleman who was highly respected in our community by both English- and Spanish-speaking residents," Rackley says. "We print the product and sell the advertising, and he supplies the copy. In return for his efforts, we provided him with advertising space for his three businesses."

The new publication was greeted with enthusiasm, Rackley says. "We were thrilled as we nearly profited from the first publication even after buying enough newspaper racks to cover eight counties." He also says the *Independent* felt they had "beaten all the other [traditional community] newspapers out of the starting gate." (Rackley made no mention of Robert Dickson's *Acento Latino*, which began publishing two years prior to *El Heraldo Hispano*).

However, Coello and his counterparts in Clinton quickly learned that just taking copy from the *Independent* and translating it for *El Heraldo Hispano* didn't work. The Latino readers wanted "stories from their homes in Honduras, Mexico and El Salvador," Rackley explains. "They also wanted information from the Department of Motor vehicles . . . [and] stories about immigration . . . so we adapted our product to fit their needs."

While the *Sampson Independent* and *El Heraldo Hispano* succeeded in finding the formula for editorial content, the same cannot be said for the advertising area. A Latina ad representative made good progress securing ads from the Hispanic businesses in the area, but, Rackley says, "she felt uncomfortable approaching English businesses because her English was at best 'fair.' " After several months, she left to continue her education. And since that time, Rackley says, *El Heraldo Hispano* has struggled to find a competent bilingual ad salesperson, possibly because their ad salespeople work entirely on commission. "For the last year we have tried five different methods of soliciting ads from the Spanish community," Rackley notes. "But today our Hispanic publication is basically 85 percent funded by English businesses. However, our goal was to draw in undiscovered revenue from new advertisers—not move around funds from current advertisers."

In the last year *El Herald Hispano* has grown in circulation by 1,000 copies and expanded into three more counties towards the coast. An online edition was also launched. Rackley says proudly, "Our Hispanic print product still produced a profit," and "we are thrilled about our new venture."

In spite of these accomplishments, *El Heraldo Hispano* is in jeopardy at the *Sampson Independent*. "We have reached a crossroads," Rackley concedes. "We are currently analyzing whether our efforts should continue with this publication or should we place these efforts into other products like the Internet where we have witnessed some re-energized growth?"

It is reasonable to speculate that this has to do with the core newspaper's ownership status. Fueling this uncertainty are the reported on-again-off-again sales of CNHI's North Carolina properties, including the *Sampson Independent*. This insecurity is most likely having a chilling effect on all operations at both the *Independent* and *El Heraldo Hispano*. Until the ownership situation stabilizes, everything in Clinton appears to be on hold.

Update: As anticipated, the *Sampson Independent* suspended publication of its Latino newspaper and was later purchased in spring 2004 by Heartland, a small group out of Florida. *Independent* editor Sherry Matthews reports that currently there are no plans for creating another Spanish-language publication.

More Than Just Ink-on-Paper Community Journalism

The Chapel Hill *News*, a free 23,500-circulation chain-owned (McClatchy) twice-weekly, has a long history of groundbreaking community journalism in its liberal university town of 38,000.

Not long after the 2000 Census figures got everyone's attention, the *News*, led by publisher Ted Vaden and editor Sharon Campbell, began publishing front-page bilingual columns by local Latino advocate Maria Palmer. That was followed by simple, illustrated Spanish lessons that appeared regularly in the paper, supplied by a local Spanish-language advocacy group.

From the beginning the *News*' Latino coverage has been folded into the mother product, because, Vaden says, he knows his typical reader, whom he describes as probably "the spouse of a faculty member." So the *News* is covering the Latino community for its traditional audience, and unlike its counterparts in Raeford and Clinton, it is making no real pretense at courting Latino readers or advertisers with a stand-alone Spanish-language publication.

Speaking to the N.C. Press Association summer convention in July 2003, senior writer Kirk Ross explained, "We've tried for several years to involve writers and people from the Latino community in the newspaper. We find it's a two-way street. Not only do people in the Latino community want to know what's going on, but people in the traditional community want to know what's going on with their new neighbors. So we took that approach and did a lot of work with a series on how churches and schools have changed with new members of our community."

But the *News* really got in the trenches in 2001 when it became clear that local businesses were laying off many Hispanic workers because of improper paperwork. Ross says, "In late November 2001 a local minister told me that she had heard about wholesale layoffs at the grocery stores of Latino workers . . . and we found it had to do with 9/11. Basically it was a Social Security double-check that had been tightened up—and we're talking about hundreds of people who are losing their jobs. It involved a thing called a 'no-match letter,' which basically says your Social Security number doesn't match the one we have on file.

"And you find this a lot. People get hired. They have a number. They may have

The state press association cited the Chapel Hill (N.C.) *News* for excellence because of this in-depth series titled "El Dilema Laboral," covering the layoffs of many local Latino workers who weren't properly documented. (Courtesy of the Chapel Hill *News*)

obtained it illegally; it may be their brother's number, or something like that. But the employers were getting these letters, and it wasn't just the major employers. It was going to restaurants, grocery stores, construction companies.

"And so we found that a lot of employers who had integrated Latino workers into their workforce, and who were moving along nicely, were suddenly faced with losing half their people or in some cases almost all their people."

"El Dilema Laboral," an award-winning 20,000-word series involving as many as 60 stories that appeared for several weeks during the spring of 2002, dealt with what Ross describes as "the double standard in which we invited these folks to come be with us, but politically and legally we have put them into a black market system." The entire series was translated into Spanish and repackaged in a tabloid format. It won the Community Service Award, the top statewide award for community news-papers. Judges commented that the series was "sophisticated" and that any of the larger dailies in the state would have been proud to publish it.

Beyond ink-on-paper journalism, the *News* also got involved with the Latino employment issue by sponsoring a well-attended town forum. Publisher Ted Vaden moderated the forum, which was called "El Dilema Latino: Seeking Local Solutions." Ross says, "We really tried to bring together employers, immigration lawyers, community leaders, a representative from the Mexican consulate and congresspeople to discuss this issue."

Ross is hopeful about the outcome, but he has no illusions. "In the end change will have to come from Congress," he says. "It won't come from the Chapel Hill *News* or the Chapel Hill Town Council."

The labor story also opened the doors to other stories. "As we got into the labor issues," says Ross, "we learned more about the cultural issues." Reporters discovered that many of the Latinos in the Chapel Hill–Carrboro area were from one little village of Guanajuato, Mexico.

So the *News* sent its editor, Sharon Campbell, to Guanajuato along with Steve Thompson, a Spanish-speaking freelance journalism student-writer to "flesh out the human stories behind this." Ross explains that in Guanajuato wives and children await "that check from Carrboro, N.C., or that phone call from Pittsboro, N.C." He adds, "So there's a whole other story on other side of the border."

Finally, Ross thinks there's a value-added component to the Latino coverage the *News* has done. He concludes, "We've really tried to look for resources within the community, and we've found that they're there. And it's that reaching out that helps lay the groundwork so that when a big story breaks in the Latino community, you have the resources, you can get out there, and you can make it relevant for folks."

Update: Since the seminar in 2003, Ross has moved on to become managing editor of the *Independent*, a highly successful local urban alternative weekly in the Chapel Hill–Durham–Raleigh area. *News* publisher Vaden adds to the update: "We provided Spanish lessons on site for all our staff. This year, we published a three-part series called 'East Meets South' about the Asian community in Chapel Hill–Carrboro, whose growth is the same as that of the Latino community. We discovered that Orange County's Asian population was the fastest growing in North Carolina in the last decade. Among the interesting stories: 'The Myth of the Model Majority,' which examines the stereotype that Asians are all smart, driven, successful and financially comfortable, which was not at all true for a lot of the folks we talked with and impairs their access to community services."

The Chapel Hill *News* Web site is <www.chapelhillnews.com>.

Because It's the Right Thing to Do

Editor Bob Stiff describes his Lexington *Dispatch* as "a weekly newspaper that comes out six afternoons a week." The 12,500-circulation daily, owned by the New York Times Regional Publishing Group, is located well west of Chapel Hill, Raeford and Clinton in a bustling county seat town (pop. 20,500), which is famous for its barbecue.

Before the 2000 Census results came in, the *Dispatch* created *Nuestro Pueblo*, a bilingual news page, every third Tuesday of the month.

Explaining the page's origins, Stiff says, "A few years ago I noticed that we were having a lot of arrests for open container laws, and they were all Spanish-sounding last names. And it occurred to me that our visitors, who are now our residents, are probably not aware of a lot of our laws that would be different from how they are in Mexico, and that we should find some sort of way of assimilating them in what we call *Nuestro Pueblo*, our town.

"So I thought why don't we have a page with all this information in it that will help them? Let's do a feature on them being here and something that they're doing that can draw them to the page to get this information. We didn't do it for any other reason than to make people feel a little more comfortable in our home."

Like other editors and publishers, Stiff says he found the census numbers to be significant. "We've got a large percentage increase over the last census," he says. Stiff estimates the county has an 11 percent Latino population, while estimates run as high as 16 percent for Lexington, prompting the editor to observe, "Those are significant numbers, and we want [Latinos] to feel comfortable with our community."

For two years Ana Agud, a Spanish-speaking reporter, was responsible for *Nuestro Pueblo* until she left the *Dispatch* for a higher-paying job with a hospital group. As luck would have it, Stiff discovered her replacement in his own backshop when he found a part-time ad makeup man with Spanish-language skills. This summer Stiff is using a Spanish-speaking student intern from the University of North Carolina at Chapel Hill to handle the bilingual page.

Says Stiff, "We do it in both Spanish and English because I knew our English-speaking readers would wonder what it was that they couldn't read and understand. What were we doing that we weren't making them a part of? So. I think it does what we intended it to do."

The *Dispatch*'s effort is a low-key operation, according to Stiff. "We've done very little promotion. We do rack cards once in a while. And there's been very little reaction." In spite of the fact that "it hasn't made a penny for us," Stiff remains committed to the monthly bilingual page, saying, "It's just simply the right thing to do."

Update: The *Dispatch*'s Latino page, *Nuestro Pueblo*, has been moved from the third Tuesday to the fourth Wednesday of each month.

For more information contact Bob Stiff at <bob.stiff@the-dispatch.com>. The paper's Web site is <www.the-dispatch.com>.

Speaking for Our People

Steve Buckley is the publisher of the Burlington *Times-News*, a 30,000-circulation chain-owned (Freedom) daily in a city of 71,000, within a county of 147,000, located in the heart of the busy Piedmont. Burlington is bracketed by the Research Triangle of Raleigh, Durham and Chapel Hill to the east and the Piedmont Triad of Greensboro, High Point and Winston-Salem to the west.

Even in this media-rich setting, publisher Buckley saw a need for a Latino community newspaper that would serve the Spanish-language readers in Alamance County. *La Voz de Alamance*, a free 5,000-circulation twice-monthly, is unique in that it is the only broadsheet-format Spanish-language publication in this study. *La Voz* also has a Web site.

Buckley created *La Voz* almost two years ago for several reasons. Reflecting the statewide growth, Alamance County's Latino population has mushroomed, and now is estimated at 10 percent. Latinos' impact on his county can't be overstated. To illustrate the point, Buckley says, "Two years ago I was traveling with a friend who owns a hosiery mill, and he said, 'Oh boy, do I have trouble. I just heard from the Department of Labor that I've got 115 invalid Social Security numbers.'

"I said, 'How many Latinos do you have working down there?'

"And he said, 'about 120.'

"I mean this was going to shut his plant down!" exclaimed Buckley.

Latinos now make up the bulk of the work force in the construction, landscaping and food service industries, Buckley says, adding, "I'm convinced that in Alamance County we'd have a huge problem if suddenly there was a huge sweep and all the Latinos were picked up and taken away. We'd have things that wouldn't open the next day. Period."

Buckley acknowledges that many Latinos are in the United States illegally, but he is a staunch believer in being supportive, explaining, "They're all contributing to the society. They're making a positive economic impact on a lot of things in Alamance County that wouldn't be happening if we didn't have our Latino population. . . . It's more important as far as I'm concerned to talk about them as people."

Buckley says Latinos' traditional distrust of government has hampered their advancement in American society. He cited a recent Latino issues community forum held at the Paramount Theater in downtown Burlington and co-sponsored by Elon University. It was attended by the head of the local Latino advocacy group, the North Carolina governor's director for Hispanic/Latino affairs, as well as local community and school leaders. But according to Buckley, "The only thing they didn't have was very many Latinos in the audience—because they thought the INS would be outside the door, ready to pick people off!"

As a newspaper publisher who must run a successful business, Buckley also saw the creation of *La Voz* as a "great marketing niche." But he is quick to add, "There's a moral obligation to do this, as well. Here is a significant segment of the population who needs to be served with information and needs access to honest information, and we felt it was important to do that."

Not all of Buckley's traditional readers agree, he says candidly. "It is not warmly received by all of our white readers. There's this one guy, for example, who has told me he'll re-subscribe [to the *Times-News*] as soon as we stop publishing this paper [*La Voz*]. We've got a county commissioner who frankly I've come to the point where I had to say [to him], 'Look, I'm not going to change my opinion, and you're not going to change your opinion, and I can't argue with a bigot, so stop calling me about this.'" Buckley seems unfazed by his critics. "It's a real issue," he says, vowing, "but we're going to continue to do this."

A typical eight-page edition of *La Voz* has a splashy color front, with the motto "El periodico que habla por nuestra gente" ("The newspaper that speaks for us") beneath the nameplate of the paper.

The front page contains stories about soccer both in Alamance County and Latin America, pictures of local entertainers, reports about recent house fires that killed local Latinos, the opening of a new food distribution plant, a police report detailing the detaining of local illegal immigrants, and a feature about the three Latino athletes who play on the local minor league baseball team. Inside is a full, live local editorial page, including a personal commentary by *La Voz* editor Jose Luis Arzola, one of two Latino freelancers who provide the editorial content for *La Voz*. The other staffer is graphics editor Monica Meza, whom Buckley calls "our in-house advocate . . . my angel . . . my conscience as well." Following two pages of the local Latino news, *La Voz* features wire service copy from "Latin America and the World."

Buckley's involvement with *La Voz* has pushed him to start learning Spanish. With a rueful grin he says, "Frankly, it's a little bit disconcerting to publish a paper that you can't read. I have minimal Spanish skills, and I listen to tapes in my car, and I'm trying to learn more . . . [because] when [*La Voz*] arrives in my office I sometimes wonder what's in here? How am I going to get bitten on this deal? Fortunately we haven't had any problems, and the feedback has been really good. So I'm relying on Monica to be our conscience as well . . . and she's done a good job. And when things aren't going well, if she feels she isn't getting the support or *La Voz* isn't getting the support it needs, I hear from her—and that's great, because she's the advocate."

With regard to the economic side, Buckley says, "We are making money on it. We didn't make it overnight, but it's beginning to grow. The biggest setback we had in our advertising effort was using our regular sales staff to sell [*La Voz*]. Buckley says the solution is a separate ad rep dedicated to selling *La Voz*. "When that happens," Buckley predicts, "we'll probably increase the publication frequency to weekly."

For more information, contact Steve Buckley at <sbuckley@link.freedom.com>.

The Granddaddy of Them All

Durham *Herald-Sun* executive editor Bill Hawkins says he didn't have to see the 2000 Census to tell him what he already knew. "Most of us in Durham," Hawkins wrote in a column from March 2001, "didn't need the census to recognize this new wave of immigrants, who have played an important role in filling jobs that have fueled our booming economy over the last decade."

Hawkins' Durham *Herald-Sun*, a 57,000-circulation family-owned daily in the blue-collar city of 190,000, didn't wait for the census to get their journalistic attention either.

As far back as 1997, the *Herald-Sun* initiated a series called "New Faces, New Voices." The pioneering series, written by Miriam Stawowy, a young reporter from Colombia, ran over a period of several months and addressed issues related to the then new phenomenon of the Latino influx in Durham.

Following the series, Hawkins asked Stawowy to write a column, which they named "Nuestro Pueblo." It became the state's very first bilingual column. The twice-monthly column was edited by then night metro editor Mark Schultz. After Miriam Stawowy returned to Florida to be closer to her family, the *Herald-Sun* continued the bilingual column using a team of Latino writers, and Schultz became the driving force behind the *Herald-Sun*'s Latino coverage initiative. Describing what happened next in 1998, he says, "We took the page weekly. . . . We added a new story and weekly calendar. All local, all bilingual." Schultz also added three more Latino writers to his original stable of three, expanding what was once only a column into a bilingual full page, published on Fridays.

Hawkins observes, "The page has been very well received in our community and is a powerful teaching tool in our schools, especially in English as a second language classes. But we also knew that the column was not reaching many newcomers, for whom a newspaper in English is not yet an option. That in turn led to our monthly *Nuestro Pueblo* publication that is entirely in Spanish and distributed separately from the *Herald-Sun*."

Hawkins notes, "It started simply in the form of a four-page section distributed at La Fiesta del Pueblo in September of 2000." Since that humble beginning, *Nuestro Pueblo* has grown into a free 8,000-circulation, 12- to 16-page tabloid going to 60 different locations primarily in Durham and Orange counties.

Schultz was honored for his work on *Nuestro Pueblo* in October 2001 when the Latin American Resource Center of Durham presented him the media award.

At that time, Hawkins lauded Schultz, saying, "We are very proud of this award in that it recognizes the exceptional leadership of Mark Schultz in creating and editing our growing *Nuestro Pueblo* edition. It is really through his determination and his compassion that the *Herald-Sun* has been able to play a positive role in helping Latinos bridge the cultural gap in one of North Carolina's most diverse communities."

Schultz notes that when the 2000 Census came out, it served as a validation. He explains, "Durham's Hispanic population had grown from just over 1,000 people (less than 2 percent) to 17,000 (nearly 8 percent) in 10 years. And by then we had already been doing our page for two years!"

Hawkins credits Schultz for assembling a talented team of eight local columnists, whom Hawkins calls "smart people with really varied backgrounds. They hail from Mexico, Chile, Costa Rica, Peru and Bolivia, mirroring the multinational face of our Latino community." Hawkins notes that translations of *Nuestro Pueblo* stories are provided by the Chapel Hill Institute for Cultural and Language Education, with final proofreading by editorial assistant Leonidas Cordova.

Schultz outlines the goals of *Nuestro Pueblo*: "to be a bridge between the Spanish-speaking and non-Spanish-speaking communities, and not to 'ghettoize' Latino news. We did not want to say we had a Spanish or bilingual page once a week and be done with it. In fact having the weekly page has improved our coverage of Latino issues seven days a week."

But *Nuestro Pueblo* faces many challenges. What began as a public service must now compete successfully with other profit-driven Spanish-language media that have sprung up in Durham in the last four years, Schultz says, including several newspapers, a Spanish-language FM station, two Spanish-language AM stations and a Spanish-language open-air broadcast station. Schultz, however, remains confident. "But none can provide the local content we do." Ideally Schultz would like to have the resources to take *Nuestro Pueblo* to a weekly.

Hawkins concludes, "All of this is a big undertaking for a newspaper our size, and Mark is determined to see that it gets even bigger. We support *Nuestro Pueblo* wholeheartedly and know that our efforts place the *Herald-Sun* in an important leadership role."

Update: The Durham *Herald-Sun* was purchased in December 2004 by Paxton Media Group of Paducah, Ky. The next month Paxton summarily terminated 23 percent of the paper's workforce, including the publisher and executive editor. The new leadership discontinued the monthly *Nuestro Pueblo* publication because it "didn't seem to be getting much traction with readership, and sure wasn't getting much with advertising," explains the *Herald-Sun's* new editor, Bob Ashley. As to the weekly bilingual Latino page, Ashley says it is "on hiatus right now," adding, "Whether we're able to resume it in the near future depends on finding (or acquiring) someone on staff with the Spanish skills to carry it forward. It's still a project under discussion, but its future is uncertain at the moment." Former *Herald-Sun* executive editor Bill Hawkins landed on his feet—as executive editor of the Charleston, S.C., *Post and Courier*. And Mark Schultz was hired away by McClatchy. He is now editor of the Chapel Hill *News* and the Orange County Bureau of the Raleigh *News & Observer*.

Other Voices; Other Newsrooms

Federico van Gelderen is publisher of the Triangle edition of *Que Pasa*, an extremely successful Spanish-language newspaper in the Raleigh–Durham–Chapel Hill area of North Carolina. Originally a businessman from Argentina, van Gelderen moved to the United States in the 1990s and became involved with social issues among the Latinos in his area, which eventually led him to the community newspaper and radio business. As you will read, van Gelderen believes the Latino media have a primary mission of helping the new immigrants become assimilated and acculturated into American society while still celebrating their cultural values. *Que Pasa*, launched in 2001, is a 20,000-circulation free weekly. A sister publication was started several years before in Winston-Salem, and a new edition was created in Charlotte in 2004. Van Gelderen makes no apologies that *Que Pasa* is dedicated to advocating and speaking for the voiceless. In his own words:

On the role of Que Pasa *in central North Carolina:* "I think it is vital. The state is going through an amazing immigration process that is changing our social map. Our newspaper is helping in this process of redrawing this map, by helping with the transition, trying to inform, educate and entertain our readers."

What are the main challenges facing your community?: "Isolation based on a federal law that has to do with Latinos' legal status language and cultural barriers, and lack of leadership."

On the mission of Que Pasa: "Commitment to go wherever it takes to get to the truth, to be the voice for the voiceless, to be willing to invest what it takes in order to be the best for those whom we serve."

On the relationship between his community and Que Pasa: "It's very dynamic. We give them a voice, and they are starting to feel what that means. It's very interactive, and we get a lot of their feedback."

On the culture of community at Que Pasa: "Everyone in the company needs to understand and share our values. Our corporate culture is based on the belief that devotion to serving our community will lead to solvency. Our commitment is to content, so everyone is an eye and an ear. They need to see what is going on and listen, since a story can be around any corner, so we need to be able to breathe and sweat with the community we serve. In our case it's important to make sure that our employees understand that we are making history, that the added value of this experience will pay off in the future, and that what they are doing now is worthwhile."

On the role of the publisher at Que Pasa: "To be very focused and organized, to make sure you understand your priorities, and be willing to work 24/7 and to do whatever it takes to put the best paper on the street with the resources you have. To make sure that your team never forgets your core values and the community we serve."

On thinking outside the box, outside the paper: "We have begun partnering with the Anglo media to learn more about the community at large, and to better serve the integration process of the Hispanic community. We participate in all kinds of events that help create awareness of the new diversity we have in our state, and the need to make the changes that will lead to a more fair and better place to live. I spend a lot of my time in the schools, going through the paper with the students. They are our future leaders, and they need to understand what is going on with *Que Pasa*."

On mentoring: "It is the key to success. In North Carolina we need to nurture our next generation in order to have more diverse newsrooms, by working with elementary, middle and high school students, getting their attention about our media, getting them involved in writing about things that affect their community."

On leadership: "I am the first one willing to get involved, to maintain our core values to help work with anyone who needs me, to be focused and set up goals and accomplish them. I exercise humility, I am a great listener and the first one willing to learn and serve. Every decision has to be made in consistency with our values, and we will never compromise content for the sake of increased revenues."

What are the challenges ahead for Que Pasa?*:* "Remaining independent when the big media companies make this market a money game; remaining focused that local is the key, regardless of how extended is your area of coverage; and understanding the dynamics of the immigration process and being able to be one step ahead of it.

"We must also try to understand the questions and have the answers for what is coming next. For example, will the second or third generation of Hispanics start using the mainstream media? What is going to be our relationship with the Anglo media? What is our content going to look like in order to keep our first generation interested and also have the new ones having an interest in it? Bilingual is an option. Local, local local for sure is one."

On the best thing Que Pasa *has done so far:* "Our project itself, now that we see our papers in almost all our state; our commitment to making content our first priority; to maintain our values of integrity, commitment, honesty, trust and accountability; understanding that our devotion to serving our community will at some point pay for itself—I think is our most special accomplishment."

Your Town; Your Turn

1. If you work at a mainstream community newspaper, what is your newspaper doing to give minorities a voice?
2. How ethnically diverse is your newsroom?
3. How has the multi-ethnic nature of your community changed in the last 15 years?
4. If there have been dramatic changes in the demographics in your town, are those changes being reflected in the pages of your paper?

TWENTY

The Great Good Paper

Sociologist Ray Oldenburg is in love with "third places." Not the home-place (your first place) or the work-place (your second place), but that other informal social place—a third place, where you go to hang out, chill out, recover, recoup and reload: the café, tavern, pub, bookstore, bowling alley or neighborhood coffee shop. When a third place is an inclusive, welcoming, nurturing and vital center of the community, Oldenburg calls such a place not just a good place, it becomes a GREAT good place.

I'm thinking that Oldenburg will not only forgive us for co-opting his title concept, but will also applaud us for making the leap. In my travels and through my research I've come to know plenty of *good* community newspapers, but I've also been exposed to many *great* good papers.

So the questions have inevitably risen to the surface like Kurt Vonnegut's "bubble in the Prell bottle." What are the characteristics of a great good paper? How did they become great? How do they keep on keeping on at that level of excellence? What can be learned from those who lead great good papers? What are some examples of what great good papers do that set them apart?

With apologies to Dr. Stephen Co-vey (author of *Seven Habits of Highly Effective People*), I've distilled the best practices of community newspapers into bullet points.

10 Habits of Highly Effective Community Newspapers

- Uncompromising dedication to EXCELLENCE: "We'll always be small-town, but we'll never be small-time."—D. Woronoff
- Open ACCESS: A reciprocity with readers, both on the page and through the front door.
- FLEXIBILITY: Flexible thought, leadership and flexible hours.
- Senior MENTORING: Feedback, inspiration and tough love.
- RESPECT: Not treating your people like pizza delivery boys.
- PEOPLE-ORIENTED LANGUAGE AND DECISIONS: Not talking about your newspaper as a PRODUCT and the community as a MARKET.
- Viewing the newspaper as a PUBLIC UTILITY. Articulating the core values of the paper to the staff. A mission statement that is taken seriously. Take the example of the McComb (Miss.) *Enterprise-Journal*: "The one newspaper that cares the most about McComb."

- A HAPPY SHOP: A work hard, play hard ethic, from the top down.
- Staffers as STAKEHOLDERS: All ideas get heard with respect, no matter how gonzo.
- HIGH RETENTION: Sharing the rewards, both tangible and intangible, internal and external, resulting in low turnover.

It all adds up to a healthy, nurturing, creative culture of community within the newspaper.

That's just my list; you can make your own. Stephen Byers, former editor and now a lecturer at the University of Wisconsin–Milwaukee Urban Studies program, offers the following principles to work and live by:

- Know what your readers care about.
- Repeat stories.
- Take sides.
- Be proud to be different.
- Localize.
- Know how your community communicates.
- Don't forget the education function of the community newspaper.
- Be a leader. Make news yourself; be identified with leading and changing, not just reflecting change. Remember, a newspaper is a unification tool.
- Never forget your readers. The ads will follow.
- Change or die.

Jim Kevlin, executive editor at the Norwich (Conn.) *Bulletin* and past president of Connecticut's Associated Press Managing Editors, created a handout for his newsroom with this rallying cry on the front: "LOCAL PEOPLE are our franchise." Inside, he reminds his reporters to keep in mind the three major points derived from a regional strategic long-range planning session: "The Future of the Region, Generation X and Young Families; and Newcomers/Diversity." Then he reminds his staff to pay attention to the four major population centers amid the nine towns in their coverage area.

From the Readership Institute at Northwestern University's Media Management Center, Kevlin prioritizes "What People Read":

1. News about ordinary people
2. Health, home, food, fashion, travel
3. Politics, government, international
4. Natural disasters, accidents
5. Movies, TV, weather
6. Business, personal finance
7. Science, technology, environment
8. Police, crime
9. Sports

And Kevlin closes with a checklist for what he wants to find in the first five grafs of his staff's stories:

1. News
2. Impact
3. Context
4. Human Dimension

Great Ideas from Great Good Papers

Don't just think outside the box—"think outside the paper."

For a community paper to truly flourish, it must do more than just "smear ink on dead trees," as the expression goes. (Of course, there is no substitute for solid, consistent, comprehensive local news, sports, features, lifestyle, commentary and visual coverage.) But what separates the merely good community papers from the truly great ones? Again, it's "thinking outside the paper."

Here is a small collection of great ideas that created win-win situations for superior community newspapers.

A Miracle in Whiteville

On the morning of July 4, 2001, roughly 1,500 people got down on their hands and knees on main street, Whiteville, N.C., to create what is believed to be the longest, largest copy of the Declaration of Independence. And they wrote it in two minutes and 29 seconds on 1.25 miles of newsprint (donated by the newspaper) laid right through the middle of town.

It was the brainstorm of a local reporter.

"I must have been insane," wrote staff writer Mark Gilchrist just hours after a wild notion he had had only six weeks before resulted in what many participants called their best July 4th ever. "Any sane person would have said that it would be impossible to organize 1,500 people, have them line up for more than a mile, and in only a few minutes handwrite a 1,500-word document."

But they did pull it off, and the result—a front-page photo of the humongous document in a parking lot surrounding by waving cheering people—took up the entire top half of the next Whiteville *News Reporter*, an award-winning locally owned 10,200-circulation semiweekly known for its enlightened management, led by publisher Jim High, editor Les High and news editor Lee Hinnant.

Gilchrist recalls, "When I first went into Mr. High's office in late May to pitch this idea, I fully expected them to kick me out (and I nearly hoped they would). But they went for it, and they went for it with vigor."

On the editorial page of that same edition, the *News Reporter* gave an editorial

An extraordinary front page from an extraordinary day. Let's shut down the main street, get the whole town together and see how fast we can make the world's largest copy of the Declaration of Independence. And what made this even more unusual? The entire scheme was the brainchild of Whiteville *News Reporter* staffer Mark Gilchrist. (Courtesy of the Whiteville *News Reporter*)

"Thumbs up" to Gilchrist: "To our own Mark Gilchrist, who spent countless hours and sleepless nights tediously organizing the Whiteville Independence Day celebration and to the City of Whiteville and the Greater Whiteville Chamber of Commerce's Special Events Committee. It was a monumental task, but it shows what can be done when people see the big picture, then pull together to make something special happen."

The Good News

It's the week after Christmas. You have just published the fat, ad-chocked seasonal whopper, and all you and your exhausted staff want is to go home.

But you've got a paper to put out. So what if there were an easy, fun and profitable way to accomplish that? There is.

The Annual Good News Issue of the Aledo (Texas) *Community News* is eagerly awaited by readers—and a lifesaver for the hard-pressed *News* staff at holiday time. (Courtesy of the Aledo *Community News*)

Welcome to the annual Good News Issue.

Editor-publisher Randy Keck of the weekly Aledo (Texas) *Community News* says he came up with the idea about a year after he purchased the paper in 1995. "It was basically born of necessity," he explains. "Some newspapers I know of don't publish the last week of the year, but I just couldn't do that. (My joke is always that as sure as I decide *not* to publish, that will be the week the UFO lands at Aledo City Hall.)"

The annual Good News Issue (they've done nine of them, so far) "is based on the idea [that] the one thing people seem to have no shortage of is bad news," Keck says. "I felt it would be a good idea to reserve one issue of the paper for only good news.

"As the years have gone by, the idea has caught on, and readers have made us aware of unsung heroes and good news stories that might not otherwise find their way into the newspaper.

"The city council reports, news and opinions can wait. For now, it's all about the people who live nearby. Turns out, there is a lot happening."

So the annual Good News Edition contains stories such as a longtime local volunteer master gardener being honored by the town, an Army couple home on leave from Korea getting to see their 1-year-old twin boys, a local Boy Scout earning his Eagle badge, a local teacher winning top national honors, a toddler receiving a revolutionary hearing device, and two local ministers who fell in love, got married and now happily serve as preachers for two different local denominations.

Keck tells his readers: "While it may be tempting to say that next week we will return to 'the real world,' the stories you will read this week are just as real as any 'bad news.' We hope that over time people will consider them just as newsworthy."

From a production standpoint, Keck notes that they usually start working on the Good News Edition in November. "The idea has been to set an early ad deadline and to get the 'Good News' issue out as soon after the previous week's issue as possible," he says. "That gives me the option of giving the staff a couple of extra days off during the holidays."

And that is really good news.

The Local Style / Fact Book

Just as every place is different, so too is every newspaper. How then is the new reporter/photographer/editor to learn all the ins and outs of both (all the while reporting and writing as if he or she knows everything that counts)?

The local style/fact book is one of the answers, says Frank Fee, associate professor of journalism at the University of North Carolina at Chapel Hill. Fee, a former copy desk chief, says, "It takes a lot of work, but it's well worth it."

In addition to spelling preferences, punctuation and local abbreviations, the local style section of the book sets rules for consistency regarding such items as local terminology for governmental, social and law enforcement agencies. For instance, is it the "Town of Forest City" or the "City of Forest City" . . . ?

Example: The police chief in Chapel Hill, N.C., spells his name "Gregg," with two "g's" at the end, and his name is misspelled in the local phone book.

Other examples: How does the paper handle sexist language, suicides, photos of dead bodies and newsroom sacred cows that otherwise go largely unspoken. For instance, many beach community newspapers forbid photos of seagulls, a photographic cliché and a favorite subject of amateurs. Likewise, at the Jackson Hole (Wyo.) *News and Guide*, says publisher Michael Sellett, it is strictly verboten to come back with an IFOT (In Front of Tetons) photo, as might occur "when the photographer [shoots] anything from a cowboy on horseback to the winners of the local quilting contest using the Tetons as a backdrop. That photo should never see print."

The local fact book section contains entries of great use to the newcomer and veteran alike: How many seats are there in the local civic auditorium. What are the names of local landmarks? For instance, it would be valuable in the Pittsburgh, Pa., area to know the names of the three rivers that flow together to form the Ohio River in the center of town. How do you spell their names, and in what direction does each flow? (The Monongahela flows north, the Allegheny flows south and the Youghiogheny flows northwest.)

Getting the Community into the Community Paper

The Asheboro (N.C.) *Courier-Tribune* annually chooses a panel of local guest columnists that this year included a business professor, a retired county elections director and a National Guard officer. Community journalism student Christina Rexrode reports that the paper also has a rotating weekly religion column written by local preachers. Former editor and columnist Bob Williams told Rexrode these twice-weekly guest columns help the staff keep in touch with what readers are thinking.

Scaring the Bejabbers out of the Young Drivers

Community journalists from great good papers are *visibly* involved in the towns they serve. Tom Terry, former editor-publisher of the weekly Geneseo (Ill.) *Republic*, involved himself very poignantly in the driver's education program at his town's high school.

"I took in our obituary form and passed it out to the kids, mainly sophomores, ages 15 and 16," Terry recalled. "Then I asked them to fill in all the blanks. Education, accomplishments, children, and so on. 'Not much on that sheet is there,' I told them after they were done. 'Of course not, you haven't even begun to *live* yet.' You could hear a pin drop in the room; then I hit them with my best shot. 'I wish you could see the faces of your parents when I stop by your house after one of you has been killed in a car crash because you were driving too fast or you were drinking or you were on drugs. They will age 20 years in their faces as they hand me the best photo they have of you to put in the paper.' Some of the girls would begin to cry at this.

"The teacher was usually someone I had known for years and sometimes the man who had taught me to drive. We would then 'chat' for a couple minutes about the kids we both knew and the circumstances of their deaths. The ones who tried to beat a train to a crossing, the one who missed the turn two blocks from the high school and slammed into a tree in front of a building that used to be the Rivenburg Funeral Home, the student who was going too fast at a T intersection in the country and was decapitated by her seat belt because she hadn't secured the lap belt portion, the twins who died in a small car because they were driving in the middle of the road as they crested a hill. Let me tell you, that was hard, but if it saved one life," Terry says, his voice trailing off.

Hear Ye, Hear Ye

So you've got aging readers who can't see so well anymore. But they're still your readers, right? So how do you get them the community news they crave? Publisher Donald Q. Smith and his good people at the 3,000-circulation Monticello (Minn.) *Times*, an award-winning independent weekly, participate with the local Lions Club in a public service project they call "the *Times* on Tape" in which volunteer readers from the Lions Club read the *Times*, creating cassette tape recordings that are then distributed to the *Times'* visually impaired readers each week.

Something Old, Something New / Something Borrowed, Something Blue . . .

Every issue of the paper should have something in it that makes the reader exclaim (to paraphrase Bronx, N.Y., weekly newspaper editor Bernard Stein): "Hey Maw! Lookit this!"

Such is the Milestones page of the Lebanon (Mo.) *Daily Record*, a 5,000-circulation independent daily. You can't take your eyes off it: then and now photographs of couples celebrating their 25th and 50th wedding anniversaries. The couple in the 1950s when they got engaged; the couple now. How they've changed, or haven't changed.

If it's true what media pundits say—that newspapers sell "eyeballs on pages"—then here's one great idea that's sure to have people hollering, "Hey Maw . . . !"

Every Picture Tells a Story

Old family snapshots create great reader interest. "A Day in History," a long-running and extremely popular feature of the 17,200-circulation CNHI-owned Port Arthur (Texas) *News*, features at the top of page two every day a vintage historical photograph submitted by a reader. Guidelines stipulate that "images must be on photographic paper. Submitters must print a description of what is in the photo and include their name and phone number. Include a self-addressed, stamped envelope for return. Send to . . ." Obviously, this takes someone at the paper committed to making this sort of component of the paper function smoothly and consistently. But it's worth it.

Juxtaposing then and now photos of the couple: What a great way to give anniversaries more reader appeal. (Courtesy of the Lebanon [Mo.] *Daily Record*)

A Best Practices Toolkit

So now, let's get specific. How do leaders of great good papers do it? Eight outstanding community journalists answer the big questions. They are, in alphabetical order:

Bob Buckel, publisher of the Azle (Texas) *News*, an independent 4,880-circulation weekly.

Linda Gilmore, a former editor of the Junction City (Kan.) *Daily Union*, a 5,500-circulation daily.

Andrea Hurley, editor of the Marthasville (Mo.) *Record*, a 2,500-circulation weekly.

John Grey Montgomery, president and editor of the Junction City (Kan.) *Daily Union*, a 5,500-circulation daily.

Don Q. Smith, publisher of the Monticello (Minn.) *Times*, an independent 3,000-circulation weekly.

Patsy Speights, editor of the Prentiss (Miss.) *Headlight*, a 2,803-circulation weekly.

Tim L. Waltner, publisher of the Freeman (S.D.) *Courier*, a 2,000-circulation independent weekly.

David Woronoff, publisher of *The Pilot* of Southern Pines, N.C., a 15,000-circulation independent tri-weekly.

What's the difference between a merely good community newspaper and a truly great one?

WALTNER: Going beyond the obvious in every aspect of news reporting and photography. Paying attention to the diversity in your community. Commitment to an editorial page. A willingness to change along with the community. A willingness to challenge the community it serves by provoking thought through every aspect of the paper.

SMITH: "A man's reach must exceed his grasp." By that I mean, the best papers are also reaching to be better—in news, layout, writing, editorials, columns, special sections. They can't stand the status quo.

WORONOFF: Great community newspapers are like Avis—they try harder. The truly great paper is willing to take risks and engage in some kind of journalistic experiment, whether that's new products outside the paper or new features in its pages. That creates a vibrancy and vitality that readers find compelling and makes the paper more relevant. I believe that the mission of the great community newspaper should be in service to the community that it serves. At *The Pilot*, we list our priorities as (1) community and readers, (2) advertisers, (3) ownership. Unfortunately, these days most newspapers are owned by huge corporations and oftentimes their priorities are in the reverse order of ours.

MONTGOMERY: Creativity.

BUCKEL: Good community newspapers can put out a pretty package and cover all the beats. Great community newspapers—and I'm privileged to be in between two of the best in the Wise County *Messenger* in Decatur and the Hood County *News* in Granbury—reinvest a huge amount of their profits in making the paper better for the readers, day in and day out. I think that's a function of commitment on the part of ownership: the decision to build equity by making the product consistently better, or to siphon off profits, have a nice paper and a nice life.

HURLEY: Being there! Being on a first-name basis with residents and community leaders. Being relentlessly local and leaving the wire stories for the city papers. Good school coverage, a local editorial page, a strong sports page and a reader-friendly design. And five little words—photos, photos and more photos. Everyone loves to pick up a newspaper with lots of really good photos sprinkled throughout. It's not unusual for the *Record* to do a photo page three times a month.

GILMORE: A great paper (of any size) finds the surprising stories and tells them well. A great paper is always trying to improve. A great paper tries to reflect its community as completely as possible. A great paper is willing to admit when it makes a mistake and takes steps not to make that mistake again. A great paper respects its readers and recognizes them as part of the community conversation.

How is community journalism different from journalism as practiced by large-circulation major metro newspapers?

WALTNER: The size of the community provides an automatic edge to smaller papers, giving the news a more intimate feel. The stories will generally resonate in a more personal way with readers in smaller communities. Weeklies have the luxury of time to provide more perspective and background; you often get scooped on big stories, but you can usually offer better context.

SPEIGHTS: You rub shoulders with your readers every day, at the bank, in the grocery, at the dress shop, at church and clubs.

SMITH: The closeness to the audience; getting immediate feedback, caring about the community and its people—often more than leaders and readers may care about the newspaper.

BUCKEL: We have to look people in the eye, day in and day out. We live with them. They're like our family, warts and all. As a result, we can't see them as merely "stories"—they're people. I learned this early in my career when I ran a photo of a DWI accident on the front page in Andrews, complete with a young man's feet sticking out from under a blanket in a field littered with broken beer bottles. It was a powerful photo, but I got to spend about 15 minutes across the desk from that young man's mother after it came out. He was more than just a pair of feet under a blanket, more than a drinker—he was an honor student, a football player, a kid who was going to start college that fall, a good son. You have to tell that part of the story, too. I think major metro dailies, by the way, have gotten much better at that.

MONTGOMERY: Connectivity. You can really see your world in a community newspaper. Sometimes you may not like it; but it is, unmistakably, your world.

HURLEY: It's personal. We live in the community, so we truly have a stake in its future. We walk the same streets every day with the people we write about, stand in line with them at the supermarket and sit next to them in the dentist's waiting room. Because of this, we know how our stories are perceived and can tell when we're getting off track. The people are our touchstone.

GILMORE: Community journalism recognizes that readers are more than just numbers on a readership survey. Readers are people who come in and talk to you— and you're glad they do, even when they disagree. Community journalism recognizes that even the seemingly mundane or unimportant stories matter to somebody. You can't cater to everybody, but you can try to get as wide a range of community events and news into the paper as possible.

How would you characterize the role of your newspaper in the community?

HURLEY: We don't merely have a role in the community; we are a vital part of it. Within that framework, our role is to offer our readers what they can't get in the nearby "big city" daily—local news, local editorials and local columnists. We try to give them the information necessary to be well-informed about the issues that affect them "right where they live." We don't take the phrase "relentlessly local" lightly.

SPEIGHTS: We are vital for information. The town has no TV and only a small radio station with only a couple of hours of "live" DJs.

SMITH: We are the reporter of news, chronicler of local history and platform for public opinion.

WALTNER: By providing news coverage, advertising services and offering a public forum for community discussion, the *Courier* provides a "weekly conversation" between the diverse groups in the community. As a community organ we strive to transcend the natural divisions such as age, gender, ethnicity, school loyalty, status and denomination affiliation. No other community institution has a better opportunity to provide that link than a community newspaper.

GILMORE: The *Daily Union* tries to reflect the community "in all its complexity and wholeness" as (the editor) says. Sometimes we do that better than others. But we try to tell the good news, as well as the hard news, and we try to help the community understand how decisions are made, and what they need to know to live their lives. We try to get diverse voices into the newspaper through our local columnists and through covering different organizations, such as a recently formed support group for gays, lesbians and transgendered people and their friends and families.

WORONOFF: Caring communities like ours don't happen by accident. They're built on the backs of civic-minded folks, whose exploits are celebrated in all three of our editions every week. We're not content to sit back and observe the community with journalistic detachment. This is our home. We live here, and, with a little luck, we'll die here. We are determined to leave this special place that we are so fortunate to call home in better condition than we found it. Whether it's volunteering to chair the United Way campaign or helping to build Habitat for Humanity houses, someone from *The Pilot* will be a part of the action. Those activities—not our involvement—inevitably find their way into the pages of the newspaper.

BUCKEL: We're the community bulletin board, the only strictly local means of communication and the catalyst that—we hope—makes a whole bunch of good things possible in our community. I think to . . . a large extent we're the glue that holds the community together.

What are the three major challenges facing your community?

SPEIGHTS: Economics: Wal-Mart killed our downtown. Racism still exists. Young people moving away.

MONTGOMERY: (1) Few young people are moving back. (2) Economy is stagnant. (3) We don't have a coherent plan for our community's development.

BUCKEL: Growth, leadership, and retaining our uniqueness in the face of suburban creep coming this way. The newspaper can and must play a key role in all those areas.

HURLEY: Growth: Warren County is growing rapidly and we're struggling to keep up with it. Crime: Meth labs are a real problem, especially in our rural areas. Voter apathy: low voter turnout, especially in municipal elections. One of our cities couldn't even come up with a candidate for mayor during the last election and ended up with a mayor elected by seven write-in votes!

WORONOFF: (1) Managing growth. (2) Maintaining ambiance. (3) Keeping unique communities united.

GILMORE: The economy, housing, a vision for the future.

WALTNER: Declining population. A decline in the number of retail businesses. Lack of dynamic vision.

SMITH: (1) Growth—more residential than commercial versus preservation of small-town community. (2) Outside ownership of businesses—owners who thus have less interest or "ownership" of the community and its institutions. Gone: Mom 'n' pops. (3) Identifying a new generation of leaders to succeed those now in their 50s and 60s who gave so much to Monticello.

How would you describe the relationship between the newspaper and your community?

HURLEY: Up close and personal. Our coverage area (all of Warren County, Mo.) includes three cities and is one of the six fastest-growing counties in the state. Even so, we make every effort to be 100 percent accessible to everyone in the county. Because we are "out there" as much as possible, our readers and area officials know us well and are confident that they can count on us.

WORONOFF: It's a participative one. We pride ourselves on being accessible to our community. We define accessibility as making our columns available to our readers as well as by making our people available to listen to their suggestions and concerns. Also, our aggressive editorial voice makes us a player in the community's affairs.

GILMORE: I think it's pretty interactive. People can walk in and talk to the reporters and the editor. The public is invited to our daily news meeting, which we have when we're done with the day's paper. People call the paper for information, such as contact information for our legislators. People expect us to be their news source.

WALTNER: The *Courier* has a strong presence in the community with solid penetration; we have a circulation of nearly 2,000 in a town of 1,300 residents. While well-received, the service the *Courier* provides to the community is largely taken for granted.

MONTGOMERY: Mostly good. We have made a lot of changes to the *Daily Union* in the past two years. Unfortunately, I think that has displeased some readers. Others I think are still getting used to the more frank tone of the *Daily Union*.

BUCKEL: Like most newspapers, it's love-hate. We make people angry at times because we publish things they'd rather we didn't, such as their name when they get arrested for drunk driving. But it's truly like a family in the overriding sense: we fuss, we fight, but we love each other. I know we love the community fiercely, and I think a lot of them love us. Years ago when a city council member died, I wrote an editorial about what a great lady she was, but at the same time a real curmudgeon who had chewed me out the last time I saw her (she then sat down and we talked about our families, etc., and hugged when she left). On the street at our Main Street Festival the weekend after the paper came out, a fellow city council member approached me with his jaw clenched and tears in his eyes, grabbed my arm so hard it hurt (I thought he was mad) and through clenched teeth said, "I *love* my local newspaper." One moment like that makes up for a lot of the other kind.

What are the three major challenges facing your newspaper?

BUCKEL: (1) Being able to continue to sell ads as corporate retail takes over our community and threatens to knock out the mom-and-pop stores where we can walk in the door and talk to a decision maker. We have to learn how to play the big-stores' game. (2) Remaining profitable and affordable at the same time. (3) Continuing to build circulation as the community constantly churns and new people come in who (a) do not know there's a newspaper here, (b) did not come from a community with a strong local paper and therefore don't realize and appreciate what they have here, and/or (c) just aren't newspaper readers. That's why NIE [Newspapers in Education] is so important as we try to build new readers and help young people develop that habit. If they don't know what a treasure they have in a strong, local community newspaper, they won't miss it if we go away. We have to be part of their lives.

SPEIGHTS: Dying subscription base and continuing to find ways to attract young readers. Attracting young people who want to work at the paper. Finding quality college graduates to train and take over.

MONTGOMERY: (1) Circulation has dropped during the past year. (2) Online readership is way up; we need to begin charging for online subscriptions. We hope this will also help point (1), but before we do that we need to revamp the site. (3) The retail economy is weak, could hurt advertising in the long run.

HURLEY: (1) Finding a way to cover an expanding community with a staff that isn't. (2) Advertising revenue—digging up ad dollars can be difficult, especially with a "free, throw-out" paper in the county. Our competition is part of the Suburban Journals of St. Louis (Pulitzer Publishing—the *St. Louis Post-Dispatch*) chain, and they can offer advertising deals that we can't. (3) Location—we're located in the far southern end of the county, in the most rural of the three communities. We actually have a natural barrier between us and the rest of the county—Hopewell Hill. The mountain and its dangerous, curvy highway is between us and the county seat 21 miles away!

WORONOFF: (1) Continuing to exceed the community's expectations. (2) Managing growth without losing what makes us unique. (3) Effectively hiring successors to our top three managers, who are all in their 60s.

GILMORE: Staff, staff, staff. I know it's hard to maintain quality when the staff turns over frequently.

WALTNER: Declining population—readership. A decline in the number of retail businesses—revenue. Staying current with technology.

SMITH: (1) Erosion of local advertising base due to the arrival of outside owners and chain businesses. (2) Record levels of outside competition selling advertising, including the metro daily 40 miles away. (3) In a growing community in computer-land, there is minimal interest in the affairs of Monticello, and thus [people] don't buy or read the newspaper.

Do you have any tips for creating and maintaining a "happy shop"—a creative, fun and productive newsroom?

SMITH: Continually stressing the importance of teamwork. And involving every reporter (full and part time) in planning of stories and special sections.

WORONOFF: Newspapering is supposed to be fun. In fact, we made "fun" one of our core values. I like to hear a lot of laughter in the hallways and banter back and forth between departments. One way we foster our kind of atmosphere is through our interior decor. We have lots of natural light streaming into the building, and we've made the office open so that everyone can see each other from just about anywhere in the building. That way everyone can gain an appreciation for what the others do every day. We try hard to instill in our folks that we are all interdependent on each other. We tell all employees on their first day of work that they are either working to put out the paper or working to put out the bills. If we fail to do either one of those things, we can't do the other.

HURLEY: It begins during the hiring process. We have a "happy shop," and I truly believe that's because we have the right mix of personalities. That's a task that's never easy, especially in a small office such as ours. Our regular staff is four, count 'em, four, and we work very closely together. It helps that we enjoy each other's company and are working toward a common goal—making the *Record* the best possible newspaper it can be. We're more than co-workers—we're friends.

SPEIGHTS: Talk to each other. Know when it's time to play and when it's time to work. Since I *am* the newsroom—I talk to myself in the mirror.

GILMORE: We try to go to lunch together every so often. Grey [the president of the paper] invited the news staff to his house after Christmas for a belated "holiday meal" in recognition of our hard work under difficult conditions. (A managing editor left, then another staffer left and for a while we were down to six on the news staff—a few bones short of a skeleton crew, as we liked to say). We keep a bowl of gummy bears on the sports reporter's desk. We talk and laugh a lot.

WALTNER: Create a relaxed and comfortable atmosphere by example. Pay attention to aesthetics and a pleasant working environment. Request, don't order. Say thank you. Admit it when you make a mistake. Be flexible, particularly on matters involving personal issues like family. Take a genuine interest in the lives of your staff. Have fun together. Empower your staff to make decisions. Seek and welcome input from your staff. Share information about the newspaper openly. Encourage a feeling of ownership and pride.

How do you nurture and maintain a "culture of community" at your newspaper?

BUCKEL: I'm convinced you have to find people who not only bring skill to the job, but who fit into the culture. Our culture here is laid-back, but highly productive, and when people jump in here, sometimes they don't realize they're jumping onto a pretty fast track. We have fun, but we're dadgum good at what we do—and newcomers find quickly that the way to be respected and fit in is to carry your share of the load. All that isn't totally top-down, although I work as hard as anyone here. I've been blessed with employees over the years who have led by their example to get us to that point. The one thing that is top-down is that in 17 years here, no one has ever seen me lose my temper or yell and scream at an employee. I treat them with respect, and therefore I can demand that they treat me, and each other, with respect. I think my employees would tell you, if you asked them, that it's a privilege to be part of this team, working with good people and producing a newspaper they can be proud of.

SPEIGHTS: Be involved. Go to church, be a member of the Chamber of Commerce, never miss a funeral and shop in town.

HURLEY: Involvement. As a community paper, we make every effort to be an actively engaged member of the community. We sponsor Senior Day at the county fair and underwrite a portion of the cost of printing the program for the fair. This year we sponsored a contestant in the Fair Queen contest and also purchased market livestock at the livestock auction and donated the meat to local charitable organizations. For the past two years we've entered a float in the county fair parade. During this year's Lewis and Clark Bicentennial, we were a sponsor for the local Lewis and Clark Rendezvous at La Charrette. Individually we also take a role in local events. Each year during Deutsch Country Days (an educational festival celebrating the area's German heritage), three members of our staff volunteer at that event. This year we'll be churning butter and making apple butter. We attend every event possible in the community and maintain an open door policy in our office—everyone is welcome to stop in and tell us how we're doing.

What are some tips you can offer for inspiring your newsroom?

BUCKEL: Send/take them to some good conferences through your press association, SPJ [Society of Professional Journalists], the Freedom of Information Foundation or other organizations. They need to understand that what they do is important and that they're not alone. And they need to see you do some really, really good work from time to time. Your newsroom veterans have to set a standard that the new ones can aspire to meet and exceed.

HURLEY: We sit down at the beginning of the year and set a goal—this year it's to become indispensable to our community.

WORONOFF: We want our employees to be what author James Michener once called "masters at the art of living who make no distinction between their labor and their leisure." We try to create a sense of fun and adventure here. That's because we believe that at its heart producing a newspaper is a creative endeavor. It's hard to be creative if you don't enjoy what you create. We try to be relentlessly energetic and enthusiastic. We hire people who possess those personality traits. We try to give our employees autonomy and freedom. We tell them to manage their departments as if they own them. Then we tell them that we expect them to love their job, and if they don't, there is no shame in leaving it. Folks spend more time awake at work than they do awake at home. Life is too fleeting to spend it being miserable. Besides that, no one wants to work with a bunch of folks who act like Eeyore.

SMITH: In every way, make sure young reporters believe they have a stake in the paper. They share ownership in news columns. And by having a column every three weeks, they have visibility and stature in a small community.

How would you define your leadership style? And what are some of the guiding principles that help you make management decisions?

SPEIGHTS: Lead by example. Use of common sense and strong Christian beliefs. Knowing the difference between right and wrong.

HURLEY: Hands-on but laid-back. I'm just one of the guys until it's time to make the tough decisions—then I carry the ball and take the flak if necessary. My guiding principle—KISS.

WORONOFF: An old farmer once told me that the best fertilizer is your footprints in the field. I agree with him. That's why I practice management by walking around. The first thing I do every day is to walk through every department and speak with everyone. Sometimes we talk about business, and sometimes we talk about the Tar Heels, and every time I learn something new. I care what my folks think and want them to feel like they can speak respectfully but candidly with me. That participative style has helped create a cohesive operation that makes folks excited to come to work every morning. I have a healthy respect for the traditions of the newspaper business, but I'm not bound by them. I try to be innovative in coming up with solutions to the challenges we face every day. The one thing I do is to figure out what our competition can't do or won't do, and then I try to find a way to do it.

BUCKEL: My style is that we're all co-workers. I don't have to be the best writer, the best ad salesman or ad-builder or page-builder in the shop, but I'm pretty dadgum good at all those things. I want the people who work for me to see me work, and do good work, and to be proud to be on my team. I'm not a yeller or even much of a rah-rah guy, but I do look for opportunities to talk about what we do, often one on one, and try to pass on a little inspiration and information. My guiding principles are to ask people to do things, instead of telling them, to set a good example, to be collegial and respectful in my dealings with people, and to be decisive and bold when that's called for. I try not to waste too much time doing what others could do, but to focus on the things that only I can do, because that's the role they need me to play.

WALTNER: Lead by example. Lead, don't dictate. Inspire, don't demand. Think. Think again. Don't be afraid to get input from others. Don't ask anyone to do something you wouldn't do. Don't forget to listen.

SMITH: Democratic, participatory, open to ideas. And every year every employee gets a reminder of Don's Ten Commandments beginning with (1) Honesty, (2) Professionalism—and including also: Support our advertisers, speak positively about the community, volunteer, read the *Times* (including our shopper and the Internet site). Never say, "It's not my job," and support the team.

What does it take to be an effective community newspaper publisher?

WORONOFF: An effective publisher must have an affinity for and knowledge of all aspects of the newspaper's operation. The publisher must get as excited about a big ad sale, an on-time press start and an employee's new baby as for a big news story. First and foremost, the newspaper is a business. It will never live to be a community institution if it is not successful as a business. So, the publisher must be adept at growing the company's revenue and circulation bit by bit every day. We believe that the best way to do that is by putting out a first-rate newspaper. Good journalism is good business. To me, a newspaper publisher should be engaged, enthusiastic and energetic.

BUCKEL: It takes a lot of time, a very even temper, an understanding and flexible spouse, and a relentlessly positive outlook coupled with an ability to be realistic in your assessment of a situation. I think it takes a pack mule rather than a thoroughbred—someone who can just keep on slogging away, year after year, through all the ups and downs, the encouraging and the discouraging things, and work to make a community better. And that's the most important piece: it takes a true love of the community, a true desire to make it a better place to live, work, raise kids, grow old and have a life. Without that love, the rest is worthless. On top of all that, it takes enough business savvy to make the newspaper a successful business, because unless you stay in business, pay your people and your press bill, and return a profit to your stockholders, you've defaulted on your responsibility to your community. As my old partner James Roberts once said, "A newspaper with a bunch of plaques on the wall and no money in the bank is like a prostitute in a white wedding dress." You can't be the fearless truth teller you need to be when a guy who runs a quarter-page ad can threaten to pull it out and bring you to your knees financially.

WALTNER: Stay in touch with your community. Stay in touch with your staff. Stay in touch with the industry. Be truthful. Be fair. Be willing to lead. Be willing to listen. Pay attention to the business. Don't take yourself too seriously.

What traits, characteristics and abilities do you look for in a great community newspaper editor?

WORONOFF: I joked when we hired our editor from a good-sized daily paper that we were going to beat the daily out of him. By that I meant that he would have to spend more time figuring out a way to say "yes" to our readers. A good editor must be accessible, energetic, enthusiastic and independently minded as well as have the ability to communicate with folks in person and in writing.

GILMORE: I think a good editor needs to understand how *not* to reinvent the wheel. The staff has ways of doing things that make sense to them, and I think a new editor should try to learn how things have been done, and give it a try, before changing everything. If it's not broke, don't fix it. And if an editor has shown a willingness to learn the system, the staff will be more willing to make changes when there's a real need. I think a great editor will take the trouble to find out what the staff members' strengths are and work with them.

SMITH: You have to love newspapers, be willing to go the extra mile; you have to care, and you have to be thick-skinned.

BUCKEL: A high energy level and a burning desire to get the story. In a community newspaper, he or she also needs to have a personality that will enable them to get along with the folks they have to go back to, week after week, for information—an abrasive personality doesn't play well in most small towns. They need to be thorough enough to make the calls, get the sources and get people on the record. And at times they need to be willing to do the best thing for the community even when it isn't necessarily the best thing for the newspaper—i.e., putting out the fire instead of just letting it burn and taking pictures for the front page.

What advice would you give a young or new editor just starting to work at his or her first community newspaper?

BUCKEL: The world is your oyster! There is a story behind every face. To me, it's the most exciting job in the world. Be fearless, get the story and get it right, and write it in a style that makes you want to read it yourself. And take good pictures.

HURLEY: Get out from behind the desk and get your butt out on the street. Have coffee at the café on the corner, go to knee-high football practice and meet some of the parents, walk through the schools and find out how much school has changed over the years! Live in the community and don't just work there—play there too.

MONTGOMERY: Pace yourself, be patient, be thick-skinned.

WORONOFF: Be active. Be accessible. Be visible. Care about your community and your paper.

WALTNER: Visit with a variety of people in the community. Spend time with a local historian. Read the papers from the past three years. Never be afraid to ask a question about something you don't understand. Rely on the people in your office.

GILMORE: Get to know the community—hang out at softball games and high school sporting events, church potlucks, community festivals, wherever people gather. Be curious and be accessible. Don't try to change the world in one issue. Small communities change slowly over long periods of time. You can make a difference, but not overnight.

What are some of the characteristics you look for in entry-level staffers?

MONTGOMERY: Creativity, intelligence, passion, energy, technical skill.

HURLEY: Ethics, energy, enthusiasm and empathy. If those characteristics are there, everything else falls into place. Poor spelling and lousy grammar can be fixed— but you can't teach someone empathy and enthusiasm!

WALTNER: Intelligence, honesty, a willingness to learn and a strong work ethic.

BUCKEL: I'd almost settle for literacy! No, really, it's the same as an editor for editorial staffers. They need to be interested in the kind of news that small towns generate (every entry-level news staffer at a community paper ought to have the privilege of spending a couple of days with Jock Lauterer!) and willing to make the extra phone call, develop the source, persuade someone to go on the record. We also need for them to be decent photographers as well. If they're . . . positive and upbeat and willing to learn (and literate) we can usually mold them into a decent reporter in about two years.

SPEIGHTS: Honesty, self-motivation, independent worker, natural writing skills, desire to work.

WORONOFF: Energy, enthusiasm and curiosity.

GILMORE: I think curiosity and a willingness to learn are important. A firm grasp of the fundamentals of grammar and story construction certainly helps, but those things can be learned and honed as time goes by.

What recruiting and retention tips can you offer?

MONTGOMERY: We have had great hiring success with our state universities. Young adults bring a lot of energy, enthusiasm, creativity and fearlessness. Retaining them is tougher because we are often their stepping stone. But I accept that. I believe we can help our retention by treating people well, [by] giving them a fun work environment and by giving our very top performers more aggressive pay raises.

SPEIGHTS: Look for local people and treat them right.

WALTNER: While people need to be compensated fairly in pay and benefits, the key to getting and keeping good people is to provide a working environment in which people feel fulfilled and that their contribution to the work of the newspaper has worth. Allow—. . . and challenge—. . . people to grow into broader responsibilities. Promote a feeling of ownership within your staff.

HURLEY: Recruiting is mainly by word of mouth. Since we are a relatively small county I tend to know what's out there, and one of my most valuable recent hires worked with me at another newspaper. I knew he was perfect for an opening I had coming up, so I simply gave him a call and asked if he'd like to come on board! Retention—I've learned that unless you challenge people, they tend to get bored. Once they're bored, you're likely to lose them. In addition, I've found broadening a job description can work wonders. My office manager was relegated to answering phones and typesetting, but I learned that she was a talented artist with a love of history. Before you know it, I had a feature writer and an amazing photographer. On top of that, she loves to go out on the accident calls!

BUCKEL: Hire people from your community when you can. Our award-winning society editor is a lady who started for us doing the darkroom work, moved away, moved back and was rehired to do our Photoshop and electronic imaging, moved away, moved back and told me she was a writer. She is. She takes great pictures, too, and Photoshops them herself. Our award-winning sports guy was a full-time firefighter in a nearby city until he retired last year. We worked around his schedule because he was worth it. The only other advice I would offer is to participate in internship programs whenever you can. I have two reporters who first came through the door as interns. We're fortunate in that the University of North Texas, which is just 30 miles away, requires their students to get work published and to do an internship before they can graduate (that's how our editor originally found us). It helps the young people, helps our profession and gives you a chance to get to know someone who may one day come back and ask you for a job. Anytime you can hire a known, versus an unknown, it's a huge advantage.

WORONOFF: We try to talk with college-aged folks about using us as a training ground. We tell them that if they give us a few years and perform well, we'll help them move up to a larger paper when the time comes. Over the years, we've gained the reputation for delivering on that promise. We think that makes us more attractive to young college grads.

Talk about mentoring at your paper—how important is it? How is it done?

HURLEY: It's very important, and it's not rocket science. Mentoring is all about caring—caring about your staff and your newspaper. Since our paper has such a small staff, mentoring comes naturally. I try to give some guidance and a little advice, but I find that my staff is quite effective at letting me know what they expect from me. I try to teach by example whenever possible.

MONTGOMERY: Mentoring is very important because so many of our news staffers are in their first jobs. Mentoring is a total experience. It's like being a good parent, teacher or coach. You don't just worry about how the staffer is doing in his or her work; you worry about his or her life around the clock. Young staffers take on so many new experiences in their first jobs. The real world is very different from college, and the adjustment is probably even more difficult outside of the newsroom than it is inside the newsroom. Awareness is the key. Editors must walk the floor a lot to keep a pulse on people. Ask what they did over the weekend. Ask how they are doing. Make casual conversation. You can pick up many clues that way.

SMITH: As publisher I'm meeting regularly with the news editor; I'm religious about leaving Post-it notes of praise and gratitude, and I write columns and editorials myself.

WALTNER: While we have a small staff, we've had the opportunity to work with a number of young journalists. Most have stayed in the industry. It's important to give them a chance to practice real journalism. Ask for their advice. Discuss their work in a positive, constructive way. Give them a chance to offer input on your own work . . . you might learn something. Find a balance between assignments that they will be comfortable with and assignments that will challenge them.

Every community has its annual festival, county fair or local celebration that must be covered year after year. What innovative things has your paper done to make for fresh coverage?

HURLEY: This year at the county fair, our sports editor took part in the demolition derby (at my suggestion) and then wrote about it. The readers loved it, and we're hoping we can get him to take part in the fair rodeo next year! By volunteering at events, such as Deutsch Country Days, we have a good time while getting great images for our pages—not to mention making great contacts for future feature stories.

SMITH: The week after this year's River Fest, we did an editorial with each reporter contributing three to four paragraphs on a theme like "the best River Fest moment," etc.

WALTNER: We have invited reporters and photographers from outside the community to be part of our staff for those special events to provide "fresh" coverage. We look for the "yet unexplored" aspect or perspective. We seek to identify the new or unique aspect of this year's festival.

GILMORE: With the Sundown Salute (the annual 4th of July festival here), we tried to include "best bets" for each day (it lasts the whole weekend) and included a schedule in the paper each day. Last year, we had people submit their own patriotic photos and printed the best of them on a color page in the paper.

MONTGOMERY: We struggle with this. The best example that comes to mind was our "10 things you need to know to survive Chautauqua 2004." We simply came up with 10 common questions that one would need answered to plan adequately for the event and we answered them in a Q and A format.

*Of all the successful projects at your paper (not just limited to print), is there one
special accomplishment that stands out in your mind?*

SMITH: The *Times'* participation in our community's "adopting" three families who
lost members on 9/11. That led to editor Laurie Dennis visiting New York City
and D.C. for in-home interviews.

BUCKEL: The one we do that pushes the most good buttons in our community is a
Fine Arts Section that comes out each spring. It started out as a double-spread to
go along with Fine Arts Week in the schools. We did a photo and bio on every
elementary music teacher and interviewed four or five people in the community
about what the arts had meant in their lives. We sold ads at the bottom. A couple
of years later Mike Hodges, now executive director of the Texas Press Association,
did an ad seminar, and one of the things he talked about was have a section where
kids draw the ads. We decided to combine that idea: we sell the section in advance
and then take a "client" to each class in the fifth and sixth grades in our school
district. The kids all draw an ad; then we take their work back to the advertiser,
and they pick the one that runs in the paper. That kid's picture and a brief bio run
with the ad. Many of the businesses interact with the class, and I've been to
businesses where those ads—every one they got, not just the one that ran—are
plastered on their walls year round. To introduce the concept, I do an assembly
for each grade at each school and talk to them about the newspaper business, the
media in general, the role advertising plays in our economy, the difference between news and advertising, the First Amendment and what makes a good ad. I
even sing a song for them. We moved it back into May to get past the testing our
state is so obsessed with, and the teachers love it as a fun, creative activity for their
kids. For the news content, we do stories on all the music, art, dance and other
fine arts–related programs in the schools, and we also track down features on artists within the community—singers, sculptors, painters, etc. We've been dumb-
founded at the abundance of art all around us, every year. This year I found Azle
High School graduates who work in the National Museum of the American
Indian (part of the Smithsonian) and the Getty Museum in Los Angeles. The
section was a 24-page broadsheet, with lots of color. Over the years we've won a
lot of awards with it, but the biggest benefit is that it puts the newspaper in front
of every kid in our school district and gives them a chance to have their art in the
paper. At a wedding I attended last week, one of the ushers, a junior engineer-
ing student at Texas Tech, brought up to me that in the sixth grade his ad was in
the paper.

WALTNER: We celebrated the 100th anniversary of our newspaper, the Freeman
Courier with "Freeman in Print," a 13-part series chronicling the news reported
by the *Courier* going back to 1901. We published 13 special 40-page sections, one a
month over a 13-month period starting with our 100th anniversary issue. Each of
the first ten issues was devoted to a specific decade (1901–1910, 1911–20, etc.).
Each of those issues included a timeline based on news items gleaned from every

issue published and selected reprinted articles, photos and artwork from that decade. The 11th issue was devoted to "Photos of the Century," the 12th was a general overview, reprinting feature stories and photos from issues published over the century. The 13th issue was a "progress issue" with the emphasis on the future. Community response—. . . as well as the advertising response that made it possible—. . . was very positive. It created a strong sense of community, renewed interest in history and generated goodwill for the *Courier*.

HURLEY: The *Record* includes some aspects every week that require reader input— "Shot of the Week" and "Who's This?" "Who's This?" is simply an old photo from our files (actually a couple of Rubbermaid storage containers tucked away in the corner of the sports editor's office) taken who knows how many years ago. We run one every week and ask readers to identify the people in the photo. They can call or e-mail their response, and we print the correct response (along with the names of the first five people to correctly make the ID) in the following week's issue. It's enormously popular, and people rush to call us. Our paper is printed at 8 A.M. Thursday, and it's not unusual to have the first call by 11 A.M. "Shot of the Week" is another reader input project. Every month readers submit their photographs (we have a different category each month, for example: outbuildings, sunrise and sunset, odd angles, animal antics, etc.). We choose one each week and run [it] in color on the back page. Once a month we choose one from the previous month to appear on our weekly color community calendar insert. The reader/photographer whose photo is chosen for the calendar receives a prize package from area businesses.

Can you give some examples of how you "think outside the box—think outside the paper"? Examples: create a newspaper read-aloud program at rest homes, fund a scholarship at the community college, print the high school paper for free, etc.

HURLEY: We sponsor Book Buzz, a reading program for children that offers free books to children who submit book reports.

BUCKEL: We do print the high school paper for free. We sell the ads, and they do the news and opinions. They've won lots of awards, and our readers—even the senior citizens—have expressed how much they enjoy being able to see it (we insert it in the paper). It's just one more example of how we try to be the glue that ties the community together—bridging the gap between the teenagers and the schools, and those whose only connection is the taxes they pay. We have funded scholarships for high school graduates in the past, and we try to take part in everything positive and good that goes on in our community.

WALTNER: We speak to classes at our schools on a variety of subjects, including (naturally) journalism, photography and writing, but also community history; we are seen as community historians. We conduct a student election at our schools that coincides with the general election . . . and publish the results.

MONTGOMERY: Our best in the community project will be our upcoming 15-month civic journalism project. We are partnering with Wichita State University to study what Junction City residents want their city to be in 5, 10, 20 years. We will survey [and] conduct focus groups and town hall meetings. Our hope is to make citizens more a part of the city planning/building process than they have been in the past.

A Template for Excellence

Here's a painless way of seeing how close your paper is to being a "great good paper." Mea Culpa: as you'll see, the following rating scale totally reflects the bias of the author. That being said, I'm still hoping you find it a fun and useful exercise.

INSTRUCTIONS: Evaluate your newspaper by assigning 1–5 points for each question, using either scales for Never to Always (N–A) or Poor to Excellent (P–E). There are also several Yes-No questions with assigned point values. Here's the point guide system:

THE NEVER TO ALWAYS SCALE

1 Never

2 Rarely

3 Sometimes

4 Often but not regularly

5 Always (regularly)

THE POOR TO EXCELLENT SCALE

1 Poor

2 Less than average

3 Average

4 Above average

5 Excellent

THE YES-NO SCALE

0–5

News

Does your newspaper's front page usually contain no more than five stories?
Never–Always Scale

1–5

Does your newspaper's front page usually have no more than three photos?
N–A

1–5

Is there usually a dominant image above the fold on the front page?
N–A

1–5

On the front page: Is there usually a hierarchy of heads? That is to say, a clear lead story with big headlines, and smaller headlines toward the bottom of the page?

   N–A

   1–5

(For weeklies) Is the front page content usually all local?

   N–A

   1–5

(For dailies) Is the front page content usually at least 75 percent local?

   N–A

   1–5

Rate the design and effectiveness of your paper's flag.

   Poor–Excellent Scale

   1–5

Does your paper run ads on the front page?

   Yes   O

   No   5

For each edition of your paper is there usually a budget session where staffers discuss content?

   N–A

   1–5

How often does your paper take on important though controversial local stories?

   N–A

   1–5

Rate your paper's coverage of law enforcement, crime and courts.

   P–E

   1–5

Rate the quality of writing in your paper.

   P–E

   1–5

Rate the quality of editing at your paper.

   P–E

   1–5

How often does your paper contain typos and mistakes?

   N–A

   1–5

Does your paper run corrections prominently and promptly?

   N–A

   1–5

Perfect score = 70

The Editorial Page

Does your paper usually have an all-local editorial page (not counting the edit cartoon)? An "all-local" page means all copy generated either by your staff or by regionally relevant columnists.

N–A

1–5

How often do your editorials take on important controversial local issues?

N–A

1–5

Does your paper have its own exclusive editorial cartoonist?

Yes   5

No   0

How often does your paper generally generate live editorials?

N–A

1–5

How often does your paper require all staffers to write personal columns or commentary?

N–A

1–5

If your paper does include personal commentary by staffers, are there accompanying mugshots?

N–A

1–5

Is the staffbox/masthead usually clearly displayed, along with names, phone numbers and e-mail addresses of staffers?

N–A

1–5

Does the editor or the publisher write commentary discussing issues related to newspaper policy and content?

N–A

1–5

Is there an average of three letters to the editor in any given issue of the paper?

N–A

1–5

Does your paper regularly display a letters to the editor policy box?

N–A

1–5

Does your paper print canned editorial copy without explaining what, for instance, "the John Locke Foundation" or "Minuteman Media" is?

   Yes 0

   No   5

Does your paper provide an identifying tagline with contact information for regionally relevant writers of editorial copy? Example: Scott Mooneyham covers the N.C. Legislature and may be reached at . . .)

   N–A

   1–5

Perfect score = 60

Features

Rate the features in your paper.

   P–E

   1–5

Does the paper regularly run features of local general interest to your readers?

   N–A

   1–5

Perfect score = 10

Lifestyle

Does your paper run free obituaries?

   N–A

   1–5

How often does your paper run free photos with obits?

   N–A

   1–5

Does your paper run free wedding stories and photos?

   N–A

   1–5

Does your paper run free anniversary stories and photos?

   N–A

   1–5

Does your paper run free engagement stories with photos?

   N–A

   1–5

Do most of the photos accompanying weddings, engagements and anniversary stories run 2 columns wide?

   N–A

   1–5

Does your paper regularly display a wedding/anniversary/engagement policy box?

   N–A

   1–5

Does your newspaper have a lifestyles editor or someone who is editorially responsible for weddings, engagements and anniversaries (not just a clerk or a secretary)?

   Yes   5

   No   0

Is "social news" run in the paper in a timely fashion (within two weeks of the event)?

   N–A

   1–5

Perfect score = 45

Sports

(For weeklies) Does your sports page or section contain all-local content?

   N–A

   1–5

Are you able to get a story from every high school in your coverage area every time a major sports event occurs? (Usually this is baseball, basketball and football.)

   N–A

   1–5

Does your paper have a sports editor/writer?

   Yes   5

   No   0

Does your paper's sports coverage contain action photographs of local sports?

   N–A

   1–5

Does your sports page/section include a local sports column?

   N–A

   1–5

Does your paper send someone to cover local teams on out-of-town trips beyond the regularly scheduled high school games? (Example: local Little Leagues going to district/regional/state playoffs)

   N–A

   1–5

(For dailies) Rate your lead sports page (the section front if you have one) for local to nonlocal content balance.

100% local	0% nonlocal	5
90% local	10% nonlocal	4
80% local	20% nonlocal	3
75% local	25% nonlocal	2
60% local	40% nonlocal	1

Perfect score = 30

Photography

Rate the photography in your paper.
P–E
1–5

Rate your paper's photo-reproduction.
P–E
1–5

How often does your paper run photos of civic, church, school and sports groups with complete identifications?
N–A
1–5

Rate your paper's use of full-page photo-spreads of local people, events and stories covered visually.
P–E
1–5

When confronted with the choice of whether or not to run controversial local photos (dead bodies, gore in wreck photos, etc.), how often does your staff discuss the options?
N–A
1–5

Perfect score = 25

The Vital Intangibles

(Harder to quantify, but nonetheless revealing about the culture of your newspaper and important to its future.)

Access: Can readers walk in and see a staffer without permission or being screened?
N–A
1–5

Location: How reader-friendly is the location of your paper's office?
P–E
1–5

Phones: When readers phone the paper during regular office hours, do they get someone live?
N–A
1–5

Involvement: How involved are you or others at your paper in civic affairs related to the betterment of the community?
N–A
1–5

And does your paper's culture encourage and reward such outside civic activity by staffers?
N–A
1–5

Outreach: Does your newspaper sponsor events and nonprofit and civic groups that contribute to making life better in your community? Examples: community concerts, floats in local parades, Special Olympics, Relay for Life, Big Buddies, Habitat for Humanity.
N–A
1–5

Education: Does your newspaper participate in the Newspaper in Education program?
Yes   5
No   0

How often does your newspaper provide regular space for high school columnists?
N–A
1–5

How often does your newspaper provide regular space for school news from individual high schools in your coverage area?
N–A
1–5

Diversity: Rate the gender equity in your newsroom.
P–E
1–5

Rate the ethnic diversity of your newsroom.
P–E
1–5

P–E

1–5

Perfect score = 60

How Did Your Paper Rate?

Add it all up. A perfect score is 300. How did your newspaper score? Here's how to assign your paper a grade:

A: ranges from an A+ at 300 down to an A− at 270. Congratulations, you work at a great good paper.

B: ranges from a B+ at 269 down to a B− at 240. Your paper is good, but it can be better.

C: ranges from a C+ at 239 down to a C− at 210. There's much work to be done just to become "good."

D: is from 209 down to 180. This is one sad puppy.

Anything below a 180 means you work for a turkey!

TWENTY-ONE

The Evolution of a Community Newspaper

When developmental psychologists track the growth and maturation of a child over a period of years, they call such a process a "longitudinal study."

What if we who study newspapers could get to watch a newspaper grow and mature as well? In this chapter we'll do just that—visiting a remarkable little paper three times at roughly five-year intervals.

The First Visit to the World's Smallest Daily

Thursday, July 8, 1993: When publisher Jeff Byrd arrived at the main street offices of the Tryon *Daily Bulletin* at 8 A.M. Thursday, assistant pressman Tony Elder already had printed three runs of the Friday paper. But then, at the *Bulletin*, a run is an 8½″ × 11″, four-page flat sheet. It's a 73-year-old, sheet-fed, letter-sized operation, and notably, the *Bulletin* is the self-proclaimed "World's Smallest Daily Newspaper."

Seated at a computer, working on getting accounts squared away, Jeff observes, "Basically, we're a weekly that comes out five times a week. We don't carry any wire copy or national news (or photos). It's all local. It's a community paper. That's what people want here."

Jeff, at 37 already a veteran community newspaperman, bought the paper in 1989 and has recharged the *Bulletin*'s batteries with youthful vigor, but for the most part has run it with an if-it-ain't-broke-don't-fix-it attitude.

Prudently, he hasn't tinkered much with the formula for success pioneered by Seth "Pop" Vining, who started the *Bulletin* in the retirement village of Tryon, N.C., in '28. Back then, the paper was printed from hand-set type on an old Kluge and was about half its present-day size—hence the hyperbole.

Folks still think of Byrd as the "new kid," but his boyish charm and head for numbers are paying off. The *Bulletin*, a 4,300-circulation, five-day-a-week daily (3,450 mail, approximately 850 street sales), seems to be thriving—and what's more, "everybody in town reads every single word," Jeff says proudly but not boastfully, turning back to his work.

Meanwhile, the *Bulletin* seems to run itself with the familiarity of an old team that has been together a very long time—as indeed they have been. The average tenure of a staffer is a dozen years.

Here's how it works for them: Jeff

tried being the news editor (in addition to his duties as editor-publisher) at first, and then took over the business side a year ago, and initiated an unusual job-share arrangement. He hired two news editors (managing editors, basically) and assigned them to different days. Claire Wharton takes Monday and Friday, while Kate Larken does Tuesday, Wednesday and Thursday. It's an unorthodox system, but the editors dovetail smoothly, are compatible, and mostly, it works. In addition, Reen Smith serves as associate editor–reporter to round out the writing staff.

The Gemini editor system works because Jeff has a solid backshop. He bought into a dependable, stable and cheery production crew—a factor not to be taken lightly by would-be buyers. Jeff will be the first person to acknowledge that he was plain lucky.

That the *Bulletin* is a happy shop is easy to see. On entering, you are greeted by Robin Lawter who's "been here forever and knows everything," Jeff says thankfully. The spacious front office is dominated by an immense window and high ceilings. The first-timer is immediately struck with the sense that here is a place of solidity, continuity and grace under pressure. Indeed, the turn-of-the-century office is a former bank. A faded blue and white banner from the 1942 Duke University Rose Bowl season hangs prominently on one wall; on another is a primitive wood-burned sign proclaiming "The Tryon Daily *Bulletin*."

There is an unpretentious homey feel to the place. The brown carpet is stained comfortably with printer's ink and the detritus of comings and goings in all weather. Down the hall to the left, the news editor du jour has a cubbyhole. Immediately to the right across the hall is Jeff's office, not the least bit grand or ostentatious. The darkroom opens right into his place, allowing the sweet, un-mistakable smell of offset developing chemicals to waft through the publisher's office. Jeff's only concession to status is a large, golden-oak desk left by the former publisher, whom they all call reverentially "ol' man Vining" or "Mister Vining."

Down the hall and to the right across from the coffee machine and snack table, the composing room is busy. By 9 A.M. Bobbie Briggs, the typesetter and computer whiz, and Joyce Jones, the ad composer and paste-up czar, are in the thick of it, talking to themselves in concentration as their monochrome computers respond to PageMaker 4.0. "Real news for real people, OK," mutters Bobbie with a wry sense of humor that will be best understood by community journalism folk in the business for a long time.

A bank of two layout tables dominates one wall. Between the tables sits a worn, once-white waxer, years of heat having turned its plastic surface to shades of yellow. The pungent odor of printer's wax permeates the room like something cooking. To the left, one wall is festooned with local advertising logos. Joyce, who's been there 18 years, knows her personal filing system inside out. Beside that, more logos and "standing art" are plastered to a giant, heavy steel door. On closer inspection, one sees that it's a vault, the vault of the old turn-of-the-century bank. Scrolls and a roaring lion dominate the lintel. On the other wall, no fewer than 80 styles of border tape hang on nails.

Tryon (N.C.) *Daily Bulletin* editor-publisher Jeff Byrd tries to get accounts straight but is interrupted by a phone call. In 1993 his office was in the hallway.

The *Bulletin* has been computerized for only one year now. Bobbie taught them all. Now Joyce says, "I love it. I don't know how we did it before."

In fact, they did it like everyone else: Compugraphic Justowriters, 7200's for headlines, and a lot of scissors and wax. Now, they do it with a combination of PageMaker and news galleys. But on Fridays, just to ease into total pagination, they experiment and do it all in PageMaker.

It's a brave new world for the world's smallest daily.

Still, the flag remains from the old days, as with the standing art sig from a local calendar and the news item roundup, "The Curb Reporter," both of which, Friday's news editor Kate says, "have been a part of this paper for a ka-jillion years."

Farther back down the main narrow hall, Jeff is found working on paying accounts. Over his head hangs a faded Norman Rockwell painting from the *Saturday Evening Post* depicting the country editor at work, circa 1946. Except for the computers, things don't look much different outside the frame. While he toys with his computer, Jeff is talking to a local columnist about a rural neighborhood's problems with a broken water system that resulted from a mudslide down the mountain.

He is interrupted by Kate, who wants to know how to handle a sticky situation: she's got on the phone an elderly woman who's so old she can't write but who wants to run a letter to the editor. Will Kate just help her write it over the phone? Kate agrees, but after she has taken the time and effort to compose the woman's letter on the computer, she discovers the old woman doesn't want to sign the letter. Now she asks Jeff, what to do? Jeff tells Kate unequivocally, no signature, no letter. Kate nods, and goes back to the phone. The old woman declines to sign the letter.

10 A.M. Kate opens the morning mail, sorting through the pile, laying possible news copy to the left and "money stuff" to the right for Jeff and bookkeeping. Watching her would make any PR person quail. Some of the mountain of mail she

trashes almost immediately upon opening. "I doubt if the retirement community of Tryon cares about the Coneheads coming to Carowinds," she quips, flipping a PR release and photo into the recycling bin.

Letters to the editor, which typically begin with "Dear Jeff," are run under the identical 14-point head, "Communication." Many stories come from club secretaries and volunteers; these are tagged at the end "Community Reporter," set in italics.

Kate, clad in shorts, sockless tennis shoes, a blue denim workshirt, hair back in a pony tail, returns to her office, scans the area dailies for local news they might have missed, as well as local obits.

The phone rings; she talks to the caller and takes notes. Hanging up, she exults, "I love this place," mimicking the Burger King baseball-hat-backward-dude. The call had come from the local golf course, where someone had just made a hole in one. Turning to the computer, Kate knocks out a two-paragraph bright. Before she is finished, she is interrupted by Joyce with another set of galleys to be proofed. She quickly scans the stories, makes corrections and returns them to composing.

Every time any four pages are ready at the *Bulletin*, they are put together, shot on the copy camera and run on the little press. The paper is thus built from four-page runs. Production has only a rough idea how many pages any given paper will contain. Because of this inherited, unorthodox and yet effective system, the *Bulletin* contains no page numbers or jumps, with the exception of front to back. Basically, everything has to fit on each page; it makes for a dicey puzzle in layout. The *Bulletin* doesn't win awards for design and graphics. But while it may not be pretty, it works. And, more importantly, it's what people in Tryon are used to.

Just ahead of 11 A.M. copy deadline, associate editor Reen Smith arrives with an envelope containing a story and photo about the Bi-Lo 24-hour grocery store's opening. Inside the envelope are a Polaroid shot and a 3½-inch disk. Waving the disk gleefully, Kate says, "This is the only way to go."

Ad deadline, 11 A.M. A local merchant rushes in, as the second hand swings up to 12. She snakes her way back through the hall, past *Bulletin* staffers to find Jeff beneath the Norman Rockwell.

11:15 A.M. Four more pages are ready. Charles Barnett, the pressman and copy camera operator, takes the two flats through Jeff's office into the darkroom. There squats an old faithful NuArc vertical "Rocket," which has been the paper's copy camera since the *Bulletin* went offset in '72. Loading the pages into the easel, Charles turns out the white lights, plunging the room into red safelights, activates the vacuum, loads the page film on the vacuum back, slides it shut and hits the start button. The room is flooded with arc lamps for 18 seconds. And then he flips open the back of the copy camera and slides the exposed film into an open tray full of developer, rocking the deeply stained tray back and forth to keep fresh developer on the negative. In the eerie red safelights, Charles looks like something out of a submarine warfare movie. Then in about 30 seconds, the page begins to "come up" and develop fully. He reaches in the solution with one bare hand, grabs a corner and holds the dripping negative in front of the safelight for close inspection—then, satisfied, plops it into the second tray containing fixer (which makes the negative light safe). He repeats the operation until the other two pages are done. Then, he washes them briefly in water, and laughs. "Our negative dryer is out . . . I just use a hair dryer."

He isn't joking. Carrying the two new page negatives into the backshop, Charles lays them on the light table, goes over each with a paper towel and pulls out a Clairol women's hair dryer and begins a back-and-forth motion over the page negs. "Well, it works," he says matter-of-factly, "and sometime we even use it for hair!"

He makes the two plates, and takes these to Tony, who loads them on the daffodil-yellow Solna flat sheet-fed press. As soon as a sheaf of several hundred pages has been run off, Charles loads them on the folder. Meanwhile, as each man runs his respective machine, they are both hand-inserting the sections that have been run. Flap-flap, flap-flap goes the methodical papery sound of inserting sections as Charles and Tony rock back and forth on their feet.

They each work on old layout tables that appear to date from the paper's genesis in 1928; built of solid oak, the tables are now smooth with time and printer's ink. The surfaces are heavy slabs of ink-stained marble or granite. Talk of the table reminds Charles, a 27-year veteran at the *Bulletin*, about old hot-type days. Before about 1972, the paper still used a Linotype to set type. Charles laughs and says he's got that wonderfully clattering old machine at the house, and he's trying to get it running again, sort of as a hobby.

The shushing and whooshing sound of the press and the folder resounds through the high-ceilinged pressroom, spilling over into the hall that leads down to the main offices, filling the building with a sense of purpose and urgency. Charles has to holler to talk. Yes, the air conditioner sure makes a difference. With a grin, he shouts, "I don't remember when it was they put in the air conditioning, but I remember when it wasn't."

It was so hot they'd have to open those two large back windows and hope for a breeze. Except for the presses and the AC, it appears that very little has changed in the pressroom in 66 years. The walls can only be described as once-beige, and the plaster is cracked, peeled and eroded in a most artful state of decay. The large windows are framed by catalpa and ivy growing outside.

Today's paper will require eight to ten runs. Five have been done already. It takes about 35 minutes per run. Between runs there is about one hour per run of make-ready. Charles calculates mentally, "At this rate we might just make the P.O. by 5 P.M. If we're later than 5, we take 'em down to Landrum and Campobello ourselves. And sometimes on Thursday, our biggest night, we're here into the night."

Maybe someday Jeff will think about converting to a web press, Charles hopes.

Joyce sticks her head in the pressroom and hollers, "Alright, y'all're having too much fun back here!"

Noon. Jeff must run to Spartanburg, 45 minutes away, to pick up a 2 × 4 ad that has to run in the Friday paper. They could fax it, but they need the clean ad slick.

Along the way, Jeff muses on how he came to be the editor-publisher of the world's smallest daily. A northern Virginia native, he graduated from the University of Colorado with a bachelor's degree in journalism, then came back east and worked as a reporter and then as an editor at a half-dozen weeklies in Virginia and Maryland, fell in love and got married along the way, did a stint as a reporter at the daily Roanoke *Times-World*, and then got picked up by the *Charlotte Observer* for his community journalism expertise to start their Neighbors edition and a bureau in Statesville, N.C. It sounded like a good idea at the time, somewhere in the decade that Jeff calls "the eighty-somethings."

He liked the idea of having his own paper. Maybe the Iredell County bureau would be something like that. "I've always liked community journalism. I've always liked it that you had to be one part reporter and about two parts being involved. You got to be involved with the community; you gotta be out there." He says it with a conviction that comes from experience.

Jeff thinks most reporters either don't want to do that, or don't care, or maybe they don't know about community journalism. Regardless, the experience in Statesville was "the worst of both worlds," he says.

"At the bureau, there were two types of people working for me: They were either on their way up or on their way out. The ones on their way up hated it (being in the bureau, and thought they deserved to be downtown where all the action was). The ones on their way out hated it, hated me, and saw their posting there as a demotion."

After three years there as bureau chief, Jeff decided it was time to take his dad up on an old standing offer to help him buy his own paper. Jeff says it was during the annual family beach trip; he and his father were out in the ocean. "Hey Dad," he said, out of the blue, "remember you said maybe someday you'd help me buy a paper . . . how about now?"

And when the answer was yes, they started scouting around, settling on a weekly in Henrico County outside Richmond, Va. But after three years, Jeff could see it wasn't working and sold out, but continued to work there for the new owners.

Mid-story, real time—Thursday, July 8, 1993—Jeff arrives at Southern Advertising Agency in Spartanburg and picks up the ad. But it's a 2 × 7, not a 2 × 4. He calls Joyce to tell her of the change and to leave more space than what they had originally allotted, and that he'll see her in 45 minutes. They're literally holding the presses for a 2 × 7 ad.

On the road heading back to the *Bulletin*, Jeff resumes the story. In 1989, almost by a fluke, a broker friend told him about Tryon and flew Jeff down to see the place with only a vague interest. But when he walked in the office, Jeff says he was immediately impressed with the homey feeling. "Hey!" he recalls saying to himself, "this is like I'm back in my grandmother's parlor. I like that window. I like that view. I like this light, I like this counter . . . this would be cool."

Looking around town he couldn't help noticing the cultural enlightenment of the population. "I've worked at cruddy little weeklies in the rural South," Jeff says, "but this place is different. We could be happy here."

In November 1989, the Vinings accepted Jeff's offer, and a deal was struck.

His wife, Helen, at first reluctant to leave Virginia because she liked Richmond, had fallen in love with the Tryon area too. Besides, it was a great place to raise two children, ages 3 and 5.

"We bought an old house. Helen's got a good job, we've got good friends. It's just worked out real great. It's the lifestyle we really like."

By the time Jeff gets back to the paper at 1 P.M., 28 pages (seven four-page runs) have been printed and inserted. He gives the ad to Joyce, who lays it on the page, and takes it to Charles to shoot, and the day's last pressrun is soon under way.

While Jeff was gone, news editor Kate ran the front office so Robin could go to lunch. "Jeez," Kate exclaims later, "I couldn't do that job. People were coming in asking me all sorts of questions I didn't know anything about."

By around 2 P.M., the last run of the day's paper is done. The staff huddles around the layout table looking at it. There doesn't really seem to be a lead story. The standing column, "Curb Reporter," anchors the top left of the four-column front, as it has for 66 years. Five stories on the front all carry identical weight 14-point heads. What catches your eye are two mugshots of sisters in a summer theater production of *Barnum!* The only hard news on today's front page is a two-inch story about a stolen pickup truck's recovery. The other three stories are about bridge club results, herbs in bloom at a local nature center and the Class of '73 reunion plans. The paper really does look like its namesake, a bulletin board, with notices tacked up in random fashion and with no particular weight given to news judgment.

Who decides what goes where?

They all look at each other. Joyce shrugs. "I guess I do. Mr. Vining liked children; he always liked to put them on the front."

"It's community news," says Jeff, adding, "besides, it doesn't matter where a story goes. We put classifieds right in there with the news because we know that's what this community is used to, and they read it cover to cover."

Joyce agrees. "People read every single line." And they catch everything.

Charles laughs about the most famous typo of the paper's history, back in hot-type days when part of the flag broke off and the day's paper came out with "The Tryon Daily *Bull*" across the top. More recently, after the snowstorm of the century in March 1993, Jeff good-naturedly took flak from friends for a headline describing Tryon's survival and clean-up efforts during "The BIZZARD of '93."

3 P.M. Jeff interviews a new radio personality in town, and then talks with Kate about doing some kind of weather-related burning story. If it's 102 degrees, aren't the forestry people worried? How about a fire tower story? Kate tells him they don't staff the towers in the summer. Jeff and Kate brainstorm. OK, we'll find another angle.

Reen, the associate editor, stops by to pick up a copy of a local author's new book she wants to review for next week. Bobbie and Joyce are already at work on the next day's paper.

From the back, the sound of the press and folder thrum and shush busily. For Charles and Tony, the rest of the day is spent inserting and mailing. With the aid of a Star Trek new labeling and mailing machine, they'll easily make the P.O. by 5.

For the editor-publisher, the day is far from over. At 4:15 P.M. Jeff still has the payroll to cut and five school board stories to write. "I guess I'll do the stories tomorrow morning." He concedes the stories will be late by *Bulletin* standards, but will still scoop the weekly from the next town. "We're just as timely as we can be with what we've got," he notes.

Jeff Byrd sees the handwriting on the wall and knows it's on newsprint. "I'm building for the future," he explains thoughtfully, and then says it again: "We're a little daily paper, but we're really a weekly that comes out five times a week. . . . We carry all the little chicken-dinner-news. No national stuff. It's what people want. But someday some medium is going serve this area—why shouldn't it be the one that's locally owned and operated?"

A New Press

Four months after that day in July 1993, publisher Jeff Byrd went to an American Press Institute (API) seminar in Reston, Va., and after doing some cost comparisons between sheet paper and web newsprint, had something of an epiphany. He decided to start looking for a good used web press. It didn't take him long to find a King Press out of Nashville, Tenn.

To make room for the double-unit stacked web press, Jeff had the building's old basement renovated. Two months later, the sleek green press was in place, and printing 32 pages at a time.

In addition to saving on paper, the new web press saves on time and work. A typical day's edition used to take eight hours to run, fold and hand-insert. Now it's all done in one hour, with no folding or inserting. And how do they like their new press? Tony Elder says with satisfaction, "It runs like a Cadillac."

The Second Visit: Growing into a Real Newspaper

Six years later, editor-publisher Jeff Byrd can look back at a period of remarkable growth from 1993 to 1999.

Growth in every sector—news coverage quality, circulation, ad revenues, staff size, updated equipment and renovated facilities. The '90s were good to the *Bulletin.*

Most noticeably, the *Bulletin* has turned into a *news*paper; the bridge club report won't be found on the front page nowadays. That's because Jeff has hired enough full-time reporters and editors to cover the community in the way it deserves to be. Sample front pages now carry stories on the new police chief, the county courthouse renovation and a town council meeting, plus a photo of a private plane that crash-landed on a local highway miraculously with no one injured.

Of course, Jeff has maintained the *Bulletin*'s essential personal touches, such as the traditional front page column of commentary and news items titled "Curb Reporter." In the July 1, 1999, edition, "Curb" editor Judy Lanier notes: "Another blessed event has occurred at the *Bulletin*. Press room assistant Louise Stierwalt has become a grandmother again . . ."

The paper's newsy feel can be credited to Jeff's having been at the paper long enough to feel good about turning over some of the responsibilities. The news chief now is Rob Lattimore, titled associate editor, but he really handles the day-to-day duties of an M.E., including photography. "Rob has really grown into the position," praises Jeff.

Whether it's front office, sales, newsroom, prepress or pressroom, Jeff has added depth in every department. Some of the cast members from 1993 are still at the paper, and typical of any business, some have moved on.

Improvements in the new *Bulletin* abound. Right away you'll notice it looks better. The photography, still all black and white, has improved dramatically. That's because Jeff hung up the old Polaroid, bought a new Nikon N90 and trained his news staff how to use it. Judy Lanier, layout and special projects editor also take photographs and scans negatives.

Something else new about the paper: The *Bulletin* now regularly covers local prep sports. Chris Dailey joined the *Bulletin* as staff reporter and sports editor (and photographer), covering the two local high schools. Jeff says the next level will be to "branch out now into Recreation Department sports."

The news department is bolstered by Caroline O'Neil and other stringers. Pam McNeil has moved on to become production chief. Bobbie Briggs, the information systems manager, oversees the new integrated computer system. While there is still some cut and paste, the production crew is completely up to date now, scanning photos and negatives and putting out much of the paper with latest version of PageMaker.

The *Bulletin*'s success has allowed Jeff to start a weekly editorial page, something the paper was sorely lacking. At a town meeting in the mid-'90s, he heard readers say they wanted the paper to have a voice and to provide a public forum. "It took me a while," Jeff concedes. "I had to have help doing the day-to-day work . . . to get over the hump." Then, Jeff had to be convinced that as a newcomer he "had the right to have a say about life in this community."

Folks in Polk County aren't the only ones who have noticed the *Bulletin*'s improvements. The paper has won 13 state press awards since 1992, five of those coming last year alone.

Polk County High finishes in top ten of Wachovia Cup standings, *page 50*

Tryon Daily Bulletin
The World's Smallest Daily Newspaper

Vol. 77 / No. 127   Tryon, N.C. 28782   Friday, July 30, 2004   Only 35 cents

CURB REPORTER

Here's what is happening:

Today

American Red Cross holds free blood pressure screenings from 10 a.m. to noon every Friday at Owen's Pharmacy in Tryon.

An exhibit of **Elaine Pearson's work** continues through Sept. 20 at Simply Irresistible, 66 Ola Mae Way, Tryon.

The gallery at Tryon Fine Arts Center is currently showing an exhibit of watercolor paintings by Jane Voorhees. The exhibit continues through Aug. 9.

"Lazy Summer Days," works by Lenore Barnett, Mark Haines and Kate Thayer, is currently featured at Conn Gallery, 108 E. Rutherford St. in Landrum.

American Legion weekly Bingo games, 7 p.m. Fridays at
(Continued on page 2)

Inside Today

- Zendik Arts group moving out of Polk County, page 13
- Polk schools reduce teacher turnover rate more than 50 percent, page 14
- Polk students to get longer summer break in 2005, page 16

Polk County Sheriff's Office starts SWAT-like team for crisis situations

by Leah Justice

When a hostage was freed in Spartanburg last week after almost 13 hours with no life-threatening injuries to anyone involved, Polk County law enforcement officials were paying close attention.

In an effort to ensure that Polk County has the specially trained and equipped officers to handle such situations in an equally effective manner, the Polk County Sheriff's Office has formed a new Special Response Team (SRT).

Lt. Chris Beddingfield of the Polk County Sheriff's Office says it's not a matter of "if," but "when" a major situation occurs in Polk County, and that's why the SRT is needed to help keep everyone safe.

Polk County's SRT unit consists of team leader Beddingfield, assistant team leader Det. Sgt. Grayson Edwards, Dep. Josh Denton, Sgt. Randall Hodge, Dep. R.G. Butler, Sgt. Dennis Bishop and Det. Sgt. James Waters. Also on the team are county paramedics Jason Wilson and Jennifer
(Continued on page 4)

Dep. Josh Denton, Det. Sgt. Grayson Edwards and Dep. Matt Prince practice entering a building during a recent training session for the new Special Response Team of the Polk County Sheriff's Office held at Link Medical in Columbus. (photo by Leah Justice)

Nearly 300 celebrate start of Bright's Creek

by Jeff Byrd

Nearly 300 people turned out to celebrate the beginning of the Bright's Creek Golf Club community near Lake Adger Tuesday.

Polk County board chairman Kim Talbot joined developer Barton Tuck and golf course designer Tom Fazio in making brief remarks before hoisting golden shovels for the ceremonial

groundbreaking.

Boy Scout Troop 659 from Columbus presented the flags, charter member Bill Ennis said a blessing and Kay Crowe of Greenville, S.C. sang a medley of patriotic songs.

With official business finished,

"It will be a spectacular end product."
— Tom Fazio

the crowd quickly returned to socializing, eating barbecue and beans and enjoying the fiddle and bass music of Hickory Grove. In all, a perfect summer evening for an historic occasion.
(Continued on page 6)

Serving Polk County and Upper Spartanburg and Greenville Counties

The Tryon *Daily Bulletin* is
more newsy than ever.

Jeff says the paper gets its economic vitality from business manager Wanda Cash and sales manager Mike Edwards, the latter of whom joined the *Bulletin* in 1995. "Mike has made all the difference . . . he's the reason we've been able to do all this," Jeff notes. Edwards is aided by a second full-time salesperson plus two special projects salespeople.

The proud publisher can't say enough about his business manager. "Wanda Cash *is* the Tryon *Daily Bulletin* . . . she grew up with the *Bulletin* . . . she's been here forever," he says with a grin, "People call up here and they want to talk to Wanda—not to that new kid."

Additionally, the newspaper's fine old turn-of-the-century building, located prominently on main street, has undergone a dramatic facelift. Over a period of several years, Jeff has tapped into the building's innate qualities: hardwood floors, big windows, high ceilings and old brick. In addition to the visual appeal, the renovation has tripled the *Bulletin*'s work space: expanding the press room–paper storage area in the basement and moving the news department to a formerly unused second floor. Jeff's spacious, tastefully decorated office is up there now, well away from the smelly darkroom.

Except for the front office (staffed by long-time receptionist Pam Edwards and new hire Phil Katrosh), the *Bulletin* doesn't look anything like it did in 1993.

The "new kid" has been in town for 10 years. Jeff is 43 now, and the paper has matured and flourished along with him. Page counts range from 16 to 64 pages. Daily circulation has grown from 3,500 in 1989 to 5,000 ten years later. Jeff estimates penetration in Tryon Township is about at saturation level. "I figure 85 percent with the other 15 percent getting pass-along copies from family. I mean, there are some people who *every day* stop by grandma's to get her copy of the paper after she is finished." Outside Tryon the *Bulletin*'s penetration drops off to around 50 percent; there are competing weeklies in neighboring Landrum and Columbus.

Every bit the small-town editor-publisher, Jeff relishes his role. He's the incoming president of the local sheltered workshop for the handicapped and has recently joined the Rotary Club. He's at Rotary at noon Thursdays singing the National Anthem and saying the Pledge of Allegiance—the whole enchilada—receiving compliments and fielding criticism, but always aware of the *Bulletin*'s profound impact on and vital importance to his community.

Simply put: Tryon would not be Tryon without the *Bulletin*.

What's next? Jeff thinks it's about time for the World's Smallest Daily to go online. Stay tuned . . .

That Was Then; This Is Now

In the 11 years since our first visit to the *Bulletin*, we've watched the World's Smallest Daily improve in content, add a new printing press, upgrade its technology to digital and give the physical plant a lovely makeover. But through all that, Jeff Byrd concedes that staff loyalty and subsequent turnover was a continuing issue. "There was a lot of weirdness for years," he says frankly.

Then, quite without knowing the formula, Byrd struck upon the key ingredient. Instead of looking only at applicants with journalistic talent, he began recruiting also for old-fashioned "stick-to-itive-ness."

"I wanted to establish a newsroom that *wanted* to be there," Jeff says, slapping his hands together for exclamation. "I don't want to be a training ground. I want people with loyalty!"

But finding that magic mix has been daunting. "It's almost like making popcorn," Jeff says, "You gotta keep adding new popcorn to the mix, and taking out the kernels that don't pop."

Jeff's recipe must be working.

"Since your last visit here, we've locked into a staff that works together well," Jeff says with a satisfied grin. "They've gelled; it's a great team."

Jeff begins naming staffers and attaching superlatives to each, starting with "fantastic" editor Chris Dailey and "unstoppable, unflappable" writer Leah Justice, and then mentally running through the lineup from front office to business to production and printing, handing out accolades left and right, finishing with "I know they're not gonna blow up; they're gonna work it out."

Not just work it out, but work more.

Publisher Jeff Byrd, at far left, joins the staff of the Tryon *Daily Bulletin* for a team photo in front of the paper's handsome office on main street. A quarter-fold newspaper, the *Bulletin* prides itself on being "The World's Smallest Daily Newspaper," which bears the motto *Multum in parvo* (Much in little).

"I don't know how we get so much local news in the paper," Jeff admits happily. "Our news staff [Jeff, Chris and Leah] generates about 12 pages a day before you get to the community contributions."

On this day, there were 16 pages of local news, also chocked full of display ads—plus the *Bulletin*'s idiosyncratic practice of placing classified ads free-form throughout the paper, thus guaranteeing high readership. It may not be pretty, but as Jeff says, "I don't care if it's slick. I want people to read it!"

It worked in 1928, and it's still working now.

Finally, there's another positive dynamic that Jeff's dependable staff has made possible. "With the realization that the paper's in good hands," he says, "and because my staff is so competent, I know I can let them go . . . ," thus allowing Jeff to turn his attention to community building, a factor the mature publisher now sees as vital to his role and to the future of the *Bulletin*.

So, in the last 11 years he has taken on multiple civic roles outside the newspaper. While Jeff modestly points out that he is just one of many such involved local citizens, his list is impressive. He has served as president of the local Chamber of Commerce, helped start a wildly successful annual barbecue and bluegrass festival and is currently the president of the Tryon Downtown Development Association, which has pushed through a streetscape project; he is also head of "e-Polk," a local group that has secured a $375,000 state grant to install a fiber optic network in the county. Jeff thinks the introduction of new tech to his county will lead to a downtown business renaissance.

Agreeing with the concept of "Think outside the box; think outside the paper," Jeff explains, "If these things [the above projects] keep the area vital, that's more important than adding a new column [in the paper]—and it's *fun*."

Plus, the outside contacts keep him in the know. He says, "Because of my public involvement, I *know* what's going on—and that's led to stories and scoops."

He also acknowledges that this involvement might leave him open to charges of conflict of interest. But as a successful community newspaper publisher of 15 years, Jeff Byrd is comfortable with that duality: "I've got one toe in the world, and one toe in the paper."

And, some would say, another toe in cyberspace. Check out <tryondailybulletin. com>.

TWENTY-TWO

A Johnny Appleseed Community Journalism Roadshow

Taking the Classroom to Newsrooms across the State

Seventy-five brightly colored pins dot the wall map of the Old North State in my office—each pin represents a town, each town one of the 189 community newspapers that blanket my state, over 500 miles from the misty mountains to the pounding surf.

Since its creation in 2001, the annual summer Community Journalism Roadshow has taken free, on-site journalism workshops to the newsrooms across North Carolina, aiming to inspire the mediocre, encourage the good and applaud the great.

Ask any gathering of community newspaper editors or publishers what they want for their newsroom staffs—and you'll hear a resounding chorus: more affordable and accessible training. Indeed, studies reveal that community newspaper staffers themselves crave feedback, encouragement and continuing education, and—most surprisingly—that this job satisfaction factor can be as important as salary.

Without such mentoring, community journalists, particularly young staffers, are more likely to become dissatisfied, burn out and leave their paper and the profession. But even if they know this, publishers say their hands are tied.

At community newspapers, where resources are typically tight, publishers say it's all but impossible to send reporters, editors and photographers to the American Press Institute, Poynter, or the workshop at the distant state press headquarters or State U. That's where the annual Community Journalism Roadshow comes in.

Now in its fourth summer, the event is a vital component of a larger effort of the Carolina Community Media Project, sponsored by the School of Journalism and Mass Communication at the University of North Carolina at Chapel Hill. As director, I've had as my goal to support, nurture and empower the state's community media through teaching, research and outreach.

A typical day-long workshop begins in the morning with a "Community Journalism 101" session, followed in the afternoon with individual coaching sessions covering writing, photography, layout and newsroom management. Last summer, I was joined by Assistant Professor Chris Roush, the new business journalism guru at UNC-Chapel Hill, who taught sessions at several larger community papers. Response from community journalists

The Roadshow in Mayberry: At a workshop led by the author, standing at the back, the staff of the Mount Airy (N.C.) *News* strike a playful pose, wearing the instructor's ice-breaking Pac-Man "news antennae." (Photo courtesy of Phil Goble, Mount Airy *News*)

statewide has been enthusiastic. One editor said, "The reporters were thrilled. . . . [The project] helped restore their commitment to our mission of serving our community."

Inspired by the pioneering "circuit riders" program at Kansas State University in the early 1990s, I liken myself to a latter-day Johnny Appleseed, crisscrossing my state dispensing seeds of journalistic learning wherever I find fertile ground.

Thus the playful title, "The Johnny Appleseed Community Journalism Roadshow," evolved with a new road warrior added each summer until now it has become an entirely unwieldy mouthful: "The Johnny Appleseed, Charles Kuralt, Willie Nelson, 'Possum-Dodgin' Community Journalism Roadshow."

And a wonderful thing happens when "the perfesser" ventures out from the cloistered halls of academe: The learning goes both ways, and I am treated to slices of life from community journalism's real world.

Like Moses in the Bullrushes

At the Wallace *Enterprise*, I met the ageless editor, Sammie Carter, who had been working at the third-generation, family-owned, 7,189-circulation semiweekly for "51 years and one month." A newspaperwoman with a considerable sense of humor, she vowed that as a newborn she was "left out there on the sidewalk [outside the paper's office] in a basket woven from newspapers so they'd find me." And of the

Not a check presentation, but a "pig presentation"—in which the author is receiving an honorary chunk of typesetting lead (called a "pig" back in hot-type days) from co-publisher Mary Hart O. Blackburn of the Wallace (N.C.) *Enterprise*, as 50-year veteran editor Sammie Carter looks on. (Photo by Gail Bullock)

1937 visit to Wallace by then First Lady Eleanor Roosevelt when Sammie was only 2 years old, she quipped, "Of course, I was there to cover it." At the end of my workshop, Sammie insisted on planting a big kiss on the top of my bald head. And they pay me to do this?

A T-Shirt with an Attitude

At the *Sampson Independent* in Clinton, a 9,000-circulation chain-owned six-day-a-week daily, editor Sherry Matthews and her fine staff compete with two nearby major metros—both called the *Observer*. So when the folks at the local paper created a bunch of T-shirts with "*Sampson Independent*" on the front, this is what they put on the back: "Get Your News from a Neighbor, not an Observer."

The Real Motto

At another newspaper, which shall remain nameless, the spunky newsroom staff told me the paper's true motto (the one they don't dare put under their flag): "Taking Names and Kicking Butt since 1890."

The folks at the Whiteville (N.C.) *News Reporter* believe in the First Amendment so much they put it on the side of their building.

A Tasty Couple

At the Archdale-Trinity *News*, a 3,132-circulation, chain-owned weekly, editor Kathy Stuart told me about the mom whose write-up of her daughter's "Harley wedding" included the following sentence: "The bride and groom were toasted over a bonfire . . ."

A Real Digital Darkroom

At the Roxboro *Courier=Times*, an 8,450-circulation family-owned semiweekly, award-winning photojournalist Ken Martin converted to digital a couple of years back. But he loved his old darkroom so much that he just figured he'd put his Mac, scanner and printer in the old photo lab where there used to be chemical trays and enlargers. Ken's workspace is a literal "digital darkroom."

High Country High Tech

High tech has come to small-town America. At the Sylva *Herald and Ruralite*, a terrific 7,000-circulation weekly high in the mountains, editor Lynn Hotaling and feature editor Rose Hooper proudly showed me their Web site, which featured a customized search engine that could plumb the depths of the extensive *Herald and*

Shortly before his death in 2005, 93-year-old publisher emeritus Ashley Futrell of the Washington (N.C.) *Daily News* is seen pounding out yet another editorial on his trusty 1947 manual Royal typewriter. Futrell estimated he'd written about 30,000 editorials for the "Voice of the Pamlico."

Ruralite morgue. You just typed in some local person's name, and, voilà, there were all the "clips"—electronically speaking.

Riding Out the Storm

In "Little Washington" I learned how they rode out Hurricane Floyd. When the Tar River flooded in September 1999, the water came perilously close to the waterfront town of Washington (called "the original Washington" by natives). Publisher Ashley "Brownie" Futrell of the 10,000-circulation family-owned Washington *Daily News* says that staffers "slept at the paper for three nights" to ensure that the Pulitzer Prize–winning community daily still came out. And most gratifying, Brownie recalls, was that three neighboring publishers, independently of each other, "called me to offer help." Happily, they didn't need it; Brownie and company rode out the storm in true "Down East" fashion.

They've Got Hollering Room

When it came time for renovation at the 8,450-circulation semiweekly *Franklin Press*, publisher Ralph Morris decided to "take down the walls; we're a team, and there are no elitists here. It's made the difference." With a wide-open "quad" newsroom arrangement of computers around a central server, everybody can see and hear each other, so if someone has a news or story tip, the whole newsroom can be in on it from the get-go. Editor Barbara McRae loves it. "People can holler at me, and I can holler back," she says with a grin.

Letters, We've Got Letters

At *The Pilot* of Southern Pines the flourishing 15,000-circulation tri-weekly gets so many quality letters to the editor that publisher David Woronoff came up with the idea of honoring the 12 best monthly letter writers with an annual formal banquet, featuring an outstanding speaker and an Oscar-like ceremony where the winning letter writer receives *The Pilot*'s "Lighthouse Letter of the Year" plaque.

No Space for Tiger

Speaking of "relentlessly local" coverage, at the Brunswick *Beacon*, a 16,263-circulation chain-owned coastal weekly in Shallotte, which is surrounded by golf courses, editor Ben Carlson told me the week I visited that they had four pages of golf, about 140 inches of copy, "and Tiger Woods' name was never mentioned." What was printed in the *Beacon* were the names of "about 500 local golfers," Carlson said proudly.

Raining Kittens

At the *Courier-Tribune* in Asheboro, I met Bob Williams, whose four-day-a-week front-page columns are immensely popular. His "slice of life" pieces are full of the vagaries that make a community worth living in—including one memorable column about literally "raining kittens." Seems a mama cat had climbed in a tree and started having her newborn litter in the branches. Folks came out to catch falling kittens. Human interest? You betcha.

You Can Tell It's a Community Newspaper If . . .

Speaking of cats, when I visited the *Transylvania Times*, an 8,150-circulation semi-weekly in the mountain town of Brevard, I was greeted by "Miss Kitty the Paper Cat," sprawled contentedly across the paperwork of the desk of the veteran editor-publisher Stella Trapp, whose wall displayed numerous awards from local civic groups for years of consistently vigorous community-building coverage.

A Happy Ending

Not everyone is cut out to work at a major metro paper. And even if they are, sometimes life has a way of giving you diamonds in the rough.

For 20 years Bill Rollins worked for the mighty *Charlotte Observer* as a sportswriter, until he realized he wanted something more—besides, he had a book in him. Leaving the metropolis, Rollins moved home to little Warsaw (pop. 3,051), in deep eastern North Carolina, to be with his aging mother and write the Great American Novel.

"So there I was in Warsaw," Rollins says, with a rueful grin, "when the folks at the paper asked me if I could cover my old high school's football games." One thing led to another . . . and, as Rollins, now associate editor of the 4,119-circulation weekly Warsaw-Faison *News*, says, "The book didn't happen. But I found a life, a good job—peaceful yet demanding."

Work is not all that Rollins has found in Warsaw. Through the Web site <class mates.com>, he became reunited with his old high school flame. And this summer they got married. Not too shabby.

It Doesn't Get Any Localer Than That

One of the highlights of the Roadshow came last summer when I got to help the Tryon *Daily Bulletin* cover the 10th Annual Barbecue Festival—a delicious assignment at the "World's Smallest Daily." I shot 15 rolls of film and gained five pounds. My column for that event went like this:

> In a world of SARS, monkeypox, Iraq and terrorism, there is room for "The Barbecue."
>
> Not only room—but a real need.
>
> In these perilous times, the annual "passion for the pig" is a welcome diversion—and I would argue, a therapeutic release.
>
> As a first-timer to this, the 10th annual Blue Ridge Barbecue Festival, I was struck by several dominant themes that ran through the event as clearly as the Pacolet River through the Harmon Field valley.
>
> HIGH GOOD HUMOR
>
> If a visitor from another planet (and according to some folks, since I'm from Chapel Hill, I qualify) beamed down to Harmon Field, and his/her/its first contact with *Homo sapiens* happened in the midst of your barbecue festival, I bet E.T. would get a good, though zany, first impression of the human race.
>
> Everywhere I went, though a rank stranger, I was received warmly and with good humor:

Example: "Hi, I'm Jock Lauterer, I'm a professor at UNC, and I'm here helping Jeff cover the festival . . ."

Typical response: "Oh well, that's alright. We won't hold that against you."

Just the names of the cooking teams 'cue you to the true nature of the festival. Though the cookers are dead serious about their business, their names are designed to make you chuckle: "the Tennessee Butt Rubbers," "Wastin' Away Again in Porkaritaville," "Butts R Us," "Smoke, Sweat & Tears," and "the Wild Bunch Butt Burners."

I was put in the proper mood first thing Thursday by the first cooking team I met. When I told Ed Britton I was looking for a local cooking team, he said, "We're from here; it doesn't get any localer than that!"

Localer. I like that.

I got lucky Thursday getting to watch and photograph the Drunken Parrot Heads of Tryon set up their booth as if it had been decorated à la Jimmy Buffett. And when it was time for the flag raising over "Fort Parrot Head," as Winky Mintz called it, someone suggested a classic pose. Chuck Britton and Reggie Drake joined Ed and Winky, and with veteran Howard Greene giving Old Glory the salute, click, there it was: the front-page photo for the *Bulletin*. Are we having fun yet?

HARD WORK

With all due respect to founder and BBQ guru Jim Tabb, no one person made this thing happen by himself overnight. Everywhere I looked—from the field set-up to the stage to the parade to the rides to the parking organization to the crafts fair to the judging of the cooking—I witnessed literally hundreds of local people involved somehow with making the festival a success.

It struck me that the whole blooming county was there working "The Barbecue."

And though I'm sure this is not entirely true, at least to the outside observer everything appeared to work like a well-oiled machine. Equally important, of the thousands of people I saw, photographed and met in the three solid days that I was there, I encountered only one grumpy person. And I think a jar of butt-rub would take care of her.

A SENSE OF COMMUNITY

As a college teacher whose specialty is "community" in general and "community journalism" in particular, I have spent a good deal of research time and effort studying various aspects of what this nebulous word "community" means.

And I can tell you this. Scholars seeking a definition of community should throw away all their books and journal articles, and come to The Barbecue to experience the "thrill of the squeal."

Your festival was all about community. As an outsider, I will never really know the thousand of people-hours it took to put this event on. But I can tell you this:

that in spite of my distant perspective, it was patently obvious that the BBQ fest is larger than any one person, that it has a life of its own and that "it takes a village to raise . . ." an event of this magnitude. I can only imagine the blood, sweat and tears (or smoke, sweat and tears) that it takes to make it happen every year.

So I salute you, Polk County. In the BBQ festival, you have something very special. May it ever be thus.

The Roadshow Goes On

And finally, on the way to papers like the Sylva *Herald and Ruralite* or the *Standard Laconic* of Snow Hill, you have to get off the interstates and onto the "blue highways." It is there that you will find roadside vernacular like this: In front of a Church of God the sign read, "For Sale by Owner."

I've heard that it takes so long to paint California's Golden Gate Bridge that when the painters get "done," they just turn around and start painting again in the opposite direction. North Carolina is like that huge bridge, over 500 miles from Wolf Creek to Whalebone. I figure by the time I've completed workshops at all 189 papers, it will be 2011—and time to start over.

So the road goes on, and with it, the Community Journalism Roadshow: helping strengthen community journalism in North Carolina, one newspaper at a time.

TWENTY-THREE

Two Case Studies of Community Newspaper Start-Ups
One Home Run, One Sacrifice Fly

Ya Gotta Want It Bad

For years the Black Knights of Robbinsville High School have been a football powerhouse. It remains something of a mystery how a tiny mountain community in the Blue Ridge Mountains can consistently generate great teams. Sure, the coaches can and should get a lot of credit, but something else is at work here too.

Right after the Big Game with their archrivals at the end of the regular season, one unremarkable-looking split end was telling a reporter why he thought Robbinsville won. The kid said, "I guess we wanted it badder'n they did."

You could shake a stick at every big city newsroom across this nation, and out of each would fall a sprinkling of midlevel editors, reporters, photographers, business and ad people harboring the secret dream of having their own paper. "To have your own little weekly someday" is a standard newsroom cliché. And for good reason. Having one's own paper is something of the manifest destiny of journalism. It's what a marathon is to a runner: the ultimate achievement, even if it is a cliché.

But sometimes clichés come true.

So, how do you break out and get your own paper? Should you get a broker? Hock the farm and buy a paper? Or should you throw in with some crazed buddies and start a paper from scratch? Where to start? How to find partners? Isn't that risky? Maybe you'd better just plod along here where you know you'll get a regular paycheck.

Whatever you do, remember the Black Knights of Robbinsville.

You've got to want it bad. Yes, even badder'n they do.

Who's they? The competition. And you will have competition.

A Tale of Two Cities

This chapter alone is worth the price you paid for this entire book. It may save you from yourself; save you from flushing bucks down the commode. On the other hand, it may turn you on so badly you won't be able to sleep; might even get you off that fence you've been straddling. What follows are case studies of two community newspaper start-ups with which I was intimately associated. One was a grand-slam homer, and the other a towering hit that turned into a sacrifice fly. The run scored, but we were out.

But, to the story . . .

I always knew I wanted my own paper. I was lucky. Sitting in Ken Byerly's Community Journalism class my junior year at the University of North Carolina at Chapel Hill in 1967, I had a revelation. This is what I would do. This is what I already was.

I'd been raised in the Chapel Hill *Weekly* backshop, doing everything from setting heads on the hot-type Ludlow to running the copy camera, in addition to doing the regular black-and-white photography darkroom work. I worked my way through college doing paste-up, layout, and all the copy camera work at the *Weekly*.

As far back as my high school days, *Weekly* editor Jim Shumaker had told me: "You're going to Carolina to major in journalism and then come back and work for me."

My junior year summer I interned at the twice-weekly *Transylvania Times* in Brevard, N.C., and was smitten by western North Carolina and the mountains. I'd found my region. Back at college I fell in love with a mountain girl who shared my dream of having a paper back home.

Following graduation and a year with Shu on the *Weekly*, I found my first mountain weekly—a one-man job in Sparta, N.C. But the eight-page *Alleghany News* was stifling. The publisher, who lived in the next town over the mountain where we printed, wouldn't let me run my photos big, as I was accustomed to doing at Shu's *Weekly*. Many pointless hollering matches ensued. Within three months of taking the job, I was plotting to start my own paper in Sparta.

Then events took over. At the publisher's Christmas party dinner in Forest City, I found myself seated by the crew from the Forest City *Courier*. When I told them of my plans, they said, in so many words: 'No, you're not going to start a paper in Sparta; you're going to come down here and start a paper with us.' I saw the logic of joining in with these guys; they were spark plugs. And Forest City I knew to be ripe for a competition paper. It was worth the gamble. Besides, it was less of a roll of the dice because Bill was from Rutherford County. He was the existing business/ad manager of the *Courier*, and Ron was the existing editor and had been there two years. In other words, they were dug in and had done the research. I was simply the icing, the element that would add zip to an already great idea.

Along with the help of a local "silent partner," we pulled together about $10,000, a ludicrously low figure by today's standards, and started putting together the makings of our own paper.

What happened over the next three months was something of a running miracle. Ron Paris, a genius on the news side, and Bill Blair, the solid rock of the business side, left the *Courier* and set up shop literally across the street. They found bargain used equipment, purchased new equipment that we needed, and either hand-built layout tables or had them locally constructed. By the time I got there on March 1, they had everything ready except the darkroom, which I supervised. As the photographer, I brought cameras, an enlarger and the darkroom equipment, and we added a small vertical copy camera and an automatic screened print photo processor.

Ya gotta want it bad. In some areas of community newspaper work, there's very little separation between front- and backshop. *THIS WEEK* co-founder and co-editor Ron Paris bends to the task of press installation.

As the rest of the country leaned into 1969, what the hippies called "the summer of love," down on Mill Street in Forest City it was the spring of dreams. We had set up shop in a former beauty parlor. There was no space for individual offices, so Ron, Bill and I all crowded in the front of the place with used desks and old manual typewriters. For years I used a Smith-Corona portable manual. The tiny hole-in-the-wall newsroom also included a very old Addressograph machine, a slow but serviceable Morisawa (Morris) headline machine, and the loudest punch tape type-setting system ever invented. At first, we didn't even have air conditioning, except in the darkroom. Our 8′ × 12′ backshop consisted of a homemade light table, a waxer on a table I brought from home and a two-sided layout table. Later, I think we actually went out and bought a commercial light table.

Everybody pitched in for Vol. 1, No. 1. Coincidentally Ron's wife, Janice, and my wife, Maggie, were both pregnant and were so big they had to type at full arm's length.

What about circulation? A stroke of pure brilliance on somebody's part—Bill? Ron? I don't remember which. The idea was to make the nationally renowned East High School marching band the sole seller of subscriptions and give them a cut. It

The "newsroom" at *THIS WEEK* in 1969. We're all one happy family, and we'd better be, because there's nowhere else to go. Co-editors Paris (seated), Lauterer (foreground) and business manager Blair wade through another all-nighter during the paper's infancy.

was a huge success. This was due largely to the intense loyalty the blue-ribbon band members felt for their band director, their music and their precision marching. In addition they were supported by a large cadre of dedicated band parents and a huge following of fans all over town. How could anyone say "no" to the Marching Cavaliers? They sold hundreds of subscriptions before we even printed the first paper.

Our first edition hit the streets on March 17, 1969.

And then, it's not a hyperbole to say, the subscriptions just poured in like rain. The town was so thirsty for a good paper that they literally embraced us. Those were heady times.

Ron named it *THIS WEEK* and subtitled it "Rutherford County's Modern Newsweekly." As if to say, we're *offset*, and the competition wasn't. And as if to say, "*THIS WEEK* is an odd name for a paper, but, well, that's modern for you."

Bill handled everything on the business side: sold the ads, pasted them up, did the billing, did the books, paid the bills and basically kept us afloat.

As I've already mentioned (in Chapter 11), the *Courier*'s "society editor," Virginia Rucker, left that paper and joined us at *THIS WEEK*. She gave us instant credibility and a maturity we needed.

Ron and I called ourselves co-editors, but that term was misleading. Ron, the older and more experienced and locally better known, was the de facto managing editor. I was sort of a glorified feature editor with a big title and a roving camera. But as co-editors, we did have one working rule: He didn't tell me what to do, and I didn't tell him what to do. Mostly, it just worked. Here's how we split up the coverage.

First of all, in our county with three municipalities and three high schools, there was no way we could cover the whole county with what we had. In effect we drew a vertical line through the middle of the county and said we'd cover everything to the right of this line: the eastern half of Rutherford County, Forest City and two high schools. Then someday, if and when we grew, we'd start covering Spindale and the county seat of Rutherfordton with another high school there. County commissioners met at the county courthouse in Rutherfordton, and Ron covered that. But for years we felt like we were in enemy territory when we'd go cover something in Rutherfordton.

EDITORIAL PAGE

We filled the editorial page each week with local copy—without a shred of canned stuff. We even used local cartoons when we could find them. Not an easy task. Each co-editor did a column, usually humorous, light-hearted, slice-of-life commentary. Additionally, we shared the editorial space with initialed edits so we could have differing opinions on the same question. Also, there was no shortage of letters to the editor.

SPORTS COVERAGE

We knew we couldn't afford the luxury of a sports editor at first. So each of the co-editors took a high school. I took East Rutherford and Ron took Chase High. We decided to go whole hog for high school football, and gave each school a *whole page each week* for each game. Ron and I each wrote (and photographed) an exhaustive game story, did a postgame coach interview and prepared an advance story on the upcoming week's game. When East played Chase, we combined our efforts for the cross-county rivalry with a two-page spread.

In addition, to whip up public interest, I'd rush back to the darkroom, develop and print the pictures late Friday after the game, and put them in the window of Smith's Drug Store on Main Street by 10 A.M. Saturday morning. Once the word got out, the entire ball team started showing up in front of the drugstore every Saturday morning to see the 20 or so prepublication 8 × 10s. It may not have been CNN, but for that little town in 1969, next-day photos from the big game was a big deal. Plus, it was a subtle way for a weekly to partly scoop the semiweekly *Courier*, which otherwise scooped us on football coverage with their Monday edition.

That sports coverage arrangement spilled over into our school coverage. We each took "our" respective high schools. We quickly found that the East and Chase journalism classes wanted to produce their own copy, so we let them, and took photos to bolster their stories. Each school had its own page about once a month. It was another of THIS WEEK's unheard-of practices that paid off.

COMMUNITY CORRESPONDENTS

Through Ron's and Virginia's contacts from the *Courier*, we were able to put together a corps of community correspondents who basically reported on visits, church news and the so-called chicken-dinner circuit. Most all wrote for the paper for eons, and some, such as Mrs. N. C. Melton, are still at it. One of the most beloved community correspondents, Mrs. Charles Self of Sunshine–Golden Valley wrote such colorful stuff that we quickly realized the only way to handle her copy— and everyone else's—was to publish it unedited. For to edit it would have been to destroy that very thing that made the copy wonderfully individual. In time, she became the most popular feature of the paper. People read Mrs. Self even if they'd never been to Sunshine–Golden Valley. And they'd tell us to our faces that the first thing they read was Mrs. Self. The following example recounts a birthday party with a very special surprise guest:

> Rev. Billy Rich preached real good sermon on Sunday, at Mountain View. After services the Church went to Sunshine Club House for dinner. It was Appreciation Day for the Pastor, Rev. Rich, it was his birthday. A beautiful Birthday Cake was made for him. I don't believe the Pastor knew about the birthday dinner, until He got there.

PRODUCTION

Ron did the front page, hard news, local news and governmental coverage, and took photos if needed. I took the second front, B-1, and each week filled it with whatever I wanted from a feature angle. No ads were allowed on that page. I was also in charge of coordinating the photography and doing darkroom work.

When it came to production on Tuesdays, after Bill pasted up ads, Ron took over his pages, and I took mine. If I finished my areas sooner than Ron, then I'd take other inside pages. Meanwhile I shot PMTS (screened prints, short for Photo-Mechanical Transfers, or Veloxes, as they were called back then) for ads, and half-tones (to be stripped into knock-out blocks for the sake of photographic reproduction quality), and finally page negatives, which I hand-developed by tray in the same tiny darkroom, which on Tuesdays was converted into an offset darkroom. (All my photos had to be out and printed from the same darkroom by Monday.)

The newspaper was an instant success. No one complained then or later about staying up all night on Tuesdays to get the thing out, reminding me of the old maxim "On the day of victory, no one is tired."

We'd drive the negatives down to the Gaffney (S.C.) *Ledger* where the paper was run off on a King offset press for $130 an issue. At our first edition, I remember Ron standing there cussing as the first papers came off the press. If I remember correctly, I think he was upset by the goofy hyphenation our typesetting machine produced. Instead of leaping for joy as I did, his response was to be openly and vocally critical. Not at anybody in particular, it was just his own inner critic with its high standards giving vent. "*Damn!*" he snarled at the first paper as I danced around, happy as a spotted pup.

But that example served as a metaphor for how opposites could combine to work toward a common end. Ron was the practical, rational, unemotional quality-control manager. I was the wild, intuitive, impulsive one. Together, through this yin-yang process, we somehow complemented one another. The synergy may have been a happy accident. Regardless, we put out some great papers.

That first year in the state press association competition, *THIS WEEK* won an unprecedented 10 awards, many of them firsts, too. From then on, "those boys from Forest City" were on the map. Not only were we the best weekly in the state, but quite possibly the best nondaily, the best community newspaper in the state. People started watching what we did. Heady times, indeed.

Growing Like Topsy

The paper grew like Topsy. Within two years, we rented the place next door, knocked a door through the brick wall, redid the front to look like a real newspaper office instead of a bunch of fly-by-nighters in a former beauty shop/cab stand. We got air conditioning. We paneled the new side and hung our awards on the walls. We made the backshop distinctly separate from our office, though the three of us still shared the same area. Because we had doubled our space, we felt like kings. The paper continued to prosper and grow, while the competition across the street went through a raft of short-time editors. In the words of Andy Griffith: "They'd tote one in—and tote another 'n' out."

Still, the *Courier* hung on doggedly. In the words of Texas publisher Bob Buckel, "That paper was like Listerine: People hated it, but they used it."

The *Courier*, with its Monday and Thursday publication cycle, scooped us on Monday, but then we scooped them on Wednesday. But the real difference was how the two papers looked. They were either hot-type or stereotype printed in Morganton. In short, their photo reproduction was terrible. And it was made worse by comparison because not only were we offset, but we were the best offset you could be. We took the extra time and effort to shoot halftone negatives individually and strip each one in on knock-out blocks on the page negatives for the maximum reproduction quality. People noticed. Pictures looked better, ads looked better, type looked better.

By 1974 and the OPEC oil embargo, when all printing and printing products doubled in price, we were strong enough to survive and absorb the financial shock. The web size got smaller, the news hole shrank, and we tightened our belts and slid right on through. The competition suffered, though, and was forced to consolidate with the smaller weekly Spindale *Sun* into the *Courier-Sun*. They finally went offset, but we'd already had the jump on them for six years. The next year, we turned the corner. In April 1975 we bought a big building up on Main Street that let each of us have our own office. The building's real strength was its full concrete basement—perfect for a press. We began looking for a used Goss Community. We found three units and a folder in Metarie, La., got a whopping big loan and took the biggest leap a community publishing outfit can make.

Maybe the news got out, and maybe that was the proverbial straw that broke the camel's back. In early summer we began to get overtures from the competition through their lawyer. Back to the bank we went again. And on Aug. 27, 1975, we announced the purchase of the *Courier-Sun*.

The following week, after we'd figured out the details of combining the two staffs—who to keep and who to let go and how to tell them—the new (used) press arrived.

Ron wrote in an editorial, "The events of this week have been monumental ones for us."

By the fall of '75, we were up and running smoothly with our own press thrumming away in the basement. For the next three years, *THIS WEEK*, with its own press, with an enlarged staff and almost no competition in sight, entered its glory days.

By now we had hired a sports editor. We made Virginia Rucker associate editor and kept the women's editor from the *Courier* to do engagements and weddings. We added two production women in typesetting and ad paste-up, two men on the press and—glory be—a receptionist. Up until then, we were answering our own phones and meeting walk-ins.

This was in lockstep with the fortuitous development of the entire county. The community college built back in the mid-'60s was growing and gaining community support. Our paper put its back to the wheel and did everything we could to help. The result: another symbiotic relationship that was mutually beneficial for the college, the community and *THIS WEEK*.

Also, a vigorous community Arts Council got cranked up the same year we started *THIS WEEK*, and the paper got on that bandwagon too. Full-scale community theater productions of *Camelot*; *Jesus Christ, Superstar*; *Oklahoma*; *South Pacific* and *the Wizard of Oz* received reams of coverage. We sold papers like hotcakes. And the community found itself in something of a backwoods cultural renaissance.

Meanwhile, a new four-lane bypass from Shelby up to Rutherfordton finally was completed. "Progress is going to march right up that road to you," a Chamber of Commerce gathering had been told prior to the road's opening. The speaker was so correct. The business community now had somewhere to expand. It may have been strip-growth, but it was growth, and that meant increased ad revenues. We tried being a semiweekly briefly, but quickly reverted.

By the summer of 1978, a mall had been built, and we were putting out 60- and 72-page weekly editions, printing sections and inserting our lives away. Something had to give.

That fall, the merchants at the new mall put out the word to us and the *County News*: Whoever has the most toys wins. The *Rutherford County News*, owned by a South Carolina chain, began publishing the *Enterprise*, a free, total market coverage shopper with canned Copley News Service stories that made it *look* like a newspaper. What were we going to do? "Progress" had marched up that road, all right, and now was in our face. If we didn't keep pace with the economic development of the business community, no matter how great a newspaper we were putting out, the new mall merchants were going to run off and leave us standing there with our awards.

Unless we went freebie too, we'd never have the numbers of the *Enterprise*. The only other thing we could do to meet the competition was to fight back with frequency. That meant going daily.

Bill was for it. Ron saw the practical necessity. And I was dead set against it. But eventually even I realized the old weekly had to pass. We'd outgrown it. Or perhaps the county's economic growth had made the weekly obsolete. In the face of this challenge, if we didn't go daily, we might not survive. Reluctantly, I threw my vote in for the conversion. In November 1978 we began publishing five days a week.

I think it was the right thing to do, financially and journalistically. But my heart just never got on board. I did my best for two more years to get excited about the new daily, which we named the *Daily Courier*, but my passion for the new daily was muted compared to what I'd felt for *THIS WEEK*.

The *Gazette*: A Towering Hit—but a Sacrifice Fly

Author's note: For reasons of privacy and fairness, the following segment uses fictitious names. As with any newspaper failure, there are still some hard feelings. But one learns infinitely more from failure than from success.

By late 1979 I had become easy prey for a new dream, no matter how implausible. At all costs I wanted another weekly. Looking around, I immediately was taken with the possibilities of the nearby town of Bosco. The county seat of a neighboring county had an entrenched, but truly wretched twice-weekly, the *Times*, owned by a relatively small chain that seemed to care about nothing but the bottom line. The long-time editor of the *Times* was feared and openly disliked by many Bosco people with whom I spoke—merchants and governmental, educational, civic and church leaders. Great. The idea looked better and better. We would have an immediate base of support.

Optimistically projecting my desires on the new community, I decided the Bosco *Times* was vulnerable. Why not? If *THIS WEEK* could take the entrenched *Courier*, why couldn't I repeat the miracle with the *Gazette*? All I had to do was duplicate the *THIS WEEK* formula for success—with one twist: This time we would be the total market coverage (TMC) weekly.

The idea was fairly novel at the time. To our knowledge, no other paper in the state had tried it: to be distributed free, going to every household in the county through the mail (third-class presort to enhance delivery time). We would take advantage of the shopper concept, but in all actuality be a true community newspaper with a generous news hole filled with our own copy and pictures. Since we knew of no papers that had tried this approach, my Forest City partners quite rightly thought me a little daft to step so boldly off that ledge, and they kindly bought me out at a quickly agreed-upon fair price; I left the *Daily Courier* with no hard feelings.

Now all I had to do was to find clones of Ron and Bill. I went through all my files and names of people wild enough to take such a risk. I settled on Jim, an older man (he was in his late 30s) with little journalism experience but with a great deal of raw talent, drive and sense of humor. Having spent 11 years behind the helm as a founding co-publisher and co-editor, I became uneasy with sharing the reigns equally with such a relatively untested man, in spite of his age. Since I owned 60 percent of the paper, I summarily promoted myself to editor in chief and named Jim as news editor. His wife, a younger woman, would work part time keeping the books and serving as receptionist. He seemed to accept the arrangement.

To find my business manager–ad salesman, I called a nearby university school of journalism and asked the business professor for any recommendations. He had a bright prospect who was currently an ad salesman on a nearby big-city daily. Within two days I'd arranged an interview with Bob. The young man, several years out of college, impressed me with his drive and his apparent grasp of the business side. In addition, he wanted to have his own paper, too. In spite of the fact that he was from urban California, I hoped that the rural, Southern mountain town of Bosco would learn to like and accept Bob. Besides, Bob's wife wanted to sell ads, and she was from the region. It seemed like a fit.

In addition, with my wife doing the women's page and Jim's wife handling the front office, we had a real extended family team thing going on. If the three couples could stay together and get along, I felt sure the *Gazette* would be an instant success.

And in many ways it was.

But, first, I had to put together the shop. I found a vacant former law office on main street at the right price. I bought a used Justowriter (typesetter) from the *Courier*, a reconditioned Compugraphic 7200 for headlines, a new vertical copy camera, a new light table, a new waxer, an ancient Addressograph machine and an even older plate maker, a slew of used typewriters, used desks and chairs—and, with some help from Bob and Jim, partitioned offices and layout desks and a darkroom.

All three of us shared the job of circulation manager. From public records in the county tax office, we got names and addresses and began constructing a mailing list and making Addressograph plates of approximately 10,000 households in the county. Making the labels alone was a huge undertaking. It seems that the three men and three wives were typing labels for weeks prior to the premier issue of the *Gazette*. Then, with the advice of the local postmaster, we sorted them by zips and postal routes. We realized we would have to make a profit early, since the monthly mailing bill was huge. We were the P.O.'s largest customer in town.

Part of my payoff at the *Daily Courier* had been six months of "free printing," so from March until September we had no printing bills. We went to Forest City with pages already shot and on negatives with halftones stripped in, or "plate-ready."

On Wednesday, March 19, 1980, we published Vol. 1, No. 1 of the *Gazette*, a 24-page broadsheet full of nothing but local news, columns, editorials and photos. Our ad percentage started at a scant 17 percent. No grocery stores. To win, we knew we'd have to get all four of the biggies with their full-page ads.

Within three months, we had three of the four.

Heady times in Bosco. The community hungrily embraced the *Gazette*. We were constantly told things like "You're the best thing that's happened to Bosco in 50 years." On the business side, we were winning. Our ad percentage had gone from that 17 percent at the start to a healthy 48 percent.

Not until then did the competition start to take us seriously. Just as in Forest City, the competition had sat back, fat and smug when we started up, waiting for us to fall on our faces. In both cases, the competition did nothing in response at first, when we were the most vulnerable. And in both cases, we lapped the *Times* before they knew what had hit them.

When the *Times* did respond, it was out of desperation. They did the thing we couldn't do: They lowered ad rates to get advertisers back. And in some critical cases, they gave away ads and "gifts." We refused to play that game. We started losing ads. We were further hampered by our ad-rate structure. Because of our huge circulation and mailing costs, we had to construct our ad rates higher than the competition did. That's always a dangerous thing for a new paper to try. And now that the *Times* was playing hardball all over town with its ad rates, making deals left and right, different rates for different people, we became increasingly positioned as the expensive and at times the out-of-reach alternative.

And nine months after start-up, we were forced to change printers. Our response was to shake things up: go twice-weekly and convert from free to paid circulation. It seemed to work, but gone were the fat 24-pagers with the expansive news hole of the first six months. Then, after a year, Bob informed Jim and me that he didn't like selling ads. Stunned by the suddenness of it all, we agreed Bob should sell out quickly. Luckily, we found a new business partner in Ted, a well-liked and respected business and community leader who'd been laid off by a large local factory. But even Ted's wise handling of the books and selling ads could not stop the recession of 1981–82. We felt as if we were caught in the jaws of something huge and malevolent.

I remember one night sitting there at my typewriter, trying to write something creative but so worried—because we had just lost the third and final grocery store ad to the *Times*—that all my creative juices had frozen solid. Writer's block? Terminal burnout? Publisher's night-terror? Whatever, I couldn't write anymore. I just went through the motions.

In desperation, we tried buying the competition. And at times, it seemed as if the out-of-state chain managers were willing to sell. But in the end, they were just stalling, while we lost more and more money. At last we realized that while the *Times* could be bought, they were too proud to sell to us—just as we were too proud to sell out to them. We were like two bloodied fighters standing on Main Street slugging it out, each refusing to fall or admit defeat.

At last, Jim wisely engineered a third-party deal in which another out-of-state chain, Park Communications Inc., accepted our invitation and came to town and soon bought both papers. We were saved. Jim was hired by the new outfit as a mid-range editor. Ted landed on his feet and was quickly snapped up as an executive for a local industry. The *Times* was converted to a five-day-a-week daily and our dear old *Gazette* relegated to a freebie shopper.

Bitter and emotionally devastated, I left town—"evacuated" would be a better term. I never wanted to see the place again. I felt as if two-and-a-half years of hard work had been for nothing. I knocked around the region for a year in a series of newspaper jobs until, out of the blue, in 1983 the university offered me a teaching position.

What Went Wrong?

Wrong people in the wrong place at the wrong time.

Three outsiders in a town not ready for a great paper, with a recession looming on the economic horizon.

From the very start, we weren't "dug in" at all. We were three complete unknowns, outsiders in a community that distrusted outsiders. Even though Jim and I were from the region, to the folks from Bosco, we might as well have been from Mars. While we definitely caused a newspaper revolution and a creative renaissance in Bosco and won some hearts, we didn't win enough of the ones that counted, the big advertisers who caved in to the *Times* under pressure. What I didn't know about Bosco: that most of the population was fiercely xenophobic and unwilling to welcome newcomers.

The town and county had such a bad self-image that if someone actually chose to move there, the residents' first reaction was: "What or who are you running from?"

Why would anyone want to live here? There must be something dark and sinister behind your reasons." We wasted a lot of energy just trying to justify our existence in Bosco.

In picking partners for a start-up, always go with as much experience as you can find and afford.

As I've said, part of my buyout at the *Courier* had been six months of printing for the new *Gazette*. While this sounded like a good idea at first, when it came to tax time, I got soaked for capital gains. This occurred initially because of poor financial counseling, but I still should have been canny enough to have figured this out for myself. Finally and most importantly, we were undercapitalized. We started the *Gazette* for about $35,000 (and my part of that was $21,000 in "free printing") and the remainder wasn't enough to float us very long—especially after those first six months of artificially optimistic and inflated P&L (profit-and-loss) sheets. This was especially hurtful in a situation where our overhead was so steep due to high costs for mailing.

Also, we were undercapitalized in the face of the type of competition we went up against. We misjudged their emotional resolve and financial ability to hang on. A larger chain than the one that controlled the old *Courier*, the owners of the *Times* had more resources to draw on.

If we'd had more financial reserves, the *Gazette* might have been able to ride out the recession, and then to have either strengthened or bought out the *Times*.

Comparisons and Contrasts

Start-up Funds. Both newspapers were undercapitalized at start-up. The difference was not just paid versus free circulation, but also the times. In the early '70s you could still make a little go a long way. When prices for film, paper, ink and chemicals skyrocketed after the oil embargo, it became a different ballgame. For a start-up today, depending on the size of the paper, you'd be wise to have a generous financial safety net. Say, at least six months of padding.

Circulation. Although both papers were weeklies, their methods of distribution were different. Forest City was paid circulation, mailed out second class and sold in racks around town. Bosco was free—and, most important, it was distributed through the mails to every household in the county via "controlled circulation," a third-class presort classification that was relatively fast and very, very expensive. Both methods have their risks. Starting out with paid circulation means you begin literally with zero circulation and build; you have no "numbers" to show potential advertisers. But on the other hand, it's the most economical way to start. You're basically mom 'n' pop-ing it. Starting small and growing. In some cases, that's the right way to do it. With TMC, you have huge overhead tied up with the post office or your delivery system, but in return you have instant numbers with which to sell to advertisers. It's hard for an advertiser to say "no" to a paper that goes to every household in the county. The gamble is that ad revenues will recoup your delivery expenses because of your impressive numbers. That's the shopper concept. It's the hit-the-ground-running approach. If you're up against stiff competition and you've got a big bankroll, that might be the way to go. But be forewarned: You're at the mercy of the U.S. Post Office, which can and will raise rates and change classifications and delivery times without regard for your paper's survival.

Researching and Backgrounding the Community. Starting or buying a paper is like buying a house. According to the old saying, when you buy a house, there are three important factors: location, location, location. In Forest City, Bill and Ron had done their homework. They had been dug in, taking samples, gathering information, taking the community's pulse, getting the feel for the business community's response to the idea of a new paper—all very quietly and thoroughly. You just can't beat that. In Bosco, I projected what I wanted to see: another Forest City. But that was not to be the case.

Timing. Both papers started in the spring. That's when one of the cyclical advertising surges occurs. That's good. But the other factor in timing is this: How long have you been planning and plotting and researching? In Forest City, the team took its time and waited until they were really ready. In Bosco, the team rushed onto the playing field, bright and eager and naïve. Perhaps a closer examination of the competition, the market, and prevailing economic trends would have warned us away from Bosco.

The Competition. No matter how you proceed, whether with a start-up or a buyout, you are going to run into competition somewhere. You need an honest appraisal of that competition. Is it a family-owned operation? Then they may be more vulnerable. Is it owned by a chain? Which one? How big is it? Where is it headquartered? What is the chain's typical response to competition? Does it just sit there passively or does it respond proactively? For instance, a small, family-owned chain run by a single elderly CEO might be more vulnerable than a fairly large, aggressive chain run by a younger management team. Before you take on a paper, project a worst-case scenario involving the competition. What would you do if the competition started a TMC shopper in response to your entry into the market?

Partners. In Forest City, Bill and Ron knew the community, and the community knew them. The most important familiar face must be your ad person. In spite of all the weight some of us newsies tend to give the editorial side, it's the success of the business side that drives a start-up. In Forest City, our ad man was a known factor. Not only was he a native, but he'd worked there all his life. I can't overemphasize the importance of this factor. On the other hand, in Bosco, our ad man was from another region of the country, which only compounded the fact that every single person on the staff was an out-of-towner—strangers, if you will. A friend who bailed out of his paper after only six months cited "a lousy partner" as his reason. "It's like marriage," he said. "Once you've said, 'I Do,' you're stuck with the sucker.

You've got to live or die by your choice." Had I realized early how suspicious Boscoites were going to be of the *Gazette*'s personnel and purposes, I might have scuttled the whole project.

Update and Follow-Up

As this book goes to press in 2005, the evolution of these newspapers continues.

The new owners of the Bosco *Times* and *Gazette*, Park Communications Inc., sold the papers in 1997 to Media General Inc. The *Times* is currently a 5,155-circulation morning daily, and the *Gazette* remains a weekly shopper, with a free circulation of about 8,000.

Back in Rutherford County, the still independent *Daily Courier* continued to prosper. In the '90s they bought out their main competition, the Rutherford County *News and Enterprise*, and in 1998 they introduced full-color fronts. Later that year, Ron Paris and Bill Blair sold the *Daily Courier* to Paxton Media Group LLC of Paducah, Ky., a chain that owns 30 dailies in Kentucky, North Carolina, Georgia, Arkansas, Indiana, Louisiana and Tennessee, plus several dozen weeklies in roughly the same area. Within the first year, the new corporate management completely redesigned the paper, doubled the single-copy price of the *Courier*, and converted to a morning publication schedule.

The co-founders of *THIS WEEK* and the *Daily Courier* are enjoying their early retirement: Bill loves his golf more than ever, and Ron is active in local civic affairs, including the United Way, the community college and Habitat for Humanity.

And most fittingly, Ron and I still work together.

When in 2001 I created the Carolina Community Media Project at the School of Journalism and Mass Communication at the University of North Carolina at Chapel Hill, I asked Ron to be on the Project's board of advisers.

I still have a second home, an old log house up in Rutherford County, so it's easy to get together with Ron to discuss the Project over lunch at a local eatery. And more often than not, when local folks see us huddled over our sandwiches, they stare and whisper. Isn't that . . . ? What are they up to now . . . ?

We just look across the table at each other and grin.

TWENTY-FOUR

Speedbumps and Troubleshooting

When's the Last Time You Changed Your Oil?

Your car needs gas, maintenance and periodic oil changes. You know all too well what happens if you don't put gas in the car: You find yourself on the side of the road when you least need to be stranded. If you defer maintenance, you really can get into trouble. And not changing your oil means Old Betsy won't be long for this world.

The irony is that people tend to be better to their cars than they are to themselves.

In community journalism, we're running flat out all the time. We're red-lining it. Our tachometers are pushing the limits every time a paper comes out. So, when's the last time you changed your oil?

Retired UNC-CH professor of journalism Stuart Sechriest tells the story of the late editor Louie Graves writing about the 25th anniversary of the Chapel Hill *Weekly*: " 'With this issue I have been putting out the newspaper for 25 years—and I'm damned sick and tired of it.' "

People at community papers face a different set of problems than folks at big-city dailies and people in the electronic media. Therefore our response must be different too. Here is a sampling of questions most often asked by community newspaper people I encounter.

Where Do I Draw the Line on Community Involvement?

As has been said several times in this book, community newspaper people have to be involved with their communities at a level far more complex and personal than our brothers and sisters at the big papers. And that means we can't enjoy the relative obscurity and anonymity of the big-city reporter. When we go to Bi-Lo, everybody knows us. When we go get gas, we are recognized. Wherever we go in the paper's coverage area—be it to play, shop, worship or socialize—we are known and recognized. People are likely to treat us more in terms of what we do than of who we are as individuals. Our professional identity is our personal identity.

For instance, what church you join will be noted by the community. Some will accuse you of giving your church more coverage. Some in your church will expect you to give it preferential treatment.

If you join the Rotary Club and give too much coverage to their activities according to the Woodmen of the World, you are going to hear about it. Will you be able to defend your coverage? You'd better be ready.

How to deal with that?

The solution is prioritization. Your first allegiance is to journalistic fairness and balance. Just be aware of your special responsibility to keep your news judgment fair and equal. Remember, the word is *balance*.

The higher up the editorial or publishing ladder you go, the more prudently you should be making these choices. This is not a job you can take off and hang on a peg each night. Your involvement with civic clubs and schools and your kids' involvement with Little League, scouts, band—everything—should be thought out carefully. No need to get overly paranoid, but editors and publishers must be aware that people are watching the paper's coverage.

And your kids better know that they too are being watched. Any preferential treatment given them in the paper will go down poorly. They need to know that if they get busted, their names will be in the police report.

And an inviolate rule of community newspaper involvement: absolutely no politics. The quickest way to wreck your paper's credibility is for you or one of your staffers to get involved in politics.

How Do I Develop My Talent When There's No One to Help Me?

If you're at a paper where you're not getting edited, or where you're the top dog but want to improve and are committed to not turning into mush . . .

- Never be satisfied with your work. That means: Take some joy and satisfaction in what you do, but don't get smug about it.

   If you're not putting your full heart, talents and effort into your work because you figure, "Well, it's just a little weekly . . . just wait until I get to the *Washington Post*," what makes you think that you'll ever get to the *Post*? And if you do, that you'll be able to turn on the talent juice like a faucet? Instead, you should do like Democratic party campaign adviser James Carville, who says, "When you hire me, you pay for my head; I throw in the heart for free."
- Take compliments graciously but with a grain of salt. Just the way you take criticism: Do you really respect the source?
- Read and look at everything you can get your hands on outside of your own area—other papers, larger papers, magazines, books and especially trade magazines such as *Editor & Publisher*, *American Journalism Review* (*AJR*'s Web site is particularly useful, with links galore), *Columbia Journalism Review*, *Quill*, *Grassroots Editor* and *Publishers' Auxiliary*. Also stay up to date with the media news in weekly newsmagazines such as *Time* and *Newsweek* or the *New York Times*' Week in Review. The best radio news is undisputedly on NPR. Great community newspaper Web editions can lift you up too. A favorite: <stateportpilot.com>.

- Strike up friendships with journalists your own age at other papers. They are likely facing the same challenges you are. Peer-counsel each other. Exchange clips and comments.
- Does your paper belong to the state press association? Such an organization can be wonderfully helpful with advice, contacts and newsletters. Make sure you get plugged in with that outfit. In addition, its contests can be useful in getting you psyched up for your work and giving you feedback, though you shouldn't regard the contest results as gospel. However, every so often it's good to go out there and take a risk at being judged.
- Seek out workshops and short courses offered by state press associations and colleges and universities. Don't wait for them to come to you. Is there someone at a nearby J-school who teaches community journalism? Make contact with such teachers, encourage them in their work, volunteer to guest lecture, host students at your paper, initiate internships.
- Finding a role model, and certainly a mentor who is willing to critique your work, is probably the scariest yet most useful way of staying sharp or getting back your edge.
- Pass it on. "Each one, reach one," says Kenny Irby of the Poynter Institute. You'll get a real charge out of advising and mentoring local high school newspaper classes. Maybe your paper could even print the high school paper. You never know what you know until you teach it. And then guess what? Teaching will get you psyched about your job.

How Can I Establish Credibility?

Credibility is a function of accretion. It takes lots of accuracy, trust and time to build up. It will come to you. You can't chase it and catch it. Lots of good works over a period of time will establish your credibility. Newcomers and recent journalism school grads: There are no shortcuts here.

There's Knowing, and Then There's Deep Knowing

The *Bugle*'s new writer-photographer, Rachel, was out shooting in the park and got a cute photo of a mom and dad pulling their 4-year-old in a kid seat under an umbrella. Rachel swears she heard the mom say they spelled their name Youngklaus with a "k" . . . and so she turned in the caption, confident that she had the name correct.

But it was Faye, the features editor, who spotted the name in the caption, and because she knew otherwise, said politely, "Isn't it Youngclaus with a 'c' . . . ?"

And yes, there it was in the phone book, Youngclaus with a "c."

And Rachel had been so careful!

But you can never be too careful. And there's no substitute for the *deep knowing* of a place.

To acquire that level of knowing, a reporter, editor, or photographer must get "dug in" to the community, as Stuart Byers likes to say.

No "parachute journalist" is every going to have that sort of encyclopedic grasp of community facts and feel. As publisher Peter Wagner of the *N'West Iowa REVIEW* says, it takes three years until a reporter's networks really start kicking in.

The first year, you learn *where the restrooms are*.

The second year, you learn *who's who in the zoo*; you begin to figure out the town, who's where, who does what, how the community works, where the real power spots are, what the community's major issues are.

The third year, it all begins to make sense, and *you soar*. That's when all the networking you've done kicks in. Experienced gardeners know this three-year rule as *Seep, Creep, Leap*.

> *Seep:* The first year you plant, and the garden gathers its strength, but it's not much to look at.
> *Creep:* The second year, the plants get adjusted as they put down deep roots and tentatively venture out.
> *Leap:* The third year—watch out! Pow, you've got a garden.

That's what publisher Wagner says. And he ought to know. His *N'West Iowa REVIEW* has been repeatedly honored as the best weekly in the nation.

If you leave a job before the third year, you're not giving the community a chance to fully reveal itself to you, and probably you'll never get to "leap." You'll blame your lack of success on the community or the paper. And you'll probably pull the same from-the-frying-pan-to-the-fire stunt at your next paper. Without those three-year networks and deep knowing, you won't do your best work. So stick around. Give your town a chance.

That's Youngclaus with a "c."

How Do I Develop My Sense of Curiosity and Precision?

"We're sorta in the truth business," says veteran editor Kirk Ross. But then he stops and thinks, and has another go at it: "No, we're *in* the truth business."

Without precision, without accuracy, there is no reason to continue working in the news business. Yes, the truth business, as nearly as we can determine it. What we're about is full, fair, balanced and accurate coverage. Otherwise, people could get their news from reading tea leaves or by listening to gossip or by believing everything they see on the Web. Ours is a goal worth striving for. And you can never let down your guard, no matter how experienced you are.

Without curiosity, we might as well be mollusks. The extent to which we are good as journalists is a function of our curiosity. We're only as good as our questions.

"The trouble with college kids these days is that they think they have all the answers—and they *don't* have the answers," says Lockwood Phillips, co-publisher and general manager of the Carteret County *News-Times*, a 10,217-circulation independent tri-weekly. Phillips wants to see more "passion and curiosity" out of recent J-school grads.

If you're not born inquisitive, then it may be something you have to nurture. Usually journalists self-select; newspaper people tend to get into this crazed business because we are curious—about life, about what makes things tick, about how government works, about who pays for what, about where our money goes, about what old men think about when they sit on porches, about what went through the quarterback's mind in the last five seconds of the game, about what it was like to live in your town in 1920, about what it's going to be like to live in your town in 2020.

Okay, I've Read the Book—Now What?

If you're a student completing a college course in community journalism and you feel like this line of work appeals to you, perhaps you're asking yourself where and when do I start? The answers are as immediate and accessible as our business can be: now and close to home.

Start by introducing yourself to your own hometown community newspaper editor. Tell him or her about this class and your interest in community journalism. Show the editor your clips and inquire about an internship, either now or during the summer. Perhaps there's an opening for a stringer. You could even go so far as to volunteer. Many community papers are short-handed and would welcome such an offer. If you hang in there, it might get parlayed into a paying position.

I've Had It with This Rag—I'm Outta Here

If you're a working pro at a community paper and feel like you're ready to move on or up, the watchword is common sense. Before leaving your own newsroom, make sure there's no room higher up. Start by going to your editor or publisher and expressing your interest in advancement or change within the structure of your paper. Speak forthrightly. After all, what do you have to lose? You might be surprised by his or her response. Unbeknownst to younger employees, many bosses yearn for and welcome such honest, constructive discussions.

But if you get a negative response and do choose to make the jump, ask yourself the questions listed below (and try to write down your answers—your most honest answers). Remember, though, just leaving doesn't guarantee that a new job will be better than your present situation. Sheer change for the sake of change can be counterproductive. Changing jobs is not something to be entered into lightly; moving is stressful and life-boggling (especially if there's a "relt" involved). So now . . .

- Why do you really want to leave?
- How does money figure into your decision?
- What do you want/need from a new position?
- Why can't you get all of the above where you are?
- What will you be giving up (what will you miss) if you leave this job?
- What kind of paper do you want to work on (size, publication frequency)?
- What kind of community or city do you want to work in?
- Does it matter where it is geographically?
- How would you describe your ideal job or dream job?
- Who in your personal life will be affected by your leaving? How do they fit in?

Finally, keep your résumé current, get your clips in order, make sure your presentation is professional, put the word out to your media friends, watch the want ads in trade magazines and network-network-network. Your new job will most likely come as a result of one-on-one contacts you've made over the years in community journalism.

Epilogue

No Epilogue, I pray you, for your play needs no excuse.
—SHAKESPEARE, *A Midsummer-Night's Dream*

No excuses, Will—just one man's final hurrah for the future of community journalism.

The legacy of 15 years of community newspapering—an old log cabin and a chunk of mountain land—lures me away from the rarified air of academe, keeping the "perfesser" grounded with the real state he's in. (Bill Moss of the Hendersonville *Times-News* once introduced me as follows: "This is Jock Lauterer: He was raised in Chapel Hill and then moved to North Carolina.")

Here in my favorite greasy spoon in little Green Hill (no stoplights . . . yet), one of my favorite games is to buy the local paper and watch folks read it, while I see if I still recognize names and faces in the café and the pages.

The *Daily Courier*, started by friends and me back in 1969, invariably informs, delights, infuriates and entertains me every single time I immerse myself in the inky pages. And from the comments of readers in my café, I am not alone. A sampling from today's paper, called by the locals the "COO-we-yur":

- There was a big electrical storm with high winds and dangerous lightning yesterday that caused two house fires just up the road from Green Hill, which explains all the downed branches in my front yard.
- The local community college will be offering a bartending class, and the paper makes a point of noting that "colored water will be used in class."
- Alexander United Methodist Church will hold a fish fry/outdoor singing, with vocal entertainment provided by "The Christian Motorcycle Association and others."
- In the police blotter I read that sheriff's deputies arrested a suspected thief at 3 A.M. yesterday morning after he was spotted driving down main street on a stolen riding mower.
- A playfully sarcastic letter to the editor from "Pappy" Bedford makes me chuckle as he chides the *Courier*'s editorial writer for a gross mistake in state geography, a gaffe a native with deep knowledge would never have committed.
- Then I read the caption under the heading "Go Fish" accompanying a photograph of proud fisherman Ken Bailey of Spindale holding up a huge

muskie. The fish is described in the caption as measuring "52 feet, 5-inches long." Wow. That *is* a big fish.

- And finally, my real reward. It is my delight to pick a random photograph from the paper and see, if after all these years, I still recognize the names. Yes, there is batsman Chad Flack, slapping a double for good old East Rutherford High School. No doubt the grandson of Chuck Flack, a renowned local civic leader whom everybody in Forest City knows.

As the old boy said, "It doesn't get any localer than that."

Yes, I may be a Rutherford County ex-pat, but I'm still connected, thanks to the *Daily Courier*, now anointed by spilled grits and coffee. And as I watch other folks, like me, poring over *their* paper, I am reminded again why community journalism, the only game in town, is not only surviving but flourishing.

Long live community journalism!

A Community Journalism Glossary

ad: Short for advertising. "There's a big ad on that page."

agate: The smallest type in the newspaper; usually reserved for stock listings and sports box scores.

air: The space around headlines, photos and copy. "We need to air out this front page." See "whitespace."

all caps: A headline containing all big or "uppercase" letters.

art: Broad term used to describe any image to accompany a story, whether it be a chart, graph, map, illustration or photograph. "Do you have art with that story?"

attribution: The spoken word of a source: quotations can be direct, partial or paraphrased.

background: Information that gives a story its context; material gathered for a story before the interview; also used to refer to "off the record" information in the term "deep background."

backshop: The production area of a newspaper; often behind the newsroom in the front office, hence the name.

banner: A large, front page headline that runs across the top of the page; usually the lead story.

beat: An area or a topic assigned to an individual reporter, as in the cops beat, the city hall beat, the lifestyle beat. "Brian's got the Latino beat."

body type: The main text of the story. Usually Times Roman 8- to 10-point type.

boldface: Type that is thicker, darker and more imposing than standard type.

box: Any content that is enclosed in a rectangular border. Boxes often contain informational graphics, featured quotes called "pull quotes" or material an editor wants the reader to notice.

break: To break a story is to publish it, usually first. First publication is called a "scoop." "We broke that story yesterday."

breaking news: Coverage of an event that is unfolding as it is being covered; a "running story"; the term usually used in reference to "hard news" and not features.

bright: Usually a short, humorous story, with a human interest angle.

bulldog: The first run or edition of a newspaper.

byline: The writer or reporter's name that goes at the top of the story, very often now accompanied by the writer's title and e-mail address. "Put a byline on that story."

caps: Stands for capital letters; also known as "uppercase."

caps and lowercase: A line of type that appears with standard English capitalization: First letter of the first word of the sentence and proper nouns; also called "clc." "Make that headline clc."

caption: The brief, succinct information accompanying a photograph, usually written in present tense and containing the 5W's. At community papers captions are written by the photographer, who may very well be the reporter too. See "cutline."

circulation: The actual physical delivery of the newspaper.

circulation figure: The number of newspapers printed in each publication cycle. The figures may be "sworn," meaning the publisher has provided them, or they may come from the Post Office or the Audit Bureau of Circulations (ABC, the most reliable).

clarification: The little cousin to the correction. A clarification is an explanation usually supplied at the first publication opportunity by the editor after there has been a misunderstanding or a small mistake in a story. Major mistakes get a correction. Sometimes "clarifications" are used as a disingenuous way of apologizing.

clip: A story that is cut from the newspaper, usually for a reporter's or photographer's personal file use. "Do you have your clips together?"

cold type: Refers to the photographic "offset" method of printing, the opposite of letterpress or "hot type." This method of printing first became popular in the 1960s at community newspapers. "Where were you when cold type came in?"

column: A vertical deck of body type. Every newspaper page is divided into decks of type, with six columns being the most popular now. Also refers to a type of editorial and/or commentary writing. "Did you see Mary's column today?"

copy camera: A large photographic device used to make full-sized negatives of photographs and whole laid-out pages for the offset printing process.

copy flow: How a story moves through the production process. Usually from reporter to copy editor to layout—depending on the size of the staff and the division of duties.

correction: When a reporter makes a mistake in a story, the newspaper corrects that mistake, usually in the next publication and usually in a standard location where readers know to look.

correspondent: A reporter who sends in information or stories from a distance, whether it be a "country correspondent" from a rural community or a high school sports correspondent. Usually not a formal part of the newsroom staff. At community papers, many times correspondents are volunteers.

coverage area: The geographical area that your media outlet attempts to cover regularly with news coverage; your turf. Usually corresponds to the area of circulation. "Hillsborough is outside the *Bugle*'s coverage area."

crop: To edit out the edges of an image, usually a photograph; to cut off the sides to emphasize content in the middle.

cut: To delete material from a story. A "cut" is also an old-fashioned term for a photograph. Hence the term "cutline."

cutline: The information under a photograph; better known as a caption.

dateline: The location of a news event, most commonly used to signal the reader about the story's origin; and most often not used if the story comes from the paper's town of origin. Many community papers don't use datelines at all.

double-truck: When copy and photos spread across two adjacent pages, usually a center-spread so the two pages are on a single large piece of paper.

dpi: Dots per inch; the higher the dpi, the sharper the printed image's resolution. See "high resolution."

ears: The space on either side of the "flag" or "nameplate." Sometimes used for text or graphic "teasers" that lead readers to interesting stories inside the paper. "Let's put a sports teaser in the right-hand ear."

edit: See "editorial."

edition: A particular version of the same day's newspaper.Only larger community dailies that can afford to, or feel the need to, publish more than once a day or for various areas ("zoned" editions). "That story was in the Orange County edition."

editorial: Copy that is purposefully subjective, written from a distinct point of view, with the purpose of not only informing but also seeking to persuade. Sometimes editorials are "signed" (a byline at the end or initials of the writer), but most often they are not. Very often called simply "edits." Confoundingly, the term is also used to refer to any copy in the newspaper that is not advertising.

exclusive: When a reporter gets access to a source and no other media outlet does. An exclusive refers to the publication or release of that story. "We got an exclusive on the mayor's firing."

exec. ed.: Newspaper shorthand for "executive editor."

feature: A story that is not "hard news"; very often about a lighter subject; written not only to inform and explain but also to entertain, typically with a dominant human element. "I'm doing a feature on the tractor-pull at the county fair." Also used to mean "highlight," as in "The *Bugle* is going to feature the checkers tournament in next week's edition."

file: To submit a story to the editor. "I filed that story yesterday." Also, to send your story to a wire service, such as the AP.

filler: If when laying out a page, the ads and the copy don't fit, an editor may put in extraneous material, such as a "house ad," to fill the space so that the page has no holes.

5W's: Stands for Who, What, Where, When and Why (and sometimes How), the most basic questions the story must answer. Often found in the lede.

flag: The name of the newspaper, also called the nameplate; almost always located at the top of the front page in the largest type of all.

flak: A not entirely complimentary nickname for someone working in public relations. "She's a flak for Senator Fudnucker."

flat: A page that has been completed in the prepress production process. "He carried the flats to the printer."

free advertising: When a reporter includes in a story material that promotes a commercial product or business. "At the *Bugle*, we say 'facial tissues,' not Kleenex."

graf: Abbreviation for paragraph. "Hey Ralph, I need two more grafs at the end of your story to make it fit."

Goss Community press: The flagship "offset" press of the community newspaper industry.

halftone: The printing method used for reproducing a photograph, whether in color or black and white. A special screen is placed over the original image, thus converting it into millions of tiny dots of varying sizes.

handout: A story written for news outlets by the source itself; very often for public relations purposes; most often rewritten by the news staff. "Did you get that handout from the Chamber of Commerce?"

hard news: News that is not scheduled; usually about disaster, tragedy, conflict, death, dying and human injury. Also called "spot news" because the reporter or photographer must be on the spot to capture the news event.

head: See "headline."

headline: A large title above the news, feature or editorial copy that announces the story's topic to the reader; also called a "head" or "hed"; usually written in present tense, clc, with articles omitted. As in "Jones triumphs again in track meet," even though the event occurred yesterday.

headshot: A photograph of a person's face, usually cropped to show only head and shoulders; also called a "mugshot" or "mug." "Don't forget to put Bill's headshot with his column."

high resolution: An image with an intense concentration of dots per inch; usually used in reference to photographic digital files.

hot type: A traditional method of printing that used molten lead/zinc to cast letters in lines of type, which were literally "hot" when they came out of the Linotype machine; also called "letterpress". Most community papers converted to "offset" printing in the 1960s.

human interest: One of the factors of news judgment; something about a story that contains an element that is appealing because it tugs at the heartstrings; usually a lighter tone. "Did you see Bob's column about the cat that had kittens in a tree? That was a great human interest piece."

italics: Type that slants to the right; also called "ital" for short; used to differentiate or emphasize a brief line of type for editorial reasons.

JPEG: The type of digital computer file most commonly used for photographs; short for Joint Photographic Experts Group. "I'm sending that to you as a high-res JPEG file."

jump: When a story that begins on one page must be continued to another. "We're going to have to jump your story to the back."

kill: To cancel the publication or release of a story or photo.

KISS: Keep It Simple, Stupid.

knock-out block: The clear rectangular shape on the page negative where a photo will be placed; used in the offset process; largely rendered obsolete by "pagination."

layout, lay out: The arrangement of body type, headlines, art and whitespace. Used as both noun and verb: "What's the layout look like for P-1?"; "I'm going to lay out the front page now."

lead: Because there are so many uses and meanings of this word, you may find some editors using "lede" to refer to the opening paragraph of a story, usually no longer than 34 words, containing the 5W's, with the express purpose of enticing the reader to read on. "I'm having trouble with this lede."

The word also refers to the metal, lead, that was used in the hot-type era prior to the 1960s to insert space between individual lines of copy. So you might still hear the term used like this: "You need to add leading to that story."

"To lead" also means to start the broadcast or to headline the paper with a single big story. "We're going to lead with the fire story"; or, "Our lead story tonight takes us to the school board meeting."

And finally, "lead" can mean a hunch about a developing story; or a bit of information that a reporter suspects may lead to a larger story. "Heather thinks she's got a lead on the coach's dismissal."

lede: See "lead."

letters to the editor: Short commentary written by readers expressly to make a point; printed on the editorial or op-ed pages of the paper; in community newspapers usually of political or local interest and almost always must be signed.

live: Any content created locally by your newspaper's staff, as in a "live edit"; as opposed to wire-service or "canned" copy.

localize: To emphasize how an event will impact your coverage area with hometown or regional names and places.

lowercase: The small letters; opposite of uppercase.

makeup: The layout or design of the newspaper. "Have you done the page makeup yet?"

masthead: The box that contains the contact information for the newspaper, usually found on the editorial page; the term is commonly misused in reference to the flag or nameplate.

M.E.: Newspaper shorthand for "managing editor"; the hands-on, day-to-day, in-the-trenches editor.

morgue: The newspaper's file of old stories or back issues.

mugshot: See "headshot."

nameplate: See "flag."

news hole: The space left after the ads have been placed on the layout. "The *Gazette* has a generous news hole in its Sunday edition."

newsprint: The type of paper used by newspapers. Less expensive, more porous and of a lower grade than magazine or graded stock paper.

nut graf: The paragraph in the story that says it all; the heart, the kernel, the essence of the story. In a news story, the nut graf often is the lede and contains many of the 5W's, but in a feature story, the nut graf often follows the lede.

obituary: A story that formally announces a person's death, along with standard information including the 5W's, next of kin, place and time of visitation, funeral, memorial service and/or burial; often called an "obit."

offset: Photographic-based printing method whereby the page image on an aluminum plate is transferred through the oil-and-water process to a series of rubber rollers and thence to the paper or "newsprint"—thus the image is not direct from type to paper, but "offset."

off the record: When a source wants to tell a reporter something but doesn't want the quote to appear in print, he or she might say, "Now this is off the record . . ." (See chapter 10 for how to handle this.)

opaque: A dark correction fluid used to fill in unwanted spots or holes on page negatives.

op-ed page: The page that follows the editorial page; *not* the editorial page; usually a right-hand page that contains secondary editorial matter including commentary and more letters to the editor.

orphan quote: A misleading one-word direct quote; to be avoided. "He said no one 'understands' him."

pagination: Computerized newspaper page layout; the current technology that has replaced paste-up.

paste-up: Before pagination, pages had to assembled much like an old-fashioned scrapbook, with galleys of copy trimmed with scissors and X-Acto knives, and affixed to full-sized layout sheets with adhesive wax. At many smaller weeklies, you can still find paste-up going on, but it is quickly fading from the backshop scene as papers convert to pagination.

PDF: Stands for "Portable Document Format"; a computer file that contains full-page images.

pica: A printer's unit of measure: 6 picas to an inch.

pica pole: A printer's measuring device, usually one foot long, marked with picas, points and inches.

pixel: Short for "picture element"; the smallest dot on the computer monitor; most screens are 72 dpi.

plate: The aluminum sheet that bears the image of the page. In the offset printing process, the plate is like an aluminum photograph of the page.

plate-burner: The machine that develops the photographic image on the plate.

plate-ready: When a smaller newspaper is printed at another location, if the pages arrive already converted into negatives, ready to be burned into plates, we would say, "We're coming plate-ready."

point: Most often used as a printer's unit of vertical measure for type; 12 points to a pica and 72 points to an inch. "This is set in 12-point type."

points of entry: Doors into the newspaper: Photos, captions, headlines—items that command first attention and thus get readers deeper into the newspaper.

prepress: Any production activity that occurs between the newsroom and the pressroom. Also used as a noun to denote a department or area in the newspaper facility: "She's over in prepress."

press release: A handout from an outside source intended for publication; usually rewritten with "spin" edited out. "Did you get the press release from the Chamber of Commerce?"

printer's devil: A term for a printer's assistant used in the days of "hot type." Usually a young boy trying to learn the trade by starting at the bottom; his main task was sorting out the old hand-set type and placing the type to be melted down again in a bucket called the "hell box."

puff, puffery: Overly complimentary coverage.

rail: A thin vertical column of type, usually on the front page, set in a different width, font, weight or point size from the rest of the page. Often used to accent short content such as briefs, brights, the index, weather and teasers.

refer: A line of type alerting the reader to related content elsewhere in the newspaper. Used as a noun and pronounced "reefer," much to the delight of newsroom wags.

running story: Ongoing coverage of a story that is happening as it is being covered; a breaking story.

semiweekly: Same as twice-weekly.

SID: Short for "sports information director"; the person at the college or university level responsible for all sports information content.

sig: The name or logo of a business. Sig is short for a "signature ad," one that is usually small and displays little more than the name of the business.

slant: To write a story with a point of view or bias or "spin"; to not be objective.

slick: An expression referring to a single completed ad in the prepress process.

slug/slugline: To tag a story with a broad topic line at the top so the editor knows its subject matter. Once a head is written, the slug is removed. "I'm sending you a story slugged 'Election.'"

source: Where a reporter gets his or her information; usually refers to people.

spin: See "slant"; often used to describe over-the-top public relations. "That story came from the spin doctors down at City Hall."

standing headshot: A head-and-shoulders photo of someone featured regularly in the paper, most often a columnist; also called a mugshot or mug.

stringer: Originally, a part-time reporter who was paid by the number of inches he or she produced as measured by the editor using a string with knots tied to mark the inches. Now more commonly it simply means a volunteer or part-time reporter. "We're using a high school kid to string for us at that Central High game."

strip: A horizontal box of copy or headline, usually on the front page, alerting readers to some inside content. Also used as a verb: "We'll strip it across the front."

stripping: In pre-pagination days, when the halftone negative was placed on the page negative, it was called "stripping" or "stripping in." Thus the person who performed this function was a "stripper"; the term was the source of many backshop jokes.

style: A commonly agreed-upon set of rules for capitalization, abbreviations, spellings and punctuation used by reporters and editors for the sake of consistency. While most papers use the *AP Stylebook*, many have their own individual in-house versions.

TMC: See "total market coverage."

total market coverage: A circulation method in which every household in a paper's circulation area receives a copy of the paper; also called TMC.

thumbnail: A photograph, usually a headshot, that is half a column wide.

waxer: A heating device that melts adhesive wax, used in pre-pagination days to stick copy to layout pages. See "paste-up."

web: A printer's term. The paper that is used for printing newspapers comes in a huge roll and is threaded through the press; thus the configuration of the paper as it winds through the press is called the "web," and the type of press itself is called a "web press." In this sense, the term has nothing whatsoever to do with the Internet.

whitespace: The space around photos, copy and headlines; also called "air."

widow line: A single line of body type standing all by itself at the head of a column; to be avoided.

wire: Short for the wire services such as the Associated Press or Reuters, press associations that provide coverage the news outlet couldn't otherwise obtain. "We're getting our coverage of the Olympics from the wire."

More Resources and References
for Community Journalists

American Journalism Review. University of Maryland. <http://newslink.org>.

American Press Institute. Reston, Va. <http://www.americanpressinstitute.org>.

American Society of Newspaper Editors. @ *Small Newspapers*. Reston, Va.
<http://www.asne.org>.

———. 1999. *The Local News Handbook*. Reston, Va.

Beittel, K. 1992. *Zen and the Art of Pottery*. New York: Weatherhill, p. 27.

Belden Associates. 2000. *North Carolina Statewide Readership Survey*. Conducted for
the North Carolina Press Services, Raleigh.

Boyer, E. 1990. *Scholarship Revisited: Priorities of the Professoriate*. Princeton: Carnegie
Foundation for the Advancement of Teaching, pp. 75–81.

Bressers, Bonnie. May 2003. "Pinching Pennies: Small papers find creative solutions in
a slow economy." *QUILL* (Indianapolis).

Brooks, David. 2004. *On Paradise Drive: How We Live Now (and Always Have) in the
Future Tense*. Simon and Schuster.

Burd, G. Winter. Winter 1994. "Building Bridges: Emerging technologies may be forming a new definition of 'community' for today's editors." *Grassroots Editor* (Brookings, S.D.), pp. 7–12.

———. Spring 1979. "What Is Community: A look at new meanings of the word 'community' which could shape local news decisions." *Grassroots Editor* (Brookings,
S.D.), pp. 3–5.

Byerly, K. 1961. *Community Journalism*. Philadelphia: Chilton.

Carolina Community Media Project. Jock Lauterer, director. School of Journalism and
Mass Communication, University of North Carolina at Chapel Hill. <jock@
email.unc.edu>; <http://www.jomc.unc.edu/specialprograms/community.html>;
<http://www.unc.edu/~jock.

Center for Community Journalism. Oswego, N.Y. <http://www.oswego.edu/ccj/>.

Central Carolina Community College. Sanford, N.C. <http://www.cccc.edu>.

Chideya, F. Spring/Summer 1999. "An Incomplete Picture." *Media Studies Journal*
(New York), p. 32.

Columbia Journalism Review (New York). <www.cjr.org>.

Community Journalism Interest Group. Jock Lauterer, head. Association for Education
in Journalism and Mass Communication. <jock@email.unc.edu>;
<http://comjig.blogspot.com>.

Conniff, R. October 1995. "It Comes Out Only Once a Week, but the *Sun* Never Sets:
Can a weekly paper in rural New Mexico raise enough hell to keep its readers
hungry for more, issue after issue? Don't ask." *Smithsonian* (Washington, D.C.),
pp. 89–98.

Critchfield, R. 1991. *Trees, Why Do You Wait?: America's Changing Rural Culture*. Washington, D.C.: Island Press.

Editor & Publisher International Year Book. Part 1: Dailies; Part 2: Weeklies; Part 3: Contact Directory. 2004. New York: Editor and Publisher.

Etzioni, A., ed. 1995. *New Communitarian Thinking: Persons, Virtues, Institutions, and Communities*. Charlottesville: University Press of Virginia.

Facts about Newspapers: A Statistical Summary of the Newspaper Industry. 2004. Reston, Va.: Newspaper Association of America.

Farrar, R. 1988. *Mass Communications: An Introduction to the Field*. St. Paul, Minn.: West Publishing Co., pp. 95–114.

Fox, H. B. 1975. *The 2000-Mile Turtle, and Other Episodes from Editor Harold Smith's Private Journal*. Austin: Madrona Press.

Gibbs, N. July 1997. "America: The Inside Story; the Backbone of America." *TIME* (New York), pp. 40–99.

Goodman, P., and P. Goodman. 1960. *Communitas: Means of Livelihood and Ways of Life*. New York: Vintage Books.

Grassroots Editor. International Society of Weekly Newspaper Editors. Missouri Southern State University, Joplin, Mo. <www.isne.org>.

Harrington, D. 1986. *Let Us Build Us a City: Eleven Lost Towns*. San Diego: Harcourt Brace Jovanovich.

Heller, R. Summer 1994. "Nine Great Small Paper Designs." *Visual Communications Quarterly* (Columbia, S.C.), pp. 4–7.

Hosie, R. Spring 1997. "Why the Hell Do They Do It?: Editors from the smallest of the small say why." *APME News* (Fort Worth, Texas), pp. 18–22.

Huck Boyd National Center for Community Media. Kansas State University. Gloria Freeland, director. <gfreela@ksu.edu>; <http://huckboyd.jmc.ksu.edu/>.

Institute for Rural Journalism and Community Issues. University of Kentucky. Al Cross, director. <al.cross@uky.edu>; <http://www.ruraljournalism.org>.

Lamb, D. 1993. *A Sense of Place: Listening to Americans*. New York: Times Books.

Mayhew, S. 1997. *A Dictionary of Geography*. 2nd ed. Oxford: Oxford University Press.

Meyer, Harold D., and Charles K. Brightbill. 1964. *Community Recreation: A Guide to Its Organization*. 3rd ed. Englewood Cliffs, N.J.: Prentice-Hall, p. 169.

Meyer, Phil. 2004. *The Vanishing Newspaper: Saving Journalism in the Information Age*. Columbia: University of Missouri Press.

Miami Theory Collective. 1991. *Community at Loose Ends*. Minneapolis: University of Minnesota Press.

National Newspaper Association. *Publishers' Auxiliary*. Columbia, Mo. <http://www.nna.org>.

Neal, R. 1939. *Editing the Small City Daily*. New York: Prentice Hall.

Newspaper Association of America. 2004. *Facts about Newspapers: A Statistical Summary of the Newspaper Industry*. Reston, Va. <http://www.naa.org>.

North Carolina Press Association. *2004 North Carolina Newspaper Directory*, Raleigh, N.C.

O'Brien, Meredith. May 2003. "Covering a Community from Within: Many small-town editors say there is no other way." *QUILL* (Indianapolis).

O'Brien, R. June 1999. "Spanish Language Press May See Explosive Growth in Readership." *NEWS* (Arlington, Va.: Freedom Forum and Newseum), p. 10.

Oldenburg, R. 1989. *The Great Good Place: Cafés, Coffee Shops, Bookstores, Bars, Hair Salons and Other Hangouts at the Heart of a Community*. New York: Marlowe.

Orlean, S. September 11, 1995. "Her Town: Since Heather Heaton came to Millerton, it's been a one-woman story." *The New Yorker* (New York), pp. 44–53.

Peck, M. Scott. 1987. *The Different Drum: Community Making and Peace*. New York: Touchstone.

Porter, C. 1995. *Community Journalism: Getting Started*. Washington, D.C.: Radio and Television News Directors Foundation, p. 1.

Poynter Institute for Media Studies. Annual course catalogs. St. Petersburg, Fla. <http://www.poynter.org>.

Project for Excellence in Journalism. 2004. *The State of the News Media 2004: An Annual Report on American Journalism*. <http://www.Journalism.org>.

Raspberry, W., and A. Etzioni. December 9, 1995. "Community of Communities' Best." *Centre Daily Times* (State College, Pa.), p. 4A.

Rheingold, H. 1993. *The Virtual Community: Homesteading on the Electronic Frontier*. Reading, Mass.: Addison-Wesley.

Richardson, Jim. May 2004. "Pulling Together: 30 Years in the Life of Cuba, Kansas." *National Geographic* (Washington, D.C.), pp. 30–54.

Schultz, T., and P. Voakes. Spring 1999. "Prophets of Gloom: Why do newspaper journalists have so little faith in the future of newspapers?" *Newspaper Research Journal* (Columbia, S.C.), pp. 23–40.

Sewell, E. 1968. *Signs and Cities*. Chapel Hill: University of North Carolina Press, p. 31.

Stack, Carol. 1996. *Call to Home: African Americans Reclaim the Rural South*. New York: HarperCollins.

Stebbins, C. 1998. *All the News Is Fit to Print: Profile of a Country Editor*. Columbia: University of Missouri Press.

Strupp, J. July 3, 1999. "Welcomed Visitors: E&P study shows newspaper Web sites busier than ever, but still learning the ropes." *Editor and Publisher* (New York), pp. 22–28.

Thomas, S. 1990. *The Rating Guide to America's Small Cities*. Buffalo: Prometheus Books.

Voakes, P. 1997. *The Newspaper Journalists of the '90s*. Reston, Va.: American Society of Newspaper Editors.

Walters, E. V. 1988. *Placeways: A Theory of the Human Environment*. Chapel Hill: University of North Carolina Press.

Walton, M. May 1999. "The Selling of Smaller Newspapers." *American Journalism Review* (University of Maryland), pp. 58–78.

Welty, Eudora. 1965. "Why I Live at the P.O." *Thirteen Stories*. New York: Harcourt Brace.

Yankelovich, D. 1991. *Coming to Public Judgment: Making Democracy Work in a Complex World*. Syracuse: Syracuse University Press.

Index